World Yearbook of Education 1986

World Yearbook of Education 1986

THE MANAGEMENT OF SCHOOLS

Edited by Eric Hoyle (Guest Editor)
and Agnes McMahon (Assistant Editor)

Kogan Page, London/Nichols Publishing
Company, New York

Previous titles in this series

World Yearbook of Education 1980
Professional Development of Teachers
Edited by Eric Hoyle and Jacquetta Megarry
US Consultant Editor: Myron Atkin

World Yearbook of Education 1981
Education of Minorities
Edited by Jacquetta Megarry, Stanley Nisbet
and Eric Hoyle
Subject Adviser: Ken Eltis

World Yearbook of Education 1982/83
Computers and Education
Edited by Jacquetta Megarry, David R F Walker,
Stanley Nisbet and Eric Hoyle

World Yearbook of Education 1984
Women and Education
Edited by Sandra Acker, Jacquetta Megarry,
Stanley Nisbet and Eric Hoyle

World Yearbook of Education 1985
Research, Policy and Practice
Edited by John Nisbet, Jacquetta Megarry and Stanley Nisbet

First published in Great Britain in 1986 by Kogan Page Limited
120 Pentonville Road, London N1 9JN

British Library Cataloguing in Publication Data

World yearbook of education — 1986
    1. Education — Periodicals
    370'.5   L16

    ISSN 0084-2508
    ISBN 1-85091-064-2

First published in the USA 1986
by Nichols Publishing Company
PO Box 96, New York, NY 10024

Library of Congress Cataloging in Publication Data

Main entry under title:
World Yearbook of Education; 1986
    1. Education — Periodicals

    ISBN 0-89397-234-7
    LC Catalog No. 32-18413

Printed and bound in Great Britain by
Anchor Brendon Ltd, Tiptree, Essex

Contents

List of Contributors

Part 1: Overview

1. The management of schools: theory and practice

Eric Hoyle

Summary: Practitioners in school management have potential access to theories of education, educational policy, curriculum, innovation, management and organization. The chapter is concerned with the last three of these areas. Although organization theory and management theory have different intellectual origins and different orientations — the former essentially concerned with understanding, the latter with guiding practice — there has been much common ground. However, recent trends in organization theory have enhanced our understanding of schools as organizations but have diverged considerably from management practice. The relationship between the two remains strongest with the link between the concept of organizations as loosely coupled systems and contingency theories of management. This nexus has important implications for practice but the impact of theory on practice remains relatively weak because we have not yet explored fully the ways in which knowledge is generated, negotiated and utilized in professional practice and in professional training. The most promising approach in recent years has come specifically through approaches to the management of change which have created contexts in which head teachers and principals have engaged with substantive problems in collaboration with colleagues and professional peers, backed by various forms of professional support. Chapters in the *World Yearbook of Education 1986* describe some of the most promising developments in this area.

Introduction

The growing preoccupation in many societies with the problems entailed in the management of schools can be largely attributed to the increasingly turbulent environment in which schools function. In North America there has been a longstanding concern with theory, research and training in the field of school management but in Britain and Europe, and in those Third World countries to which colonial systems of education have been exported, there has been much less interest in this domain largely due to cultural differences in attitude towards management in general and to the styles of leadership appropriate to schools in particular. Head teachers in these systems have not been expected to have had any training in management; experience as a teacher plus certain personal qualities, diffuse and undefined, have been regarded as sufficient for the successful head. However, there has been a steady growth of concern with management in Britain, Europe, Australia and the Third World over the past 20 years. The British Educational Management and Administration Society and the Commonwealth Council for Educational Administration have both fostered interest and activity in their respective constituencies. And such agencies as the Organization for Economic Co-operation and Development (OECD) and the International Movement for the Training for Educational Change (IMTEC) have sponsored research and development in Europe and the Third World on the management of school change. These trends have now accelerated and in many countries school management training has become a major element in governmental attempts to improve the quality of schooling (see Bailey, Chapter 16).

The increasing importance which is being attached to the training of head teachers has been stimulated in large part by the perceived need to equip them to cope with substantive problems with which schools have to cope. These problems differ from society to society, and are sometimes the exact reverse in some societies than others. Thus, while schools in many Western societies are having to cope with the problems of falling enrolments, schools in many developing societies are having to cope with rapid acceleration in enrolments. Some of the other problems which schools are facing include those social developments which are affecting the behaviour of young people (for example, substance abuse), the constant need for curriculum change (forced by high unemployment in many industrialized societies), the requirement that schools should seek to equalize opportunities for ethnic minorities and girls and, in newly in-dependent societies, the problem of balancing a curriculum for nation building with the more universal needs of pupils (see Maravanyika, Chapter 15). Schools are generally experiencing much more direct political inter-vention than in the past, and the shrill demand for accountability is to some extent matched by the growing militancy of teachers at school level (see Lyons, Chapter 10).

It is assumed that training better enables the head teacher to make a professional response to these substantive problems and, if it is accepted, despite the doubts of some students of the professions that such a response involves recourse to a body of theoretical knowledge, one must ask what bodies of theory are available to the head and how these inform, or might inform, practice. The fact is that there are diverse theories available, including curriculum theory, organization theory, manage-ment theory, theory of innovation, etc, which are developed to varying degrees and related to each other somewhat loosely. We can explore further this range of available theory.

The theoretical basis of school management

Figure 1 (see p 00) shows some of the areas of relevant theory. It must be immediately stated that this diagram is simplistic and used here only for heuristic purposes. *Theory of education* represents the most philosophical

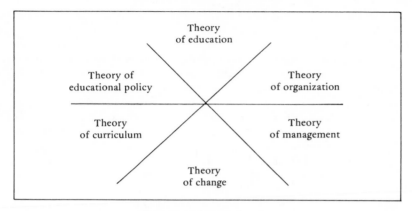

Figure 1 *Relevant theories*

level. It includes theories about the ultimate purposes of education and is thus an enormous field. *Theory of educational policy* is concerned with what the general arrangements should be for achieving educational aims in a particular society at a particular time. It would include theories about, for example, states of transfer, the role of examinations, the schooling of minorities and the relationship between education and industry. *Theory of curriculum* includes all areas related to content and trans- mission. It could be further subdivided in many ways to include, eg, theories of learning and theories of pedagogy. The distinction made between *theory of organization* and *theory of management* may not be immediately obvious. However, as the distinction is discussed in some detail below, suffice it to say here that *theories of organization* are seen as being concerned with all the components of an organization (eg a school) while *theories of management* are concerned largely with one domain of organization centring on authority, decision making, etc. Similarly, one might quibble that the remaining vector, the *theory of change*, is really a subsection of management theory, and this is a per- fectly reasonable point. However, an admittedly crude distinction can be made, not least because international initiatives in this area have ensured its more rapid development in many societies than broader aspects of management theory. Its affinity has often been more with theories of curriculum and their renewal than with management theory.

Insofar as practitioners draw upon theory, one may imagine that there will be variations in the degree to which individual heads will draw upon the different bodies. One can perhaps produce the sections on the above diagram as a sort of pie-chart with 'slices' of varying size, or of vectors covering different proportions of the equal divisions. For example, one head may give priority to educational theory, a vision of what education can accomplish, and be little concerned with, say, theories of manage- ment, while another may have a good organizer as a self-image and thus be concerned with management theory. In any case, the mix of theoretical concerns will, insofar as this influences practice, generate different styles. Hodgkinson (1983) in *The Philosophy of Leadership* has developed a model of leadership concerns of a much more sophisticated kind than the above and discusses various archetypes, eg *the poet* or *the technician*, which represent different priorities. However, these are heuristic categories, different in nature and intent from the research-based models of educational leadership of, say, Leithwood *et al* (1984) or Hall *et al* (1984).

Many of the substantive problems of head teachers, referred to earlier, would obviously involve recourse to the three distinctively 'educational' vectors, ie theories of education, educational policy and curriculum. It might well be that the training of heads should focus on these areas on the assumption that if the head can handle these issues the more 'managerial' tasks are of less importance and can be relegated to a minor concern. However, this chapter is concerned with the other three areas presented in Figure 1 and we can now turn to consider their nature.

Theories of organization, management and change

Organization theory and management theory have different intellectual origins. Organization theory is essentially a sociological tradition, with Max Weber as one of the founding fathers. Management theory stemmed from the writings of practitioners. However, the distinction is a crude one and over time there has been considerable intertwining between the two strands of organization and management theories with a degree of overlap at a notional 'centre' from which the two traditions diverge. They differ basically in terms of range and function.

Organization theory is a broader type of theory. Organizational structure and management process are central components of an organization but still only two of a set of components. Organization theory is also concerned with cultural aspects of organization: symbols, language, the ways in which participants define their situation, etc, together with the micro-politics of organizations: the strategies which participants use in pursuit of their interests, and with the informal dimension of the organization; peer groups and their values, etc. Management theory is, on the whole, limited to a concern with organizational structure and the management process. However, there has long been a concern with organizational climates and, increasingly, an interest in culture and micro-politics is developing. Thus, there is a degree of overlap in the concerns of the two bodies of theory.

The different functions of the two types of theory can be indicated, in an admittedly over-simplified way, by conceiving organization theory as *theory-for-understanding* and management theory as *theory-for-practice*. Organization theory consists of a number of different perspectives by which we might better understand the nature of organization as social units and the reality of life in organizations. Organizations are objects of inquiry, and the organization theorist an interested but neutral party.

Management theory, as a practical theory, is concerned with enabling the practitioner to improve the effectiveness of organizations and, simultaneously, the work satisfaction of members. Thus its focus is on organizational design, leadership, decision-making processes, communication, etc.

Of course, this distinction in terms of function is over-simplified. Organization theories are rarely value free. Organizational theorists naturally hope that their work will lead to improvement in effectiveness and satisfaction. However, within the category of organizational theory there is a great variation. Some theories are virtually indistinguishable from management theory, while at the other end of the continuum are those which are grounded on Marxism, critical theory or social phenomenology which are critical of the most fundamental characteristics of organizations. It is a moot point whether these should be termed 'organization theories' at all, though they are certainly social theories about organizations (see Burrell and Morgan, 1979, for an excellent discussion of the full range of organization theories, and Willower, 1980, as well as Chapter 2 of this book, for a discussion of their place in the educational domain).

In dubbing organization theory *theory-for-understanding* one is not, of course, implying that management theory is not concerned with understanding. It would be foolish to seek to improve organizations without such understanding. However, whereas some management theories seek to embrace all organizational components, most are limited and, at the end of a continuum which stretches from the middle ground occupied by both organization and management theory, there are those theories which are highly mechanistic and unformed by 'engineering' models of organization.

The dangers of each type of theory for the practitioner are clear. Management theories can be so mechanistic as to be almost wholly detached from the realities of organizational life. One still encounters management theories which are splendidly rational blueprints for an unreal world. On the other hand, the understandings yielded by organization theory could easily bemuse and confuse the practitioner who tries to struggle with philosophical disputes within fields marked by an arcane scholasticism. One of the paradoxes of organization theory at the present time is that, as it enhances our understanding, it is thereby undermining some of the rationalistic assumptions which underpin much management theory and guide most practitioners. Three such developments can be discussed.

Social phenomenology, a perspective which has been much debated in the literature on education organizations for over ten years (eg Greenfield, 1975; 1980; Gronn, 1983; Willower, 1982), is less an organization *theory* than a *perspective* on organizations which questions some of the basic tenets of mainstream organization theory (see Burrell and Morgan, 1979, for a 'placing' of phenomenology). Whereas organization theory is predicated on the assumption that organizations are entities about which generalizations can be made, and have internal structures which are independent of those who people a given organization at a particular point in time, social phenomenology deplores this misplaced concreteness and holds that an organization, though it has a location and a membership, is essentially a social construct with different sets of members construing the same 'organization' differently. Thus for the phenomenologist the appropriate focus is not the properties of organizations but the varying definitions of members, say the head teacher and a group of low-achieving pupils. Although one cannot at this point debate in detail the relative merits of the 'phenomenological' and 'systems' approaches one can suggest that the former, in challenging the prevailing systems perspective, has enhanced our understanding of organizations.

The second development can be called, albeit with some hyperbole, the 'arationalist' approach. Elsewhere the present writer (Hoyle, 1986, forthcoming) has described 'organizational pathos' as the inevitable gap between the rationalistic perspective of those who design and manage organizations and the reality of organizational life which, from their perspective, is 'irrational'. In fact the 'irrational' behaviour of organizational members is usually 'rational' according to other criteria. That there are cognitive and logical limits to rationality in organizations has long been recognized (eg March and Simon, 1958; Lindblom, 1959). These limits have been much discussed in the literature on social policy (eg Allison, 1971; Olson, 1965; Hirschman, 1981). The philosophical aspects of this have been discussed in a fascinating and scholarly manner by Elster (1978; 1979). Perhaps the best-known exploration in the field of organizations, particularly educational organizations, occurs in March and Olsen (1976) whose striking metaphors of 'garbage can' modes of decision making, 'organized anarchies' and 'backward-running' organizations have caught the imagination. Again, there is no opportunity here to discuss the degree to which organizations are rational systems, but one can simply note again the point that, although it may enhance understanding, it is not obviously helpful to practitioners who have to cope with the daily running of a school.

The same problems are generated by the third development, the micro-politics of organizations (see Gronn, Chapter 3 of this book, and the contributions to the British Journal of Educational Management and Administration 10:2,1982). In the latter volume the present writer (Hoyle, 1982) seeks to explore the symbolic nature of management and micro-politics in organizations. The existence of micro-politics in all organizations is widely recognized in talk of 'hidden agendas', 'rigging meetings', 'massaging the minutes', 'making offers which cannot be refused', etc, but the study of these phenomena, not least because it is difficult and sensitive, has remained recessive to the more dominant organizational theory.

Each of the above developments in the field of organization theory clearly diverges from management theory. The implications of these trends away from the more practical theories of management will be discussed below.

One further theme which can be raised in this section can perhaps be best expressed by drawing a distinction between *understanding schools* and *understanding schools as organizations.* The implication of this is that schools are much more than those components which are the focus of even the broadest organization theories. In the 1960s it was optimistically assumed that organization theory would substantially enhance our understanding of schools (eg Hoyle, 1965). There is now a widespread view that this promise has not been fulfilled (eg Davies, 1982). Certainly, some of the studies which best illuminate the nature of schools have made little use of organization theory. Much cited British studies are those by Hargreaves (1967), Lacey (1970) and Ball (1983) which have focused essentially on the nexus of grouping for instruction, peer groups and their cultures. Bernstein, whose approach to an understanding of schools is Durkheimian rather than Weberian, wrote an early article (Bernstein, 1967) specifically as a counter to the organizational approach to schools, and has continued to develop an understanding of schools through what is essentially a structuralist approach to the curriculum (Bernstein, 1975). There is a view, particularly a Marxist view, that schools are best understood not through the ideologies which these processes sustain. This view holds that the focus should be on what functions the school performs in relation to society, particularly its relationship with the means of production and the sustaining hegemony (eg Bowles and Gintis, 1976).

Thus there are several approaches to an understanding of schools which treat their structures and managerial processes as relatively unimportant domains. One can envisage a model of the school which is shaped like an hourglass. In the top section is the management domain. In the bottom section is the domain of curriculum and pedagogy. Organization theory and management theory focus on the top section and make the implicit or explicit assumption that this upper section ultimately influences the lower. Other theories hold that the upper section has relatively little effect on the lower which is much more influenced by external forces which are perhaps mediated through management as an ideology. The task is to explore the extent to which the upper section influences the lower. We will return to this later. In the meantime we can explore some of the contributions which organization theory appears to have made to the structure of schooling and how this is congruent with recent developments in management theory.

Loosely coupled systems and contingency theory

A prevalent theme in the application of organization theory to the school is the following. The key structural characteristic of schools is that a powerful central management unit is balanced by a number of components — departments, classes, pastoral units, etc — which have a high degree of potential autonomy. Bidwell (1965) noted the structural looseness of the school; Katz (1964) noted that schools were as much characterized by autonomy as bureaucracy; Lortie (1969) wrote of the balance between control and autonomy in the primary school; Litwak (1961) and Litwak and Meyer (1974) depicted schools as conforming to a 'professional' model: one part bureaucracy and one part human relations. And Weick (1970) included educational organizations as being in the category of *loosely coupled systems*, a concept which has been central to much recent discussion of schools as organizations (see Willower, 1980, Chapter 2).

If one accepts that, as a matter of observation and research, schools *do* tend to have the property of structural looseness, one can treat this knowledge in various ways which have a different relationship to practice. At one end of a theoretical continuum there stands a *description* of one structural characteristic of schools. One appreciates that descriptions of the social world are never 'simple' — in that those who observe and report bring to bear potentially distorting lenses of assumption, presumption and even ideology, and although there may be consensus among a number of observers this does not guarantee that the observation is therefore 'correct'. However, with this proviso, let us assume that the observation about the loosely coupled nature of schools is valid. As description it has little or no implication for practice. It is a datum on which practice might well draw, but something must be done to the datum before it impinges on practice. One of the things which has to be done is to explain the datum. One form of explanation is *historical*. The present structure of schools is thus because it has certain historical antecedents. Whether such an explanation can have practical implications depends, of course, on one's theory of history, and only if one adopts an historicist view which sees any current phenomenon as part of the working out of some teleological purpose can one link this explanation to practice. And even then one can either accept the present situation as a manifestation of historical inevitability, or one can give inevitability a helping hand.

Another form of explanation is *functionalist*. One form of functionalist explanation is that schools display loose coupling because that system is what works, that it is the best form of organization for achieving the purpose of schools. This form of functionalism obviously has a conservative cast to it. A more radical form of functionalist explanation is that schools are structured as they are because this is functional for achieving the ends of schooling which has been determined by ruling groups. Obviously these two versions of functionalism are in conflict with each other. This can be illustrated by reference to the 'free school' movement of the 1960s. There are two basic forms of social control in organizations: the rule-governed control of a vertical bureaucracy and the norm-governed horizontal control of a collective of peers. The free schools of the 1960s aspired to the latter form of control in which boundaries which had previously existed between school subjects, categories of pupils, teachers and pupils, the physical parts of the school building, the temporal stages of the school day, school and non-school, etc, were abolished. Such schools constituted a brief historical phenomenon and relatively few now exist. A conservative functionalist explanation for their decline would be that this move to a tight coupling based on naive consensus and close integration removed boundaries which were essential to the effectiveness of schools. A radical functionalist explanation would be that this mode of integration implied a shift in the tasks of schools which was ideologically unacceptable to ruling groups who therefore, by various means, destroyed these schools and ensured the *status quo*.

These different forms of explanation would generate a lively debate among practitioners. Their function would thus be to sensitize them to a number of issues related to schools as organizations about which they had not thought before. This would be at the levels of philosophy and policy (see Figure 1, p 13). At the same time, this organizational approach begins to merge with the dominant managerial approach of *contingency theory*. This theory of management is essentially a theory for understanding combined with a framework for organizational design. Its basic assumptions are that organizations exist in a turbulent and relatively unpredictable environment. Even schools, for so long 'domesticated' organizations, now function increasingly in the 'wild' (Carlson, 1964). The basic tenet of contingency theory is that there is no eternally 'right' way of structuring and managing organizations. Effectiveness is relative to environment. The pioneering study of Burns and Stalker (1966) illustrated how mechanistic firms could succeed in stable environments but that organismic firms were better able to adapt to changing environments. Since then, contingency theory has come to dominate the field of organizational design (Lawrence and Lorsch, 1967; Pugh and Hinings, 1976). Although we have not a great deal of direct evidence of the effectiveness of contingency-oriented schools, that which exists (Derr and Gabarro, 1972; Hanson and Brown, 1977) suggests that it is as effective in education as elsewhere.

Hanson and Brown's (1977) formulation of the assumptions which underpin contingency theory can be summarized as follows. Organizations are open systems influenced by their environments and have overlapping goals. While all organizations have universal problems they also face problems which are unique. Hence effective performance involves a match between external requirements and internal constraints. This has to be achieved in a context in which a manager can rarely take on problems from their outset and never knows all that is going on around him. Thus leadership style needs to vary with the problem. Structures need to be flexibly differentiated, since different problems are best handled by appropriate, and thus different, structures. There is little doubt about the *heuristic* value of contingency theory sensitizing head teachers and principals to the general characteristics of the contexts in which they function. However, contingency theory would seem to offer little specific guidance at a practical level or predictive power at the theoretical level. Insofar as the central tenets are those of balance and adaptation, much still depends on the judgement and flexibility of the head teacher. These will be enhanced in two ways: through reflection on experience and through rehearsing the potential of alternative courses of action. However, the impact of contingency theory on practice is unlikely to be direct.

Like other theories, it will impinge on practice only indirectly and as mediated through contexts in which heads engage with substantive problems in collaboration sometimes with colleagues, and sometimes with peers — supported by those in training roles of different kinds involving different forms of expertise. These contexts are being developed in current approaches to management training which themselves have emerged as part of the development of theories of innovation and change.

Theories of innovation

Theories of innovation can be crudely divided between those which are essentially part of a broader theory of social change, eg the diffusion of innovations, and those which are essentially theories of the management of change. In effect, the latter are, or should be, simply variants of management theory. *Management* here connotes the activity of 'moving' an organization rather than keeping it ticking over, a definition which has in the past led to distinctions being made between, eg, *administration* (change) and *management* (routine) (Lipham, 1964) which, though useful, have not become universal. On one view, therefore, theory of management is *ipso facto* a theory of innovation. However, a distinction persists because over the past 20 years theories of innovation in education have developed independently of theories of management and have, in fact, had a substantial influence not only on the theory of school management but also on school management *practice*.

This distinction has arisen because theory of innovation has been perhaps more closely related to curriculum theory and theory of professional development than to management, the latter becoming almost a residual category. The story is familiar: the uprush of innovation in curriculum, pedagogy, pupil grouping, etc, from the late 1950s led to a recognition of the problem of uptake by schools and teachers. It was fairly obvious that one problem was that the individual teacher was regarded as the target of change and amenable to strategies ranging from unplanned diffusion through to planned dissemination. In fact, the more appropriate target of change was the school. It was recognized that innovation was more likely to be effective where teachers became actively and collectively involved in the process of change, that this involvement was predicated on professional development which would enable teachers to acquire professional skills, including the skills of achieving organizational change. Thus there was an interaction between curriculum development and organizational development. Theory, research and practice in relation to this nexus has generated substantial literature (see Hoyle, 1970; Havelock, 1973; Fullan, 1972; 1982; Dalin, 1973; Dalin and Rust, 1983; Bolam, 1982; Hoyle and Megarry, 1980).

There would appear to have been a considerable interplay between theory and practice in the area of educational innovation in the 1960s. Throughout North America, Britain, Europe and Australia a large number of schemes for supporting heads and teachers in their attempts at change were initiated and many schools today take this challenge seriously. The approach chimed well with emerging theories of school management, and it may well have been, though there is no way of knowing, that this particular trend had a substantial impact on management practice. One's judgement would be that in Britain, at least, it had a greater impact on management practice than courses in management training, which were few in number at this time, and a greater impact than management theory as such.

Perhaps the main problem in this otherwise powerful approach to change was the relatively weak relationship with mainstream organization and management theory. It certainly did not take enough account of prevailing theories of leadership, particularly the contingency theory of leadership. Nor did it take sufficient account of the implications of structural looseness and contingency theory. It is likely that many development projects and efforts at school-based change were implicitly informed by theories of loose coupling and contingency, but there can be little doubt that many attempts at innovation were not so informed and in some cases disaster ensued.

Management training in education

Emergent theories of organization, management and change present considerable problems for those who devise training programmes for head teachers, principals and senior staff. The contingency element in these theories suggests that managerial effectiveness depends very much on a capacity for judgement — an elusive quality and not one which is likely to be inculcated by a rationalistic, one-right-way approach via a training package of predetermined skills. Certainly skills training has its place in management training when properly contextualized, but it is not in itself sufficient. Neither are the understandings provided by organization theory or theories of management themselves sufficient. As Fullan (Chapter 5) points out, there is a world of difference between understanding the cause of change and actually achieving it. Moreover, much of the training of the head teacher or principal needs to be focused on substantive knowledge of policies, curricula, pedagogy, etc. Among some writers of educational management in the 1960s there was a rejection of the *adjectival* view of management in favour of a universal concept of management which was relevant to all contexts. That view is no longer current (see Al-Khalifa, Chapter 17). It is generally recognized that educational management, the adjective now restored, is a very different activity from industrial management. After all, those who manage educational institutions are not balancing massive budgets or deploying huge physical resources, or constantly negotiating with trade unions in pursuit of well-defined goals. As institutions or cultural transmission the management of schools is, or ought to be, of a different order. It is concerned with a much more

diffuse form of leadership related to the creation of meaning rather than
to profit and loss. The symbolic function of school leadership may be met
by a leader of vision and charisma, but it would generally be held that
vision is preferably informed by a good grasp of the realities of the educational world: forces in the situation, subordinates, the environment, as
well as forces in the leader himself or herself — to use the formulation of
Tannenbaum *et al* (1961). All this means that we should not assume that
the major task involved in training managers is transmitting business skills
or even the skills of managing and motivating people. It is important that
management training provides ample scope for reflection and discussion
about educational issues.

Contingency approaches to management suggest the need for flexibility
and, by implication, the avoidance of training to formula — except perhaps in relation to certain limited and specific skills. This implies that
training should focus on enabling heads and principals to become aware of
their needs and their problems. This is a broad, even vague, injunction,
but it does suggest that although specific training techniques, eg simulation, team building, etc, have their place, this place is that of a number
of activities supporting what must be the central strategies of training,
that of enabling heads and principals to work through these problems
with groups of people who share them: occupants of the same role in
other schools and immediate colleagues in their own schools.

This approach is far from novel. Many of the available techniques have
long been used and advocated by people such as Schmuck and Miles
(1971). They have, however, taken off outside the United States as a result
of the pressures towards increased training. Moreover, while the 'person'
component of this approach remains, the 'task' component has been given
more emphasis, particularly in relation to the substantive problems. The
chapters in Section 5 of this book indicate the emergence of a particular
approach to management training, the major characteristic of which is to
provide contexts in which head teachers and principals can address the
problems which they are confronting at the level of policy: coping with
ethnic minorities, introducing a new examination system, responding to
demands for accountability, assessing teacher performance, etc.

In this endeavour, some common approaches are emerging with these
characteristics:

(a) Central and/or regional institutions for research, development
    and training.
(b) A mixed strategy of on-site and off-site training.
(c) On-site training directly related to substantive problems being
    confronted.
(d) On-site training conceived as part of a broader process of collec-
    tive staff development linked with organizational and curriculum
    development.
(e) Off-site training organized to ensure maximum interaction with
    professional peers in problem-solving activities and, in some
    instances, involving teams of immediate professional associates.

This approach to training meets with a positive response from participants as assessed by various feed-back techniques, though external evaluation remains underdeveloped. The ultimate aim of training for school leadership is the improvement of quality in schooling. This is a difficult task to be sure, but progress is being made in establishing the relationship between management and instructional programmes (see Bossert, Chapter 8). Progress towards identifying the choices made by effective school leaders is being made by, for example, Astuto and Clark (see Chapter 4) whose work is informed by the concept of the school as a loosely coupled system. Progress in an approach to training for the management of change which abjures ready-made rationalistic solutions in favour of a more contingent approach is discussed by Fullan (Chapter 5).

Conclusion

One way of assessing whether progress has been made in relating theory to practice is to compare the contents of this book with that of the National Society for the Study of Education (NSSE) Yearbook published over 20 years ago (Griffiths, 1964). The latter displayed optimism that educational administration was at the point of generating a body of quasi-scientific theory which, when absorbed by practising administrators in the course of their training, would guide practice. Although the 1964 collection epitomized the 'new movement' in educational management and administration which brought a new vigour to the study of this domain, even its main protagonists would not now claim that it constituted quite the breakthrough which it appeared to be at the time. The progress which has been made since 1964 has been divergent and the theory-practice relationship remains very much with us. There has been a rich development in theory, both about management and about organizations. However, these theoretical advances, in their emphasis on phenomenology, micro-politics, symbols, and competing rationalities, though yielding improved ways of understanding organizations, provide little help in the practicalities of running a school and indeed could inhibit the head teacher's capacity to *act*. They add interest to training programmes and probably fascinate more participants than they repel, but this relationship to practice is complex, some would say dubious, and others would say non-existent. Greenfield (1980) writes that the function of management training is to give the educational administrator a transcendental view of the world and his place within it — true perhaps, but hardly a course objective likely to appeal to funding agencies.

Although it is difficult to adduce hard evidence, the training of heads and principals has probably improved considerably in contexts in which practising administrators can engage with rather than substantive problems with support and professional guidance. It is likely that if there has been an improvement it has been linked at least as much with developments in the area of the theory and practice of handling change through staff and organizational development as with mainstream theories of management training and practice.

There are a number of optimistic trends as indicated in several chapters in this book. Other trends include a concern with 'knowledge utilization' and detailed ethnographic studies of how head teachers and principals spend their time (eg Woolcott, 1973; O'Dempsey, 1976; Willis, 1980; Sproull, 1981; Martin and Willower, 1981). However, more work is needed on the data, theories, beliefs and assumptions which inform their actions. Detailed studies of professional practice (eg Freidson, 1975) reveal the complexity of the relationship between knowledge and practice. It is naive to assume that theory and research impinge directly on practice. As the present writer has pointed out elsewhere (Hoyle, 1985), the knowledge which informs professional practice is generated, or at least negotiated, in various contexts including certain kinds of training programmes, structured forms of professional exchange and school-focused action research projects.

References

Allison, G T (1971) *Essence of Decision: Explaining the Cuban Missile Crisis* Little, Brown: Boston, Mass

Ball, S J (1983) *Beachside Comprehensive: A Study of Comprehensive Schooling* Cambridge University Press: Cambridge

Bernstein, B (1967) Open schools, open society? *New Society* 14

Bernstein, B (1975) *Class, Codes and Control III: Towards a Theory of Educational Transmissions* Routledge and Kegan Paul: London

Bidwell, C E (1965) The school as a formal organization *in* March (1965)

Bolam, R ed (1982) *School-focussed In-Service Training* Heinemann: London

Bowles, S and Gintis, H (1976) *Schooling in Capitalist America: Educational Reform and the Contradictions of Economic Life* Routledge and Kegan Paul: London

British Journal of Educational Management and Administration (1982) 10: 2

Burns, T and Stalker, G M (1966) *The Management of Innovation* Tavistock Publications: London (second edition)

Burrell, G and Morgan, G (1979) *Sociological Paradigms and Organizational Analysis* Heinemann: London

Carlson, D (1964) Environmental constraints and educational consequences: the public school and its clients *in* Griffiths (1964)

Carlson, R (1965) *Change Processes in the Public Schools* Centre for Advanced Study of Educational Administration, University of Oregon: Eugene, Oregon

Dalin, P (1973) *Case Studies of Educational Innovation IV: Strategies for Innovation in Education* OECD/CERI: Paris

Dalin, P and Rust, V D (1983) *Can Schools Learn?* NFER-Nelson: Windsor, Berks

Davies, B (1982) Organizational theory and schools *in* Hartnett (1982)

Derr, B and Gabarro, J (1972) An organizational contingency theory for education *Educational Administration Quarterly* 8

Elster, J (1978) *Logic and Society: Contradictions and Possible Worlds* John Wiley: New York

Elster, J (1979) *Ulysses and the Siren: Studies in Rationality and Irrationality* Cambridge University Press: Cambridge

Etzioni, A ed (1969) *The Semi-Professions and their Organization: Teachers, Nurses, Social Workers* The Free Press: New York

Freidson, E (1975) *The Profession of Medicine* Dodd, Mead: New York

Fullan, M (1972) Overview of the innovative process and user *Interchange* **3** 2-3: 1-43, 70

Fullan, M (1982) *The Meaning of Educational Change* Teachers College Press, Columbia University: New York

Greenfield, T B (1975) Theory about organizations: a new perspective and its implications for schools *in* Hughes (1975)

Greenfield, T B (1980) The man who comes back through the door in the wall: discovering truth, discovering self, discovering organizations *Educational Administration Quarterly* **16** 3: 26-59

Griffiths, D E ed (1964) *Behavioural Science and Educational Administration* 63rd Yearbook of the National Society for the Study of Education. Chicago University Press: Chicago

Gronn, P (1983) *Rethinking Educational Administration: T B Greenfield and his Critics* (ESA 841 Theory and Practice in Educational Administration) Deakin University: Geelong, Victoria

Hall, G E *et al* (1984) Three change-facilitator styles. Paper presented at the Annual Meeting of The American Educational Research Association: New York

Hanson, E M and Brown, M E (1977) A contingency view of problem solving in schools: a case analysis *Educational Administration Quarterly* **13**

Hargreaves, D H (1967) *Social Relations in a Secondary School* Routledge and Kegan Paul: London

Hartnett, A ed (1982) *The Social Sciences in Educational Studies* Heinemann: London

Havelock, R G (1973) *The Change Agent's Guide to Innovation in Education* Educational Technology Publications Ltd: Englewood Cliffs, NJ

Hirschman, A O (1981) *Essays in Trespassing: Economic Politics and Beyond* Cambridge University Press: Cambridge

Hodgkinson, C (1983) *The Philosophy of Leadership* Blackwell: Oxford

Hoyle, E (1965) Organizational analysis in the field of education *Educational Research* **7** 2: 97-114

Hoyle, E (1970) Planned organizational change in education *Research in Education* **3**

Hoyle, E (1982) Micropolitics of educational organizations *Educational Management and Administration* **10** 2: 87-98

Hoyle, E (1985) Educational research: dissemination, participation, negotiation *in* Nisbet, Nisbet and Megarry (1985)

Hoyle, E (1986) *The Politics of School Management* Hodder and Stoughton: London (forthcoming)

Hoyle, E and Megarry, J eds (1980) *The World Yearbook of Education: the Professional Development of Teachers* Kogan Page: London

Hughes, M G ed (1975) *Administering Education: International Challenge* Athlone Press: London

Katz, F E (1964) The school as a complex organization: a consideration of patterns of autonomy *Harvard Educational Review* **34** 3: 428-55

Lacey, C (1970) *Hightown Grammar* Manchester University Press: Manchester

Lawrence, P R and Lorsch, J W (1967) *Organization and Environment* Harvard Graduate School of Business Administration: Cambridge, Mass

Leithwood, K and Montgomery, D J (1984) Patterns of growth in principal effectiveness. Paper presented at the Annual Meeting of the American Educational Research Association: New Orleans (April)

Lindblom, C E (1959) The science of muddling through *Public Administration Review* **19**

Lipham, J (1964) Leadership and administration *in* Griffiths (1964)

Litwak, E (1961) Models of bureaucracy which permit conflict *American Journal of Sociology* **67**

Litwak, E and Meyer, H J (1974) *School, Family and Neighbourhood* Columbia University Press: New York

Lortie, D C (1969) The balance of control and autonomy in elementary school teaching *in* Etzioni (1969)

March, J G *ed* (1965) *Handbook of Organizations* Rand McNally: Chicago

March, J G and Simon, H A (1958) *Organizations* Wiley: New York

March, J G and Olsen, J P *eds* (1976) *Ambiguity and Choice in Organizations* Universitetforlaget: Bergen, Norway

Martin, W J and Willower, D (1981) The managerial behavior of high school principals *Educational Administration Quarterly* **17** 1: 69-90

Miles, M B (1965) Planned change and organizational health *in* Carlson *et al* (1965)

Nisbet, J, Nisbet, S and Megarry, J *eds* (1985) *Research, Policy and Practice. World Yearbook of Education 1985* Kogan Page: London

O'Dempsey, K (1976) Time analysis of activities, work-patterns and roles of high school principals *Administrator's Bulletin* **7** 8: 1-4

Olson, M (1965) *The Logic of Collective Action* Harvard University Press: Cambridge, Mass

Pugh, D S and Hinings, C R *eds* (1976) *Organisational Structure, Extensions and Replications: The Aston Programme II* Saxon House: Farnborough, Hants

Schmuck, R A and Miles, M (1971) *Organizational Development in Schools* National Press Books: Palo Alto, Cal

Sproull, L S (1981) Managing educational programs: a micro-behavioural analysis *Human Organization* **40** 2: 113-22

Tannenbaum, R, Weischler, I and Massarik, F (1961) *Leadership and Organization: a Behavioural Science Approach* University of Illinois Press: Urbana, Ill

Weick, K (1970) Educational organizations as loosely-coupled systems *Educational Administration Quarterly* **21**

Willis, Q (1980) The work activity of school principals: an observational study *Journal of Educational Administration* **18** 1: 27-54

Willower, D J (1980) Contemporary issues in theory in educational administration *Educational Administration Quarterly* **16** 1-25

Willower, D J (1982) School organizations: perspectives in juxtaposition *Educational Administration Quarterly* **18** 3: 89-110

Woolcott, H F (1973) *The Man in the Principal's Office. An Ethnography* Holt, Rinehard and Winston: New York

Part 2: Theoretical Perspectives

2. Organization theory and the management of schools

Donald J Willower

Summary: Theory and research on school organizations and their management are considered in four areas: environment, organization, culture and position. In connection with environment, institutional organization theory is critiqued, along with the concepts of normative and technical legitimation. In the section on organization, the loose coupling metaphor and studies of bureaucratization are examined. The concept of organizational culture is applied to schools and explored in terms of the relationships of a particular school's culture to existing subcultures, such as those associated with teacher and student groups. Studies of the managerial position that deal with activity, talk, grapevines, rule bending, politics and conflict, among others, are discussed. The importance of treating concepts as variables and examining contingencies is stressed. Questions are raised concerning the political effectiveness and style of school managers and on the staying power of school cultures that are dependent on individual leaders rather than on long-term organizational supports. Finally, some philosophical positions currently being advanced in educational administration that bear on the study of school management are considered. They include neo-Marxism, subjectivism, and versions of pragmatism.

Introduction

There are many ways of thinking about schools as organizations. An array of theories, concepts, images, and metaphors has been employed. There is exciting theoretical and empirical work going on, as well as some lively controversy that is essentially philosophical in nature.

The first section of this chapter deals with theory and research on school organizations and management. Four general topics are considered: environment, organization, culture, and position. In the second section, some questions are raised and a few speculations are advanced relative to the theory and research. The third and final section is a brief commentary on philosophical positions that bear on organization theory and school management.

Theory and research

In exploring theory and research, the aim has been to present major ideas and trends. For this reason, and because of space limitation, the treatment has been highly selective. It has been necessary to omit some good work.

Environment

Virtually everyone agrees that schools reflect their societal and community environments. Meyer and Rowan (1977; 1978) see schools as examples of institutional organizations. Such organizations are creatures of the society, legitimated by shared beliefs and normative conformity rather than by technical efficiency (Meyer, Scott and Deal, 1983). Waller (1932) long ago called schools museums of virtue, a label picked up by Tyack and Hansot (1982) who depicted school superintendents as managers of virtue. Wolcott (1973) characterized school principals as monitors for continuity who maintained societal values. Willower (1982; 1985) described school administrators as threshold guardians because they countered behaviour that threatened to exceed normative limits; he likened schools to secular churches with school managers as their chief clergy. Reproduction theorists contended that schools reinforce dominant societal structures (Bowles and Gintis, 1976; Giroux, 1983). All these perspectives in their various ways assert the primacy of the community in its relationship with schools.

The other side of the coin consists of the efforts of school organizations and their personnel to insulate themselves from societal interventions and maintain a degree of autonomy. Theories of political economy or public choice claim that school personnel (and others) act essentially to promote their own interests rather than the public interest or the interests of their clients (Boyd, 1982b; Michaelsen, 1981). It has also been argued, with some empirical support, that the professionalization of school management has increased the power of school managers relative to their communities (Boyd, 1982a).

One way that schools can protect internal leeway is by maintaining legitimacy in the eyes of their communities. Ordinarily, this requires symbolic and behavioural affirmation of dominant social values. However, many societies are becoming more pluralistic and for this reason, among others, normative change and conflict occur. Meyer and Rowan (1977; 1978) ignore this pluralism and take legitimation as ritualistic and as given rather than as problematic. Nevertheless, their emphasis on the importance of external legitimation for schools is consistent with earlier and current work. When school managers are cautious about risk taking (Brown, 1970), monitor their environments (Pitner and Ogawa, 1981), anticipate the reactions of community groups to potential courses of action, and employ rhetoric that pays homage to shared societal values (Willower, 1982; 1985), they can be seen as engaging in behaviour that protects organizational legitimation. Such activity also fits Thompson's (1967) theory that organizations behave so as to reduce uncertainty.

Despite Meyer and Rowan's emphasis on normative conformity over technical efficiency, it is possible for technical efficiency to become a

cultural value (Bates, 1981). The effective schools and school improvement literatures (Clark, Lotto and Astuto, 1984) suggest just such a
possibility. Moreover, in the case of schools, technical efficiency in the
form of improved student outcomes can provide grounds for organizational legitimation. After all, such outcomes are at the heart of the
schools' purposes and their attainment, or even verbal commitment
to them, should enhance legitimation. In any event, a clear implication
is that school managers should be politically astute individuals who can
cope with multiple demands from the environment and fashion some
sort of negotiated order (Day and Day, 1977) that features external
legitimation and support and the internal autonomy required for responsive decision making.

Organization

In Meyer and Rowan's (1977; 1978) view, despite the shared normative
structures that signal the dominance of society over its schools, school
organizations are characterized by internal dissensus. One of its features is
the separation or decoupling of organizational supervision and goal attainment. Other writers have also depicted relationships within schools in
terms that run counter to theories that emphasize consensus and control.
For instance, Weick (1976; 1980) has advanced the idea of loose coupling,
a concept similar to, but more encompassing than, Bidwell's (1965)
notion of structural looseness, and March and Olsen (1976) have applied
the organized anarchy metaphor to educational settings.

Weick (1976) emphasized loosely coupled systems. This meant a focus
on the independence of subsystems. While thinkers like Parsons (1958)
discussed community, managerial, and technical subsystems, and pointed
to their articulation as a problem in educational organization, writers on
loose coupling have considered a variety of connections, or rather the
lack of them. For example, Hannaway and Sproull (1979) found loose
coupling between central office and building administrators, and between
administration and instruction. Rowan (1981) reported that loose coupling
in instruction was related to the demands of the institutional environment.
In general, loose coupling studies have neglected the processes of articulation that Parsons stressed.

Even though Weick (1976) saw loose coupling as an alternative to
functionalism, it has been suggested that some loose coupling in such areas
as administration and instruction (Martin and Willower, 1981), and in
information processing by administrators and teachers (Ogawa, 1984),
might be functional for educational organizations. Criticisms of loose
coupling have not been lacking (Boyan, 1982) and some writers (Metcalfe,
1981) have offered lists of its disadvantages. Willower (1982) suggested
that teachers and other school personnel are aware of the rules of the
game and usually play by them, thus avoiding organizational responses
characteristic of tight coupling. This gives the appearance of loose coupling,
but if teachers ignore the rules of the game and cross the thresholds of

normatively proscribed behaviour, administrators quickly react. This was consistent with empirical data on principals' reactions to teacher misbehaviour (Stetter and Willower, 1985).

The trick is to discover in what areas and under what conditions schools are loosely coupled and when they are tightly coupled. Work along these lines was done by Herriott and Firestone (1984) who reported that elementary schools were more bureaucratic while secondary schools were more loosely coupled. Abramowitz and Tenenbaum (1978) also described high schools as loosely coupled systems.

Meanwhile, work on structural and bureaucratic features of school organizations showed some support for loose coupling, but also found that tightly linked schools tended to be perceived as effective (Miskel, McDonald and Bloom, 1983). Research by Hoy and his associates indicated that bureaucratic structure in schools is not unitary but multidimensional (Sousa and Hoy, 1981). Bureaucratic structures defined in terms of high formalization and high centralization were positively related to teacher alienation (Hoy, Blazovsky and Newland, 1983). Studies of bureaucracy in education follow the general pattern found elsewhere; that is, they commonly document bureaucratic dysfunction.

Culture

The topic of organizational culture has become increasingly popular (Administrative Science Quarterly, 1983; Deal and Kennedy, 1982). This popularity has been spurred by the success of books in business management that called attention to the concept (Ouchi, 1981; Peters and Waterman, 1982). In education, writing on organizational culture was foreshadowed by work on schools as social systems. Waller's (1932) treatment of the school as a miniature society emphasized common norms, values, and symbols (see also Sarason, 1971). There are also some similarities between organizational culture and organizational climate (Anderson, 1982).

In addition, the concept of organizational culture has appeared in the literature on educational management in connection with the relation of school culture and school improvement defined largely by student outcomes. This has been most noteworthy with regard to the school principalship (eg Leithwood and Montgomery, 1982) but the idea of culture has also been employed in analyses of national educational reform. Thus Deal (1985) contended that commission reports on education in the US will have little effect unless the proper ceremonies and symbols are created at the grass roots level.

Willower (1984) argued that the concept of organizational culture cannot be divorced from theoretical considerations that take into account the structural characteristics of school organizations as well as their constituent groups. These groups have themselves been examined in cultural terms. Student subculture studies (Cusick, 1973; Lacey, 1970; Peshkin, 1978; Willis, 1977) are perhaps best known, but there is also work on teacher and administrator subcultures (Lortie, 1975; Willower, 1971; 1985). Some of this work shows each group having norms and values that protect its interests. This can be antithetical to broader educational aims (Rutter, Maugham, Mortimore and Ouston, 1979; Cusick, 1983).

While the notion of a culture that is specific to a given school is intriguing because it provides desirable directions for practitioners of school management, the concept is underdeveloped in theoretical and research terms. There are also philosophical issues at stake, since the wrong kind of cultures could restrict critical thought and individual initiative.

Position

Managerial positions in school organizations have been studied in numerous ways and from a variety of perspectives. Two lines of research focus on administrator activity. One asks what schools managers do; the other asks what they say. Work on action usually follows the structured observation procedures of Mintzberg (1973). Studies have been done on elementary school principals (Kmetz and Willower, 1982; Morris, Crowson, Porter-Gehrie and Hurwitz, 1984; Peterson, 1978; Phillipps and Thomas, 1982; Thomas, Willis and Phillipps, 1981), secondary principals (Martin and Willower, 1981; Morris, Crowson, Porter-Gehrie and Hurwitz, 1984; O'Dempsey, 1976; Thomas, Willis and Phillipps, 1981; Willis, 1980), and school superintendents (Duignan, 1980; Friesen and Duignan, 1980; Larson, Bussom and Vicars, 1981; Pitner and Ogawa, 1981), among others. These studies document the varied, fragmented, interrupted character of managerial work. They show that preference goes to issues that are current, lively, and quickly handled. Much of the work gets done in brief, unscheduled meetings, although superintendents engage in fewer and longer sessions than principals. Principals spend more time on managerial than instructional duties, with elementary school principals giving the most time to instructional matters. Compared with the principals, superintendents have more contacts with organizational outsiders. These studies show that the managerial world is a verbal one.

The research on administrator talk (Gronn, 1983; 1984) was done on principals. It suggests that principals' talk is used to engineer consent and to loosen and tighten administrative controls. It also supports the idea of students of bureaucracy that authority colours others' perceptions of managers' talk.

The investigations of managerial activity and talk are limited by their methodologies. Indeed, more sophisticated procedures for treating administrator talk have already been suggested (Levine, Donnellon, Gioia and Sims, 1984). Such small-sample research has problems with representativeness. Still, it provides insights into a neglected area of administration: the work lives of managers.

Numerous studies have examined one facet or another of administrator behaviour. For example, Licata and Hack (1980) found that the grapevine structures or information networks of elementary school principals were based on personal considerations like friendships, while those of secondary principals were grounded in professional considerations such as specialization. These structures were labelled 'clan-like' and 'guild-like', respectively. Bredeson (1985) reported that the metaphorical perspectives of principals could be grouped under maintenance, survival, and vision, areas, he argued, that reflected the ethos of the position. Hoyle (1982) depicted school principals as practitioners of micro-politics, reflecting the conflict of authority and expectations principals typically face. Crowson and Porter-Gehrie (1980) showed how principals cope by developing organizational shortcuts, by rule bending, by flexibly interpreting policies, and by extending and redefining their roles.

Burford (1985) found that when principals were perceived to have good senses of humour, teacher loyalty and judged school effectiveness were higher. Smedley and Willower (1981) reported a relationship between a humanistic style of pupil control behaviour by the school principal and the robustness of school for students.

Blumberg (1985) depicted school superintendents as educational politicians thoroughly involved in conflict that is both internal to the organization and an integral part of the schools' environmental relationships. Cuban (1976) provided a vivid picture along these lines in connection with the large urban superintendency. Williams and Willower (1983) reported that female school superintendents were similar to their male counterparts in the way they perceived their work. However, the women had to overcome subtle forms of discrimination. Miskel and Cosgrove (1985) examined studies of managerial succession, an area studied earlier by Carlson (1961). They concluded that succession research could furnish insights not supplied by investigations of leadership, because studies done during periods of relative calm do not tap the range of organizational and leadership problems that can emerge during successions.

Blumberg and Greenfield (1980) studied effective school principals and inferred that, while each principal had a particular style of managing, there was a functional equivalence of style that featured tolerance for ambiguity, expressive abilities, skills at collecting and analysing data, vision and initiative, and physical energy and psychological strength. Lipham (1981), among others, provided a similar type of listing, but with different content. However, Bossert, Dwyer, Rowan and Lee (1982) pointed to the complexity of instructional management, arguing that the behaviour of the administrator is only one variable among many others that stem from context, climate, and organization. In his comprehensive review, Boyan (1982) concluded that studies of managerial effects in school organizations have been inconclusive.

Despite its selectivity, this review provides a sampling of current work on school organizations. Clearly, thought and research in this field are characterized by multiple perspectives and methods. That is all to the good, especially if scholars and practitioners are willing to employ a variety of theories and methods to explore problems (Immegart and Boyd, 1979). To understand a particular phenomenon more fully, it makes sense to examine it using more than one set of lenses. In addition, it is well to bear in mind that scientific generalizations are always provisional, fated to be edged aside by new ideas.

Questions and speculations

Next, some questions stemming from the work explored are considered. A few speculations are added where appropriate. Comments are organized around the schools' external and internal concerns.

External

When describing schools as reflections of their societies and as politically vulnerable, vulnerability should be thought of as an environmental contingency (Hanson, 1985: 151-172) that is a variable. From a comparative viewpoint, differences in political pressures on school managers in various kinds of societies, for instance Western democracies and Marxist or military dictatorships, have been neglected. Within societies, differences in school responses to various interest groups (Bacharach and Mitchell, 1981; Ratsoy, 1980), as well as differences in the tactics and strategies employed by these groups, should be studied. For example, are school managers more likely to respond to taxpayers' groups with information and to civil libertarians in a symbolic manner? A larger question is whether school managers employ a political style akin to a leadership style.

A lot of attention has been given to the problem of managerial effectiveness, but mostly in terms of internal relations and student outcomes. What constitutes political effectiveness on the part of the school manager? It might be speculated that an apolitical stance on the part of administrators could have political value. Scholars who have debunked the myth that school administration has not been political may have neglected the political consequences of this myth. It might enhance legitimacy by using a language that puts the schools above politics, just where many citizens want them.

In fact, it is reasonable to argue that school administrators gain legitimacy when they speak as educators rather than as managers or politicians. These administrators are also spokespersons in the school and community for shared values. Here, too, they fight political battles from high ground and enhance organizational legitimacy. However, pluralism has sometimes meant the clash of accepted values, for example, equity and excellence. In these circumstances, the schools reflect social conflict and might respond to mixed signals in a confused manner or not respond at all and simply maintain the *status quo*. If legitimacy is central to the school's relation with its environment, greater attention should be given to how legitimacy is maintained and what its special characteristics are for educational institutions. Such work might lead to better recognition of the importance of administrator articulation of educational ideals publicly expressed, and reflected in school programmes. Legitimacy may have both symbolic and technical aspects.

Internal

The concept of legitimacy is also useful in exploring the school's internal relations. Loose coupling with regard to supervision of teachers in schools might be partially explained by professional norms that question the legitimacy of managerial intervention in classroom activities. Moreover, instruction is characterized by soft rules (Lortie, 1969) that temper administrator intervention. It seems likely that the tightly coupled areas in schools involve students and the more routine aspects of teacher activity. Studies that examine the particulars are needed.

Needed also is research that looks at the effects of various contingencies on the blend of autonomy and control in schools. Peterson's (1984) work, which concluded that increased school district size resulted in increased impersonal controls but decreased supervision, is an illustration. Another is March's (1981) study which suggested that different spheres of control were associated with different organizational positions. A third is Hallinger and Murphy's (1984) investigation of variations in school principals' instructional leadership that relate to school socio-economic status.

The concept of organizational culture stands in stark contrast to Meyer and Rowan's (1978) notion of internal dissensus. Organizational culture applied to schools suggests many questions. For instance, if there are teacher, student, and even administrator subcultures, how do they fit organizational culture? Do strong subcultures inhibit the development of an organizational culture, and does the development of an organizational culture require changes in the subcultures? Is there a cultural limit in collectivities, such that a strong organizational culture precludes strong subcultures or vice versa? Can an organizational culture coexist with the subcultures with each having separate spheres?

Another set of questions concerns the ends served by school cultures. It cannot be assumed that a strong organizational culture will unambiguously serve educational ends. Some configurations of culture might be dysfunctional for some desirable student outcomes. For instance, school cultures that stress academics might stint critical thinking or social skills.

What difficulties are likely to be faced by school principals who intentionally strive to build school cultures in harmony with particular educational aims? One concern is the potential clash of narrower teacher interests with organizational purposes. A strong organizational culture would likely limit autonomy and require commitments of teacher time and energy far beyond the ordinary. Another concern is the stability and staying power of a school culture dependent on an individual leader and lacking long-term structural supports in the organization. An empirical literature on organizational cultures in educational settings is needed, as is more writing on what have been called the subcultures, especially the adult ones.

The work on the allocation of attention and on talk should begin to treat results as variables and examine relationships. For instance, under what conditions is fragmentation or variation increased or decreased, and what influences greater or less attention to instructional or managerial activities? What organizational circumstances elicit administrator talk directed toward control? Under what conditions is such talk increased or reduced? Even more fundamental for the talk studies, it can be asked what factors affect the discrepancy between talk and perceived meaning, and questions can be raised concerning the cues, gestures, tones, and other special features of talk that give similar statements different significance. Both the activity and talk research have had limited theoretical under-pinnings, and the talk studies lack rudimentary classification typologies. One is tempted to call for combined activity and talk research, but its intensity might channel the behaviour of participants in an on-stage (Goffman, 1959) direction.

Given the relentless pace and pressures of managerial life, the contin-gencies that affect deliberation and purposeful administrator action should be explored. Also, more needs to be known about how managers think and react on the job. If they do not overtly spend much time pondering the consequences of various decisions and courses of action, how do they make managerial choices? Is their lack of deliberation more apparent than real? Do managers develop a repertoire of skills and clues that enable them to render sensible on-the-spot decisions? There is a lot of work to be done on a range of topics related to this subject.

Philosophy

There has been considerable ferment (Griffiths, 1979) and debate in educational administration in recent years that is essentially philosophical. This debate concerns the epistemological basis of thought and research in the field and issues of value, among others.

A number of conflicting philosophical positions have been set forth. One is a form of neo-Marxism with roots in the work of the critical theorists, mainly of the Frankfurt School (Jay, 1973; Held, 1980). This point of view has also been influenced by the new sociology of education in Great Britain (Karabel and Halsey, 1977).

One thrust of the neo-Marxists in education is the examination of the impact of dominant social classes on the management and curriculum of the schools (Apple, 1979; Giroux, 1983). Another is based on the argu-ment that current theories of school organization reflect idological biases (Bates, 1980) which neglect social issues, such as the neutralization of power that prevents equal opportunity (Foster, 1980). Neo-Marxists reject traditional theories from functionalism to symbolic interactionism and distrust empirical studies. For many of them, truth is bound up with

historical struggle (Held, 1980: 191) and is not solely a question of veri-
fication in the scientific sense.

The work of the neo-Marxists has been extensively criticized. Their
most vociferous critics have been more traditional Marxists (Hoffman,
1975) who criticize their deviation from certain orthodox Marxist doctrines.
Non-Marxist scholars (Rockmore, Colbert, Gavin and Blakeley, 1981)
have noted that dialectical analysis, the method claimed by Marxists, is
not a method at all but a social ontology, and also point out that Marxists
grant themselves a plenary indulgence from the influences of ideology that
they believe corrupts other perspectives.

It is worth noting that there is an extensive literature written from
non-Marxist viewpoints on topics that concern Marxists. Early studies of
social class (Hollingshead, 1949) and recent work on racism or gender
inequities (Shakeshaft and Nowell, 1985) are examples.

A second philosophical approach in educational administration is
represented by scholars like Greenfield (1975; 1978; 1980). This strand of
thought is essentially subjectivist. It is phenomenologically oriented but
not connected to Husserl's philosphical phenomenology. An effort at
genuine phenomenological analysis in educational administration can
be found in Vandenberg (1982).

People espousing a subjectivist view have been critical of what they
call positivistic science which they see as a fruitless effort to achieve
knowledge through quantification and controls. They believe such work
neglects the realities faced by individuals in organizations. They believe
also that organization theorists reify organizations, making them into
something more than collections of individuals and providing grounds for
an oppressive ideology. They call for studies of individuals in the ethnographic and field observation modes. Hodgkinson (1978) adds an emphasis
on values which he sees as central to educational administration.

Subjectivism was criticized early by Griffiths (1975) and later by Hills
(1980) and Willower (1980). One criticism is that the subjectivists attack
a primitive, essentially extinct, notion of science — for example, the idea
that there is a single theory true for all time, an idea which is rejected
today and which runs counter to the very ethos of inquiry (Merton, 1973).
More recently it has been contended that both Greenfield's (Lakomski,
1985b) and Hodgkinson's (Evers, 1985) positions employ positivistic
assumptions. Just as there has been much research on social class and
equity that is not Marxist, there is considerable work on administrator
perceptions, feelings, and attitudes that is not connected to the subjectivist critique. Similarly with regard to methods, the first ethnographic-
type study in educational administration was done more than 30 years
ago (Boyan, 1951) and scholars like Griffiths (1959: 35) have been calling
for more studies of that type for almost that long. It should be noted
that there is virtually no disagreement on the point that values are central
to educational administration. The main issues concern which values and
the place of values in preparation programmes. Also, more research is
clearly needed on the topic (Enns, 1981).

Alternatives to the neo-Marxist and subjectivist approaches that are non-positivistic have been proposed by Willower (1981; 1983) and by Lakomski (1985a). The first was described as a blend of naturalism, instrumentalism and pragmatism, while the second was described as a combination of pragmatism and materialism. Both reject Marxist, subjectivist, and positivist doctrines and subscribe to conceptions of science that recognize the human fallibility of inquirers and the tentativeness of their conclusions, but see the process of inquiry and its cumulated conceptions and results as providing grounds for the assessment of theoretical ideas and hypotheses.

No one currently writing on philosophical issues in educational administration subscribes to traditional philosophical positivism. This is not surprising since the position is unfashionable in philosophy proper. However, it remains a convenient target.

The philosophical debates going on in educational administration mirror similar debates in administrative science, the social sciences and philosophy itself. However, work on the management of schools continues while the debates go on. Some writers like Sander and Wiggins (1985) offer broad frameworks that draw implications for educational administration from several philosophical approaches. Their main interest is the examination of implications, not the finer points of philosophic discourse. Other scholars simply do their research unconcerned about philosophy. Trends in the field of organization theory as it applies to schools are only partly tied to philosophical discussion. Thus, in a major review, Boyd and Crowson (1981) reported a trend from work on processes to a focus on outcomes and organizational effectiveness, a trend that appears unrelated to the current debates.

Nevertheless, change is occurring, and scholarship on the philosophical bases of educational administration can help to direct that change (Allison, 1983). At the same time, it is important that those of different persuasions communicate in a civil way with one another. It would be a disservice to educational administration if the field was divided into continually warring camps. Tolerance for the viewpoints of others is needed, as well as recognition that no one person, theory, or philosophy has all the answers.

References

Abramowitz, S and Tenenbaum, E (1978) *High School '77* National Institute of Education: Washington, DC

Administrative Science Quarterly (1983) Issue on organizational culture **28** 3: 331-499

Allison, D J (1983) Toward an improved understanding of the organizational nature of schools *Educational Administration Quarterly* **19** 4: 7-34

Anderson, C S (1982) The search for school climate: a review of the research *Review of Educational Research* **52** 3: 368-420

Apple, M (1979) *Ideology and Curriculum* Routledge and Kegan Paul: London

Bacharach, S B ed (1981) *Organizational Behavior in Schools and School Districts* Praeger: New York

Bacharach, S B and Mitchell, S M (1981) Critical variables in the formation and maintenance of consensus in school districts *Educational Administration Quarterly* **17** 4: 74-79

Bates, R J (1980) Educational administration, the sociology of science and the management of knowledge *Educational Administration Quarterly* **16** 2: 1-20

Bates, R (1981) Power and the Educational Administrator: Bureaucracy, Loose Coupling or Cultural Negotiation. American Educational Research Association Annual Meeting Paper: San Francisco

Benson, J K ed (1977) *Organizational Analysis: Critique and Innovation* Sage: Beverley Hills, Cal

Berliner, D C ed (1981) *Review of Research in Education* American Educational Research Association: Washington, DC

Bidwell, C E (1965) The school as a formal organization *in* March (1965)

Blumberg, A (1985) *The School Superintendency: Living with Conflict* Teachers College Press, Columbia University: New York

Blumberg, A and Greenfield, W (1980) *The Effective Principal* Allyn and Bacon: Boston, Mass

Bossert, S T, Dwyer, D C, Rowan, B and Lee, G V (1982) The instructional management role of the principal *Educational Administration Quarterly* **18** 3: 34-64

Bowles, S and Gintis, H (1976) *Schooling in Capitalist America: Educational Reform and the Contradictions of Economic Life* Basic Books: New York

Boyan, N J (1951) A Study of the Formal and Informal Organization of a School Faculty. Doctoral dissertation. Harvard University: Cambridge, Mass

Boyan, N J (1982) Administration of educational institutions *in* Mitzel (1982)

Boyd, W L (1982a) Local influences on education *in* Mitzel (1982)

Boyd, W L (1982b) The political economy of public schools *Educational Administration Quarterly* **18** 3: 111-30

Boyd, W L and Crowson, R L (1981) The changing conception and practice of public school administration *in* Berliner (1981)

Bredeson, P V (1985) An analysis of the metaphorical perspectives of school principals *Educational Administration Quarterly* **21** 1: 29-50

Brown, J S (1970) Risk propensity in decision making: a comparison of business and public school administrators *Administrative Science Quarterly* **15** 4: 473-81

Burford, C T (1985) The Relationship of Principals' Sense of Humor and Job Robustness to School Environment. Doctoral dissertation, Pennsylvania State University: University Park, Penn

Carlson, R O (1961) Succession and performance among school superintendents *Administrative Science Quarterly* **6** 3: 220-27

*Clark, D L, Lotto, L S and Astuto, T A (1984) Effective schools and school improvement: a comparative analysis of two lines of inquiry *Educational Administration Quarterly* **20** 3: 41-68

Crowson, R L and Porter-Gehrie, C (1980) The discretionary behavior of principals in large-city schools *Educational Administration Quarterly* **16** 1: 45-69

Cuban, L (1976) *Urban School Chiefs Under Fire* University of Chicago Press: Chicago

Cusick, P A (1973) *Inside High School* Holt, Rinehart and Winston: New York

Cusick, P A (1983) *The Egalitarian Ideal and the American High School* Longman: New York

Day, R and Day, J V (1977) A review of the current state of negotiated order theory *in* Benson (1977)

Deal, T E (1985) National commissions: blueprints for remodeling or ceremonies for revitalizing public schools *Education and Urban Society* **17** 2: 145-56

Deal, T E and Kennedy, A A (1982) *Corporate Cultures* Addison-Wesley: Reading, Mass

Drabick, L W ed (1971) *Interpreting Education: A Sociological Approach* Appleton-Century-Crofts: New York

Duignan, P (1980) Administrative behavior of school superintendents *Journal of Educational Administration* **18** 1: 5-26

Enns, F (1981) Some ethical-moral concerns in administration *Canadian Administrator* **20** 8: 1-8

Etzioni, A ed (1969) *The Semi-Professions and Their Organization* The Free Press: New York

Evers, C W (1985) Hodgkinson on Ethics and the Philosophy of Administration *in* Rizvi (1985)

Foster, W P (1980) Administration and the crisis in legitimacy *Harvard Educational Review* **50** 4: 496-505

Friesen, D and Duignan, P (1980) How superintendents spent their working time *Canadian Administrator* **19** 5: 1-5

Giroux, H A (1983) Theories of reproduction and resistance in the new sociology of education *Harvard Educational Review* **53** 3: 257-93

Goffman, E (1959) *The Presentation of Self in Everyday Life* Anchor: Garden City, New York

Greenfield, T B (1975) Theory about organizations: a new perspective and its implications for schools *in* Hughes (1975)

Greenfield, T B (1978) Reflections on organization theory and the truths of irreconcilable realities *Educational Administration Quarterly* **14** 2: 1-23

Greenfield, T B (1980) The man who comes back through the door in the wall: discovering truth, discovering self, discovering organizations *Educational Administration Quarterly* **16** 3: 26-59

Griffiths, D E (1959) *Administrative Theory* Appleton-Century-Crofts: New York

Griffiths, D E (1975) Some thoughts about theory in educational administration *University Council for Educational Administration Review* **17** 1: 12-18

Griffiths, D E (1979) Intellectual turmoil in educational administration *Educational Administration Quarterly* **15** 3: 45-65

Gronn, P C (1983) Talk as the work: the accomplishment of school administration *Administrative Science Quarterly* **28** 1: 1-21

Gronn, P C (1984) I have a solution . . .: administrative power in a school meeting *Educational Administrative Quarterly* **20** 2: 65-92

Hallinger, P and Murphy, J (1984) Instructional leadership and school socio-economic status *Administrator's Notebook* **31** 5: 1-4

Halpin, A W (1958) *Administrative Theory in Education* Midwest Administration Center, University of Chicago: Chicago

Hannaway, J and Sproull, L S (1979) Who's running the show?: coordination and control in educational organizations *Administrator's Notebook* **27** 9: 1-4

Hanson, E M (1985) *Educational Administration and Organizational Behavior* Allyn and Bacon: Boston

Held, D (1980) *Introduction to Critical Theory: Horkheimer to Habermas* University of California Press: Berkeley and Los Angeles

Herriott, R E and Firestone, W A (1984) Two images of schools as organizations: a refinement and elaboration *Educational Administration Quarterly* **20** 4: 41-57

Hills, J (1980) A critique of Greenfield's new perspective *Educational Administration Quarterly* **16** 1: 20-44

Hodgkinson, C (1978) *Towards a Philosophy of Administration* Basil Blackwell: Oxford

Hoffman, J (1975) *Marxism and the Theory of Praxis* International Publishers: New York

Hollingshead, A B (1949) *Elmtown's Youth* Wiley: New York

Hoy, W K, Blazovsky, R and Newland, W (1983) Bureaucracy and alienation: a comparative analysis *Journal of Educational Administration* **21** 2: 109-20

Hoyle, E (1982) Micropolitics of educational organizations *Educational Management and Administration* **10** 2: 87-98

Hughes, M G ed (1975) *Administering Education: International Challenge* Athlone Press: London

Immegart, G L and Boyd, W L eds (1979) *Problem Finding in Educational Administration* D C Heath: Lexington, Mass

Jay, M (1973) *The Dialectical Imagination: A History of the Frankfurt School and the Institute for Social Research 1923-1950* Little, Brown and Company: Boston

Johnston, G S ed (1985) *Thought and Research in Educational Administration: The State of the Art* University Press of America: Lanham, Maryland

Karabel, J and Halsey, A H (1977) Educational research: a review and an interpretation *in* Karabel and Halsey (1977)

Karabel, J and Halsey, A H eds (1977) *Power and Ideology in Education* Oxford University Press: New York

Kmetz, J T and Willower, D J (1982) Elementary school principals' work behavior *Educational Administration Quarterly* **18** 4: 62-78

Lacey, C (1970) *Hightown Grammar* Manchester University Press: Manchester

Lakomski, G (1985a) Critical Theory and Educational Administration. American Educational Research Association Annual Meeting Paper: Chicago

Lakomski, G (1985b) Theory, Value and Relevance in Educational Administration *in* Rizvi (1985)

Larson, L L, Bussom, R S and Vicars, W M (1981) *The Nature of a School Superintendent's Work* Southern Illinois University: Carbondale, Ill

Leithwood, K A and Montgomery, D J (1982) The role of the elementary principal in program improvement *Review of Educational Research* **52** 3: 309-39

Levine, V, Donnellon, A, Gioia, D A and Sims, H P (1984) Scripts and speech acts in administrative behavior *Educational Administration Quarterly* **20** 1: 93-110

Licata, J W and Hack, W G (1980) School administrator grapevine structure *Educational Administration Quarterly* **16** 3: 82-99

Lipham, J M (1981) *Effective Principal, Effective School* National Association of Secondary School Principals: Reston, Va

Lortie, D C (1969) The balance of control and autonomy in elementary school teaching *in* Etzioni (1969)

Lortie, D C (1975) *School Teacher* University of Chicago Press: Chicago

March, J G ed (1965) *Handbook of Organizations* Rand McNally: Chicago

March, J G and Olsen, J P (1976) *Ambiguity and Choice in Organizations* Universitetsforlaget: Bergen-Oslo-Tromso, Norway

March, M E (1981) Control over educational decisions *Canadian Administrator* **21** 3: 1-6

Martin, W J and Willower, D J (1981) The managerial behavior of high school principals *Educational Administration Quarterly* **17** 1: 69-90

Merton, R K (1973) *The Sociology of Science* University of Chicago Press: Chicago

Metcalfe, L (1981) Designing precarious partnerships *in* Nystrom and Starbuck (1981)

Meyer, J W and Rowan, B (1977) Institutionalized organizations: formal structure as myth and ceremony *American Journal of Sociology* **83** 2: 340-63

Meyer, J W and Rowan, B (1978) The structure of educational organizations *in* Meyer (1978)

Meyer, J W and Scott, W R eds (1983) *Organizational Environments: Ritual and Rationality* Sage: Beverley Hills, Cal

Meyer, J W, Scott, W R and Deal, T E (1983) Institutional and technical sources of organizational structure: explaining the structure of educational organizations *in* Meyer and Scott (1983)

Meyer, M W ed (1978) *Organizations and Environments* Jossey-Bass: San Francisco

Michaelsen, J B (1981) The political economy of school district administration *Educational Administration Quarterly* **17** 3: 98-113

Mintzberg, H (1973) *The Nature of Managerial Work* Harper and Row: New York

Miskel, C and Cosgrove, D (1985) Leader succession in school settings *Review of Educational Research* **55** 1: 87-106

Miskel, C, McDonald, D and Bloom, S (1983) Structural and expectancy linkages within schools and organizational effectiveness *Educational Administration Quarterly* **19** 1: 49-82

Mitzel, H E ed (1982) *Encyclopedia of Educational Research* Macmillan and Free Press: New York

Morris, V C, Crowson, R L, Porter-Gehrie, C and Hurwitz, E (1984) *Principals in Action* Charles E Merrill: Columbus, Ohio

Nystrom, P C and Starbuck, W H eds (1981) *Handbook of Organizational Design* Oxford University Press: New York

O'Dempsey, K (1976) Time analysis of activities, work patterns and roles of high school principals *Administrator's Bulletin* 7 8: 1-4

Ogawa, R T (1984) Teachers and administrators: elements of the information processing repertoires of schools *Educational Administration Quarterly* 20 2: 5-24

Ouchi, W (1981) *Theory Z* Avon: New York

Parsons, T (1958) Some ingredients of a general theory of formal organization *in* Halpin (1958)

Peshkin, A (1978) *Growing Up American* University of Chicago Press: Chicago

Peters, T J and Waterman, R H (1982) *In Serarch of Excellence* Harper and Row: New York

Peterson, K (1978) The principal's tasks *Administrator's Notebook* 26 8: 1-4

Peterson, K (1984) Mechanisms of administrative control over managers in educational organizations *Administrative Science Quarterly* 29 4: 573-97

Phillipps, D and Thomas, A R (1982) Principals' decision making: some observations *in* Simpkins *et al* (1982)

Pitner, N J and Ogawa, R T (1981) Organizational leadership: the case of the school superintendent *Educational Administration Quarterly* 17 2: 45-65

Ratsoy, E W (1980) Environments, linkages and policy making in education *Canadian Administrator* 19, 7: 1-6

Rizvi, F ed (1985) *Working Papers in Ethics and Educational Administration* Deakin University: Victoria, Australia

Rockmore, T, Colbert, J G, Gavin, W J and Blakeley, T J (1981) *Marxism and Alternatives* D Reidel: Dordrecht, Holland

Rowan, B (1981) The effects of institutionalized rules on administrators *in* Bacharach (1981)

*Rutter, M, Maugham, B, Mortimore, P, Ouston, J and Smith, A (1979) *Fifteen Thousand Hours* Harvard University Press: Cambridge, Mass

Sander, B and Wiggins, T (1985) Cultural context of administrative theory: in consideration of a multidimensional paradigm *Educational Administration Quarterly* 21 1: 95-117

Sarason, S (1971) *The Culture of the School and the Problem of Change* Allyn and Bacon: Boston

Shakeshaft, C and Nowell, I (1985) Research on theories, concepts, and models of organizational behavior: the influence of gender *Issues in Education* 2 3: 186-203

Simpkins, W S, Thomas, A R and Thomas, E B eds (1982) *Principal and Task: An Australian Perspective* University of New England: Armidale, Australia

Smedley, S R and Willower, D J (1981) Principals: pupil control behavior and school robustness *Educational Administration Quarterly* 17 4: 40-56

Sousa, D A and Hoy, W K (1981) Bureaucratic structure in schools *Educational Administration Quarterly* 17 4: 21-39

Stetter, M W and Willower, D J (1985) School principals as threshold guardians: an exploratory study *Alberta Journal of Educational Research* 31 1: 2-10

Thomas, A R, Willis, Q and Phillipps, D (1981) Observational studies of Australian administrators: methodological issues *Australian Journal of Education* 25 1: 55-72

Thompson, J D (1967) *Organizations in Action* McGraw-Hill: New York

Tyack, D and Hansot, E (1982) *Managers of Virtue: Public School Leadership 1820-1980* Basic Books: New York

Vandenburg, D (1982) Hermeneutical phenomenology in the study of educational administration *Journal of Educational Administration* 20 1: 23-32

Waller, W (1932) *The Sociology of Teaching* Wiley: New York

Weick, K E (1976) Educational organizations as loosely coupled systems *Administrative Science Quarterly* **21** 1: 1-19

Weick, K E (1980) Loosely Coupled Systems: Relaxed Meanings and Thick Interpretations. Cornell University Paper: Ithaca, New York

Williams, R H and Willower, D J (1983) Female school superintendents on their work *Journal of Educational Equity and Leadership* **3** 4: 289-304

Willis, P (1977) *Learning to Labour* Heath: Lexington, Mass

Willis, Q (1980) The work activity of school principals *Journal of Educational Administration* **18** 1: 27-54

Willower, D J (1971) The teacher subculture *in* Drabick (1971)

Willower, D J (1980) Contemporary issues in theory in educational administration *Educational Administration Quarterly* **16** 3: 1-25

Willower, D J (1981) Educational administration: some philosophical and other considerations *Journal of Educational Administration* **19** 2: 115-39

Willower, D J (1982) School organizations: perspectives in juxtaposition *Educational Administration Quarterly* **18** 3: 89-110

Willower, D J (1983) Evolution in the professorship: past, philosophy, future *Educational Administration Quarterly* **19** 3: 179-200

Willower, D J (1984) School principals, school cultures, and school improvement *Educational Horizons* **63** 1: 35-38

Willower, D J (1985) Mystifications and mysteries in thought and research in educational administration *in* Johnston (1985)

Wolcott, H F (1973) *The Man in the Principal's Office* Holt, Rinehart and Winston: New York

3. Politics, power and the management of schools

Peter Gronn

Summary: The accomplishment of tasks and responsibilities in providing for education necessitates resort to micro-politics by school managers. Confronted by competition for scarce resources and with ideologies, interests and personalities at variance, bargaining becomes crucial. Political exchanges, which can occur at all organizational levels and in all spheres of management, formal and informal, comprise negotiations over definitions governing the content and conduct of action. Conflict between the actors takes a number of forms. It can be manifest, hidden or latent. It can even be forestalled by what turns out to be false presuppositions on the part of the actor, or thwarted by the actor's very own framework for attributing things as real. It is not clear whether such frameworks can be freely altered at will and under what circumstances this might be possible. However, some slight structural variations do exist between the politics of State and non-State systems and, in the two contrasting models which can be drawn of each, different outlooks are shown to be required of the respective actors.

Introduction

The manager has been defined by Jaques (1970: 133) as 'someone who is in a role in which he is authorized to get work done through employed subordinates for whose work he is held accountable'. Managerial responsibilities are, in turn, usually arranged hierarchically to form an executive system (Jaques, 1951: 273-297). Were compliance with managerial directives for accomplishing the work always automatic, a depoliticized system of 'pure' or even 'total' administration would be conceivable. Needless to say, unquestioning obedience is rarely, if ever, forthcoming. The norm in schools is conflict. There are always different definitions of the situation in the minds of the actors, across the span of managerial responsibility.

Reasons for politics

Four factors account for the manifestation of school politics: scarce resources, conflicting ideologies, clashing interests and personality differences.

Resources are the 'what' in the classic Lasswellian (1936) formula. They include not only the more obviously quantifiable objects like personnel, money, equipment and facilities but also intangible yet no less real qualitative things such as cultural, class and linguistic capital or 'know-how' (Gouldner, 1979: 21-27). Disputes about resource adequacy and utilization occur at the points of procurement and allocation. School and system managers frequently differ on the grounds of equity and efficiency about what is necessary and sufficient for the provision of education.

Ideologies are conceptions of desirable states of affairs held, implicitly or explicitly, in the minds of actors. Analytically, these are of two sorts: sets of beliefs about various end states in education and beliefs about the appropriate means of obtaining such states. In practice, the two coexist. Statements of ends such as classical, liberal-humanist and radical conceptions of education also include beliefs about desired modes of curriculum, pedagogy and evaluation (Bates, 1980). These ideologies are anchored, in turn, in each actor's bedrock assumptions about man, society, nature and knowledge (Burrell and Morgan, 1979: 1-37).

Interests are definitions of what is materially at stake, to be gained or lost, in any one set of circumstances for individuals and groups. Disagreement over whether interests are 'subjective' (defined by the actors), 'objective' (defined for, or imputed to, the actors) or 'real' as opposed to 'false', plague discussion (Runciman, 1970; Wall, 1975). Occupationally, for teachers, there are at least two dimensions to 'interests': personal and professional. The former include various career accoutrements: tenure, status, promotion and reward. The latter entail commitments to particular epistemologies, their organization and transmission. Interests in both these senses are legitimated or justified by particular career ideologies and may be closely related to particular macro or party political allegiances (Hoyle, 1982: 88-89).

Personality is an actor's manifest, characteristic pattern of interpersonal behaviour. Particular personality configurations or 'styles' — for example, compulsive, obsessive, impulsive — (Shapiro, 1965) emerge in response to culturally and intra-psychically induced anxiety. Residues of unresolved inner conflicts, deriving from the delicate interplay of nature and nurture in infancy, remain latent in the actor's unconscious. Stressful situations re-activate these conflicts. One then resorts to defence mechanisms and impaired judgement results (Jaques, 1955; Horney, 1950). The consequent act may be paranoid, schizoid or depressive, and can engulf the mentality of a whole organization and its management (Kets de Vries and Miller, 1984).

Forms of politics

'Each office, each fraternal order, each college faculty has its tiny conspirational clique,' writes Kenneth Burke (1969: 166). 'Conspiracy is as natural as breathing.' Schools comprise a number of interlocking arenas. There are formal or front stage arenas and informal or back stage arenas

(Bailey, 1977: 88-126; Goffman, 1976: 109-140). Formal arenas include subject departments, committees and meetings. Informal arenas include friendship and network groups. In all arenas the actors contest and negotiate definitions of the situation. For each area of managerial responsibility it can always be asked: Which definitions prevail? Whose definitions are they? Why does *this* particular definition prevail? Definitions of the situation are taken-for-granted ways of thinking and acting. Control of computers by one department (eg Mathematics) instead of universal provision, the presumption that particular subjects warrant more time-table space, and that there are budgetary priorities are examples of particular definitions. When there is a dominant coalition or group, enduring definitions solidify to form a 'paradigm' (Barnes, 1979; Brown, 1978) or 'mobilization of bias' (Bachrach and Baratz, 1970).

There are three sets of constraints on the actors in any one arena. Each actor's individual portmanteau of ideology, interests and personality will determine his or her particular framing and reading of the situation. This baggage is the outcome of class location, familial experiences and occupational socialization. Then, the prescriptions, rules and conventions which apply to individuals as role incumbents dictate the alternate courses of action open to them in the circumstances. Finally, the expectations and demands of various external provider and beneficiary groups (eg taxpayers, parents, employers, politicians) have to be confronted. The actors are continually pushed and pulled between the freedom or necessity to act.

Mechanisms of power

How do 'the struggles for advantage' (Burke, 1969: 166) and 'small politics' (Bailey, 1971: 2) work? 'Struggle' implies overt dissension and competition, yet is has been clear for a long time now, particularly since the publication of Lukes' (1974) work, that power need not only take this form. For instance, it has been shown that the *status quo* or normal course of events may be complied with because 'the dissidents either feared to enter the ring at all or had already been worsted by crooked means beforehand' (Bailey, 1965: 18-19).

There are in fact five ways in which power can be seen at work in any institution: through overt conflict, covert conflict, latent conflict, inaction through self-censorship and inaction through the failure of an idea to enter consciousness. Each is discussed in turn and illustration from schools is provided.

Action

Pluralists, like Dahl (1972), have argued that power is exercised, its exercise can be observed, the extent of its exercise can be measured and it is always clear who exercises it. 'Key' items or matters, it is said, can be isolated to see who made decisions in each case. Thus, at a departmental meeting of English teachers, it ought to be possible to demonstrate who decided (say) on particular textbooks, that emphasis be placed on grammar rather than creative expression and that literal, not numerical, assessment of student work be adopted. Factions and points of view, in this conception of power, contend until one side wins through. The new *status quo* or definition of the situation reflects a changed balance of interests.

On some occasions, in some situations, this account is no doubt an accurate one. It may not hold good, however, in circumstances where interests are vested; that is, where a group perceives itself to be threatened and seeks, accordingly, to perpetuate an existing set of arrangements. Building on Schattschneider's (1960: 71) observation that 'some issues are organized into politics while others are organized out', Bachrach and Baratz (1970) have shown that power has a second, hidden face. Measures may be taken to prevent the emergence of conflict. What is to be made, for instance, of an apparent absence of acrimony, strife and anger? Unanimity (in the case of textbooks, that a novel by a controversial author be left off the syllabus) presumably denotes consent willingly and freely given. This may not be the case, however, as Bachrach and Baratz showed in the case of the Baltimore anti-poverty programme. What may be signalled is the opposite, namely that a lot of backstage manoeuvring has gone on beforehand to silence potential critics with threats, promises or offers to help elsewhere if this matter is pushed through.

Covert action need not only take the form of a decision not to decide in the formal arena, a non-decision, so to speak. It may well be that an aggrieved party meets secretly or behind the scenes and realizes it lacks the resources or the 'numbers' to carry the day. No one stifles or worsts the group; it simply suppresses its own impulse to dissent. (This is not quite the same thing as 'anticipated reactions' — to be discussed later — because the lobbying, while covert or in stealth, is normally the subject of rumour and 'known' to be going on.) Thus, reverting to the textbook example, it is possible to speak of a hidden agenda. In one sense, for the disaffected (supporters of the controversial novel), the matter is very much on their personal agenda but it fails to get on to the official one. In another sense, the notion of 'hidden agenda' refers, in this case, to the reasons for the failure of dissent to emerge, ie that because particular pressures have been brought to bear something else is really at stake.

Some writers point to 'latent' conflicts as the next point on the action-inaction continuum. This is where concerns are felt or experienced by individuals as 'grievances' (Kent Jennings, 1968). From the dominant coalition's point of view it is best if grievances are experienced purely at the level of personal 'troubles' (Wright Mills, 1970: 14-15) rather than acted upon, because troubles, as Emerson and Messenger (1977) have shown, rapidly get out of hand and escalate into 'issues'. One interesting study of how latent disaffection informally coalesces, bubbles and simmers along, but is none the less contained, is Burns' (1955) analysis of managerial cliques and cabals in industry. Ageing, frustrated cabals begrudgingly give allegiance to the dictates of the managerial prerogative, while the impatient, upwardly mobile young Turks temper ambition in line with their superiors' presumed expectations of them. Labour relations are especially prone to 'troubles' flaring and hardening into the vicious circle of 'them or us' unless headed off early on, as Gouldner's (1955) study of a gypsum plant strike shows.

Inaction

How is it possible to get to grips with the non-occurrence of something, a 'non-event'? There are three ways this might be done. First, on the basis of experience and known cases, a range of hypothesized actions, policies or outcomes can be posited. The task is then to account empirically for the absence of these in any one place. Second, it may be possible to compare two or three sites, as did Crenson (1971) and Gronn (1979), accounting for the presence and absence of comparable issues in each case. Thus Gronn (1979: 330-340) found that in the provision of specialist teaching staff, over which school councillors exercised no official jurisdiction or sanctions, one council vigorously pursued the matter, while another cowered before the might and status of a dominant principal. The third tack is to find evidence of self-censorship or 'anticipated reactions' (Friedrich, 1963), such as in the case of this cringing council. It is clear that some actors will hesitate or refrain from pursuing their interests in the face of the presumed or reputed power of others (Hunter, 1963). The decision to abstain may be based on a misreading of the true state of affairs pertaining, but to assert that is to miss the point; for it is what the powerless take the definition of the situation to be which becomes 'real' and therefore determining.

An even trickier variant of inaction to pin down is where an option fails to occur to the actors. Lukes (1974: 24) tried to tackle this by showing that in 'shaping their perceptions, cognitions and preferences in such a way that they accept their role in the existing order of things' people can be prevented from having grievances. This is plausible because in everyday discourse people sometimes announce after the event that 'it never occurred to me' or 'it never even entered my head.' Language is the clue to making sense of this phenomenon. Pocock (1972: 46), for instance, has observed that where followers unquestioningly and automatically observe regime rituals and traditions, words become redundant. The predisposition to obey is like that of a musician in the orchestra to whom 'it no more occurs . . . to play a part other than that appointed to him than it occurs to the dancer to move to a different rhythm.' Freire's (1972) experience bears this out because it shows that oppression and enslavement are tolerated by the powerless since they lack the linguistic wherewithal with which to envisage alternative possibilities to their current condition.

When the lid of oppression is eventually lifted off, such as during violent social upheaval or in Lukes' (1974: 47) 'abnormal times', all sorts

of potentialities are unleashed. Ordinarily, however, language works to
enslave the mind within a particular 'way of seeing'. Orwell (1963: 45)
knew this well. That is why he had the Newspeak philologist, Syme, say
to the hero of *1984*, Winston Smith:

> Don't you see that the whole aim of Newspeak is to narrow the range of
> thought? In the end we shall make thought crime impossible, because there
> will be no words in which to express it. Every concept that can ever be needed,
> will be expressed by exactly *one* word, with its meaning rigidly defined and
> all its subsidiary meanings rubbed out and forgotten . . . Every year fewer and
> fewer words, and the range of consciousness always a little smaller.

Thus, the failure to act may represent a conscious or unconscious refusal
to act on the one hand or an actor's incapacity to see the need for action
from the start on the other. Far from all the dimensions of power discussed being captured by a simple locution like Dahl's 'making decisions',
evidence of the very power of definition itself is evident in designating
'making decisions' as *the* framework for conceptualizing 'power' (Brown,
1978: 376).

Discussion

Two key issues emerge from the above observations: just how free are the
actors to alter the definitions of the situation in which they find themselves, and do the patterns of power and the texture of politics vary when
the underlying legitimation of authority differs?

The first question is prompted by the observation that definitions are
always socially constructed and 'those who are in the situation ordinarily
do not *create* this definition' (Goffman, 1975: 1). Long-standing debates
have raged back and forth about the relative weight to attach to the
realms of freedom and necessity in accounting for varieties of human
action, between various species of voluntarists and determinists in social
theory. The latest version of this argument, which continues to defy
resolution, has been carried forth by Giddens (1979) and Archer (1982)
and is now couched in terms of a dichotomy between 'agency' and 'structure' and the relative importance accorded to each. Schools are of fundamental importance to the terms and outcome of this debate because they
are pointed to by protagonists as key mechanisms by which any society
endeavours to perpetuate (or 'reproduce') its underlying basis and format
or to modify and change it. Indeed, beliefs about a school or a school
system's capacity to do either of these things lie at the heart of school
managers' and teachers' ideologies about the *desirability* of so doing.

However it is chosen to address the issues of politicization raised by
the first question, there is little doubt that managerial reality is more
intractable and impervious than might at first be thought. Part and parcel
of the above power phenomena are components like 'drift' (the impercep-
tible feeling that the ground is shifting beneath the actor's feet), 'routines'
which 'have their own momentum' (Parry and Morriss, 1974: 331),

'precedent' and 'custom', all of which in some sense lock the actors in. Then, what is to be made of 'ruling' or 'reigning' as types of governing or managing? Are such modes to be equated with action, as in the phrase 'the powers that do' or, more subtly, are they evidence of 'the powers that be'? A useful device for appreciating the full force of such phenomena is to view managerial action linguistically, so that the action embedded in the manager's performative utterances can be seen as conforming to a spontaneous, rehearsed or unrehearsed 'script'.

The second issue is slightly less vexed. Schools operated by the State are 'bureaucratic', and sanctioned by impersonal, legislatively derived rules in a way in which church-based English and Australian versions of 'public schools' in the Arnoldian tradition are not. These latter are best seen as feudally organized fiefdoms, centred around a succession of 'patriarchs' ('very superior men' they were known as in the nineteenth century) although this is changing. Authority has usually been legitimated in terms of custom, tradition and the personal power of the 'chief'. In contra-distinction to State institutions these schools service a more homogenized market or clientele and have been seen as 'organic' to a 'ruling class' (Connell *et al*, 1982). They have been extremely successful in both societies in having their products secure control of various political and economic command posts. In that the minimizing of ideological deviance and en-suring commonality of interest among staff are central to the public school's cultivation of successful cultural capital and currency, it may be that there is more free play for the eccentricities of personality and systems of patronage in the conduct of their politics of resource management.

According to the extent to which the overarching ideological canopy is hegemonic, the conduct and content of micro-political exchanges will differ from State schools. Managerial systems of punishment and reward and mobility and sponsorship will be more informal and personalized than in a bureaucracy. There is likely to be less formal machinery provision for parity of treatment which is, after all, what sets of bureaucratic rules are meant to be devices for. This is not to say that there will be no conflict (overt, hidden or latent). What is means is that having to find favour (and keeping it) with a dominant, benevolent head becomes the ticket to success, so that any unwillingness and reluctance to 'play the game' tends to be kept in check. This is not merely because it is seen as 'bad form' or 'letting the side down' but because it is intimidating to be dependent on someone else's benevolence.

Conclusions

The argument has been advanced that politics is the vehicle by which the work gets done, in the Jaques' (1970: 133) formula. Politics in the micro-sense depicted here is not merely to be seen as a technique or a useful device; instead, an appreciation of its dimensions and scope is basic to an understanding of how schools operate as institutions. The discussion has been mainly confined to aspects of the provision of the educational 'fabric' for the schools as a whole rather than journeying into and scrutin- izing the politics of classroom pedagogy. Clearly it is difficult to keep the two domains separate in practice. It was shown how power in one or other of its forms need not be overtly 'exercised' to be present in any one situation. Furthermore, it was argued that while there are always severe constraints on the freedom of any one individual or group to act entirely freely in the pursuit of their own interests, opportunities for so doing are thrown open from time to time. Some indication was given of the circum- stances and conditions making this possible.

Finally, it was suggested that the dynamics of micro-political behaviour may well vary between different types of school. To the extent that bureaucracies are designed to ensure parity of treatment, stressing pro- cedural rights and guarantees, politics in schools of that type can be characterized as the politics of formalism. Where, by contrast, patronage and favours are more likely to be bestowed, as in the 'public schools', a politics of 'croneyism' is the appropriate model. The validity and force of these contrasting typifications are not hard to sustain. One State school councillor's lament that a principal will always get his way because 'there's a group that have louder and louder voices' and 'stick together' to support him (Gronn, 1984: 86) is evidence that a game has been lost. At least there is a game. But when a retired head, long a doyen and archetype amongst his peers, can admit to a wide-eyed general public that, in respect of his school council's executive committee ('where the real authority lay'), 'I wrote the minutes beforehand with the anticipated decisions [and] the system worked well' (Wood, 1976: 257, 258), he is not simply obviating the need for bargaining, he is defining it out of existence by resort to his very own personal fiat. To survive the system the neophyte in the former case contrives to become an *apparatchik* acquiring the rudiments of an organizational calculus sufficient to master the machine. In the latter instance, when the institution is more likely to be fuelled by whim and friends are required at court, the individual aspires to be an indispensable identity, a pedagogical *éminence grise*.

References

Archer, M S (1982) Morphogenesis versus structuration *British Journal of Sociology* 33 4: 455-83

Bachrach, P and Baratz, M S (1970) *Power and Poverty* Oxford University Press: New York

Bailey, F G (1965) Decisions by consensus in councils and committees, with special reference to village and local government in India *in* Banton (1965)

Bailey, F G (1971) Gifts and poisons *in* Bailey (1971)

Bailey, F G ed (1971) *Gifts and Poisons* Basil Blackwell: Oxford

*Bailey, F G (1977) *Morality and Expediency* Basil Blackwell: Oxford

Banton, M ed (1965) *Political Systems and the Distribution of Power* Tavistock: London

Barnes, S B (1969) Paradigms: social and scientific *Man* 4 1: 94-102

Bates, R J (1980) Educational administration, the sociology of science, and the management of knowledge *Educational Administration Quarterly* **16** 2: 1-20

Brown, R H (1978) Bureaucracy as praxis: towards a political phenomenology of formal organisations *Administrative Science Quarterly* **23** 3: 365-82

Burke, K (1969) *A Rhetoric of Motives* University of California Press: Los Angeles

Burns, T (1955) The reference of conduct in small groups *Human Relations* **7** 4: 467-86

Burrell, G and Morgan, G (1979) *Sociological Paradigms and Organisational Analysis* Heinemann: London

Connell, R W, Ashendon, D J, Kessler, G W and Dowsett, G W (1982) *Making the Difference* Allen and Unwin: Sydney

Crenson, M A (1971) *The Unpolitics of Air Pollution* John Hopkins Press: Baltimore

Crewe, I ed (1974) *British Political Sociology Yearbook: Elites in Western Democracy* Croom Helm: London

Dahl, R A (1972) *Who Governs?* Yale University Press: New Haven

Emerson, R M and Messenger, S L (1977) The micro-politics of trouble *Social Problems* **25** 1: 121-34

Freire, P (1972) *Pedagogy of the Oppressed* Penguin: Harmondsworth

Friedrich, C J (1963) *Man and His Government* McGraw-Hill: New York

Giddens, A (1979) *Central Problems in Social Theory* Macmillan: London

Goffman, E (1975) *Frame Analysis* Peregrine Books: Harmondsworth

*Goffman, E (1976) *The Presentation of Self in Everyday Life* Penguin: Harmondsworth

Gouldner, A W (1955) *Wildcat Strike* Routledge and Kegan Paul: London

Gouldner, A W (1979) *The Future of the Intellectuals and the Rise of the New Class* Macmillan: London

Gronn, P C (1979) The Politics of School Management: A Comparative Study of Three School Councils. PhD thesis. Monash University

Gronn, P C (1984) 'I have a solution . . .': administrative power in a school meeting *Educational Administration Quarterly* **20** 2: 65-92

Horney, K (1950) *Neurosis and Human Growth* W W Norton and Co: New York

Hoyle, E (1982) Micropolitics of educational organizations *Educational Management and Administration* **10** 2: 87-98

Hunter, F (1963) *Community Power Structure* Anchor: New York

Jaques, E (1951) *The Changing Culture of a Factory* Tavistock: London

Jaques, E (1955) Social systems as a defence against persecutary and depressive anxiety *in* Klein *et al* (1955)

Jaques, E (1970) *Work, Creativity and Social Justice* Heinemann: London

Kent Jennings, M (1968) Parental grievances and school politics *Public Opinion Quarterly* **32** 3: 363-78

Kets de Vries, M R F and Miller, D (1984) *The Neurotic Organization* Jossey-Bass: New York

Klein, M, Heimann, P and Money-Kyrle, R eds (1955) *New Directions in Psychoanalysis* Tavistock: London

Lasswell, H D (1936) *Politics: Who Gets What, When, How* McGraw-Hill: New York

*Lukes, S (1974) *Power* Macmillan: London

Murray-Smith, S ed (1976) *Melbourne Studies in Education 1976* Melbourne University Press: Melbourne

Orwell, G (1963) *Nineteen Eighty-four* Penguin: Harmondsworth

Parry, G and Morriss, P (1974) When is a decision not a decision? *in* Crewe (1974)

Pocock, J G A (1972) *Politics, Language and Time* Methuen: London

Runciman, W G (1970) *Sociology and Its Place and Other Essays* Cambridge University Press: Cambridge

Schattschneider, E E (1960) *The Semi-Sovereign People* Holt, Rinehart and Winston: New York

Shapiro, D (1965) *Neurotic Styles* Basic Books: New York

Wall, G (1975) The concept of interest in politics *Politics and Society* **5** 4: 487-510

Wood, A H (1976) M L C Melbourne, 1939-1966: a personal memoir *in* Murray-Smith (1976)

Wright Mills, C (1970) *The Sociological Imagination* Penguin: Harmondsworth

Part 3: Managerial Tasks in Schools

4. Achieving effective schools

Terry A Astuto and David L Clark

Summary: The organizational literature of the last decade has begun to develop a consensus around key organizational characteristics that are associated with organizational effectiveness. This chapter argues that these characteristics are in conflict with traditional value preferences that have been emphasized in organizational theory, eg efficiency, stability, accountability, and control. In fact, the conflictual nature of the value preferences are argued to be so persistent and pervasive as to create eight paradoxes of management for the school leader, ie

1. Activity vs stability
2. Distinction vs intention
3. Variability vs regularity
4. Efficacy vs accountability
5. Facilitation vs intervention
6. Empowerment vs control
7. Disaggregation vs holism
8. Effectiveness vs efficiency.

The relationship of the preferences to achieving effective schools is explored using the literatures of organization and the educational change process. The choice options available to the school manager in each preference cluster are described as akin to the flow of decision options described in educational organizations by Cohen, March, and Olsen (1972). Choice options arise infrequently and irregularly for school managers but, when they do, the manager's choice to affirm, deny or equivocate about a preference signals the essential values held by the manager for the organization.

Proposed guidelines for school managers emphasize preferences as follows:

(a) Stimulate activity. Increase trials. Serve as an activity agent.
(b) Reinforce positive cultural elements. Encourage teachers to examine cultural alternatives.
(c) Uncover alternative value premises. Relax rules. Encourage introspection.
(d) Discover productivity through people. Foster teacher efficacy. Reward teachers.
(e) Manage unobtrusively. Entertain multiple solutions. Encourage problem solving by teachers.
(f) Diffuse power tools to teachers. Relax control. Distribute decision options.
(g) Build 'skunk' works. Seize incremental change opportunities. Make use of loose coupling.
(h) Provide time and resources for change agents and implementors. Support product champions. Use technical assistance.

Introduction

What constitutes effectiveness? What organizational conditions or characteristics are associated with effectiveness? What is the manager's role in achieving those conditions? These questions need to be answered before one can deal with the topic of the manager's role in achieving effective schools. The instructionally effective schools (IES) literature defined school effectiveness as a school that 'brings the children of the poor to those minimal masteries of basic school skills that now describe minimally successful pupil performance for the children of the middle class' (Edmonds, 1979: 16). That is too narrow for our purposes but we would support the criterion that an effective school exhibits pupil performance that relatively exceeds the achievement of other schools with comparable student populations, ie socio-economic backgrounds, and resources. To that we would add a dimension of reputation and client satisfaction. An effective school should be recognized as such by those who use its facilities and resources and by external observers who claim expertise in educational practice and/or assessment. In sum, the effective school competes favourably in terms of output, support, and reputation within its comparable cohort of schools.

The organizational literature of the last decade is developing a consensus around organizational characteristics or conditions that are associated with organizational achievement (eg Kanter, 1983; March and Olsen, 1976; Morgan, 1983; Ouchi, 1981; Peters and Waterman, 1982; Pfeffer, 1982; Schein, 1985; Weick, 1979). We will attempt to capture this consensus in eight dimensions of preference in the choice of organizational strategy for retaining or attaining effectiveness. The contention is that each of the preferences represents an everyday paradox confronted by managers. The dimensions are paradoxical precisely because each choice within a dimension taken alone can be argued reasonably to be a good choice leading to organizational effectiveness. Unfortunately for the manager, the 'goods' are potentially in conflict. The manager, then, is confronted with choosing between goods. These choices made on a daily basis determine, in sum, the likely effectiveness of the manager and the organization. They reflect an organizational strategy for excellence. In every organization, the following emphases are vying for primacy:

1. *Activity* (multiple trials and innovation) rather than *stability* (substantiality in the job setting and a focus on the technical core of the organization's activity);
2. *Distinction* (identity defined through consensus, culture, and sensemaking) rather than *intention* (identity defined through systematic, organization-level, goal setting);
3. *Variability* (divergent behaviour, the search for alternative value premises and solutions, adjustment to individual social enactment processes) rather than *regularity* (clarity of job roles, rules, policies and procedures, reliability of response across people and over time);

4. *Efficacy* (reinforcement of the creativity, productivity, and commitment of the individual) rather than *accountability* (a systematic effort to ensure individual and group productivity);

5. *Facilitation* (unobtrusive management, influencing preferences, building organizational problem-solving capacity) rather than *intervention* (the design of interventions, solving problems, ordering preferences);

6. *Empowerment* (individual autonomy and achievement, choice activity by organizational participants, shared power and rewards) rather than *control* (retention of critical choice, preference, and judgement activities at the centre of the organization);

7. *Disaggregation* (loose coupling, piecemeal change, emphasis on individuals and subgroups) rather than *holism* (comprehensive reform or change, system-wide quality control, centralization);

8. *Effectiveness* (including both measures of current productivity and responsiveness to change) rather than *efficiency* (doing the most with the least).

These strategic elements of organizational life are not a set of continua but a set of choice preferences. They are not mutually exclusive but they are contradictive. Take, for example, the emphasis on activity or stability. Peters and Waterman (1982) argued that organizations should simultaneously exhibit a bias for action and a concentration on technical core activity, ie tend to the knitting. This advice avoids the paradox by creating an anomaly. An emphasis on activity will lead inevitably away from the technical core or, at the least, will modify the processes of that technical core. The manager needs stronger advice about the paradox. In our opinion, contemporary organizational research and theory justify the assertion that activity is a choice preferable to stability. Does this mean the paradox is solved? Not all all. An organization with a sole emphasis on activity would be anarchic; a sole emphasis on stability would lead to moribundity. That suggests the happy possibility that we are not dealing with a paradox but only a balance between the two. Perhaps the issue will be no more agonizing than the choice between consideration and initiating structure turned out to be in leadership studies. No such luck: these strategic preferences are potentially in conflict. In the final analysis, the manager, and other organizational participants, have to opt for a consistent position of preference. They end up *fostering one* and *tolerating the other.* We will return to this issue in the final section of this chapter, examining further the necessity for the manager to choose a strategy distinctly and consistently.

Again, in contrast to the IES literature, the eight paradoxes suggest a more subtle role for the school manager. The assertion that the IES is characterized by strong administrative leadership implies a heavy-handed managerial posture. We should temper what might appear at this stage to be an over-estimate of what a manager can do in an organization. Basically, we believe that the influence of the designated leader of the organization is almost always over-emphasized. The leader acts within narrow constraints of influence. Followership empowers leadership. Most of the actions of the organization are determined by linkages and patterns established prior to the leader's election that will continue beyond his or her tenure. We are sensitive to Weick's admonition that 'the thrust of the organizing model is that it is easy to overmanage an organization and that it is an excess rather than deficiency of intervention that lies at the heart of many organizational problems' (Edmonds, 1979: 244). On the other hand, leaders obviously affect organizational processes and outcomes, both positively and negatively.

Managing organizational paradoxes

The following discussion of the paradoxes will review briefly the evidence supporting the relationship between strategic choices and outcomes as the manager seeks organizational effectiveness.

Activity and stability

Karl Weick argued 'that meaning is retrospective and only elapsed experience is available for meaningful interpretation. The practical implication of this is that an organization would be in a better position to improve . . . if the elapsed experience were filled with action rather than inaction' (1979: 245). Effective organizations initiate more trials. In such organizations, this increased activity is based upon 1. a sense of opportunism and 2. a proclivity toward success. Managers in effective organizations sense, and act upon, the points at which choice options are available for decision. Organizational members often report a consensus that a particular decision seemed right or was inevitable. Equally important, the choice option is made within the past experience and strength of the organization. The proposed action has a chance to succeed. The organization uses its assessment of achievements to initiate timely action and increase the percentage of successful actions.

There are a variety of reasons to argue the efficacy of activity, to wit:

(a) In some instances, trials may simply increase productivity. Peters and Waterman reported, for example, that in oil and mineral exploration, 'the number of tries counts for a great deal. Indeed, an analysis of Amoco, recently revitalized to become the top US domestic oil finder, suggests just one success factor: *Amoco simply drills more wells*' (1982: 141).

(b) Research on the change process in education has demonstrated consistently that organizations learn how to innovate from implementing innovations, whether or not the particular trial was substantively important to the institution. Organizations that innovate become better at innovation.

(c) The alternative schools movement and the instructionally effective schools experience demonstrated the impact of trying on organizational participants. Both movements were criticized accurately as poorly specified innovations. Both were adjudged subsequently as having increased the level of self-efficacy and productivity of faculty and students in these schools. Action provides a chance to break negative amplifying cycles in organizations. At a minimum it may offer a symbolic response to areas of organizational concern that cannot be ameliorated by traditional organizational processes or programmes.

(d) Over a longer period of time Weick's argument justifies the higher level of activity. Successful organizations learn more by doing more. They accumulate an understanding of themselves which is reflected ultimately in a better sense of opportunism and success.

A school manager can directly affect the level of activity in a system or building. Most obviously, although perhaps least usefully, he or she can generate choice options for the school. The manager has the advantage of physical presence at more events where decision points arise. He or she can facilitate choice — some choice, any choice in preference to no choice. The manager can consciously search out ideas and options from among organizational participants. The manager can nurture those other administrators, teachers, and students who are offering choice options, suggesting change, or volunteering to participate in new ventures. The most effective school leaders are more likely to have an agenda *to* change than a substantive agenda *for* change; they stimulate trials rather than advocating particular trials; they encourage true believers to move ahead with their ideas, although they are not, themselves, true believers.

Most schools, most of the time, are not ineffective because they are unstable organizations rife with trials. They are ineffective because they have become frozen in their mediocrity and failure. The school manager can serve the role of activity agent, if not change agent.

Distinction and intention

Schein (1985: 2) noted, 'In fact, there is a possibility — underemphasized in leadership research — *that the only thing of real importance that leaders do is to create and manage culture* and that the unique talent of leaders is their ability to work with culture'. Deal and Kennedy (1983: 16) asserted, 'We believe that the character or culture of organizations is not unlike the character of wines. Attempts to quantify important variables produce more precision and greater "rigor". But while the tightness of the metric increases reliability and reduces noise, it moves further from the essence of the organizational "truth". That truth is embedded in the meanings that humans assign to important things and events inside their own reality'. However difficult it may be to identify the elements of organizational culture, it is a truism that somehow organizations transmit a feeling that allows, for example, most educators to claim that they can sense an effective school in the space of time required for a casual visit.

The demise of the goal-based paradigm of organizations seems to have coincided with a flurry of interest in how commitment builds up through socialization and enactment processes in some organizations to generate a positive organizational culture. Perhaps the concepts are exclusive. The culture-heavy organization may have little need to explicate its goals formally or may find that an effort to do so generates dissent and tension when none existed beforehand. Organizational goals have been under attack for years as vehicles for learning about organizational behaviour. By their nature they represent sense-making at the apex of the organization; they homogenize and compromise the goals of subunits and individuals in the organization — frequently beyond recognition; they seem frequently to be reconstructions of previous action, ie retrospective rather than prospective; and they seldom control or even influence strongly organizational choice patterns. The difficulty with organizational goals is aggravated when researchers and practitioners begin to act as if none of these limitations of goals is true; when they assume, for example, that the formal representations may be incomplete but are, none the less, guides for individual choice preferences; or that the goals may be inaccurate representations of individual objectives but still reflect the consensus view of organizational participants; or that goals are prospective and represent the organization's aspirations. In short, goals become pernicious when those who examine them take them seriously; taken casually they are merely uninformative.

Effective school managers concentrate on establishing distinction through enactment processes rather than projecting or defining intent in task forces on goals. The sense of purpose and commitment found in an effective school derives from shared sense-making about 'what's going on around here'. The faculty believe that, within its competitive institutional class, this institution is the place to be. Schein (1985) suggested that leadership may be the creation and management of culture, for example:

(a) In the mature organization, the leader will be engaged in culture-management. This suggests reinforcing cultural elements that seem to be productive; and opening up the organization to the consideration of alternatives in cases where existing cultural elements seem counter-productive.

(b) Many, perhaps most, schools are culture-light. The participants seem to reflect little agreement about the essence of the school's activity and little pride in its achievement. The school leader can be imagined as a discoverer, if not an inventor, of culture, ie identifying and reinforcing the strongest elements that exist around individuals or programmes or small groups in the school. But inventor may not be too strong a description of the impact of a few charismatic leaders, and all managers can create the opportunities for the involvement and participation of teachers in cultural definition.

The important current statement to be made about organizational culture is that the manager should focus on distinction, represented by action and interpretations of action, rather than intent, represented by prospective action. Interpretations of actions are made by organizational participants over time, not by organizational leaders at a point in time.

Variability and regularity

No one need fear an underemphasis on regularity in most organizations. The bureaucratic organizational form has provided an essential structure that assumes regularity and reliability through written rules, policies, job descriptions, and standard operating procedures. The training, experience, and socialization of school managers reinforce the desirability of regularity, routine, and predictability.

But there is another view. Research on organizational innovation and change processes cites the need for safe havens and the toleration of idiosyncratic behaviour by organizational inventors and change agents. Organizational studies note the vitality and productivity of *ad hoc* work groups that are given their head. March and Olsen (1976: 81) argued for a technology of foolishness to offset the technology of regularity to make '. . . the individuals within an organization more playful by encouraging the attitudes and skills of inconsistency'.

We will argue that variability is a necessary condition for achieving school effectiveness for several reasons. Variability supports the encouragement of 'product champions' (Peters and Waterman, 1982: 202) who often require either exemption from organizational rules or exceptional institutional reinforcement, or both. Variability allows the fostering of primary work groups that are exhibiting productivity or give the promise of productivity. 'Entrepreneurs — and entrepreneurial organizations always operate at the edge of their competence, focusing more of their resources and attention on what they do not yet know [eg investment in R and D] than on controlling what they already know' (Kanter, 1983: 27). Regularity supports the application and implementation of proven skills. Variability supports the trials necessary to develop new knowledge.

March and Olsen contended that 'strict insistence on purpose, consistency, and rationality limits our ability to find new purposes' (1976: 77). Variability, in contrast, may uncover useful, alternative value premises. Since it can be argued that organizations frequently identify goals retrospectively, variability provides the opportunity to explore new directions and potential objectives. Planfulness promotes regularity; playfulness promotes variability. 'Playfulness is the deliberate, temporary relaxation of rules in order to explore the possibilities of alternative rules. When we are playful, we challenge the necessity of consistency' (March and Olsen, 1976: 77). Challenging the necessity of consistency allows the exploration of new directions and new territory.

Variability provides a place for organizational forgetfulness, a necessary feature of renewal. 'Retained information is sacred in most organizations (Grossman, 1976), and this means that routines, standard operating procedures, and grooved thinking (Steinbruner, 1974) work against the organization being able to discredit its past knowledge . . . The thick layering of routines in most organizations, coupled with the fact that departures from routine increase vulnerability, mean that discrediting is rare' (Weick, 1976: 225). Forgetfulness and doubt enhance the organization's ability to rethink past enactments and increase quality. The process of forgetfulness results in the possibility of an organization unfreezing itself — a necessary pre-condition of many forms of organizational change.

School managers, pictured in the instructionally effective schools literature as guardians of regularity, need to engage in activities designed to foster organizational variability, for example:

(a) encouraging and supporting experimentation in teaching;
(b) relaxing rules, regulations and standard operating procedures for teachers *and* students willing to try new things;
(c) participating with teachers and students in *ad hoc* efforts to challenge school routines; encouraging playfulness and shared risk in learning how to do it better;
(d) stimulating teacher participation in interactive R and D ventures with university colleagues focused upon school-level learning and experimentation.

Regularity maintains but finally traps the organization. Variability disrupts the organization but provides paths of egress to future, new forms.

Efficacy and accountability

People, individually and in groups, are the pivotal players in effective organizations. Good schools and school systems are populated by confident people who expect to succeed and expect others to perform to their personal level of competence. This shared sense of personal efficacy translates into pride and commitment to the organization. '. . . (T)here is emotional and value commitment between person and organization; people feel that they "belong" to a meaningful entity and can realize cherished values by their contributions' (Kanter, 1983: 149). The cumulative effects of this self-reinforcing cycle of success-pride-commitment-expectations for continued success are the development of shared understandings about the organization and an *esprit de corps*.

The pivotal role of people in the organization requires activities on the part of managers that support the development of this personal sense of efficacy. Peters and Waterman (1982: 238) contended that the lessons from the excellent companies' research were to, 'Treat people as adults. Treat them as partners; treat them with dignity; treat them with respect. Treat *them* . . . as the primary source of productivity gains'. Institutional efforts to enforce accountability by 1. establishing achievable goals, 2. monitoring performance, and 3. evaluating achievements overshadow efforts to promote personal efficacy. These well-intentioned accountability activities inevitably alienate people (displace individual goals with organizational goals), oppress people (scrutinize levels of performance), and threaten people (pass judgement on their performance). The tone of accountability is inhibitive. Fostering efficacy supports change and effectiveness:

(a) Change and innovation are difficult for all people. An individual is more likely to risk change when there are shared expectations for success. Managers are more likely to sense opportunities for innovation when individuals are convinced of their own abilities and those of others. 'Respect for the individual, then, is not only a matter of basic human dignity; it is also a necessity for the leap of faith required to let entrepreneurs innovate' (Kanter, 1983: 34).

(b) Although the individual may be the key actor in the organization, individual actions are related to, and frequently dependent upon, other contextual features of the organization. Shared expectations for individual and organizational success and an *esprit de corps* are necessary conditions to support proactive individual activity.

(c) Organizations can be understood as negotiated cause maps, 'Beliefs are cause maps that people impose on the world after which they "see" what they have already imposed' (Weick, 1979: 135). Thus, a shared sense of personal efficacy translates into beliefs that the organization is effective. Movement towards excellence is more likely when individuals see themselves and others as competent, productive, effective organizational participants.

School managers who wish to promote individual efficacy and *esprit de corps* practise the up-side of personnel management:

(a) Credit for success is given to individuals and/or groups who achieved it; blame is assumed by the manager;

(b) Gathering evidence about performance is not considered of sufficient importance to subvert individual and organizational achievements;

(c) Mechanisms of accountability, including a rigid chain of command, are relaxed in favour of mechanisms for rewarding excellence;

(d) Opportunities are provided for job and role diversity for high producers.

When managers focus on accountability they miss opportunities to foster the real source of productivity gains — the people. Fostering a sense of individual efficacy and *esprit de corps* places the people, the key actors, in a pre-eminent position and sets the stage for them to invest their energies and skills in the organization.

Facilitation and intervention

Weick (1979: 244) observed that conducting an orchestra is a familiar metaphor for managing an organization, and that '. . . conducting is more effective when it is tacit, unobtrusive, non-interfering, and takes into consideration control processes already woven into the orchestra'. Most managers bring to the organization a model bias in favour of hierarchy, authority, and intervention. It should be no surprise to find that managers meddle, over-manage, and get in the way. But effective organizations cannot be managed with a heavy hand. Trust in teachers to be productive and confidence in teachers' technical expertise require facilitative managerial actions for several reasons.

First, intervention presumes one best solution to organizational programmes, processes, and problems. But the ambiguities of organizational life guarantee that there is no one best solution. Cohen, March and Olsen (1972: 1) argued that educational organizations were prototypic examples of organized anarchies in which choices were problematic, technology was unclear, and participation by organizational members was fluid. Facilitation not only concedes the truth of organizational ambiguity but builds upon it as a source of new ideas and multiple solutions to dilemmas.

Second, organizations have a storehouse of multiple preferences in the sense-making activities of their participants. Intervention disregards these preferences by interjecting unilateral corrections. Facilitation seeks out personal preferences, highlights them, and provides the conditions in which mutual adaptations can occur. Intervention defines organizational change as remediating defects. Facilitation defines organizational change as testing preferences and new ideas.

Finally, in an organization populated by skilled, committed people, a directive interventionist management stance squanders the available human resources. Solutions, ideas, and potential new futures already exist in abundant supply in the expertise, activities, and ingenuity of organizational members. The necessary strategy for managers is to provide the occasion, the mechanisms, and the conditions for members of the organization to contribute and to increase their capacity to contribute.

Effective school managers facilitate the work of teachers in a variety of ways:

(a) By avoiding premature closure in considering organizational issues and concerns, time and space can be provided for uncovering multiple alternative solutions;

(b) By encouraging interactions among teachers about professional issues, the talents and individual preferences of teachers can be energized to address nagging classroom and school problems;

(c) By supporting varied opportunities for professional growth, the supply of potential solutions to school problems can be increased;

(d) By establishing mechanisms for teachers to study and reflect on the substance and processes being used to achieve effectiveness, a wider array of reasonable and useful alternatives can be invented.

'Managers who make decisions might well view that function somewhat less as a process of deduction or a process of political negotiation, and somewhat more as a process of gently upsetting preconceptions of what the organization is doing' (March and Olsen, 1976: 80). Facilitation rather than intervention requires managers to act in ways that mobilize strengths, increase the capacities of individuals to enhance organizational effectiveness, and entertain alternative, plausible futures.

Empowerment and control

Empowerment provides people in the organization with the tools needed to be innovative and effective. 'Organizational power tools consist of supplies of three "basic commodities" that can be invested in action: *information* (data, technical knowledge, political intelligence, expertise); *resources* (funds, material, space time); and *support* (endorsement, backing, approval, legitimacy)' (Kanter, 1983: 159). Effective organizations make power more widely accessible to organizational participants by establishing conditions that allow the rapid circulation of these power tools.

Providing these tools to professionals requires the relaxation of control. In effective organizations '. . . incentives for initiative derive from situations in which job charters are broad; assignments are ambiguous, non-routine, and change-directed; job territories are intersecting, so that others are both affected by action and required for it; and local autonomy is strong enough that actors can go ahead with large chunks of action without waiting for higher-level approval' (Kanter, 1983: 143). Conditions of control are replaced with conditions for sharing power.

Empowering people diffuses the initiative for action and the freedom of choice away from the managerial centre of the organization. Choice options and decision options are expanded and distributed throughout the organization, thereby increasing the number of spheres of activity and expanding opportunities for meaningful involvement and participation in organizational processes.

Empowerment assists the organization in discovering non-designated leaders. Individual autonomy and the autonomy of cooperative work groups assist the organization in generating multiple-choice options and selecting alternative decision options. The end result of distributing decision options and increasing autonomy is to enhance the capacity of the organization to be innovative and productive. Empowerment encourages innovation everywhere in the organization.

To achieve school effectiveness school managers need to empower teachers.

(a) Empowering teachers means recognizing that good schools have multiple leaders. Designated leadership positions are held by individuals who are active, committed, and frequently charismatic. But these good schools are also distinguishable because they spawn cooperative work groups and individuals who are leaders by idea and example.

(b) School managers need to support and nurture individuals within the organization and ameliorate the constraints that impede the growth of a changing organization for people.

(c) School managers need to trade-off structural organizational control mechanisms for support systems for teachers, moving the locus of control to teachers, and creating a climate that emphasizes trials and tolerates error.

Empowerment to promote productivity and innovation brings with it problems of managing participation, ambiguity, and choice. But those trade-offs are necessary to capture the full range of new ideas that arise from within the organization. Control acts as a mild depressant to innovation. Empowerment opens up the organization and creates the conditions necessary for improvement.

Disaggregation and holism

Karl Weick (1982: 674-75) contended that schools and school districts are loosely coupled systems and that these have some distinct advantages for organizational effectiveness. In a loosely coupled organization, Weick noted individual units can: 1. preserve novelty so they are reservoirs of flexibility; 2. adapt more quickly to conflicting demands; 3. improvise more effectively; and 4. respond swiftly enough to seal off some small problems before they become large problems. The literature on organizational change and innovation argues the utility of supporting change efforts in subunits of the organization, creating *ad hoc* teams (Peters and Waterman [1982] referred to them as 'skunk works') to focus on the invention of alternative solutions, and avoiding comprehensive, hyper-rational designs for change (Fullan, 1982: 91-92).

An effective, innovative organization is likely to celebrate and exploit its loose coupledness instead of viewing the condition as an organizational pathology. However, the pressure on managers to ferret out and tighten this natural condition is embedded in bureaucratic theory and the problem-solving paradigm. The effective school manager needs to heed the advice Douglas McGregor (1960: 9) offered in developing the rationale for Theory Y: 'Many of our attempts to control behavior, far from representing selective adaptations, are in direct violation of human nature. They consist in trying to make people behave as we wish without concern for natural law'. That is the point! It is unrealistic to picture an educational organization of professionals acceding willingly to tight management control or to significant changes introduced in the organization by fiat. It is equally difficult to imagine all teachers arriving at a consensus about needed changes or, if they did, being able to implement them. The predisposition of organizational participants to change and their individual ability to modify their behaviour, even if they were so disposed, suggests that routinely one should expect that some will, some will not — some can, some cannot. Disaggregation focuses on change, improvement, and effectiveness, whenever and wherever it can occur — for *ad hoc* groups, or centres, or departments, or individuals. Disaggregation embraces loose coupling for its advantages and tolerates the requisite need for integration as best it can.

School managers who embrace disaggregation act in predictable ways:

(a) They search out producers, change agents, and implementers, and support their efforts. They try to link them with others who may share similar interests.

(b) They take advantage of opportunities for change and progress whenever and wherever they arise. They do not expose ideas for change to the test of their implications for the school as a whole; that is, will it work or can it be diffused everywhere in the school or school system?

(c) They try to construct and protect sheltered locations for experimentation. They believe in the efficacy of 'skunk works' (Peters and Waterman, 1982: 201).

(d) They avoid systemwide efforts at change or qualitative improvement as unlikely, tension provoking, and damaging to organizational integrity. The only thing that an organization is likely to be able to agree upon doing is what it is already doing.

Weick (1982: 675) warned, 'Administrators must be attentive to the "glue" that holds loosely coupled systems together because such forms are just barely systems. In fact, this borderline condition is their strength, in the sense that it allows local adjustment and storage of novel remedies. It is also their point of vulnerability, because such systems can quickly dissolve into anarchy'. School managers need to attend particularly to the issues of distinction (culture) and empowerment (participation) to capture the strength of their environment and avoid its weaknesses.

Effectiveness and efficiency

Can effective schools be efficient? Probably not. Too many elements of effectiveness are conjectural to ensure the condition of efficiency. If one assumes that effective schools are innovative organizations, tolerant of variability in practice, with an emphasis on the self-actualization of participants and participative management styles, no current technological device employed to increase efficiency will accommodate such irregularities in management.

Take, for example, a 'soft', popular tool of management efficiency — management by objectives. Most such systems contend that the objectives which specify what is to be accomplished allow negotiation between manager and teacher. It is argued that specified objectives build up self-efficacy by assuring the employee that the final evaluation will be based on mutually agreed goals and activities. The system provides for in-process correction in the event of the teacher being off-course. That is enough detail for the counterpoints. The objectives are obviously not negotiated. The issue between the manager and the teacher is simple. There are a set of nomothetic goals in this organization. The teacher contributes directly to a specified subset. The teacher's performance, in the manager's judgement, is better in some areas than others. The two 'negotiators' figure out a self-improvement strategy for the teacher in some of these goals areas for the next semester or year. The manager will keep a check on progress as the teacher goes along.

This is no exchange between equals. If the teacher were to respond by saying, 'let's begin by working on a set of objectives to improve your management performance', he or she would be considered frivolous or insolent. Challenging the goals is perceived as a defence mechanism against incompetence. The integrity of the hierarchy is obvious. If the building level manager is to participate personally in an MBO exercise, it will occur not with his or her teachers, but with a central office superordinate. School administrators and students of administration have become too sophisticated to buy into simplistic time management systems, but they are still wrestling with the issue of the trade-off posed by an efficiency tool that includes an effectiveness dimension. A decade ago, March and Olsen alerted us to some of the hidden assumptions of management technology when they noted, 'Every tool of management decision that is currently a part of management science, operations research, or decision theory assumes the prior existence of a set of consistent goals' (1976: 71). Those goals, of course, are nomothetic, rational, sequential evidence of the organization's control of its processes.

There are a number of reasons to support the argument that the effective school manager opts consistently for effectiveness, even at the loss of efficiency:

(a) The change literature notes that innovation is facilitated by involvement of teachers in planning for implementation, flexible timelines for implementation, and added resources, ie staff, materials, and time, staff development and technical assistance. There is no evidence that lean and mean organizations support innovation. On the contrary, the threat of failure in such institutional settings encourages conservative responses.

(b) Effectiveness is linked inextricably to the concept of productivity through people. Focusing on the teacher as the keystone of school change and achievement means accepting inefficient management options in planning, decision making, and implementation. People are inefficient.

(c) Organizational studies demonstrate repeatedly that effective organizations foster more cooperative work groups and product champions. These organizational phenomena are not programmable elements. They emerge in organizational settings where variability that shows evidence of producing qualitative gains is seized upon as an opportunity, not merely tolerated. They are, however, inefficient in the traditional meaning of that term.

School managers can exercise options to encourage effectiveness as a preferred criterion of organizational choice. They can eschew technological management devices to achieve efficiency. They can resist efforts to eliminate resources in the organization. They can oppose hyperrational planning schemes for innovation and implementation. They can identify productive individuals and units, formal or informal, and encourage their productivity. They can convince themselves and their staff that the focus of this administration is on productivity gains at whatever cost the traffic will bear.

The margin of excellence

Managing to achieve excellence is a subtle process guided by increasingly discernible clues. Organizational theorists and researchers are accumulating evidence that the effective leader emphasizes:

(a) activity and trials;
(b) culture management;
(c) flexibility in application of rules and policies;
(d) the efficacy of the 'follower';
(e) unobtrusive, facilitative leadership;
(f) the empowerment of the individual;
(g) incrementalism in change and segmentation in structure;
(h) productivity and innovation.

What makes this list provocative is that it characterizes few leaders in education today and it conflicts with a set of equally plausible leader emphases that have dominated the technology and training of school managers, ie stability, goal-based planning, regularity, accountability, intervention, control, holism, and efficiency. In short, the emerging emphases conflict with the will-o'-the-wisp pursuit of the bureaucracy that works with the leader in control.

We suggest that you imagine each of the conflictual emphases portrayed in this chapter as elements existing in a conflictual territory. On any given day, conflict may be avoided by accident or design. The elements simply do not cross one another's path. They flow through organizational life as Cohen, March and Olsen (1972) described the independent flow of solutions, problems, participants, and choice opportunities in the garbage-can model of decision making. But from time to time, under very different circumstances (a public group meeting, a private two-person discussion, a solitary choice in resource allocation), by accident or design, involving matters of apparently great or small consequence, the leader is confronted with a choice option. The opportunity arises to affirm, deny, or equivocate upon the leader's emphasis. On these occasions, involving a small percentage of the choices exercised by the manager — perhaps 1-5 per cent of the choice options — rests the margin of excellence available to the leader. On these occasions, the leader has the chance to strike the hallmark of the institution. Flowing around, about, and through the conflictual territory are the ordinary processes of daily organizational life that seem to be leader-free, ie the choice options are habitual, the choices are unconscious, the conflict, if it exists, is unrecognized, the behaviour is an option only in a hypothetical sense — realistically the pattern followed has been enacted into the life of the institution almost aphoristically. Managing for the achievement of effectiveness, the leader should:

1. Exercise choice options as they arise that consistently reflect a preference for the active, person-centred, flexible organization.
2. Seek out and act upon choice options within the scope of the leader's role that have been made routine in support of traditional organizational emphases, eg explicitly reallocate resources to high-risk ventures.
3. Provoke occasions for institutional members to challenge habitual choice opportunities in public and private circumstances; reinforce faculty and managers who empower their colleagues and experiment on their own.
4. Institutionalize preferences as choice opportunities have arisen and been seized; create symbols that make it seem ordinary to avoid traditional choices — create new traditions.

The emergence of new evidence to support change in administrative practice and organizational behaviour coincides with an unharnessed but vocal call for educational excellence. The two tendencies should be recognized as complementary and conjoined.

References

Cohen, M D, March, J D, and Olsen, J P (1972) A garbage can model of organiz-ational choice *Administrative Science Quarterly* **17**: 1-25

Deal, T and Kennedy, A (1983) Culture: a new look through old lenses. American Educational Research Association Annual Meeting Paper: Montreal

Edmonds, R (1979) Effective schools for the urban poor *Educational Leadership* **37** 1: 15-24

*Fullan, M (1982) *The Meaning of Educational Change* Teachers College Press, Colum-bia University: New York

Grossman, L (1976) *Fat Paper* McGraw-Hill: New York

*Kanter, R M (1983) *The Change Masters* Simon and Schuster: New York

McGregor, D (1960) *The Human Side of Enterprise* McGraw-Hill: New York

March, J G and Olsen, J P eds (1976) *Ambiguity and Choice in Organizations* Uni-versitetsforlaget: Bergen, Norway

Morgan, G ed (1983) *Beyond Method* Sage Publications: Beverly Hills, Cal

Ouchi, W G (1981) *Theory Z* Avon Books: New York

Peters, T J and Waterman, R H (1982) *In Search of Excellence* Harper and Row: New York

Pfeffer, J (1982) *Organizations and Organization Theory* Pitman Publishing: Marsh-field, Mass

Schein, E H (1985) *Organizational Culture and Leadership* Jossey-Bass: San Francisco

Steinbruner, J D (1974) *The Cybernetic Theory of Decision* Princeton University Press: Princeton, New Jersey

Weick, K E (1976) Educational organizations as loosely coupled systems *Adminis-trative Science Quarterly* **12** 1: 1-19

Weick, K E (1979) *The Social Psychology of Organizing* Addison-Wesley: Reading, Mass

Weick, K E (1982) Administering education in loosely coupled schools *Phi Delta Kappan* **63** 10: 673-76

5. The management of change

Michael G Fullan

Summary: Serious research on the implementation of educational change began only in the early 1970s. Most of the early research essentially documented failures. From the late 1970s to the present the dominant theme has been descriptions of factors associated with success. A number of areas of research — implementation, in-service education, leadership and effective schools — have produced increasingly consistent findings about the nature and functioning of change in schools. Understanding change, however, is not the same as managing it. We are now at the stage of grappling with the much more complex problem of how to manage change in schools.

This chapter is divided into two main sections. The first section describes what change is and summarizes what we know about success. Three critical factors at the school level are explained: the role of professional development of teachers; the active instructional role of the principal; and the kind of culture or climate of the school as an organization that best supports the first two factors. The dynamics of change — the way in which the change process works over a period of time — is especially emphasized.

In the second section, guidelines and dilemmas for managing change are taken up. A number of guidelines are presented from recent publications. They represent helpful aids and insights to those involved in managing school change projects. In the final part of the chapter five basic problems or dilemmas are discussed — change versus changing, common versus unique aspects, plan-making, where and how big to start, and the selection and training of managers. These problems indicate intrinsic difficulties and remind us once again that change in social systems can never be managed in a step-by-step fashion.

Introduction

It is surprising to realize how short the history of serious research is on change in schools. It was not until 1971 that the first works appeared analysing problems of implementing educational innovations (Sarason, 1971; Gross *et al*, 1971). A decade and a half of intensive research has produced impressive and increasingly precise and convergent insights into the change process, yet we are just at the very beginning of deriving implications for improving the *management* of change.

In broad terms we can conceive of the past 15 years and the immediate future in three phases. The first phase — covering most of the 1970s — was essentially one of documenting failure (see Fullan and Pomfret,

1977 for a review). We learned more about what not to do than anything else. In the second phase — roughly 1978 to the present — identifying and analysing success and effectiveness in schools became the dominant theme (see Crandall *et al*, 1983; Fullan, 1982; 1985; Huberman and Miles, 1984). At first glance one might think that clear descriptions of what constitutes success is tantamount to being well down the road to solving the management of change problem. This is not the case as I will attempt to show in this paper. Managing change — the third phase on which we are just embarking — will turn out to be the most difficult problem of all.

This chapter is divided into two main sections. The first contains a summary of some things we know about successful change at the school level and the second identifies some basic guidelines, dilemmas and un-resolved issues with respect to the management of change.

What we know about successful change

The point here is not to formulate yet another listing of factors related to change. Fullan (1982) identifies 15 key factors related to successful implementation. Clark, Lotto and Astuto (1984) do an excellent job of summarizing and synthesizing the main findings from the effective schools and the school improvement lines of research. Firestone and Corbett (1986) provide an important history and state-of-the-art of our knowledge about organizational change in schools. Instead of another overview I should like to treat the matter in a more focused way. First, I will comment briefly on what change is. Second, I will discuss in more detail what we know about the three most central factors at the school level — the role of in-service or professional development of teachers, the role of principals, and a third factor that ties together the previous two: organizational culture or climate. The purpose of this section is not to tell the whole complicated story, but to consolidate some of the main things we know about change at the school level. The complications of working with these and other factors in a management sense are taken up in the second half of this chapter.

What is change?

Let us start with the example of curriculum change in the school and ask the question: What types of things would have changed if a new or revised curriculum were to get fully used? While there are a number of possible ancillary changes (eg the exam system), I have suggested elsewhere that there are three core changes as far as the individual teacher is concerned, namely:

1. learning materials
2. practices or behaviours
3 beliefs and understanding (Fullan, 1982).

In other words, when a teacher takes on a curriculum change he or she is inevitably engaged in using new materials, changing his or her teaching practices in some manner (that is, new activities, skills, behaviour, pedagogical style, etc), and altering his or her beliefs or understanding (ie philosophy, conceptual framework, pedagogical theory, and the like). Typically, when we think of curriculum innovations, we think of the first of the three aspects — the concrete materials such as textbooks that one can pick up and use. However, it is the latter two that are more fundamental and much more problematic because they involve changes in what teachers *do* (the practices and underlying skills) and *think* (their beliefs and understandings).

The individual difficulties of change are compounded when they occur in an organizational context and/or when the organizational context itself is the target of change as in the effective schools research which focuses on altering the climate, the value system and the role of leadership and collaboration within the school. These latter changes also involve new behaviours, skills and beliefs or understandings in relation to the school as an organization.

The management of change is difficult because it must contend with a personal and anxiety-ridden learning process on the part of individuals working in an organizational context. The latter is typically not only not conducive to supporting the process, but also may be downright unhelpful (Fullan, 1982). Change, then, is an individual and organizational *learning process* (only it is the adults who are expected to learn along with, or more so than, the pupils). To jump ahead for a moment: anything we know about how people learn represents a productive resource for generating ideas for managing change.

Three powerful factors related to success

Having defined change, what are the roles of professional development and the principal and organizational culture/climate in accomplishing successful outcomes?

Recall that successful change is *learning* how to do something new. Once this is understood, it is obvious why in-service education or professional development is a *sine qua non* of change, and why traditional approaches to professional development do not work. Once-only workshops, pre-implementation training (even intensive examples) without follow-up, formal professional development sessions and courses unconnected to the job and to the real life of the organization have little or no impact because they are designed to provide the ongoing, interactive, cumulative learning necessary to develop new skills, behaviour and conceptions in practice.

Huberman and Miles, in their detailed examination of 12 case examples of innovation (Huberman and Miles, 1984), put the positive case best:

> Large-scale, change-bearing innovations lived or died by the amount and quality of assistance that their users received once the change process was under

way . . . The forms of assistance were various. The high-assistance sites set up external conferences, in-service training sessions, visits, committee structures, and team meetings. They also furnished a lot of ongoing assistance in the form of materials, peer consultation, access to external consultants, and rapid access to central office personnel . . . Although strong assistance did not usually succeed in smoothing the way in early implementations, especially for the more demanding innovations, it paid handsome dividends later on by substantially increasing the levels of commitment and practice mastery (273).

In short, it is not the amount of in-service training but the *nature* of it that counts. There are numerous other examples of how successful professional development works. A clear example of how a local school district integrated in-service education and successful implementation of a science curriculum is described in Fullan (1982: 170-72). Stallings (1981) outlines the components and documents the effectiveness of her 'staff development mastery learning model': pre-test (observe teachers, start where they are), inform (link theory, practice, experience), organize and guide practice (support, assess, give feedback), and post-test. Little (1982; 1984) provides additional detail and evidence. Joyce and Showers (Joyce and Showers, 1980; Showers, 1985) have researched and developed quality approaches to in-service education with their theory-demonstration-practice-feedback-follow-up model which has catapulted 'coaching' to the centre stage of staff development in the United States. Coaching teams (teacher-teacher, consultant-teacher) are designed to enhance the understanding and use of new teaching strategies or curriculum innovations by providing opportunities for training sessions, trying new practices, peer observation, exchanging experiences, feedback, and so on (Showers, 1985).

The evidence continues to accumulate, and is as convincing as any we need, to make the general point that a new task-focused, continuous professional development, combining a variety of learning formats, and a variety of trainers and other support personnel, is evolving and is effective in bringing about change in practice. While these examples are based on much more intensive and systematic interaction than are traditional forms of in-service, there is some evidence to show that a small amount of time, used under the right conditions over a period of several months alternating between practice and training, can go a long way (Huberman and Crandall, 1983; Sparks, 1984). Still, there are many unresolved issues, most of which pertain to management questions of how to initiate, design and follow-through on what amounts to a sophisticated, highly integrated approach to professional development.

The research evidence on the critical role of the principal in facilitating or inhibiting change in schools is equally compelling. It is certainly possible for change to occur without the principal (Crandall *et al*, 1983), but it would not be difficult to assemble 100 research studies that show that when the principal is an active supporter of a change effort it is much more likely to succeed. (For reviews see Bossert *et al*, 1982: Fullan, 1982; 1985; Leithwood and Montgomery, 1982.) Virtually every line of inquiry ends up identifying the significance of the principal in bringing about change (see, for example, Clark *et al*'s 1984 comparison of school effectiveness and school improvement, and Little's 1984 and Showers' 1985 analysis of the role of the principal in successful staff development).

The operative word in the above paragraph is the principal as an *active* supporter or director of the change effort. The more recent research has begun to identify some of the specific components of what it means to be active. Firestone and Corbett (1986) describe six behavioural components of principal administrative support: locating slack time, overseeing local facility and clerical arrangements, exerting positive pressure on participants, buffering the process, encouraging and reinforcing all staff, and pressing for incorporation of the change. Leithwood and Montgomery (1986) have developed 'the principal profile', based on four levels of effectiveness (from administrator to systematic problem solver) according to the principal's skills in four domains of behaviour (decision making, goals, factors addressed, and strategies used).

There are several unresolved matters. First, when effective principals are examined in detail, the complexity and differences among those labelled effective becomes much more apparent (Blumberg and Greenfield, 1980; Dwyer *et al*, 1983). Second, while the word 'active' is an adjective agreed upon, the difference and appropriateness under different conditions of the principal as an 'active facilitator' versus an 'active director' is not clear (Fullan, 1982; see also Peters and Austin, 1985, Chapter 20 for a description of the common features of successful, dynamic directive high school principals based on Lightfoot's 1983 case studies of six principals). Third, what are the differences, if any, between effective elementary school principals (on which most of the research has been done) and effective high school principals? Some of the preliminary evidence indicates that the role of the high school principal is not qualitatively different but more complex, and involves the development of more intermediaries (eg department heads) (Berman and Gjelten, 1982; Daresh and Liu, 1985; Fullan and Newton, 1985; and Hall *et al*, 1984). Finally, the question of the most effective approaches to the pre- and in-service training of principals is one of the most pressing difficulties in the immediate future of the principalship, and one which is directly related to management issues.

The study of organizational climate — the third factor — has had a long and relatively unproductive history in educational administration, largely because it has been described and researched in a manner which has detached it from the real tasks and issues of programme improvement in the school. Recent research has provided a more meaningful description of the relationship between climate and improvement. Whether one uses the term 'ethos' (Rutter *et al*, 1979), 'culture' (Deal, 1985; Peters and Waterman, 1982) or 'climate', there is something dynamic and powerful about the shared values, beliefs and expectations which characterize effective organizations.

Stated more simply in relation to the previous two factors, climate refers to the set of values and norms within the school as an organization that foster, support and propel the kind of professional development and principal-teachers activism referred to in the previous paragraphs. Showers (1985) describes the change in these words:

> The social changes required by coaching in the workplace represent a major departure from the traditional school organization. The building of collegial teams that study teaching on a continuous basis forces the restructuring of administrators and supervisory staff (48).

And again:

> Principals must work to establish new norms that reward collegial planning, public teaching, constructive feedback, and experimentation. Professional growth must be seen as valuable and expected. Where coaching has flourished best, principals have taken very active roles in helping teams form, supporting them, providing times in meetings for sharing of teaching and planning, and providing help for team leaders (45).

Judith Little's research over the past five years reflects the same theme (Little, 1982; 1984; 1985). Mot recently she has been examining schools from the following three perspectives:

1. The school as an environment for learning to teach.
2. The school as an institution organized for its own steady improvement and for the advancement of professional knowledge and practice.
3. The school as a place for pursuing a career (Little, 1985: 1).

In effect, school climate as defined here, makes explicit the values, norms and practices that underpin effective professional development and effective principal roles, and makes it clear that what is at stake is the nature of the school as a social institution. Most schools do not function as organizations designed to support improvement, but some do. They exist and their effectiveness makes practical and conceptual sense (Joyce *et al*, 1983; Rutter *et al*, 1979; Little, 1984; 1985).

Guidelines and dilemmas in managing school change

This section is based on two themes. In the first, guidelines are presented which are derived from recent examples of success. A number of researchers have begun to build on this positive knowledge by formulating and applying the knowledge to guide change efforts. The first theme, then, contains good, sound advice for managing change in schools. In the second theme, however, we return to the full reality of change by identifying five fundamental problems which indicate that managing change is intrinsically dilemma-ridden. The guidelines and dilemmas are applicable both to change managers at the school level and to those at the school district level, although in a more refined treatment it would be necessary to spell out the differences in managing change at these two levels.

Guidelines

Several sets of recently published guidelines will be presented briefly in order to show what specific help one can obtain from the research literature, and to indicate how much overlap and consistency there is across recommendations. Loucks-Horsley and Hergert (1985) have written a very insightful booklet incorporating both the obvious and more subtle knowledge of the recent research literature on implementing innovations. They base their guidelines on seven steps:

1. Establishing the project
2. Assessment and goal setting
3. Identifying a solution
4. Preparing for implementation
5. Implementing the project
6. Reviewing progress and problems
7. Maintenance and institutionalization.

There are a number of techniques and wise pieces of advice associated with each step. The authors' underlying beliefs (derived from their intensive work in schools) presented in the introduction reflect the kind of deeper insights and more valid and useful guidelines currently available for change managers. Six are stated:

1. *Acting* is better than *planning*. Protracted needs assessment can be worse than none at all.
2. The principal is not *the* key to school improvement. Although the principal is important, so are many other people . . .
3. Thinking you can truly create ownership at the beginning of a project is ridiculous. Like trust, ownership and commitment build and develop over time through the actual work of improving a school.
4. Help and support given teachers *after* planning and initial training is much more crucial for success than the best (pre-implementation) training money can buy.
5. Coercion is not always bad. A firm push, coupled with lots of help, can launch a project on a path to success.
6. New programmes and practices imported from somewhere else offer a viable, cost-effective . . . alternative to major development efforts (Loucks-Horsley and Hergert, 1985: ix, italics in original).

Fullan (1985) emphasizes eight tasks that must be attended to, and offers a number of suggestions relative to each task:

1. Develop a plan
2. Clarify and develop the role of central staff
3. Select innovations and schools
4. Clarify and develop the role of principals and the criteria for school-based processes
5. Stress ongoing staff development and technical assistance

6. Ensure information gathering and use
7. Plan for continuation and spread
8. Review capacity for future change.

Everard and Morris (1985), in a book that contains a comprehensive range of techniques and suggestions for managing schools, list six tasks similar to the above for managing change systematically. Joyce *et al* (1983) provide a thorough analysis of school improvement on which they build a comprehensive reform agenda based on five principles (build collaborative local governance; build a climate of support; build effective training; build a sound organization; and make change familiar), followed by a series of specific tasks to be addressed. Similarly, Purkey and Smith (1985) identify 13 characteristics of effective schools (or tasks which must be attended to) such as school leadership, staff development, etc. Corbett *et al*, 1984 found eight local conditions related to success or failure: availability of resources, incentives and disincentives, organizational linkages within the school, school priorities, staff factors, turnover in key positions, a school's current decision making and instructional practices, and the influence of prior change projects. They also offer a number of specific suggestions for countering or taking advantage of these eight conditions. Most authors gear their advice to the different phases of a change process (see also Berman, 1981; Fullan, 1982).

The effective schools research in the United States, which identified a small number of school characteristics associated with success (eg instructional leadership by the principal, orderly climate, high expectations, etc), quickly led to a spate of effective schools projects designed to 'instal' the desired characteristics in all schools. While these projects have been seriously criticized precisely because they ignore the complexities of the management of change (Purkey and Smith, 1983; Fullan, 1985), recent examples are beginning to show more sensitivity to the difficulties and possibilities in the change process. Pink and Wallace (1984), after describing a successful effective schools project, suggest that six themes contributed to the success:

1. The project was grounded on a *transactional* process (by viewing change as a process requiring attention to the individual as someone acquiring the meaning of the change).
2. It was based on simultaneous *'tight' and 'loose' coupling*. (It strengthened communication between central office and schools, but gave schools considerable autonomy in deciding what to do.).
3. The project provided *time* for ongoing planning and staff development.
4. The project emphasized *reflection* (by assisting principals and staff to become familiar with the literature on school improvement, and to analyse and reflect on their own situations on a regular basis.
5. *Trade-offs* were negotiated throughout the project instead of following a pre-packaged programme.
6. A *data-driven* emphasis was maintained in which information was

constantly produced and used (see also Eubanks and Levine, 1985).

Deal (1985) argues in a novel and convincing way that we must begin to recognize, stimulate and manage directly the symbolism (the stories and rituals) associated with the development of effective organizations in order to build the all important culture or ethos of the effective school.

To sum up, we have come a long way from the days of documenting failure. We have not only identified the main factors related to effective management within schools, but also increasingly understand their nature and functioning in a process of change. In particular, at the school level, three core management tasks have been identified:

1. Planning ongoing professional development linked to specific programmes.
2. Developing the principal's role as an active instructional leader.
3. Establishing new, shared values and norms supportive of collective action.

Specific guidelines have been formulated by a number of authors. They vary in some of their detail, but the guidelines have two things in common: first, many of the underlying principles are the same — improvement is a process of developing new skills, behaviour and beliefs, requiring active leadership at the school level, and ongoing technical and social support under organizational conditions that promote interaction and the pursuit of common goals collaboratively agreed upon at some point in the process (Fullan, 1985); second, all the authors stress that change cannot be planned in a step-by-step manner, because it is not linear and the process is fraught with difficulties and subtleties. But still, there are many useful lessons and aids to be found in the recent literature on managing change.

Dilemmas and problems

There are five basic dilemmas or problems I should like to take up by way of conclusion: change versus changing, common versus unique aspects, plan-making, where and how big to start, and the key problem of the selection and training of managers.

A theory of change identifies major factors in change processes and explains their interactive functioning. A theory of changing concerns itself with how to influence, manage, and otherwise *alter* those factors known to affect change outcomes. The particular words do not matter, but one of the perennial pitfalls in the management of change is the rational and conceptual fallacy that knowing what causes change is sufficient to being able to bring it about successfully. At the very least we must begin to develop more dynamic and thoughtful strategies for addressing each factor. (For example, what are the characteristics of effective professional development experiences, and how could we possibly establish them in X or Y situations?) Beyond that, we must be more modest in realizing that just because we can explain success in one context does not mean that we can (or even should) transfer the conditions for success to another setting.

Second, and somewhat related, we must not only know the factors common to success but also have a healthy respect for the unique history, personalities and patterns in specific situations, and for the inevitability of the unexpected. This is more an attitude of orientation to change than a technique. I have referred to this elsewhere as 'leadership feel for the improvement process' (Fullan, 1985: 400). It comes from actively using research knowledge in the improvement process, and also developing one's ability to use it through experience and reflection in contending with change projects being attempted (see also Peters and Waterman, 1982). Furthermore, unexpected disruptions (eg administrator and staff turn-over, strikes, or new legislation redirecting efforts) have been found to be commonplace (Louis, 1980; Huberman and Miles, 1984; Corbett *et al*, 1984). The timing of such events is often unpredictable, but the likeli-hood of their occurrence is not. It is possible to have plans to address some of these contingencies; for example, in-service training for new-comers can be built in from the beginning. But it will also be necessary to come to expect disruptions as part and parcel of the change process.

Third, and along the same lines, is the problem of plan making. Again, the rational fallacy. It would seem obvious that, if we know that certain factors influence success, we should build a plan which addresses these factors. There are two problems with this assumption. The first is that successful schools did in fact have certain characteristics in common, but not necessarily because they formulated *a plan* and deliberately put them in place. We must not underestimate the complex and awkward ways in which effective schools have evolved. The second problem is that a plan is just that: a plan to do something, not the actual doing of it. Ironic-ally (but not inconsistent with our knowledge of managing change) one of the most frequent problems currently is 'how to implement the imple-mentation plan'. The implication is that plans, like any innovation, must develop ways so that participants come to modify and internalize them. Recent analysts of successful business organizations have come to the same conclusion: 'The architects of change . . . have to operate integrat-ively, bringing other people in, bridging multiple realities, and re-conceptualizing activities to take account of this new, shared reality . . . Here's the paradox: There needs to be a plan, and the plan has to ack-knowledge that it will be departed from' (Kanter, 1983: 305; also Peters and Waterman, 1982; Fullan, 1982; 1985). This is essentially another warning that step-by-step guidelines cannot provide the answers; if they represent sound advice they can be moderately helpful.

The question of where and how big to start has two aspects — the first concerns the proportion of users, and the second the type and magnitude of the change itself. Does one start with a small or large number of people? Should one start with volunteers or include all those affected? Should one undertake the exercise demanding large-scale changes or more modest ones? (Huberman and Miles, 1984: 280 refer to ambitiousness versus practicality.) There are, of course, no clear answers to these dilemmas. The best advice is to start small with expansion in mind. The number of participants should be small enough to be manageable, but sufficient in size to be conducive to sustained interaction among those implementing change. The scope or magnitude of the change can be quite significant, provided that people are able to start with parts of the change and build incrementally. There are a number of leverage points for the manager of change, but the most important one is to be able to foster the ongoing interaction and assistance especially necessary during the early stages of implementing a new programme or reform. In such a system peers influence peers. What is learned in first attempts can be used for improving the quality of managing second and third attempts. There are many inherent difficulties in trying to establish the right balance in a school between 'pressure and support' for change, but the goal is to make the culture of the school increasingly responsive to, and demanding of, its members to consider and follow through on selected improvements (Fullan, 1985; Little, 1985).

Also part of the fourth factor, relative to magnitude, is the issue of whether it is better to concentrate on specific innovations (eg revising the teaching of science) or on school effectiveness *per se* (in which changes in certain basic characteristics of the school are attempted directly). The relationship between the two emphases should be understood. In the innovation-focused approach the change itself is relatively narrowly defined and takes centre stage, with the effective schools factors (eg principal leadership, climate, etc) being in the foregound in that they are seen and treated as influencing the likelihood of success. In the school-effectiveness approach the so-called foreground factors *are* the innovation, and thus become the centre of attention with any particular innovation being relatively unimportant (or in any case arising from changes in the foreground factors). Whatever initial approach one takes, the advice is that both innovation and effectiveness factors should be directly addressed along the way.

Selection and training are the final problems to be considered as they are at the heart of the potential for significant reform in the effectiveness of the management of change. There is an entire section on management training in this book, so we need only make a small number of points directly related to the issues in this chapter. First, to refer to selection of principals, it is not general practice to carefully choose new principals based on their ability to manage change (Baltzell and Dentler, 1983). It appears, although there is little research evidence as yet, that selection procedures are changing rapidly to make active instructional leadership as one of the main criteria of selection. Since it is easier to select leaders with certain characteristics than to retrian existing ones, and since there will be many openings over the next ten years (in North American schools at least), we should expect some major improvements in the management of school change.

Second, no matter how careful the selection criteria, pre-job and in-service training for school principals will be critical because many of the insights and capacities will have to be developed on the job. There are some very significant developments in this respect. Buckley (1985) outlines and analyses five case studies in different countries (France, Sweden, England, The Netherlands, and Norway) focusing on the training needs of secondary school heads. Everard and Morris (1985) have written a book which amounts to a curriculum for training school leaders. Leithwood and his associates have developed a specific 'principal's profile' which they use for training as well as research purposes (Leithwood *et al*, 1984; Leithwood and Montgomery, 1986).

Third, the school effectiveness literature has brought the principal's role to the forefront, including substantial new investment in in-service training and specific expectations. Duke and Imber (1985) provide an important critique of the current tendency in the United States to equate principal effectiveness with student achievement, and suggest an alternative boader conception of principal effectiveness based on organizational efficiency, subordinate and superordinate satisfaction, as well as on goal accomplishment.

Fourth, and the main point I should like to make about training, is that we run the risk of vastly underestimating how difficult it is to conduct effective training in the management of change. Managing change requires great sophistication in contending with the dilemmas, paradoxes, contingencies, unexpected events and the multiplicity of factors operating in the organization and its environment (Peters and Waterman, 1982; Fullan, 1985). Hall and Hord (1984), for example, documented nearly 2000 interventions in one school year in a study of nine principals as each principal attempted to facilitate the implementation of a relatively simple curriculum innovation. It will be easy to repeat the mistake that was made in the widespread expansion of in-service education for teachers in the 1970s. We know now why offering direct in-service courses and workshops did not work (see the first part of this chapter). In the same vein, providing pre-job and in-service programmes to principals, even well designed ones, will not have much impact unless they incorporate some of the elements of effective professional development — ongoing interaction, back and forth between theory and practice, incrementalism, demonstration, practice, feedback, pressure and support. Barnett (1985) describes the kind of intensive in-service programme which will be needed. His Peer-Assisted Leadership (PAL) programme is based on shadowing (peer observation by another principal) and reflective interviewing in the development of specific themes for organizational improvement, using a structured technique to generate the themes. Training in application and reflection will require great effort and ingenuity to accomplish the goal of producing effective managers of change (see also Schon, 1983).

Taking stock of where we are now: it was relatively easy to document failure; it was more difficult but possible to describe and explain success; it will be infinitely more difficult to become better at managing change because we will no longer be attempting to understand situations, but to actively change them through deliberate means.

We have made great progress in a relatively short period of time, with research continuing to grow in volume and sophistication. It is important to retain a measure of humility in recognizing that change (or stability for that matter) in social systems will never be all that manageable.

References

Baltzell, C and Dentler, R (1983) *Selecting American School Principals: A Research Report.* Abt Associates: Cambridge, Mass

Barnett, B (1985) A synthesis for improving practice. Paper presented at the Annual Meeting of the American Educational Research Association: Montreal

Berman, P (1981) Toward an implementation pradigm *in* Lehming and Kane (1981)

Berman, P and Gjelten, T (1982) *Improvement Maintenance and Decline: A Progress Report* Berman, Weiler Associates: Berkeley, Cal

Blumberg, A and Greenfield, W (1980) *The Effective Principal: Perspectives in School Leadership* Allyn and Bacon: Boston, Mass

Bossert, S T, Dwyer, D C, Rowan, B and Lee, G V (1982) The instructional management role of the principal *Educational Administration Quarterly* 18 3: 34-64

Boyan, N J ed (1986) *The Handbook of Research on Educational Administration* American Educational Research Association: Washington, DC (forthcoming)

*Buckley, J (1985) *The Training of Secondary School Heads in Western Europe* NFER-Nelson for the Council of Europe: Windsor, Berks

Clark, D L, Lotto, L S and Astuto, T A (1984) Effective schools and school improvement: a comparative analysis of two lines of inquiry *Educational Administration Quarterly* 20 3: 41-68

Corbett, H, Dawson, J and Firestone, W (1984) *School Context and School Change* Teachers College Press: New York

Crandall, D P *et al* (1983) *People, Policies and Practices: Examining the Chain of School Improvement* (10 volumes) The Network: Andover, Mass

Daresh, J and Liu, C (1985) High school principals' perceptions of their instructional leadership behavior. Paper presented at the Annual Meeting of the American Educational Research Association: Montreal

Deal, T (1985) The symbolism of effective schools *The Elementary School Journal* 85 5: 601-20

Duke, D L and Imber, M (1985) Should principals be required to be effective? *School Organization* 5 2: 125-46

Dwyer, D, Lee, G, Rowan, B and Bossert, S (1983) *Five Principals in Action: Perspectives on Instructional Management* The Far West Laboratory for Educational Research and Development: San Francisco

Eubanks, E and Levine, D (1985) A first look at effective school projects at inner-city elementary schools. Paper presented at the Annual Meeting of the American Educational Research Association: Montreal

Everard, K B and Morris, G (1985) *Effective School Management* Harper and Row: London

Firestone, W and Corbett, H (1986) Organizational change *in* Boyan (1986)

Fullan, M (1982) *The Meaning of Educational Change* Teachers College Press: Columbia University: New York

Fullan, M (1985) Change processes and strategies at the local level *The Elementary School Journal* 85 3: 391-421

Fullan, M and Pomfret, A (1977) Research on curriculum and instruction implementation *Review of Educational Research* 47 1: 335-97

Fullan, M and Newton, E (1985) High school principals as facilitators of instruction. Unpublished paper, Ontario Institute for Studies in Education: Toronto

Gross, N, Giacquinta, J and Bernstein, M (1971) *Implementing Organizational Innovations: A Sociological Analysis of Planned Educational Change* Basic Books: New York

Hall, G E and Hord, S M (1984) Analyzing what change facilitators do *Knowledge Creation, Diffusion, Utilization* **5** 3: 275-307

Hall, G E, Hord, S, Rutherford, W and Huling, L (1984) Change in high schools *Educational Leadership* **41**: 59-62

Huberman, A M and Crandall, D (1983) *People, Policies and Practices: Examining the Chain of School Improvement* **9** *Implications for Action, A Study of Dissemination Efforts Supporting School Improvement* The Network: Andover, Mass

*Huberman, A M and Miles, M B *Innovation Up Close: How School Improvement Works* Plenum: New York

Joyce, B R, Hersh, R H and McKibbin, M (1983) *The Structure of School Improvement* Longman: New York

Joyce, B and Showers, B (1980) Improving in-service training: the messages from research *Educational Leadership* **37** 5: 379-85

Kanter, R (1983) *The Change Masters* Simon and Schuster: New York

Lehming, R and Kane, M eds (1981) *Improving Schools: Using What We Know* Sage: Beverly Hills, Cal

Leithwood, K A and Montgomery, D J (1982) The role of the elementary school principal in program improvement *Review of Educational Research* **52** 3: 309-39

Leithwood, K and Montgomery, D (1986) *Improving Principal Effectiveness: The Principal Profile* OISE Press: Toronto (forthcoming)

Leithwood, K A, Stanley, K and Montgomery, D J (1984) Training principals for school improvement *Education and Urban Society* **17** 1: 49-72

Lightfoot, S L (1983) *The Good High School: Portraits of Character and Culture* Basic Books: New York

Little, J W (1982) Norms of collegiality and experimentation: workplace conditions of school success *American Educational Research Journal* **19** 3: 325-40

Little, J W (1984) Seductive images and organizational realities in professional development *Teachers College Record* **86** 1: 84-102

Little, J W (1985) What schools contribute to teachers' professional development. Paper presented at the Annual Meeting of the American Educational Research Association: Montreal

Loucks-Horsley, S and Hergert, L F (1985) *An Action Guide to School Improvement* Association for Supervision and Curriculum Development The Network: Andover, Mass

Louis, K (1980) *A Study of the R and D Utilization Program* Abt Associates: Cambridge, Mass

Peters, T J and Waterman, R H (1982) *In Search of Excellence: Lessons From America's Best Run Companies* Harper and Row: New York

Peters, T and Austin, N (1985) *A Passion for Excellence* Random House: New York

Pink, W and Wallace, D (1984) Creating effective schools: moving from theory to practice. Paper presented at the Annual Meeting of the American Educational Research Association: New Orleans

Purkey, S and Smith, M (1983) Effective schools: a review *The Elementary School Journal* **83**: 427-52

Purkey, S and Smith, M (1985) School reform: the district policy implications of the effective schools literature *The Elementary School Journal* **85** 3: 353-90

*Rutter, M, Maugham, B, Mortimer, P, Ouston, J and Smith, A (1979) *Fifteen Thousand Hours: Secondary Schools and Their Effects on Children* Harvard University Press: Cambridge, Mass

Sarason, S (1971) *The Culture of the School and the Problem of Change* Allyn and Bacon: Boston, Mass

Schön, D A (1983) *The Reflective Practitioner* Basic Books: New York

Showers, B (1985) Teachers coaching teachers *Educational Leadership* **42** 7: 43-49

Sparks, G (1984) In-service education: the process of teacher change. Paper presented at the Annual Meeting of the American Educational Research Association: New Orleans

Stallings, J (1981) *Testing Teachers' In-class Instruction and Measuring Change Resulting from Staff Development* Teaching and Learning Institute: Mountain View, Cal

6. The management of school improvement

Ron Glatter

Summary: This chapter is based on reflections arising from the author's participation in the OECD/CERI International School Improvement Project (ISIP). The resonances and scope of the term 'school improvement' are considered, as well as its different connotations in different national contexts. The connection between improvement processes and routine operations is examined, and it is argued that we should focus attention on how the management of improvement and the management of maintenance relate to one another, rather than regard them as largely separate activities. It is noted that recent research on the improvement process has emphasized the importance of the more intuitive, judgemental aspects of the management task, and this is related to the broader conceptual shift from an over-reliance on rational, linear models of how change occurs in schools towards acceptance of a far wider range of explanations. Some recent schemes for classifying various 'perspectives' on or 'images' of schools are briefly discussed, and contrasts between the behaviour of those attempting to manage improvements on the basis of different images are indicated. The calls for a multiperspective view are supported, but it is not yet clear what is entailed in such integration or what it would imply for practice, training and research. The chapter ends with a few brief conclusions concerning professional development.

Introduction

This chapter is based on reflections arising from the author's participation in the International School Improvement Project (ISIP). ISIP is organized under the aegis of the Centre for Educational Research and Innovation (CERI) of the Organization for Economic Co-operation and Development (OECD). It is a collaborative project involving institutions and individuals from 14 countries which aims, through seminars, publications and other means, to develop and disseminate useful knowledge about the process of school improvement.

The project has been divided into six broad areas relevant to school improvement: school-based review; principals and internal change agents; external support; research and evaluation; school improvement policy; and conceptual mapping of school improvement. At the time of writing, the first major book arising from the project, related to the last of the above areas, is about to be published (van Velzen et al, 1985). Publications

concerned with the other areas are expected to appear before the end of
the project (December 1986). The particular focus of the author has been
on the area dealing with principals.

The chapter starts with a brief examination of the concept of school
improvement, goes on to consider some current perceptions of management, and then attempts to relate the two ideas of school improvement
and management by reference to various 'images' of schools as organizations. Finally, some implications of this analysis for the professional
development of principals and others in leading positions within schools
(who are subsequently referred to collectively as 'school leaders') will be
mentioned.

A note of caution should be entered here. Although a European contri-
butor to this book, the author is conscious that the concept of school
improvement is North American in origin, that an impressive range of
relevant empirical research has been conducted there and that there has
been valuable and promising conceptual development (Clark, Lotto and
Astuto, 1984). The European work is, by contrast, sparse (for a rare
example, see Hopkins and Wideen, 1984). One of the outcomes of ISIP
should be to initiate some correction in this imbalance. Meanwhile, this
author has found it necessary — and educative — to draw mainly on
North American sources.

The concept of school improvement

There is space to discuss only a small selection of aspects of this concept.
We might ask first what are the distinctive resonances of the term 'school
improvement' compared with those of its elder cousin 'innovation'?
The tone of 'school improvement' is more comprehensive yet more incremental, implying a broader sweep over the school's activities but less
radical in intent. There is also a clear focus on the attempt to achieve an
outcome — improvement — rather than just to introduce something new.
Thus, 'school improvement' is a term which reflects the current age in
ways 'innovation' does not.

Meanings

The definition of 'school improvement' adopted by ISIP is as follows:

> A systematic, sustained effort aimed at change in learning conditions and
> other related internal conditions in one or more schools, with the ultimate
> aim of accomplishing educational goals more effectively (Miles and Ekholm,
> 1985a).

Such a definition can clearly encompass many different varieties of change.
The authors of the first ISIP book suggest three major variables — scope,
size and scale. *Scope* refers to whether the boundaries of the change are
broad or narrow, for instance a specific curriculum change compared with

a broader reform aimed at several aspects of the school's functioning; *size* is the relative complexity of the change from the point of view of the persons implementing it; and *scale* relates to the number of units and levels of the educational system that the change involves. Quite modest changes (in terms of scope, size and scale) in 'related internal conditions' could fall within the definition. For instance, in the British context, a head teacher might feel that a strict policy on the wearing of school uniform by pupils would improve learning conditions and hence attainment. A sustained campaign to enforce the wearing of uniform would then constitute an attempt at school improvement. It certainly meets the authors' criterion of aiming at change in the school as a whole, not just in specific classrooms (van Velzen *et al*, 1985).

The example also highlights a theme familiar from innovation studies: the value-laden and political aspects of many attempts at school improvement. These aspects have probably grown sharper in recent years with, for instance, the decline in resources allocated to schools and expectations of a greater emphasis on vocationally oriented learning in secondary schools in many countries. The different connotations of a term like 'school improvement' in different national contexts are also striking. At a recent ISIP seminar such contrasting perspectives became very apparent. For instance, the Japanese view of improvement seemed to be in terms of the steady development of current activities: for them, as one Japanese speaker observed, 'School improvement is equivalent to better daily problem solving.' By contrast, in North America, improvement still frequently appeared in practice to be associated with specific curriculum (often single-subject) initiatives introduced by school districts. As a final example, in Sweden, the improvement attempt seemed to be concerned with altering the whole ethos of, and pattern of relationships within, the school. Attaching simple labels to each of these perspectives, we might select improvement (Japan), innovation (North America) and reform (Sweden).

Clearly, there are many qualifications to be made about such general perceptions. For instance, the reality at school level might look quite different and present far more common features than the sharp contrasts above imply. However, one conclusion in the first ISIP publication is that research suggests that the *process* which a school needs to go through when it improves is largely the same wherever it occurs (Ekholm and Miles, 1985). The validity of this conclusion must depend in part on how disparate are the meanings attached to 'improvement' in various contexts.

Improvement and maintenance

A relevant issue here is the connection between 'improvement' and routine operations. While the ISIP definition given above largely reflects the cultural shift from 'innovation' to 'improvement' outlined earlier, it nevertheless specifies that, to be classed as an 'improvement', a change must involve 'a systematic, sustained effort . . .' implying a sharp distinction between routine operations and attempts at change. Is improvement possible *only* through a 'systematic, sustained effort aimed at change . . .'? We have already seen that in the Japanese context such a distinction may not be wholly acceptable. March (1984), writing generally rather than with specific reference to education, has argued that administrative theory has been misleading in the emphasis it has given to this distinction, and that effective routine operations are often the main motors of organizational change. 'The theoretical rhetoric of change seems antithetical to routine, but I have argued that effective systems of routine behaviour are the primary bases of organizational adaptation to an environment' (March, 1984: 33). He urges us to recognize the impact of 'ordinary competence' and 'of the ways in which organizations change by modest modifications of routines rather than by massive mucking around' (March, 1984: 22). Change and improvement do take place through a large number of quite small adjustments, and we need to examine the ways in which this happens as well as the more overt and systematic attempts at improvement. For example, is the evolutionary adaptive process outlined by March capable of accommodating radical changes in environmental conditions or expectations?

If the old boundary between 'innovation' and 'maintenance' is becoming less firm, with the idea of 'improvement' acting to some extent as a bridge between them, this by no means implies that intervention and pressure will not accelerate change. As House observes, the nature of this pressure is a matter of debate on social as well as technical grounds: '. . . The school, being traditional, will be slow to change without pressures. How modernization should occur, through what legitimate means, and how fast, are the issues that divide people concerned about innovation' (House, 1981: 37).

The effects of school-level interventions during improvement processes have been studied by researchers, particularly in North America. In line with the trends outlined above, the activities involved appear to be more subtle and informal than is implied when, as March puts it, 'we sing the grand arias of management' (March, 1984: 23). Hall and Hord (1984) developed an 'intervention taxonomy' based on their own studies of change processes in schools and from published case studies. Although there were significant interventions at various strategic levels, the most important type was the 'incident level intervention'; for example, a short interaction between two teachers concerned with a particular change or a memo from a school leader to all teachers involved in an innovation. 'From our studies to date, it is clear that delivery and understanding of incident level interventions is of crucial importance to successful implementation . . . The number of incident interventions is so large that their combined effect appears to "make or break" the effort' (Hall and Hord, 1984: 292). Another significant type of intervention was dubbed a 'mushroom' by the authors. A mushroom is an intervention that was not deliberately initiated to influence the course of an improvement process, but turns out to do so, for good or ill: 'Mushrooms can be flavourful and nutritious or they can be quite poisonous' (Hall and Hord, 1984: 295). Examples might include: a key person taking on an increased workload and missing meetings relevant to the improvement with negative, or possibly positive, effects on its progress; unexpected staff losses or gains, with their resultant impact (Miles, 1983); personality clashes within the staff group and their effects on the improvement attempt.

Such examples indicate not only the multiplicity of influences involved but also the importance of regarding school improvement as a process. For example, studies have found that staff commitment often grows during implementation: 'Changes in attitudes, beliefs and understanding tend to *follow* rather than precede changes in behaviour' (Fullan, 1985: 393). Of course, the ultimate object of a process of improvement is to stabilize a change in state, to establish new routines (Berman, 1981: Morris and Burgoyne, 1973), a point which emphasizes the close connection between improvement and maintenance processes.

Scope

Finally in this section, we return to the suggestion that 'school improvement' carries the implication of a process that will cover the whole of the school and affect it for the better. In the real world, however, there are always choices to be made and limited funds, time and energy to be allocated in certain directions rather than others. So the *scope* of a particular school improvement attempt is an important issue. 'Devoting resources and attention to one or two objectives is certainly a good way to improve performance in those areas. But if this is done without consideration of other domains, it is likely that the latter will suffer' (Fullan, 1985: 397). Since school improvement is an ambitious-sounding concept, it is well to ask of any particular scheme: 'whether by accident or design, what is this proposal *not* intended to improve?' The answer should give guidance in assessing whether the plan might fairly be described as an attempt at school improvement.

Perceptions of the task of management

Recent writing on management, in education and elsewhere, has been reasserting the intuitive, judgemental aspects of the management task as distinct from the more technical scientific dimensions which were emphasized through much of the 1960s and 1970s. Schön, a leading exponent of this view, refers to 'the spontaneous exercise of intuitive artistry' and to managers becoming effective not mainly through studying theory and technique but through long practice 'which builds up a generic, essentially unanalysable capacity for problem-solving' (Schön, 1984: 41). (A somewhat similar assessment has been made by Griffiths [1979].) From these ideas, Schön develops his proposal for a 'reflective management science' based on the 'private inquiries' of reflective managers, supported by researchers whose primary tasks would be to facilitate and document these inquiries, synthesize their results and provide conceptual frameworks for them (Schön, 1984: 62).

The literature focusing specifically on studies of improvement and change is also increasingly stressing the less tangible, more subtle aspects of management. Glatter refers to 'the central role of imagination, judgment and a grasp of reality in management for adaptability' (Glatter, 1984: 34). Fullan identifies what he calls 'leadership feel for the improvement process' as a key variable, partly because 'processes of improvement are intrinsically paradoxical and subtle' (Fullan, 1985: 401).

Attempts to snare these elusive factors are proceeding apace. Rutherford and his associates have developed a model of 'change facilitator style' which includes not only 'behaviours' like providing for staff development and actively seeking resources but also 'attitude, motivations and feelings of adequacy for facilitating, knowledge of the task, beliefs about the role and philosophy of change' (Rutherford, Hord, Huling and Hall, 1983: 115). They consider that these factors may represent the 'inner states' to which Leithwood and Montgomery refer in their review of 29 studies of elementary school principals: 'These inner states explain much overt activity and are, in turn, affected by the consequences of that activity' (Leithwood and Montgomery, 1982: 320). Rutherford and his colleagues introduce a further 'intangible' factor as a component of their model of style: 'tone' similar to 'tone of voice'. They argue that it is not only the words in which a spoken statement is delivered which convey a message, but also the tone with which they are delivered (for instance, half listening compared with listening enthusiastically and asking an appropriate question). 'In fact, the tone of voice may carry a more powerful message than the words' (Rutherford, Hord, Huling and Hall, 1983: 116).

Setting directions

This is clearly difficult territory for researchers. There are, for instance, obvious problems in attempting to identify in any concrete terms the variables contained in this simple but striking sentence by Buckley, an experienced British head teacher and trainer who conducted a survey of European training provision for school leaders: 'A head must give a school a sense of direction and a feeling of confidence' (Buckley, 1985: 171). This conclusion is supported by a study of British primary school teachers' perceptions of, and degrees of satisfaction with, the leadership styles of their head teachers (Nias, 1980), which found that the teachers especially wanted their heads to provide a sense of purpose, direction and coherence. The style which was especially appreciated was one in which the head took the lead in goal-setting, but the teachers felt they were genuinely able to contribute to policy formation. This is resonant of the conclusion from North American research on effective principals that, in spite of often operating (as we have seen) in an informal manner, and in spite of involving their teachers extensively in decision making, their own preference is for a *task* rather than a relations orientation, emphasizing, for instance, the definition of goals related to student learning and monitoring their achievement (Leithwood, Stanley and Montgomery, 1984).

Change and stability

To try to ensure that this direction-setting task of management is adequately fulfilled, some have suggested that the 'routine' and 'improvement' aspects of management should be more clearly separated. This is related to the repeated finding that the frenetic and fragmented work pattern of school leaders (as of other managers) tends to drive out forward thinking, planning and goal definition (Glatter, 1983). In fact, Buckley identifies as the *major* problem facing European secondary school leaders 'managing the present while preparing for the future at the same time' (Buckley, 1985: 22). He argues that this problem is made more severe when training programmes increasingly emphasize the school leader's role as a change agent which the individual is expected to fulfil while preoccupied with the task of maintaining day-to-day stability, and he considers that trainers should give careful attention to this dilemma. The strains imposed by this extension of the job in terms of *time* are additional to those resulting from its extension in terms of *space*, indicated by the school's increasing involvement in, and accountability to, society and its local community (Buckley, 1985; see also Morgan, Hall and Mackay, 1984).

Pressures of this kind and scale have led to suggestions like that made by Handy, a British management specialist who undertood a close examination of secondary schools in England. He concluded that '. . . there is not enough discussion of what we are trying to do and how we should be doing it and measuring it and too much discussion of timetables, rosters and duties' (Handy, 1984: 35). He makes a sharp distinction between 'leadership' and 'administration' and argues that 'Professionals require one of their own to lead them but can, and normally should, use an outsider to administer things for them' (Handy, 1984: 23). Handy himself recognizes that the two tasks are not divorced from one another and in particular that 'An inefficient school is an ineffective school, and you notice it straight away' (Handy, 1984: 35). The dichotomy is difficult to sustain in practice, as March argued (even for timetables, rosters and duties), particularly in terms of the student's experience. Buckley's dilemmas are likely to remain: school leaders are not solely change agents, nor can they avoid maintenance activity or functions which do not have an immediate and obvious connection with the processes of teaching and learning. The detailed review of North American research on the effective principal conducted by Leithwood and his colleagues led them to the view that '. . . the principal must and ought to engage in a wide spectrum of functions, that these functions all have some bearing (positive or negative) on the quality of students' school experiences' and that the objective in carrying out these functions is to give them coherence and purpose 'in order to realize the holistic image of the educated person to which students and school aspire' (Leithwood, Stanley and Montgomery, 1984: 62). We now need to focus collective attention on how such a demanding set of requirements can be met, and on how the management of improvement and the management of current operations relate to one another, rather than regarding them as largely separate and unconnected activities.

Organizational images and school improvement

Underlying many of the trends which have been discussed in earlier sections is a broader conceptual shift, from an over-reliance on rational, linear models of how change occurs in schools towards acceptance of a far wider range of explanations. For instance, in their review of relevant American studies, Clark, Lotto and Astuto (1984) criticize the 'model bias' of much work on school improvement because of its rational, bureaucratic view of organizations, goals, leadership and accountability and its assumption of a relationship of linear causality between identified variables. Berman (1981) argues that the complex organizational sub-processes which make up the educational change process 'are loosely, not linearly, coupled'. At the level of action in schools, a prime task for management is the identification of new problems and key opportunities which, as Handy points out, 'is an activity that belongs more to the right or creative side of the brain than to the left or logical and linear bit' (Handy, 1984: 27).

Images of schools

Several writers have recently developed useful schemes for classifying the different 'perspectives' on or 'images' of educational organizations found in the research literature (Cuthbert, 1984; Davies and Morgan, 1983; Ellström, 1983; House, 1981; Miles and Ekholm, 1985b). For instance, House (1981) refers to the technological, political and cultual perspectives, while Miles and Ekholm (1985b) identify five 'images' of schools as organizations: rational/bureaucratic, professionalized/collegial; social system; political; natural system. For House, the perspectives are 'ways of seeing' organizations and they function in a changing social and political world: 'The political and cultural perspectives are made more viable by the declining belief in technology and by less social consensus on goals' (House, 1981: 20). They are therefore more open to change than scientific paradigms and are more dependent on the particular context. Furthermore, they are not mutually exclusive: 'The same person may view innovation from one perspective, then from another for another purpose' (House, 1981).

Consideration has therefore been given to the relationship between the images. Davies and Morgan (1983) regard them as relating to distinct phases of a change process, whereas Ellström (1983) suggests that they should be seen not as phases but as *faces* or 'dimensions of the same organizational reality' and assumes that the different dimensions may be differently *salient* in different organizations (for instance schools and industrial firms), in different parts of the same organization or even in the same part at different points in time. Other writers are less specific than this, and simply stress the implications for our research and our practice of viewing schools through a particular 'lens': 'Regardless of the lens we use, the real life of any particular school may be more or less like the image' (Miles and Ekholm, 1985b). Schön argues that an over-emphasis on the rational, technological aspects of management in the professional training of managers may create in them 'selective inattention' to the other aspects and the avoidance of 'situations — often the most important in organizational life — where they would find themselves confronted with uncertainty, instability or uniqueness' (Schön, 1984: 41). Sergiovanni (1984) advocates a 'multiple-perspective view' which does not involve a complete break with the technological perspective but locates it appropriately within a comprehensive theory of organization. Nevertheless, it is significant that, just when technological, 'rational' approaches to the management of school improvement are coming into increasing prominence in many countries, research-based analyses are increasingly questioning their validity and potency.

Implications for management

Some interesting contrasts between the behaviour of those attempting to manage improvements on the basis of the different images can be suggested (House, 1981; Miles and Ekholm, 1985b). The *rational image* emphasizes order and rules and assumes much consensus on interests and values. The tasks of management are then to clarify purposes and goals, to discover and specify ways of achieving them, to monitor performance and to ensure that teachers have the requisite skills and training. These managerial tasks can be carried out fairly aggressively since values and interests are not in serious dispute; structures tend to be hierarchical and authority is relatively unquestioned. This perspective is often associated with initiatives for improvement emanating from government agencies, and tends to be optimistic in its assumption about what can be achieved by management action.

The *professional/collegial image*, as its name implies, emphasizes the professional competence and expertise of the teaching staff and their collegial collaboration in meeting the needs of the clients (students). The task of management in the improvement process is largely to support the work of teaching, perhaps even to 'fade into the wallpaper' and concentrate closely on administrative and supportive activities while the professionals go about the real business. The collegial overlaps considerably with the *social system image*, but the latter stresses in addition the idea of the organization as an interdependent collection of parts interacting with each other and with the environment, and also the development of open, trusting relationships and modes of communication. The tasks of management for improvement are to lead and to facilitate, especially in terms of the *process* aspects of improvement, involving everyone in thoughtful, collaborative work.

Some of the most interesting and least explored questions arise in connection with the 'newer' political and cultural images. The *political image* emphasizes the conflicting interests which individuals and groups have in organizations, and which they pursue through building factions and coalitions and through bargaining and compromise. In the *cultural image* (called 'natural systems image' by Miles and Ekholm [1985b]) schools and school systems are seen as composed of groups with separate and distinct cultures and their associated values interacting with one another: 'The fact that schools are often slow to agree to external initiatives suggests that they own *themselves*, and the so-called "demands of society" as filtered through governments and authorities are far away, in another world' (van Velzen and Robin, 1985). Handy (1984) has argued that one way to improve large secondary schools would be to strengthen their cultural aspects by, for instance, giving them federal structures and so making them 'cities of villages'.

The cultural and political images differ from the other three, as is often remarked, in that they do not assume consensus or clarity about goals. In consequence, these perspectives imply far less 'optimism' over the extent to which improvement can be 'engineered', although they can certainly accommodate the possibility that organizations adapt effectively to their environment through routine processes, as suggested by March (1984) and discussed earlier in this chapter. Nevertheless, these perspectives seem, at least up to the present, to be more helpful in suggesting why attempts at improvement may fail — because they conflict with the values and/or interests of those who are intended to carry them through — than in indicating how such attempts may be made to succeed. Thus, it has been suggested that the political perspective is 'essentially reactive' and is antithetical to participative decision making or group problem solving because political procedures are primarily 'a method for keeping order in institutions, not for obtaining the optimal solutions to problems' (Meier, 1985: 66). Equally, the cultural perspective has been character-ized as harbouring a 'conservative, traditional view of change' because of the inherent difficulty of resolving conflict between cultures, short of political action by the stronger one (House, 1981). It is interesting, in this context, to note the increasing use of financial and other incentives in some countries to persuade schools and teachers to move in certain directions. Berman (1981) has drawn attention to US findings which suggest that innovation projects are often adopted opportunistically to benefit from external money or for political considerations rather than to solve pressing educational problems. Further data along these lines might lead us to conclude that the political perspective is rather more firmly based than the cultural!

Even in these perspectives, some tasks and requirements relevant to the management of improvement can be indicated. Conflict management is pervasive in both, though of a different kind in each, and in the cultural perspective it is akin to treading on eggshells. The political perspective implies the need for those managing improvements to have a close understanding of the interests and motives of those likely to be affected, to be willing to consider 'tailoring' the improvement to maximize political 'gains' and minimize 'losses' for key groups, and to be prepared to build coalitions and strike deals to secure support for the improvement. The notion of a 'market in political horse-trading' (March, 1974) may be remote from the conventional rhetoric of school improvement but it is clearly seen in the political perspective and widely recognized by those working in schools. The requirements for management in the cultural image include a tolerance for ambiguity and a strong sensitivity to the values and beliefs of different groups or 'sub-cultures': 'To interact effectively in a sub-culture means developing multi-cultural competence, learning what to expect' (House, 1981: 27). Although the political and cultural images of schools look somewhat different, their implications for management tasks and skills are related, in that both put a premium on factors such as sensitivity, ability to grasp situations, judgement and even intuition!

Towards integration

It is important to re-emphasize the point that 'perspectives are images of reality and not truths in themselves' and that their purpose is 'to enhance one's understanding and to illuminate one's view of the world' (Sergiovanni, 1984: 10). Much more work needs to be done to clarify and extend their usefulness for practice and research. For instance, as Miles and Ekholm (1985b) repeatedly stress, no single image is an adequate basis for understanding or action, hence the calls for 'multi-perspective' and 'integrative' views, 'comprehensive' strategies and so on. Yet it is far from clear what is entailed in such integration and how these or other 'images of reality' can most usefully be related to one another for different purposes (such as practice, training or research). Nevertheless, such classifications of perspectives seem potentially to have considerable heuristic value both to enhance understanding of our present practices and to provide a basis for further explorations into the mysteries of school improvement and its management.

Implications for professional development

There is space for only three brief concluding comments on the topic of professional development, which is taken up by others in greater detail elsewhere in this volume.

First, the discussion in the previous section would suggest some grounds for concern about professional development programmes related to the management of school improvement which are strongly focused on one or two of the images to the relative exclusion of the others. Certainly there may be contextual or other reasons to be advanced in support of the dominant focus, but legitimate questions can be asked about such a stance and the justifications might be closely examined.

Second, there are serious pedagogical and other difficulties associated with offering effective professional development relating to the political and cultural images in particular: for example, ethical dilemmas are involved in developing political capabilities (Glatter, 1982). These problems need careful study.

Third, an important aim of professional development for those concerned with managing school improvement should be to help them realize what images they are using, both in specific situations and more generally, and to encourage them to consider whether these are either appropriate or sufficient.

References

Berman, P (1981) Educational change: an implementation paradigm *in* Lehming and Kane (1981)

Boyd-Barrett, O, Bush, T, Goodey, J, McNay, I, and Preedy, M *eds* (1983) *Approaches to Post-School Management* Harper and Row/The Open University: London

*Buckley, J (1985) *The Training of Secondary School Heads in Western Europe* NFER-Nelson: Windsor, Berks

Bush, T, Glatter, R, Goodey, J and Riches, C *eds* (1980) *Approaches to School Management* Harper and Row/The Open University: London

*Clark, D L, Lotto, L S and Astuto, T A (1984) Effective schools and school improvement: a comparative analysis of two lines of inquiry *Educational Administration Quarterly* 20 3: 41-68

Cuthbert, R (1984) *The Management Process* (Block 3, Part 2 of the Open University course *Management in Post-compulsory Education*) The Open University Press: Milton Keynes

Davies, J L and Morgan, A W (1983) Management of higher education institutions in a period of contraction and uncertainty *in* Boyd-Barrett *et al* (1983)

Ekholm, M and Miles, M B (1985) Conclusions and recommendations *in* van Velzen *et al* (1985)

Ellström, P (1983) Four faces of educational organizations *Higher Education* 12 2: 231-41

Fullan, M (1985) Change processes and strategies at the local level *The Elementary School Journal* 85 3: 391-421

Glatter, R (1982) The micropolitics of education: issues for training *Educational Management and Administration* 10 2: 160-65

Glatter, R (1983) Implications of research for policy on school management training *in* Hegarty (1983)

Glatter, R (1984) *Managing for Change* (Block 6 of the Open University course E324 *Management in Post-Compulsory Education*) The Open University Press: Milton Keynes

Griffiths, D (1979) Another look at research on the behaviour of administrators *in* Immegart and Boyd (1979)

Hall, G E and Hord, S M (1984) Analyzing what change facilitators do: the intervention taxonomy *Knowledge Creation, Diffusion, Utilization* 5 3: 275-307

Handy, C (1984) *Taken for Granted? Understanding Schools as Organizations* Longman for the Schools Council: York

*Hegarty, S ed (1983) *Training for Management in Schools* NFER-Nelson for the Council of Europe: Windsor, Berks

Hopkins, D and Wideen, M (1984) *Alternative Perspectives on School Improvement* Falmer Press: Lewes, Sussex

House, E R (1981) Three perspectives on innovation: technological, political and cultural *in* Lehming and Kane (1981)

Immegart, G L and Boyd, W L eds (1979) *Problem-Finding in Educational Administration* D C Heath: Lexington, Mass

Lehming, R and Kane, M eds (1981) *Improving Schools: Using What We Know* Sage: Beverley Hills, Cal

Leithwood, K A and Montgomery, D J (1982) The role of the elementary school principal in program improvement *Review of Educational Research* **52** 3: 309-39

Leithwood, K A, Stanley, K and Montgomery, D J (1984) Training principals for school improvement *Education and Urban Society* **17** 1: 49-72

March, J G (1974) Analytical skills and the university training of educational administrators *Journal of Educational Administration* **12** 1: 17-44

March, J G (1984) How we talk and how we act: administrative theory and administrative life *in* Sergiovanni and Corbally (1984)

Meier, T K (1985) Leadership theories from industry: relevant to higher education? *Educational Administration and History* **17** 1: 62-69

Miles, M B (1983) Unravelling the mystery of institutionalization *Educational Leadership* **40** 14-19 (November)

Miles, M B and Ekholm, M (1985a) What is school improvement? *in* van Velzen *et al* (1985)

Miles, M B and Ekholm, M (1985b) School improvement at the school level *in* van Velzen *et al* (1985)

Morgan, C, Hall, V and Mackay, H (1984) *The Selection of Secondary School Headteachers* The Open University Press: Milton Keynes

Morris, J and Burgoyne, J G (1973) *Developing Resourceful Managers* Institute of Personnel Management: London

Nias, J (1982) Leadership styles and job satisfaction in primary schools *in* Bush *et al* (1980)

Rutherford, W L, Hord, S M, Huling, L L and Hall, G E (1983) *Change Facilitators: In Search of Understanding Their Role* Research and Development Center for Teacher Education, University of Texas at Austin: Austin, Tex (mimeographed)

Schön, D A (1984) Leadership as reflection-in-action *in* Sergiovanni and Corbally (1984)

Sergiovanni, T J (1984) Cultural and competing perspectives in administrative theory and practice *in* Sergiovanni and Corbally (1984)

Sergiovanni, T J and Corbally, J E (1984) *Leadership and Organizational Culture* University of Illinois Press: Urbana, Ill

van Velzen, W G and Robin, D (1985) The need for school improvement in the next decade *in* van Velzen *et al* (1985)

*van Velzen, W G, Miles, M B, Ekholm, M, Hameyer, U and Robin, D (1985) *Making School Improvement Work* Acco Pub: Leuven, Belgium

7. School self review

Agnes McMahon

Summary: School self review or evaluation, meaning the process whereby the school reflects upon and assesses its own work, can be a powerful strategy for school improvement. This chapter draws on the experience of the Guidelines for Review and Internal Development in Schools (GRIDS) project to explore a series of questions about the review and development process:

(a) When is a school ready for self review and development?
(b) What is the role of the head teacher?
(c) How can the review and development process be managed?
(d) Does self review reach the real issues?
(e) What external support is required?

What is school self review?

The term 'school self review' or 'self evaluation' is used here to mean the process whereby a school reflects upon and assesses its own work for the purpose of development with the ultimate aim of improving the teaching and learning process. Yet any such definition immediately raises questions. What is the school in this context? Is it the principal, a group of teachers or the whole staff? Does it or does it not include the pupils, the parents, members of the governing body and the local education authority (LEA)? What is the immediate purpose of such activity? Is it solely to promote internal school development, or to produce a formal report or account of the school for an external body, or both of these? If a formal report is necessary should it be submitted as soon as the review stage is complete or once some development has been implemented? Who should control the review — the principal and the teachers or representatives of the LEA? Should the review focus on the whole school or on a subgroup or particular task area? The shape of the review will be largely determined by the way these questions are answered. Yet, no matter how it is designed, self review should provide a mechanism whereby the people who work in the school rather than an external individual or group can make an assessment of it and decide what should be the priorities for development. It should foster and enhance the school's capacity for problem solving.

School self review has been identified as one of six areas of focus for the OECD/CERI International School Improvement Project. In a state-of-the-art paper for the Organization for Economic Co-operation and Development (OECD), Hopkins (1984) defined school based review as: '. . . a school improvement strategy that involves systematic diagnosis of school functioning by school personnel initiated for developmental purposes'. He went on to argue that the design and scope of any school self evaluation or review process was influenced by its purpose (development or accountability), control (internal or external) and orientation (the problem-solving capacity of the school or a specific aspect of its functioning). He pointed out that the practice of school-based review was contentious and discussed the technical and policy issues that it raises in some detail. Currently there is quite widespread interest in school self review as this report revealed. Exemplar schemes can be found in both centralized and decentralized systems. Hopkins (1984) reviewed 36 school-based evaluation or review programmes in 12 different countries: Australia, Belgium, Britain, Canada, Denmark, France, Netherlands, New Zealand, Norway, Sweden, Switzerland and the United States.

Interest in school self review is especially strong in Britain. Elliott (1984) reported that 90 of the 104 LEAs in England and Wales had initiated discussions on school self evaluation and that 44 of these LEAs had produced some form of self evaluation guidelines for the schools. Birchenough (1985) discussed the principles and practice of school-based review in England and Wales and made a comparative analysis of three schemes that are currently in use.

This interest in school self evaluation or review exists in all the OECD member countries, especially Britain and Australia. It is essentially a product of the late 1970s and 1980s and emanated from several factors, among which were the growing realization that the school must be a prime focus for change efforts and a concern on behalf of local and national governments that schools should become more accountable. Whether or not these two broad purposes of review — accountability and development — are compatible has long been a matter of debate (Nuttall, 1981). School self review in Britain has developed out of earlier work in curriculum development and school focused in-service education and training for teachers (Bolam, 1982). It became clear that school improvement strategies and school-based in-service activities required a preliminary diagnostic or review phase to establish the school's present position and clarify what action would be appropriate before new initiatives were introduced. The research on school improvement is optimistic that schools can and do improve (Clark, Lotto and Astuto, 1984; and Chapter 4 in this book). The aim in this chapter is to highlight some of the factors that need to be taken into account if school self review and development is to be a useful strategy for improvement.

The GRIDS project

Some key issues about the process of conducting a school self review and development exercise are discussed in this chapter. In so far as the issues arose from a particular approach to review and development it is a case study, but it is hoped that the issues have a wider relevance.

The chapter is based on a series of reflections about the process of conducting a school self review or evaluation, arising from work on the first phase of the Guidelines for Review and Internal Development in Schools (GRIDS) project during the period 1981-1983. (For information about the second phase of the project see Abbott, 1985.) This project was funded by the Schools Council for England and Wales and was designed to help teachers who wished to review and develop the curriculum and organization of their schools. From the outset, the project team's intention was to concentrate on the process of conducting a review and development exercise, since advice about how schools could do this was then in short supply. Most of the Britush guidelines for teachers on school self review available at that time consisted of lengthy check lists of questions but contained little or no advice about how to conduct the review. All too frequently the exercise stopped at the review stage and no action resulted. Survey feedback techniques might have provided a way forward but these appeared to be heavily dependent upon skilled outside support which was in short supply and consequently would have been rather time consuming and expensive. Hence the decision of the GRIDS team to develop simple procedures which school staff could administer themselves.

The team worked collaboratively with staff in 30 primary and secondary schools in five LEAs, and out of this experience developed a set of process guidelines for school self review which have subsequently been published (McMahon et al, 1984). The guideline materials contained structured, step-by-step advice about how to conduct a review and development exercise, though schools were not intended to follow the suggestions slavishly but adapt and amend them as required. A major purpose was to help schools move from the review stage into development. The approach was underpinned by a series of key principles, one of which was that the staff of the school should be consulted and involved in the process as much as possible. Five key stages in the process were identified: getting started; initial review; specific review; action for development; and overview and re-start (Figure 1 on p 103). The central practical recommendation was that the school should not try to tackle too much at once but should adopt an incremental strategy.

In summary, the recommended procedure was to make a rapid survey of what was happening in the school and, on the basis of this, to identify one or two areas that the staff considered to be priorities for review and development. Once a priority had been agreed there should be a careful assessment of what change should be introduced; this should be implemented and evaluated and work should then start again on another priority area.

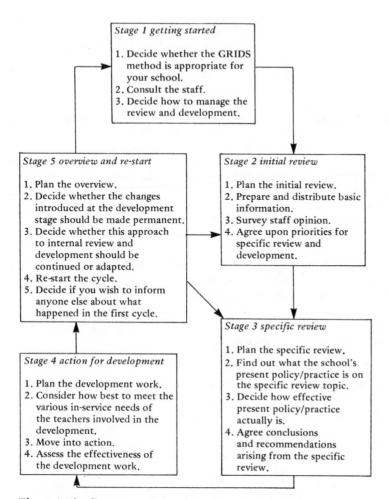

Figure 1 *The five stages of the internal review and development process*

The five participating LEAs all told the project team at the outset that they genuinely wanted to promote school review and development. In turn, the LEAs were advised by the project team to select pilot schools that wanted to work on school review and development, were prepared to pilot the GRIDS materials and were 'ready' to do so. (What was meant by readiness was never clearly articulated.) A fairly strong support structure was provided both inside and outside the school. Each school was asked to identify a coordinator and a small team of teachers to work on the review and development exercise and to promote ownership of it within the school. Each LEA was asked to identify two people from the team of officers and advisers, a supervisor and a coordinator, to manage the whole process and to support the individual schools.

The central project team adopted a particular style of working. To encourage ownership of the project at LEA and school level, and because their own resources were stretched (though there were four people in the team, only one of them was working on the project full time), most of their strategic interventions were directed at the LEA supervisors and coordinators. A series of two-day workshop conferences to review progress and discuss draft guideline materials were arranged for the LEA co-ordinators, and they in turn held meetings for school coordinators. The project team had little face-to-face contact with the teachers and usually communicated with them by mail via the central LEA team. Approximately once a term the schools and LEAs wrote a report on the progress of the review and development process and this was the key mechanism for feedback to the project team.

Five questions that were highlighted during this experience of the school self review process are discussed here. They are the following:

1. When is a school ready for self review and development?
2. What is the role of head teacher?
3. How can the review and development process be managed?
4. Does self review reach the real issues?
5. What external support is required?

These questions will arise whatever type of school self review exercise is being undertaken. The advantages and disadvantages of guidelines are commented upon in the final section.

When is a school 'ready' for self review and development?

Undertaking a formal self review or evaluation exercise is not a normal activity for a school. Though the outcomes can be very positive it consumes teacher time and energy and is potentially threatening. It is unlikely that anyone will fully understand the process at the outset. Given this situation, how does the school ever get started on a project of this kind? One way, of course, may be as a response to an external stimulus, for example a request by the local or central education authority that the school conduct some type of review or evaluation. Alternatively, the initiative can come from an individual or group within the school; most usually it will come from the head teacher. It will certainly have to be agreed by the head. Why the head teacher decides to initiate a review at a particular time is problematic. It may be that he or she judges that it is necessary and timely, but it could also be motivated by other factors, such as a desire to gain additional resources or community support. It may simply be that the person is newly appointed and wants to promote change. Indeed, Fullan (1982) points out that '. . . the most successful examples of change occur when leaders are replaced with new leaders with different characteristics and a mandate for change'. Five of the head teachers of the 15 secondary schools involved in the GRIDS project had recently been appointed to the post and their involvement presumably reflected a belief on the part of themselves or the LEA that the early years of headship are an optimum period for initiating change. However, in itself the head teacher's decision to go ahead is not enough.

The school must see it as necessary and appropriate. For example, a certain period of time should have elapsed since the previous full-scale review; it is not something that should be tackled every year, and the recommendations of any earlier review should have been implemented. This last point reflects on the credibility and track record of the head and senior managers, and underlines the message that conducting a school review and development exercise depends as much as anything else on the parties involved establishing a degree of mutual trust and confidence. The head teacher must trust the staff and be prepared to let them share in the decision making, and they in turn need to feel confident that the head will take seriously any recommendations that they make. Where this is the case, the head is more likely to gain staff commitment for the exercise. Where the process of review and development requires that the teachers work collaboratively then it is obviously advantageous if they have had some experience of doing this. A further point that seemed important was that the school should be in a period of relative stability and not engaged in several other major innovations.

Of course, these conditions are difficult to achieve. Realizing them will involve deciding on some priorities and agreeing that certain other innovations will not be taken up while the school is engaged in self review and development. The head teacher cannot always do this alone and must be protected to some extent by the LEA. This is also difficult. It could be argued that British schools are currently suffering from innovation overload. Any one LEA is likely to be involved in 30 to 40 major national or local innovations, and each school alone could be involved in eight or nine innovations. In the 1984-85 school year national government produced several major reports, all of which have implications for the schools. Yet if the school review is to be productive it needs to be kept centre stage.

Finally, it could be argued that a school's readiness for self review and development is dependent to no small extent on the availability of external support, especially from the LEA. The school can act on its own but it is likely to be in a much stronger position if the advisers and officers in the authority are aware of what is going on and are ready to provide encouragement, advice, in-service training and resources on an ongoing basis.

What is the role of the head teacher?

The central importance of the principal or head teacher as an agent of change has long been recognized. Certainly no whole school review and development exercise could get under way without at least the agreement of the head teacher. Yet Loucks-Horsley and Hergert (1985) argue that 'The principal is not *the* key to school improvement. Although the principal is important, so are many other people', and the GRIDS experience would broadly support this view. Certainly head teachers do not have to provide the day-to-day leadership and management of the review and development processes. Their role seems to be crucial at three stages: first they must agree at the outset that the exercise shall take place; second they need to demonstrate to the staff that they are actively monitoring and supporting the process and consider it worthwhile; finally they must be prepared to implement the recommendations for action. If the teachers' recommendations are never implemented then the process will lose all credibility.

None of these tasks is as simple as it might at first appear: it is not sufficient to agree that the school should begin a review and development exercise without also considering how it is to be conducted. The GRIDS project schools were asked to appoint a coordinator, and since this person was responsible for keeping an overview of the whole exercise and generally managing it the role was strategically important. The head teachers in primary schools where staff numbers are small (average seven) usually took on this role themselves, feeling that it was too important to be delegated and that they needed to work directly with the staff. In the large secondary schools, however, this task was invariably delegated, most frequently to a deputy head. Indeed, few secondary school principals would have had the time to do the job on a day-to-day basis. The head teacher's key task is to delegate efficiently and to select as coordinator someone who has both the competence to do the job well and status in the organization, as well as credibility with the staff.

While the self review and development exercise is in progress the head has to be seen to be actively supporting it. This means much more than receiving progress reports from the coordinator; it means demonstrating to the staff an ongoing commitment to the process. Possible ways for the head to do this are to discuss the progress of the review at staff meetings, join a working group, talk with teachers informally about what is happening, try to obtain any necessary resources, and set target dates when recommendations should be considered. The final task is to work with the teachers to implement the development work that has been recommended. The head teacher might not be doing the routine management of the self review and development exercise but he or she must become involved. Fullan (1982) sums this up neatly when he comments: 'As long as we have schools and principals, if the principal does not lead the development of an effective organizational process, or if he or she leaves it to others, it will normally not get done. That is, change will not happen'.

How can the review and development process be managed?

Coordinating a whole school review and development exercise is a complex task. This may seem to be self evident but it appears to be a fact that is often overlooked. The teachers who adopted the GRIDS approach to school review found that it was time consuming, lasting a minimum of a year. For much of this period they were working in small groups or teams, yet many of them found themselves undertaking tasks (for example as group leader or researcher) for which they had no previous training or experience.

The process appeared to work best in those schools where:

(a) the basic principles underlying the exercise were clearly agreed;
(b) a timetable was drawn up and adhered to;
(c) the coordinator ensured that the whole process was carefully planned and monitored and the momentum sustained;
(d) the leaders of the working groups had status in the organization and the groups were integrated into the existing decision-making machinery of the school;
(e) appropriate methods of collecting and analysing data were selected.

Basic principles

It will be impossible to predict at the outset exactly what will happen during the course of the review. Nevertheless, it seems important to set out the broad working parameters clearly at the outset, eg what is the purpose of the exercise? How will the teachers be consulted and involved in it? What will happen to any data that are collected? Once some basics have been agreed they can provide a structure for the work and should give the teachers a clearer notion of the process.

Timetabling

A school-based review and development exercise will take time and this is a commodity that is always in short supply. One of the basic GRIDS principles was that the demands made on key resources such as time, money and skilled personnel should be realistic and feasible for schools and LEAs. School coordinators were advised to draw up a timetable at the outset and set realistic targets within this. Once deadlines for the production of reports and dates when recommendations would be discussed had been agreed the coordinator was better able to monitor the progress of the review. The timetable was also a powerful motivating factor for the teachers. Change is a slow process — commonly three to five years is spoken of as a minimal period for implementation yet planning the change must not take this long. Loucks-Horsley and Hergert (1985) state this succinctly: 'Acting is better than planning. Protracted needs assessment can be worse than none at all'. The GRIDS process suggested a notional timetable of a year, and experience showed that certainly in smaller schools and in many larger ones this timetable was feasible. Teachers could conduct a quick review of the school, agree on priority areas, make a detailed review and assessment of each of these, produce a plan for action and begin to implement it within that timescale. A great deal can happen during the course of a school year — at least one cohort of children will leave the school and another one will join, and teachers leave and are replaced. Implementing the developments arising from the review can take years but if the review stage lasts for more than a year several of the key personnel may well have changed and the original purpose of the exercise may be forgotten.

Monitoring

One person, usually the head or deputy in the school, must coordinate the whole exercise and monitor what is happening. He or she will need to keep one step ahead of everyone else, trying to obtain any necessary resources, thinking through the implications of particular suggestions, advising and supporting group leaders, encouraging groups to meet deadlines and keeping everyone informed about what is happening. Not an easy role but one that is crucially important if the process is to work successfully.

Working groups

Much of the work of investigating present practice in a particular area, assessing its effectiveness and drawing up recommendations for development work, will probably be done in small groups or teams. In the GRIDS primary schools the whole staff (about seven people) frequently worked as a group, but in large secondary schools this obviously was not possible. The success or otherwise of these groups was influenced by two key factors. First, the quality of the leaders and, second, the extent to which the group was integrated into the normal decision-making machinery of the school. It was not sufficient for the leaders to be competent administrators though, of course, this was necessary; they also needed to have some status in the organization and have credibility with their peers if the recommendations were to carry weight. The group also needed somebody to report to.

Problems could occur if the review teams were not integrated with the existing decision-making machinery. For example, a review team investigating the school policy on record keeping and assessment needs to have clear links with the regular meeting for heads of subject departments.

A further management task is to provide support and training for group leaders and their teams. The group leaders will find themselves chairing meetings, drawing up agendas, writing minutes and reports and trying to build into an effective team a group of people who may not have worked together before. These tasks will be quite new to some of them and some training in group skills and team building could be valuable.

Handling data

Some of the difficulties that the schools using the GRIDS approach encountered were due to the teachers' lack of basic research skills. The data collection methods that they selected were occasionally inappropriate. For example, one team devised a lengthy questionnaire containing many open-ended questions and the members then found themselves unable to analyse the vast amount of information that they collected. Another team (in a different school) attempted to questionnaire all the parents rather than just a sample. The most difficult problem was to identify and agree criteria for assessing the effectiveness of their present practice. These are all instances where an external consultant should be able to provide useful advice and practical help. Though teachers and others can learn how to collect and analyse data by actually doing it, the task can be unnecessarily time consuming and frustrating unless some basic ground rules have been applied.

Does self review reach the real issues?

One of the main criticisms that can be made about school self review and development is that the process is insufficiently rigorous and bypasses the key issues. Protagonists of this view argue that teachers will only select 'safe' topics to investigate and will not be overly critical of their own practice. In fact this was not the experience with the schools using the GRIDS approach. The topics that the teachers selected as priorities for development were usually those where they felt dissatisfied with present practice (though they were encouraged to work on areas of strength in the school as well as weaknesses). The head teacher or LEA adviser did not always share the teachers' perception that the area or topic under review was in fact a top priority for development, but he or she usually recognized that the teachers were concerned about it (eg primary teachers' anxiety about maths). The teachers investigated hard topics to do with the curriculum and organization of the school, and collected large amounts of data. Admittedly, much of the data about classroom practice were based on teacher self report and records rather than observation and analysis of teaching, but this may come as confidence in the review process grows. The GRIDS review was intended to promote internal school development and the teachers were free to criticize their own practice where appropriate. Had they needed to produce a formal report for use outside the school it is likely that they would have been more circumspect.

Nevertheless, the schools would undoubtedly have benefited from some external validation of their review and development work. Identifying and agreeing criteria against which to measure the effectiveness of present practice was a difficult task, especially in the more creative areas of the curriculum. One way of overcoming this might be to consider asking individuals or a group (eg LEA advisers or head teachers) to make an independent assessment of work in the priority areas, the conclusions that have been reached and the recommendations for development.

What external support is required?

A school staff can undertake a school self review and development exercise without any external help, but it is difficult to do this. External consultants can provide advice and expertise that the staff may lack; they can provide an objective opinion about the process or give their perception of the effectiveness of a particular practice and they can provide ongoing encouragement and support. Nevertheless, conducting a school review and development exercise is potentially very threatening, and many teachers will be unwilling to involve consultants from the outset. Two broad types of support seem to be necessary — the first is best provided by the LEA. Ideally someone in the LEA office should be aware of what the school is doing, understand the processes involved and be able to supply resources where necessary and advice about where to get further help. Above all else, this person needs to monitor what is happening, and provide ongoing support and encouragement. Fullan (1985) recognizes this when he says, 'For school based improvement efforts to work central office staff must take an active interest in them by providing direction, assistance, and prodding and by expecting and asking for results'. One very practical way of helping is to try to provide some extra hours in the school. Teachers cannot realistically be expected to continue to use their own free time for school improvement work. Even a small gesture like the LEA agreeing to a one-day school closure so that the teachers can meet for discussion can not only enable the process to move forward but also be a powerful motivational factor for the teachers as it demonstrates that review and development is considered important and useful.

The second type of support is that provided by a general eduational consultant, college or university lecturer, teacher centre warden, teacher, etc. The GRIDS pilot schools only rarely involved a consultant to advise on the process. Usually they invited an 'expert' to advise them about how to move forward in the particular area they had selected as a priority. The task of setting up a consultancy relationship can be fraught with problems on both sides. The key recommendation for potential consultants is that they should attempt to familiarize themselves with the review and development process that the school has been following, and that they should attempt to clarify the dimensions of the consultancy from the outset. Schools need to be similarly clear about their expectations and concerns.

Are guidelines useful?

A serious criticism of the GRIDS materials, and of many other guidelines, is that they are based on a rational, problem-solving model of organizational behaviour. Hence they do not approximate to the real world as we know it, where things happen by accident or chance, where micro-political issues cannot be ignored and where formal planning can on occasions seem almost impossibly difficult.

Nevertheless, if teachers or anyone else want to tackle something like a full scale review and development exercise but have no real ideas about how to begin, suggestions in the form of guidelines can be useful. Time spent trying to establish procedures for conducting a review would probably be better used to investigate existing practice and to implement the subsequent development work. Some teachers used the GRIDS materials as a form of check list on the review and development process. Since the approach was broken down into clear stages they were better able to identify where they were at any time and could see how to re-start the process if it was interrupted (eg to prepare for a school concert). For a whole series of reasons teachers are more likely to read and use a short handbook of suggestions that seem practical and relevant than a dozen research papers. However, in the final analysis the usefulness of any guidelines for school review and development must be assessed in terms of the product. In the long term, if they do not help teachers to improve the teaching and learning in the school they will be of little or no use.

References

Abbott, R (1985) *An Introduction to GRIDS* School Curriculum Development Committee: London

Birchenough, M (1985) *Making School Based Review Work* National Development Centre for School Management Training: Bristol

Bolam, R ed (1982) *School-Focussed In-Service Training* Heinemann: London

*Clark, D L, Lotto, L S and Astuto, T A (1984) Effective schools and school improvement: a comparative analysis of two lines of enquiry *Educational Administration Quarterly* **20** 3: 41-68

Elliott, G (1984) *Self-Evaluation and the Teacher: An Annotated Bibliography and Report on Current Practice 1982 Part 5* School Curriculum Development Committee: London

Fullan, M (1982) *The Meaning of Educational Change* Teachers College Press, Columbia University: New York

Fullan, M (1985) Change processes and strategies at the local level *Elementary School Journal* **85** 3: 391-421

Hopkins, D (1984) *School Based Review for School Improvement: A Preliminary State of the Art* Centre for Educational Research and Innovation, OECD: Paris

Loucks-Horsley, S and Hergert, L F (1985) *An Action Guide to School Improvement* Association for Supervision and Curriculum Development The Network: Andover, Mass

McMahon, A, Bolam, R, Abbott, R and Holly, P (1984) *Guidelines for Review and Internal Development in Schools (GRIDS). Primary and Secondary School Handbooks* Longman for the Schools Council: York

Nuttall, D L (1981) *School Self Evaluation: Accountability with a Human Face?* Longman for the Schools Council: York

8. Instructional management

Steven T Bossert

Summary: This chapter summarizes recent research on effective schools and principals. The literature suggests that successful principals are strong, programmatic leaders who take an active part in structuring the instructional programme within their schools. Although this prescription seems commonsense, there are several conceptual and practical problems that must be addressed before an adequate formulation of the instructional management role of school principals can be developed. The chapter presents a critique of current research findings and offers a framework for examining instructional management. This framework incorporates important findings from studies of effective classroom instructional practices and suggests how school-level management can affect the daily activities in which teachers and students interact and which, in turn, produce student achievement. Current ethnographic research on principals' management behaviour is described.

Introduction

During the last few years, increasing attention has been given to the instructional management role of school principals. The old maxim, 'effective school, effective principal', has reappeared and has sparked demands for research concerning the influences that principals have on students' achievements. In the United States, where a common characterization of principals' work has emphasized non-instructional, maintenance tasks, new school improvement efforts and training programmes are challenging principals to engage actively in instructional management.

Despite this concern, little is known about how principals and instructional management at the school level affect students' schooling experience. The literature is filled with prescriptions about what a good manager should do, but few of these describe how certain management actions actually become translated into concrete activities which help students succeed in school. Management studies typically treat the learning environment as a 'black box' into which resources are poured and from which student achievements are produced, Yet the nature of the day-to-day events in which teachers and students engage, and how these are managed effectively by the principal, remain unanalysed. Unfortunately, recent advances in knowledge about effective classroom instructional practices have been overlooked. Studies have shown that curriculum pacing, time-on-task, instructional grouping, task demands and other processes can significantly influence the amount and quality of student learning. Research in educational administration and school management has focused on the school as a formal organization, thus ignoring these important schooling processes and how they are organized and managed (Erickson, 1979).

In this chapter, some of the prescriptions for instructional management are examined, especially those derived from recent studies of 'effective schools' and principals. The promises and pitfalls of this research are summarized. A framework for analysing instructional management processes and their effects is presented. This framework incorporates findings from the latest research on effective instruction and is used to describe some recent studies of the instructional management role of school principals. Finally, questions for future research on school instructional management are raised.

Effective schools research

Recent research on 'effective schools' has successfully shifted the focus of empirical studies away from largely intractable aspects of family background to alterable factors of schools. Despite nearly two decades of studies which argued that school effects are insignificant, especially when compared to the influence of family socio-economic status (Coleman, 1966; Jencks, 1972), new studies demonstrate that important school-level management effects can be found when appropriate models and research techniques are employed (eg Wellisch *et al*, 1978; Brookover *et al*, 1979; Rutter *et al*, 1979).

Specifically, comparisons of effective and ineffective schools have begun to identify factors that promote higher student achievements, particularly in the basic skills. Studies consistently report that principals of successful schools have the following characteristics (for comprehensive reviews of this literature, see Bossert *et al*, 1982; Purkey and Smith, 1983; Rutter, 1983):

1. *Goals and production emphasis.* Effective principals are actively involved in setting instructional goals, emphasizing basic skills instruction, developing performance standards for students, and expressing the belief that all students can achieve (Wellisch *et al*, 1978; Brookover *et al*, 1979).

2. *Power and decision making.* Effective principals are more powerful than their colleagues, especially in the areas of curriculum and instruction. They are seen as leaders and are effective in maintaining the support of parents and the local community (Blumberg and Greenfield, 1980; Lipham, 1981).

3. *Management.* Principals in effective schools devote more time to

the coordination and management of instruction and are more skilled in instructional matters. They observe their teachers at work, discuss instructional problems, support teachers' efforts to improve, and develop evaluation procedures that assess teacher and student performance (Clark, 1980).

4. *Human relations.* Effective principals recognize the unique styles and needs of teachers and help teachers achieve their own performance goals. They instil a sense of pride in the school among teachers, students and parents (Rutter *et al*, 1979; Brookover *et al*, 1979).

Few would disagree with the desirability of these traits. In fact, studies of business, the military and other organizations also show that successful managers exhibit these same characteristics.

Like most research, however, the findings listed above are not unambiguous. A number of troubling questions arise when one tries to apply these as prescriptions. For example, if an effective school principal helps to set high expectations for students, how high should those expectations be? Should they be set at grade level or above? Should all students be held to the same standard? Studies of motivation, as well as commonsense, indicate that effort may decrease when standards are set too high; just as achievements may decrease when standards are too low. The research has not specified at what level expectations should be set or how they can be communicated effectively.

Effective principals emphasize basic skill instruction. But how much time should be devoted to elementary decoding and numeracy tasks? What about important reasoning and social skills? Most schools have goals that go beyond basic skills learning, and too much time spent on basic tasks may detract from the higher-order thinking capacities that are necessary for success in the secondary grades (Peterson and Janicki, 1979). The most productive balance of various skill tasks has not been described.

Effective schools have strong principals. But teachers in effective schools also have high levels of autonomy so that they can provide instruction appropriate to the immediate needs of their students. How are strong leadership and autonomy managed simultaneously?

These dilemmas from the studies of effective schools and principals are due largely to limitations of their research designs. Several problems have plagued these studies (see Rowan, 1983). First, they are correlational. That is, after a small number of effective schools are identified, researchers catalogue school characteristics, hoping to find a list of shared factors among the schools. This *post hoc* method cannot readily separate those factors that *caused* effectiveness from other inconsequential, but shared items. Nor can these studies chart how important factors shaped success because the process of becoming successful is never studiied.

Second, the research has used a very circumscribed definition of effectiveness, and the techniques used to select effective schools are unreliable. Usually, effectiveness is defined by a school's average level of achievement on standardized basic skills tests. Schools are considered effective if they score higher than expected, given the socio-economic status of their students. In other words, two schools which have identical average achievement scores may not be equally effective. This definition of success is unstable. The likelihood of a school being successful for two consecutive years is nearly 50 per cent — not much better than pure chance (Rowan and Denk, 1984).

Moreover, important school goals are not assessed. The studies never examine problem solving, social, or other types of schooling outcomes. In fact, most effective school studies use only *one* achievement score at *two* grade levels (eg reading in the third and sixth grades) to measure effectiveness. Therefore, there is no guarantee that schools which are identified by this technique are also excellent in attaining all, or even most of, the important goals set by schools at all grade levels. (For an expanded list of relevant schooling outcomes, see Rutter, 1983.)

These problems do not suggest that findings from the effectiveness studies should be ignored. The cumulative evidence, as well as the practical experience of educators, supports the importance of having high expectations for students, developing a positive school climate, improving instruction, and demonstrating leadership. These are necessary, but probably not sufficient, elements of effective instructional management. Recipes or blueprints have not been developed for making a school more effective.

Analysing instructional management

How can the instructional management effects be analysed? My colleagues and I have developed a framework for examining the management behaviour of school principals (Bossert *et al*, 1982). Figure 1 summarizes the model.

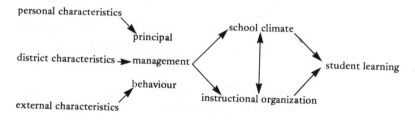

Figure 1 *A framework for examining instructional management*

It shows that a principal's instructional management behaviour affects two fundamental aspects of the school's social organization — climate and instructional organization. These are the contexts which shape teachers' behaviour and students' learning experiences. At the same time, the principal's own management actions are shaped by factors external to the school — personal, school district, and community characteristics.

For illustration, I will focus on instructional management because it is central to an understanding of how school and classroom organization affects student achievement. (Climate and contextual effects have been treated in a previous paper: Bossert *et al*, 1982.)

Instructional organization

Instruction can be conceived as the core technology of the school. Although some have characterized this technology as weak, thus limiting the effect that principals' management actions can have on learning (Deal and Celotti, 1980), recent research on effective instructional practices identifies important and manipulable factors that affect students' achievements:

1. *Time-on-task*. Studies show that the amount of time in which a student is engaged in a learning activity affects achievement and that teachers can be trained in classroom management practices which increase students' engagement rates. However, engaged time may be less important than 'success rate' — the proportion of engaged time in which students actually master the assigned task. Higher success rates produce higher motivation and achievement (Fisher, 1980).
2. *Class size and composition*. Smaller classes produce higher average achievement scores, especially when class size is reduced to below 20 students (Glass and Smith, 1978). Yet, decreasing class size does not always guarantee improved instructional opportunities for students. Without adequate in-service training, teachers may simply teach in the same fashion even when class size is reduced (Filby, 1980). Recent research indicates that the overall achievement distribution within a classroom significantly affects learning (Beckerman and Good, 1981).
3. *Grouping for instruction*. Although there is some disagreement concerning the effects of various grouping practices, especially when students are separated by ability, studies show that the size of instructional groupings within a class affects pupil achievement. Instruction in large or small groups may not affect learning of basic skills concepts, but higher-order thinking skills are best promoted in small group activities (Peterson, 1984).
4. *Curriculum*. Pacing, sequencing, and content coverage of classroom lessons influence both an individual student's achievements and the distribution of performance within a classroom. Generally, students who receive reading instruction paced at a higher level also score higher on standardized reading tests. Moreover, as time-on-task is increased, concomitant increases in material density must occur so that tasks do not become unnecessarily repetitive and do not depress student motivation and achievement (Barr and Dreeben, 1977; 1983).
5. *Evaluation*. Although the effectiveness of teacher praise is questionable, the nature of feedback and its uses have been shown to affect

students' learning (Brophy, 1981). Prompt and prescriptive evaluation of assignments and homework stimulates motivation and retention. Moreover, classrooms which provide only one or two ways to demonstrate learning (eg tests or recitation performance) may overlook certain learning styles, limit opportunities to demonstrate competence, and depress task engagement (Block and Burns, 1977; Rosenholtz and Simpson, 1984).

6. *Task characteristics.* The nature of the instructional task, especially students' perceptions of its clarity and requirements for problem solving, affects student learning. Often, 'inappropriate' learning strategies and poor performance are caused by teachers' insensitivity to students' conceptions of the activity (Doyle, 1978). And, if tasks are too complex and require extensive organization time, student learning decreases (Stallings, 1980).

Good teachers seem to know, plan, and construct their classrooms and lessons using these six factors. Although these factors operate primarily at the classroom level, it is easy to see how school-level management can affect these elements. Consider the following three examples of school-level management (for additional examples, see Bossert, 1985).

Time. At the school level, numerous things can determine instructional time in classrooms. Schools have yearly, weekly, and daily cycles that specify not only how much time can be allotted to instruction in various curricular areas, but also when evaluations and tests must be given before students can progress to new subjects and materials. Housekeeping, reporting requirements, transition time needed for special classes, and other tasks may seriously cut into students' time-on-task. The degree of coordination within the school may heighten or lessen interruptions of classroom lessons. For example, special 'pull-out' programmes for students with learning problems can fragment a child's day, interrupt important practice time provided in the regular classroom, and thus perpetuate a child's under-achievement unless the programme is carefully coordinated with regular classroom activities.

Studies of business and industry demonstrate that successful managers 'buffer' their workers during key production periods in order to guarantee maximum efficiency (Thompson, 1967). Although schools are not factories, school principals can be mediators of organizational and environmental forces that determine the amount of engaged time and student productivity. For example, the principal's role as disturbance handler, as school gatekeeper and as middleman in disputes between parents and teachers buffers classrooms from disturbances that can interrupt the flow of instruction. Principals can guarantee that all classrooms have the resources necessary to carry out the school's instructional goals so that teachers do not have to use valuable class time to secure needed materials.

Curriculum. An important area of school-wide curricular management concerns the articulation of the curriculum across grades. For example, in schools that have numerous programmes for students with special needs, principals can assist teachers in coordinating these programmes with regular classroom activities. When there is a lack of coordination, some students may experience a fragmented instructional programme. They may not be provided with opportunities to practise and accomplish the various learning tasks they are assigned. If some students are sent to remedial reading during guided spelling practice, this may guarantee that these students will continue to fail in spelling. Often the competing demands of regular and special programme teachers need to be addressed by the school principal, and not simply in terms of the teachers' conveneince.

Task characteristics. A school-wide analysis of task demands inherent in classroom instructional practices can disclose the continuities and discontinuities experienced by students. For example, a school-wide commitment to developing self-directed learning skills can be undercut by teachers who do not provide opportunities for students to exercise choice and control over their learning.

The 'hidden curriculum' in activities prescribed by textbooks can convey messages that conflict with overall school goals. For example, excellent curricular content on multi-cultural education that is designed to overcome racism and gender stereotyping and to foster cooperative behaviour can be subverted by prescribed competitive learning games and activities (Bossert, 1979; 1981).

These examples do not exhaust the ways in which school-level and classroom-level instructional management mesh. The study of how policies and practices at various organizational levels within school systems actually shape what teachers and students can accomplish is called the 'multilevel perspective'. Researchers are beginning to chart how certain structural and management factors at the school and school district levels facilitate or hinder effective classroom instructional practices (see Bidwell and Kasarda, 1980; Barr and Dreeben, 1983).

Studying principal behaviour

Using the framework presented in Figure 1 as the analytic model, staff from the Instructional Management Program at the Far West Laboratory for Educational Research and Development have been conducting studies of the instructional leadership roles of school principals. Detailed interviewing and ethnographic observation techniques are being used to characterize the management activities of effective principals (Dwyer *et al*, 1983).

This research indicates that there is no single formula for instructional leadership. Some principals exemplify a 'master teacher' role. They are active in preparing and demonstrating instructional techniques for their teachers. They spend many hours in classrooms, interacting with the students and suggesting solutions to instructional problems.

Other principals are less obvious in their instructional management.

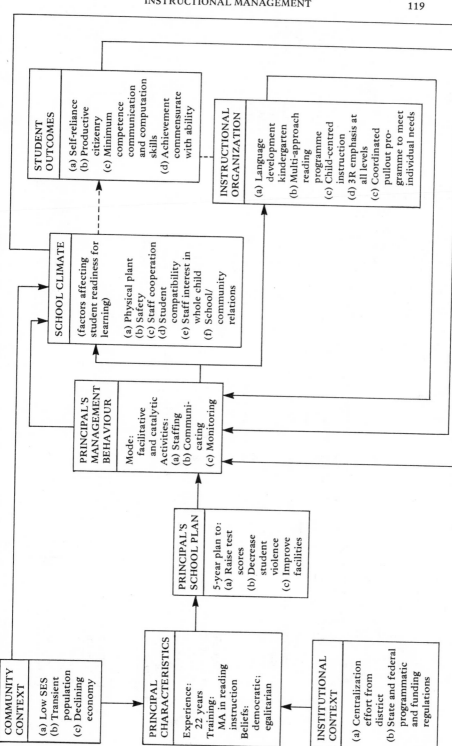

Figure 2 *Instructional management model (Jeffrey Hudson)*

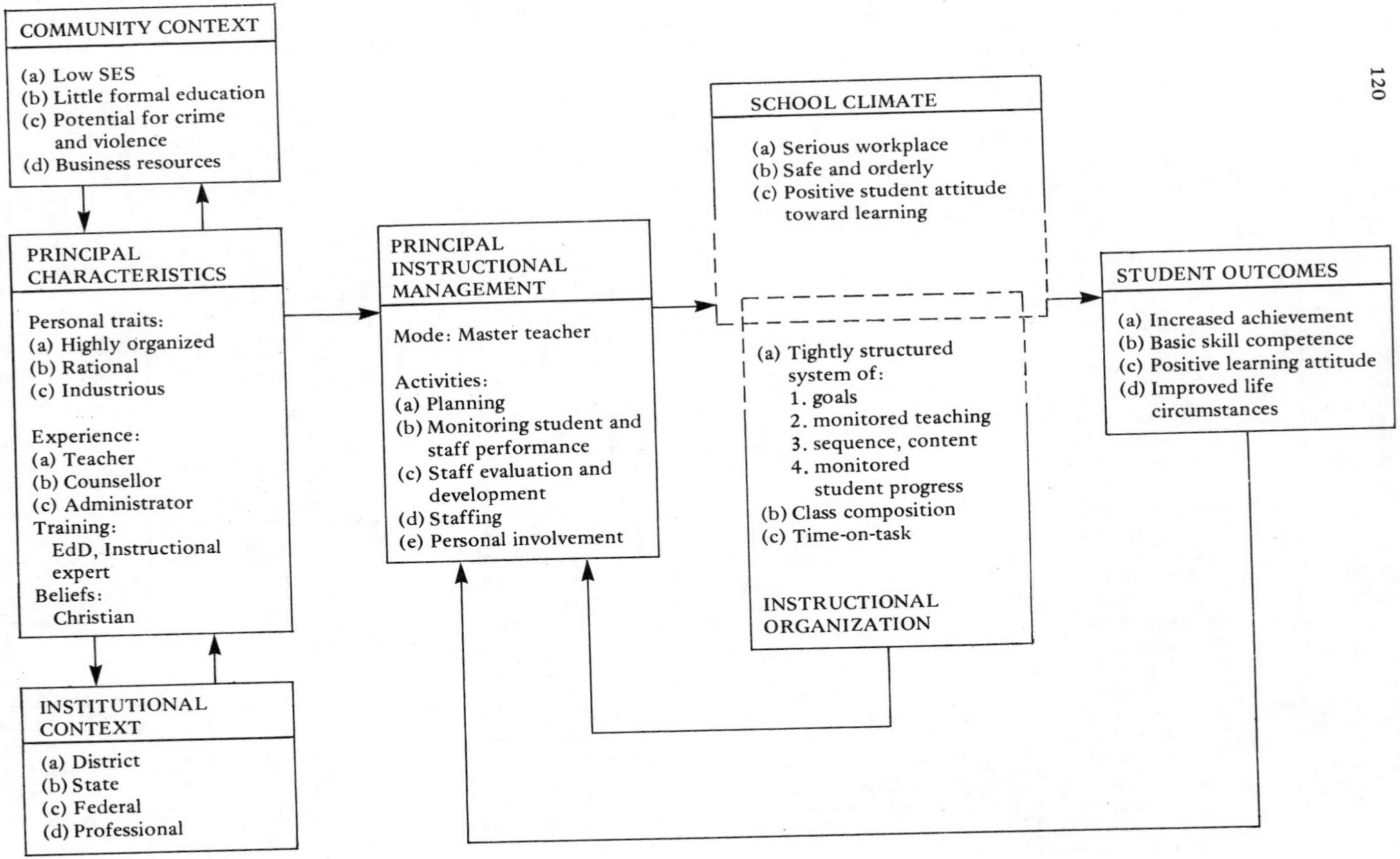

Figure 3 *Instructional management model (Harold Mann)*

Their visits to classrooms are short in duration, usually comprising only a momentary visit to deliver a message or check on an administrative detail. These principals seem to influence teaching practices indirectly. Often they plant an idea with a teacher leader and make sure he or she disseminates the idea so that it will spread to other teachers in the school.

In analysing the differences among these principals, important personal and contextual factors seem to shape how a principal manages a school. One such factor may relate to characteristics of the teaching staff. When staff are highly experienced and professional, more indirect leadership techniques are employed by school principals, whereas where staff are largely inexperienced or 'under fire' by community and district criticism to improve instruction, more direct supervision and management are desirable.

The need for different leadership styles is reinforced by research in other organizational contexts. A single method for leadership will not apply in all situations. This is called a 'contingency approach' to administration (Fiedler, 1966). Administrators who recognize the importance of this approach also realize that their own leadership styles vary over time and, in response to the exigencies of management, within their organizations.

Yet, despite differences in management behaviour, there are certain commonalities among the principals studied. One common factor relates to the principals' visibility in their schools. Usually, the principals begin each day by roaming their buildings and greeting students and staff as they arrive. As classes begin, they return to their offices for short planning meetings with assistants or to resolve student problems. But presently, they are back out into the hallways and classrooms to monitor events and communicate with their staff and the students. The principals are systematic about observing, and being seen, in just about every locale and context within their schools — hallways, classrooms, recesses, libraries and lunchrooms. Afternoons bring these principals back to their offices to handle student problems, paperwork, and parents.

This daily cycle serves a basic maintenance function for the school. It allows the principals to assess the working status of their organizations and circumvent minor difficulties before they become major problems. If 'buffering' is a key to good management (Thompson, 1967), the systematic tours of their schools provide the principals with essential information to carry out this function.

A second common characteristic shared by these principals is that this daily cycle and the information gathered during tours is constantly linked to improving instruction within their schools. Each of the principals clearly articulates direct and remote links between his or her actions and the schools' instructional systems. It seems as if successful principals always ask themselves how a particular decision will affect the learning environment within their schools and classrooms. Although each principal expresses his or her instructional philosophy differently, the elements of that guiding philosophy are strikingly similar to the factors that derive

from effective teaching research (listed above). These principals are concerned with engaged time, class compositions, grouping arrangements,
curriculum pacing and articulation, student evaluation, and the task
demands. They analyse and work with their teachers to guarantee that
school activities reinforce, rather than detract from, their classrooms'
instructional programmes.

Therefore, effective instructional management does not mean doing
something new, highly visible, or especially time-consuming. Rather it
means systematically linking everyday management activities to the critical
factors that support excellent instruction within all classrooms in the
school.

However, it is incorrect to assume that instructional leadership falls
solely on the school principal. Teachers share an equal responsibility for
assessing and contributing to the overall instructional programme within
their schools, rather than protecting the needs of their own classrooms.
Research on effective staff development clearly indicates that effective
schools are characterized by 'norms of continuous improvement' (Little,
1982). This simply means that school improvement is viewed both as an
ongoing process and as a collective responsibility shared equally among
all teachers in the school. When this exists, there is greater experimentation, less isolation of inexperienced teachers, stronger collegiality and
joint problem solving, reduced teacher absenteeism, and increased
demands for effective in-service training.

These findings support the notion that effective programme implementation requires a shared sense of commitment among a school's staff,
collegial support, involvement in planning and assessment, a sense of
ownership in the project, and administrative support.

The balance between strong management and teachers' professional
autonomy lies in a particular view of the function of school leadership.
Effective leadership helps a school's staff articulate shared values, goals,
and approaches to school improvement. But it also involves developing the
conditions in which these can be realized. The instruments that foster
improvement do not necessarily require the adoption of entirely new
models of instruction or supervision. Effective school-level management
involves knowing how to link the already present elements of good
instruction into school-wide policies and activities that support effective
classroom practice.

Research needs

If the primary function of school management is to foster an effective
instructional programme, research must address how the formal organizational milieu of the school affects schooling outcomes. This will happen
only when studies explicitly examine the linkages among management
activities, the use of resources by teachers and students in the classroom
context, and instructional practices. As has been argued, principals affect

student learning indirectly by making decisions that either constrain teachers' decisions at the classroom level or 'buffer' classrooms so that they run smoothly. Direct effects occur when the principal coordinates the overall instructional programme. Research and development models must chart these effects, looking for school-level processes that shape the potent classroom-level instructional practices. Without such models, common myths about effective school instructional management will continue to rule educational practice.

References

Barr, R and Dreeben, R (1977) Instruction in classrooms *in* Shulman (1977)

*Barr, R and Dreeben, R (1983) *How Schools Work* University of Chicago Press: Chicago

Beckerman, T M and Good, T L (1981) The classroom ratio of high- and low-aptitude students and its effect on achievement *American Educational Research Journal* 18: 317-28

Bidwell, C E and Kasarda, J D (1980) Conceptualizing and measuring the effects of school and schooling *American Journal of Education* 88: 401-30

Block, J H and Burns, B (1977) Mastery learning *in* Shulman (1977)

Blumberg, A and Greenfield, W (1980) *The Effective Principal: Perspectives in School Leadership* Allyn and Bacon: Boston, Mass

Bossert, S T (1979) *Tasks and Social Relationships in Classrooms: A Study of Instructional Organization and Its Consequences* Cambridge University Press: New York

Bossert, S T (1981) Understanding sex differences in children's classroom experiences *Elementary School Journal* 81 254-66

Bossert, S T (1985) Effective schools — the elementary level *in* Kyle (1985)

Bossert, S·T, Dwyer, D C, Rowan, B and Lee, G V (1982) The instructional management role of the principal *Educational Administration Quarterly* 18 3: 34-64

Brookover, W, Deady, C, Flood, P, Schweitzer, J and Wisenbaker, J (1979) *School Social Systems and Student Achievement: Schools Can Make a Difference* Praeger: New York

Brophy, J E (1981) Teacher praise: a functional analysis *Review of Educational Research* 51 1: 5-32

Clark, D (1980) Factors associated with success in urban elementary schools *Phi Delta Kappan* 61: 467-70

Coleman, J (1966) *Equality of Educational Opportunity* United States Department of Health, Education and Welfare: Washington, DC

Deal, T and Celotti, L D (1980) How much influence do (and can) administrators have on classrooms? *Phi Delta Kappan* 61: 7: 471-73

Denham, C and Lieberman, A eds (1980) *Time to Learn: A Review of the Beginning Teacher Evaluation Study* United States Department of Education: Washington, DC

Doyle, W (1978) Paradigms for research on teacher effectiveness *in* Shulman (1978)

Dwyer, D, Lee, G, Rowan, B and Bossert, S (1983) *Five Principals in Action: Perspectives on Instructional Leadership* The Far West Laboratory for Educational Research and Development: San Francisco

Erickson, D A (1979) Research on educational administration: the state-of-the-art *Educational Researcher* 8 3: 9-14

Fiedler, F (1966) The contingency model: a theory of leadership effectiveness *in* Proshansky and Seidenberg (1966)

Filby, N N (1980) *What Happens in Smaller Classes* The Far West Laboratory for Educational Research and Development: San Francisco

Fisher, C W (1980) Teaching behaviors, academic learning time, and student achievement: an overview *in* Denham and Lieberman (1980)

Glass, G V and Smith, M L (1978) *Meta-Analysis of Research on the Relationship of Class-Size and Achievement* The Far West Laboratory for Educational Research and Development: San Francisco

Jencks, C (1972) *Inequality* Basic Books: New York

Kyle, R ed (1985) *Sourcebook for Effective Schools* National Institute of Education, United States Department of Education: Washington, DC

Lipham, J M (1981) *Effective Principal, Effective School* National Association of Secondary School Principals: Reston, VA

Little, J W (1982) Norms of collegiality and experimentation: workplace conditions of school success *American Educational Research Journal* 19 3: 325-40

Peterson, P ed (1984) *The Social Context of Instruction: Group Organization and Group Processes* Academic Press: New York

Peterson, P L and Janicki, T C (1979) Individual characteristics and children's learning in large-group and small-group approaches *Journal of Educational Psychology* 71 5: 677-87

Proshansky, H M and Swidenberg, B eds (1966) *Basic Studies in Social Psychology* Holt, Rinehart and Winston,: New York

Purkey, S and Smith, M (1983) Effective schools: a review *Elementary School Journal* 83: 427-53

Rosenholtz, S and Simpson, C (1984) The formation of ability conceptions: Development trend or social construction? *Review of Educational Research* 54: 31-64

Rowan, B (1983) Research on effective schools: a cautionary note *Educational Researcher* 12 4: 24-31

Rowan, B and Denk, C (1984) Management succession, school socioeconomic context, and basic skills achievement *American Educational Research Journal* 21 3: 517-39

Rutter, M (1983) School effects on pupil progress: research findings and policy implications *in* Shulman and Sykes (1983)

Rutter, M, Maugham, B, Mortimer, P, Ouston, J and Smith, A (1979) *Fifteen Thousand Hours: Secondary Schools and Their Effects on Children* Open Books: London

Shulman, L E ed (1977) *Review of Research in Education* 5 Peacock Publishers: Itasca, Ill

Shulman, L E ed (1978) *Review of Research in Education* 6 Peacock Publishers: Itasca, Ill

Shulman, L E and Sykes, G eds (1983) *Handbook of Teaching and Policy* Longman: New York

Stallings, J (1980) Allocated academic learning time revisited, or beyond time on task *Educational Researcher* 9: 11-16

Thompson, J D (1967) *Organizations in Action: Social Science Bases of Administrative Theory* McGraw-Hill: New York

Wellisch, J B, MacQueen, A H, Carriere, R A and Duck, G A (1978) School management and organization in successful schools *Sociology of Education* 51 3: 211-26

9. Staff appraisal

Glenn Turner, Professor Desmond Nuttall and Philip Clift

Summary: The performance appraisal of teachers has become an important issue in many countries of the world in recent years. It serves a number of different purposes which may be broadly characterized as formative and summative and which are frequently in conflict.

This review concentrates on experiences in the USA and Britain. In the USA staff appraisal largely grew out of competence-based programmes of initial training; but it is now applied widely to all teachers in service and is sometimes used to identify candidates for 'merit pay'. In Britain, appraisal has largely been focused upon career development, as opposed to tenure or pay, and derives from practice in industry and commerce.

Extensive research into teacher effectiveness and competency-based teaching has failed to reveal consistent patterns of effective teacher behaviour, and the validity of most staff appraisal schemes remains to be demonstrated.

The methods that are most commonly used in staff appraisal, often in combination, are: assessment of pupil performance, assessing teacher knowledge, observation of teacher performance, and appraisal interviews. Each of these methods is critically discussed. The first three are widely used in the USA but only the fourth is commonly employed in Britain.

Introduction

Staff appraisal in schools and colleges has become one of the growth areas in education worldwide. Although well established in the USA, Canada, Australia and South Africa, it has only recently become a significant educational issue in Britain, where it is currently the subject of much controversy owing mainly to a proposal in the 1981 Burnham Settlement (which determines teachers' pay scales nationally each year) for linking teachers' pay to formal appraisal. The issue of appraisal has also been stressed in recent Government Policy Documents: *Teaching Quality* in 1983 and *Better Schools* in 1985. This review concentrates on the experience of the USA and Britain. A recent review of trends covering other countries as well suggests that almost all issues are common to all countries (Suffolk Education Department, 1985).

The purposes of teacher appraisal

What tends to make the issue of teacher appraisal a complex and controversial one is that particular schemes are often intended to serve several purposes. In the USA a recent survey by the Educational Research Service revealed that the majority of school districts had four main purposes in mind when developing appraisal schemes (Wood and Pohland, 1983). These are:

1. To help teachers improve their teaching performance.
2. To decide on renewed appointment of probationary teachers.
3. To recommend probationary teachers to tenure or continuing contract status.
4. To recommend dismissal of unsatisfactory tenured or continuing contract teachers.

Broadly these purposes fall into two categories: formative (1) and summative (2-4). Formative appraisal serves the purpose of professional development — the improvement of practice — while summative appraisal is geared to career decision making. In the United Kingdom, emerging schemes in schools seem to be almost exclusively geared to professional development (see Turner, 1985). However, in its policy document *Teaching Quality*, the Government has stressed the importance of career decision making and in particular the removal of incompetent teachers from the profession:

> Concern for quality demands that in the small minority of cases where, despite in-service training arrangements, teachers fail to maintain a satisfactory standard of performance, employers must, in the interest of pupils, be ready to use procedures for dismissal (DES, 1983: 25).

This particular issue has caused much controversy and has slowed down developments in many local education authorities (LEAs). Attempts by the Government Department of Education and Science (DES) to set up 'trial areas' for staff appraisal in six LEAs met with considerable opposition from teacher unions. A further move, to create pilot schemes in two LEAs, has also met with problems.

Despite these difficulties, staff appraisal has been developing considerably in Britain on an *ad hoc* basis, and has become the subject of much discussion in a number of educational organizations. The Centre for the Study of Comprehensive Schools has undertaken research into the subject and produced several publications. Education for Industrial Society has run many courses and conferences on staff appraisal. More recently, the British Educational Management and Administration Society has taken an interest in the subject. Teacher appraisal was also the subject of one of the major sessions at the 1985 conference of the British Educational Research Association. Perhaps of most significance, however, is the fact that individual schools and colleges have been experimenting with staff appraisal schemes of various kinds (see Turner and Clift, 1985) and many schools intend to set up a scheme in the near future. But, almost without exception, these schemes are formative rather than summative.

Historical trends

Staff appraisal seems to be taking a very different form in Britain from that in the United States for a number of historical reasons. In the USA staff appraisal has developed mainly along summative lines as a basis for the initial certification of teachers and for the renewal of contracts. Concern with the competence of teachers to carry out their jobs success-fully led some teacher training institutions to develop competency-based teacher training programmes. The notion of competency-based teaching has now spread throughout the USA, and beyond initial training to the appraisal of practising teachers. Many States have developed their own programmes of competency-based teaching and these are in many cases mandated either through legislation or through State Department of Education regulations. Assessment is carried out by a team of experts, usually experienced teachers, using agreed instruments of appraisal such as observation schedules and knowledge tests. On the basis of assessments made, contracts are renewed or terminated. In some cases tenured staff might even be dismissed on the basis of an adverse report. The desire to reward effective teaching has also led a few States to adopt systems for awarding 'merit pay' to those teachers considered to be achieving standards of excellence (see, for example, Burke, 1982).

In Britain staff appraisal has traditionally been the responsibility of LEAs and is carried out by a team of local inspectors or advisers who usually have considerable experience in teaching. The purposes of such appraisal of individuals have tended to be to assess probationary teachers, to advise on appointments and promotions and to look into cases of poor performance. Periodical appraisal of non-probationary teachers does not normally take place, although many LEAs carry out inspections of schools. Staff appraisal is also undertaken, in a sense, by Her Majesty's Inspectorate as part of their own inspection procedures or in cases where they are invited into schools because of problems. However, individual teachers are not identified in LEA or HMI inspection reports: concern is with the school as a whole rather than the performance of individual teachers.

Periodic appraisal of individual teachers by senior personnel *within* schools has been a recent development in some British schools. It seems to have emerged as a management tool designed, in many cases, to boost morale at a time of falling rolls when promotion prospects become much more limited and to assist redeployment. To some extent staff appraisal has developed out of moves, mainly by LEAs, to promote curriculum review and institutional self-evaluation, and so far it seems to have had much more impact within secondary schools. The models of appraisal adopted owe more to schemes in use in industry and commerce and much less to those in initial training systems than is the case in the USA. Courses run by Education for Industrial Society have helped to promote manage-ment-oriented models, with an emphasis on staff development and training rather than hiring and firing. Those schools in Britain which are adopting schemes seem to have borrowed many ideas from industrial practice and there are striking similarities between the school schemes revealed by recent research (Turner and Clift, 1985; HMI, 1985; Suffolk Education Department, 1985) and the industrial schemes revealed in company surveys such as that of Gill (1977). Common features are the use of appraisal interviews, 'target setting' and delegation of appraisal to 'middle' managers. Appraisal through observation of lessons is not a feature of many British school schemes, although the idea of mutual observation by teachers for the purpose of improvement of practice does seem to be developing; for example, in a recent Schools Council publication (Oldroyd et al, 1984), a section is devoted to techniques of mutual observation. However, the notion of competency-based teaching does not seem to have caught on in Britain at all despite promotion of the idea by the Further Education Unit (FEU, 1982).

Research into teacher effectiveness

Staff appraisal in both the USA and Britain has to some extent been informed by research into what constitutes an 'effective teacher'. There has been a considerable amount of research into this in America; indeed it has reached such proportions that a recent annotated bibliography reports on no less than 3041 studies of teacher effectiveness (Powell and Beard, 1984). According to Farrar et al (1984), most American effective schools programmes are based on research into elementary urban schools serving low income and minority groups. In the USA teacher effectiveness has been assessed partly through systems for rating teachers, but these have been subjected to considerable criticism particularly on grounds of validity (Soar et al, 1983). Attempts to validate many rating schemes in the past were not successful (Barr, 1935; Medley and Mitzel, 1959). Research on expert opinions of good teaching has also raised doubts about the validity of teachers' own notions of what constitutes effective teaching. Coker et al (1980) found that expert opinions about good teaching correlated in many cases with decreased pupil achievement. Perhaps one of the least surprising findings is that of McDonald (1977) — that the most effective pattern of teaching differs according to the subject matter and grade level.

Flanders (1977) has shown that there are many logical and technical problems in research which has sought to establish the parameters of teacher effectiveness, and Borich and Madden (1977) have identified several measurement problems in product-process research on teacher effectiveness. Borich (1977) argues that the evaluation of teacher effectiveness must be based on information gathered from multiple sources and should take into account four stages of the teaching process:

(a) the pre-operational;
(b) the immediate;
(c) the intermediate;
(d) the product.

According to Borich, few schemes in the USA deal effectively with more than one of these stages.

In Britain the effectiveness of different teaching strategies has been examined by the ORACLE project (Observational Research and Classroom Learning Evaluation). Initially concerned with the effectiveness of different styles of science teaching, the ORACLE project devoted considerable attention to primary education (see Galton *et al*, 1980). It revealed that teaching which was geared to promoting individualized learning tended to be routine, managerial and didactic, and less educationally stimulating than whole-class teaching. This tends to be more true the larger the size of the class. In classes of over 30, many pupils spend considerable periods of time working in isolation. The study emphasized the need for flexibility in teaching and for attention to be given to the *quality* as well as the quantity of pupil learning.

Research into competency-based teaching

Competency-based teaching in the USA has been the subject of considerable research. Borich (1977) argues that the relationship between a competency and pupil change must be established by empirical data. Teacher appraisal must be based on validated proficiency levels. However, research so far has validated few of these. Rosenshine and Furst (1971) identified 11 teacher variables that showed some relationship to gain in cognitive achievement, the main five being clarity, variability, enthusiasm, task-oriented behaviour and opportunity for learning. However, these are all variables requiring a high degree of inference and hence a very large element of subjectivity in their assessment. In Britain the idea of competency-based teaching has been criticized for being based on a model of teaching which is extremely narrow in its conception. Elliott (1983) has argued that evaluating teaching in this way conceptualizes it as a simple technology which ignores the need for imaginative and reflexive skills on the part of the teacher. Similarly, Wragg (1984) argues that teaching is not just the transmission of knowledge but includes fostering interest in learning, the success of which can only be assessed in the long term. He objects to existing programmes of competency-based teaching on the grounds that they simply reduce teaching to a narrow set of skills.

The research literature led a recent review to conclude:

> To make, or to help make, a teacher more effective in the job must take account of the complexity of the task of teaching; it must take account of the fact that there is, and will continue to be, a spectrum of teacher competence; that much of what a teacher does and achieves cannot be 'measured' and that some of his [sic] work, indeed, does not bear immediate fruit (Suffolk Education Department, 1985: 3)

Current methods of teacher appraisal

There have been several recent reviews of staff appraisal methods

(Haefele, 1980; Kyriacou and Newsom, 1982; Soar *et al*, 1983; Darling-Hammond *et al*, 1983). The methods that have most often been used in teacher appraisal are: assessment of pupil performance, observation of teacher performance, assessing teacher knowledge and appraisal interviews. Particular schemes, of course, often employ more than one method.

Assessment of pupil performance

Perhaps the most common method of staff appraisal in the USA is to attempt to measure teacher effectiveness by some system of assessing pupil performance. The main problem in adopting such a method is to identify only those effects that can be attributed to the performance of a particular teacher. Many different systems for appraising teachers by examining pupil gains have been adopted in the USA, but most of these have met with some objections. All the reviews mentioned above have criticized appraisal based on pupil performance, and it seems that whatever form the assessment takes raises questions of reliability and validity. Furthermore, there is a tendency for pupils who have performed well at one particular time to perform less well on the next occasion, and vice versa. Soar *et al* (1983) argue that this regression effect makes assessment of pupil gains problematic if it is to be used for the appraisal of teachers. Brophy and Everston (1977) observed the behaviour patterns of teachers known to be effective in terms of pupil performance, and found that there was a relationship between teacher behaviours and pupil outcomes in some schools but not in others. Klein and Alkin (1977) have approached the evaluation of teacher effectiveness by comparing pupil gains produced by one particular teacher with the average gains produced by all the teachers being appraised but the problem here is being able to tell how good the average teacher in a school is in comparison to teachers in other schools. Good and Grouws (1977) divided teachers into two groups – more effective and less effective – on the basis of pupils' test score gains, but found that the two groups did not differ in the methods they used. They concluded that pupils did not seem to suffer from contact with the less effective teachers!

In Britain the assessment of pupil performance has not been a formal part of teacher appraisal since the days of payment by results in the nineteenth century and, given the adverse effects of that system on teaching methods and the criticism it provoked, it seems unlikely to re-emerge as an appraisal method, except perhaps covertly in terms of appraisal of teachers according to the performance of their pupils in public examinations.

Observation of teachers

Appraisal systems which are based purely on performance testing can be criticized for taking a 'black box' view of teaching: they examine the product but ignore the process. Glass (1977) has argued that process rather than product measures are the more stable indices of teacher effectiveness. Schemes which utilize lesson observation as a method of appraisal vary from those akin to interaction analysis, which list a set of attributes for the observer to look for, to those where the observer conducts the appraisal purely on an intuitive basis. Both systems have weaknesses as a basis for staff appraisal and research into different observation-based schemes has revealed that observers can be extremely unreliable and may be biased in their interpretation of teacher actions (see Rosenshine, 1970; Brophy and Everston, 1974; Haefele, 1980; Soar et al, 1983). If observation is conducted without a predetermined set of categories it is difficult to discover what criteria are being used. Much staff appraisal in Britain seems to be undertaken in this way and its validity is assumed to lie in the fact that a head teacher, senior teacher or adviser conducting the appraisal has sufficient experience to be able to detect the characteristics of a good teacher. Observation of teachers by Her Majesty's Inspectorate also seems to be of a high inference nature. Although the criteria used by Her Majesty's Inspectorate when observing teachers have recently been made public (HMI, 1982), what has not been made explicit is how overall judgements are arrived at. American competency-based schemes tend to be much more explicit in terms of the criteria selected and the basis upon which judgements are made. Many State programmes include detailed observation schedules which have been subjected to many years' trial and development (see, for example, those of Florida, 1983 and Georgia, 1984). Soar (1977) argues, however, that we can only assess classroom processes if a relationship between product and process can be empirically confirmed, and Scriven (1977) has criticized many existing American classroom observation techniques because they concentrate on procedures which have not yet been shown to produce pupil growth. Not all State programmes are validated or subjected to tests of reliability, although that of Georgia is an exception (see Capie, in press).

Most of the schemes for teacher appraisal developed in recent years in Britain do not employ classroom observation (see, for example, Turner and Clift, 1985), and a study by Lloyd (1981) indicates that head teachers are reluctant to observe their teachers for evaluative purposes, but HMI (1985) and Suffolk Education Department (1985) are critical of this omission.

Assessing teacher knowledge

It follows logically that a teacher cannot possibly teach what he or she does not know. It is also clear that a teacher needs to have sufficient knowledge of how to teach — what has sometimes been termed pedagogical knowledge. Some staff appraisal schemes base assessment on teacher knowledge; nearly all of them on subject knowledge. An obvious example is the National Teacher Examinations in the USA. In some States, where such examinations form a part of competency-based teaching programmes, a score below a certain level is considered to be adequate grounds for dismissal. This has caused considerable controversy since many of the teachers who have failed to achieve the desired scores have successfully completed teacher training, and in many cases are considered to be very good teachers by their principals (McDaniel, 1977). Research which has tried to demonstrate the relationship between teacher knowledge and teacher effectiveness has produced inconclusive evidence (Byrne, 1983). Moreover, Kauchak (1984) has criticized these examinations on the grounds that they discriminate against black teachers.

Appraisal interviews

In the USA appraisal interviews sometimes form part of a programme for summative appraisal. One particular interview system which has been used in the USA is the Teacher Perceiver Interview (TPI), in which interviewers apply certain techniques that are designed to tease out the extent to which a person is likely to be a good practitioner. Even though it could perhaps be used for routine evaluation of existing staff, the TPI was designed as a recruitment device. How far it is a *valid* system of assessing the qualities of a good teacher has, however, been questioned (Haefele, 1978).

In Britain the appraisal interview tends to be used for periodic evaluation as a basis for professional development rather than for summative appraisal. In some of the schemes developed by particular schools, it includes a large element of self-assessment by the teacher being interviewed, something which has long been advocated in industry (see, for example, McGregor, 1957). As well as classroom practice, other aspects of the teacher's job tend to be considered, such as planning, marking, curriculum development, management tasks and extra-curricular activities. The main emphasis of many interview-based appraisal schemes in Britain is to bring about improvements in practice (Turner and Clift, 1985) and the responsibility for improvement is assumed to rest with both the appraiser and the person being appraised. In some cases both parties are expected to agree on targets for future action, the success of which can be evaluated at a subsequent appraisal interview.

Although such interviews can identify problems, priorities and training needs, much depends on the knowledge and skills of the interviewer and the ability and willingness of the teacher appraised to discuss and evaluate his or her own performance. The potential weakness of a system which relies exclusively on interviews is that it can become simply a formality and the interviewer may well have no direct evidence of the classroom performance of the person appraised.

Conclusion

Evans (1951) argues that the best way to evaluate teaching is by a composite of different methods. However, the important question is not what methods to use but what *purpose* appraisal schemes are put to. In this review a distinction has been made between formative and summative evaluation. The former is concerned with professional development while the latter is concerned with career decision making. However, the two are not easily separated and it is likely that any scheme will be adopted to some extent for both purposes.

It has been noted that in the USA staff appraisal has developed out of approaches to evaluating beginner teachers by institutions charged with initial training. Competency-based teaching programmes are increasingly being adopted by States for the summative evaluation of all their teachers and are being mandated through regulations or State legislation. The methods adopted in such programmes are mainly observation of classroom practice by experts, using observation schedules of different types, and pencil-and-paper tests to assess teacher knowledge. There has been a considerable amount of research in America to establish the relationship between the actions of teachers and pupil gains, and thus to validate competencies. However, much of the evidence from such research is inconclusive and many competency-based schemes have been criticized on the grounds that their validity has not been demonstrated.

In Britain staff appraisal seems to be emerging in a different way from the USA. In addition to traditional assessment by LEA inspectors or advisers, schools are increasingly developing their own internal schemes, many of which seem to have been influenced by industrial practice. The primary aim of such schemes appears to be formative; they are designed to promote job satisfaction, to identify further training needs and to guide future deployment. The method most commonly used is that of an appraisal interview by a senior member of staff. So far the idea of competency-based teaching has not met with approval in Britain. Nevertheless, central Government has been attempting to introduce systematic staff appraisal by employers for summative purposes. At present such appraisal is merely advocated in Government pronouncements, but the Secretary of State for Education and Science has suggested the possibility of legislation being introduced to impose staff appraisal on LEAs. Such a system would include higher pay for those deemed to be the best performers and the removal from the profession of those considered to be irremediably incompetent. Whether staff appraisal in Britain will follow the American model and be mandated, either by LEAs or by national legislation, depends in large measure on negotiations over teachers' pay and conditions of service which have been fraught with problems in recent years.

References

Barr, A S (1935) The measurement of teaching ability *Journal of Educational Research* **288**: 561-9

*Borich, G D ed (1977) *The Appraisal of Teaching: Concepts and Process* Addison-Wesley: Reading, Mass

Borich, G D and Madden, S K (1977) *Evaluating Classroom Instruction: A Source-book of Instruments* Addison-Wesley: Reading, Mass

Brophy, J E and Everston, C M (1974) *Process-Product Correlations in the Texas Teacher Effectiveness Study: Final Report* University of Texas at Austin: Austin, Tex

Brophy, J E and Everston, C M (1977) Teacher behavior and student learning in the second and third grades *in* Borich (1977)

Burke, B T (1982) Merit pay for teachers: Round Valley may have the answer *Phi Delta Kappan* **64** 4: 265-6 (December)

Byrne, C (1983) Teacher knowledge and teacher effectiveness: a literature review, theoretical analysis and discussion of research strategy. Paper presented to the 14th Annual Convocation of the Northeastern Educational Research Association: Ellenville, New York (October)

Capie, W (in press) Coming of age: systematic performance appraisal *Educational Measurement*

Coker, H, Medley, D M and Soar, R S (1980) How valid are expert opinions about effective teaching? *Phi Delta Kappan* **62** 2: 131-49 (October)

*Darling-Hammond, L, Wise, A E and Pease, S R (1983) Teacher evaluation in the organisational context: a review of the literature *Review of Educational Research* **53** 3: 285-328

Department of Education and Science (1983) *Teaching Quality* (Cmnd 8836) HMSO: London

Department of Education and Science (1985) *Better Schools* (Cmnd 9469) HMSO: London

Elliott, J (1983) *Teacher Evaluation and Teaching as a Moral Science* Cambridge Institute of Education: Cambridge (mimeo)

Evans, K M (1951) A critical survey of methods of assessing teaching ability *British Journal of Educational Psychology* **21** 2: 89-95

Farrar, E, Neufeld, B and Miles, M B (1984) Effective schools programs in high schools: social promotion or movement by merit? *Phi Delta Kappan* **65** 10: 701-6 (June)

Flanders, N A (1977) Knowledge about teacher effectiveness *British Journal of Teacher Education* **3** 1: 3-26

Florida Department of Education (1983) *Domains of the Florida Performance Measurement System* Office of Teacher Education, Certification, and Inservice Staff Development: Tallahassee, Fla

Further Education Unit (1982) *Competency in Teaching: A Review of Competency and Performance Based Staff Development* FEU: London

Galton, M, Simon, B and Croll, P (1980) *Inside the Primary Classroom* Routledge and Kegan Paul: London

Georgia Department of Education (1984) *Teacher Performance Assessment Instrument* Georgia Department of Education, Division of Staff Development: Atlanta, Ga

Gill, D (1977) *Appraising Performance: Present Trends and the Next Decade* Institute of Personnel Management: London

Glass, G V (1977) A review of three methods of determining teacher effectiveness *in* Borich (1977)

Good, T L and Grouws, D A (1977) Teacher effectiveness in fourth-grade mathematics classrooms *in* Borich (1977)

Haefele, D L (1978) The teacher perceiver interview: how valid? *Phi Delta Kappan* **59** 10: 683-4 (June)

Haefele, D L (1980) How to evaluate thee, teacher — let me count the ways *Phi Delta Kappan* **61** 5: 349-52 (January)

Her Majesty's Inspectorate (1982) *The New Teacher in School: A Report by Her Majesty's Inspectors* HMSO: London

Her Majesty's Inspectorate (1985) *Quality in Schools: Evaluation and Appraisal* HMSO: London

Kauchak, D (1984) Testing teachers in Louisiana: a closer look *Phi Delta Kappan* **65** 9: 626-8 (May)

Klein, S P and Alkin, M C (1977) Evaluating teachers for outcome accountability *in* Borich (1977)

Kyriacou, C and Newson, G (1982) Teacher effectiveness: a consideration of research problems *Educational Review* **34** 1: 3-12

Lloyd, K (1981) Quality control in the primary school: the head's role in supervising the work of classteachers *School Organisation* **1** 4: 317-29

McDaniel, T R (1977) The NTE and teacher certification *Phi Delta Kappan* **59** 3: 186-8 (November)

McDonald, F J (1977) Research on teaching: report on phase II of the beginning teacher evaluation study *in* Borich (1977)

McGregor, D (1957) An uneasy look at performance appraisal *Harvard Business Review* September/October

Medley, D M and Mitzel, H E (1959) Some behavioural correlates of teacher effectiveness *Journal of Educational Psychology* **50** 6: 239-46

Oldroyd, D, Smith, K and Lee, J (1984) *School-based Staff Development Activities: A Handbook for Secondary Schools* Longman for the Schools Council: York

*Powell, M and Beard, J W (1984) *Teacher Effectiveness: An Annotated Bibliography and Guide to Research* Garland: New York

Rosenshine, B (1970) The stability of teacher effects upon student achievement *Review of Educational Research* **40** 5: 647-62

Rosenshine, B and Furst, N F (1971) Research on teacher performance criteria *in* Smith (1971)

Scriven, M (1977) The evaluation of teachers and teaching *in* Borich (1977)

Smith, B O (1971) *Research in Teacher Education: A Symposium* Prentice-Hall: Englewood Cliffs, NJ

Soar, R S (1977) Teacher assessment: problems and possibilities *in* Borich (1977)

Soar, R S, Medley, D M and Coker, H (1983) Teacher evaluation: a critique of currently used methods *Phi Delta Kappan* **65**: 239-46 (December)

Suffolk Education Department (1985) *Those Having Torches . . . Teacher Appraisal: A Study* Suffolk Education Department: Ipswich, England

Turner, G (1985) Nascent schemes for teacher appraisal *School Organisation* **5** 2: 155-61

Turner, G and Clift, P S (1985) *A First Review and Register of School and College Based Teacher Appraisal Schemes* Open University: Milton Keynes (mimeo)

Wood, C J and Pohland, P A (1983) Teacher evaluation and the 'hand of history' *Journal of Educational Administration* **21** 2: 169-81

Wragg, E C (1984) *Classroom Teaching Skills* Croom Helm: London

Part 4: Selected Management

10. Coping with unionized staff in the comprehensive school: a framework for analysis

Geoffrey Lyons

Summary: A framework of analysis derived from Webb and Lyons (1982) and the work of Rosemary Stewart (1982; 1983) is used as a means to examine responses made by secondary head teachers in England and Wales to the increasingly sophisticated and complex tasks involved in managing staff. The opportunity of doing this was provided by data from a field survey conducted by Lyons and Stenning (1985). The context in which head teachers' actions are located, the knowledge and skills brought to the task, the differentiation of responses made by head teachers and the impact on others who share the head's role network, are all examined. The reader's attention is drawn to the flexible responses, sophisticated philosophy and the armoury of skills deployed in the coping strategies adopted by the effective head teacher.

Introduction

Earlier studies of the administrative or managerial work of the secondary comprehensive head teacher have tended to use a simplified classification or categorization of such areas as the head teachers' tasks, functions, responsibilities or leadership styles, for example Allen (1968), Poster (1976), Lyons (1974) and Hughes (1976). In these earlier works the complex and multi-faceted nature of the roles being enacted and projected tended to be insufficiently recognized. The similarities between head teachers' managerial behaviours and strategies and those adopted by managers in other sectors were rarely given sufficient prominence. These issues were identified by Webb and Lyons (1982) in developing earlier work of Mintzberg (1973). The importance for an understanding of managerial behaviour of the differentiation of job and function that regularly occurs through the exercise of individual choice was also largely unrecognized (see Stewart, 1982; Webb and Lyons, 1982).

The tasks of head teachers: an emerging perspective

Following Mintzberg, Webb and Lyons initially focused upon interpersonal, informational and decisional roles as a way of, first, identifying the knowledge and managerial skills the head teacher regularly uses in order to perform any of his or her daily tasks, and second, of gaining insight into the complexity of the role configurations adopted by head teachers, which particular circumstances of time and place dictate. Any framework for the analysis of the head teacher's managerial roles and function must recognize the ability of the head teacher to select an appropriate mode of action. This is one which reflects the circumstances of his or her own personality, experience and preferences, the practical exigencies implicit in the situation, and the likely impact on other significant individuals or groups who form parts of the extended role networks in which the head's actions are located. As Webb and Lyons (1982) express it:

> The interlocking nature of the roles adopted seems to imply a personally oriented and self conscious adoption of sets of role configurations, or perhaps, partly stereotyped and partly pragmatically determined behaviour which hard won experience has shown to be appropriate and which enables the [head teacher] to see his way towards survival with effectiveness. This choice of role configurations has to be undertaken in the knowledge, typically for those with management responsibilities, that the positions and actions taken at any moment will not be appropriate to all situations, and are likely to be rejected or misunderstood by significant sections of the populations the [head teacher] regularly deals with. The significance of such is not lost upon head teachers, for it would seem that a degree of role confusion and ambivalence is a principal characteristic of the [head teacher's] lot, given the disparate nature of the personal and professional values and interests of a large school (or college staff). These ambivalences are the products of many (contemporary) circumstances present within their environments.

Stewart (1982; 1983) in particular focuses our attention upon job differentiation as a significant means of analysing managerial work and develops a framework based on the three key concepts of *demands, constraints* and *choices.* Demands are defined as:

> 'what any person in the job must do, [and] cannot avoid doing without invoking reprisals from boss, peer or subordinates; constraints are the factors that limit what the job holder can do, including [company] policies and procedures, legislation, resource limitations and attitudes; choice involves the fact that managers in similar jobs do them differently; the differences include which aspects of the job are emphasized and neglected, how much time is spent with subordinates compared with colleagues, and how far the [manager] becomes involved in the technical aspects of the work (Stewart, 1983).

The perspectives developed by Stewart and Webb and Lyons will be used here as a basis for exploring problems currently encountered by secondary comprehensive head teachers in the managerial aspects of their roles, and as a means of accounting for differences in observed behaviours and in the coping strategies adopted. No two head teachers would necessarily deal with apparently similar issues and circumstances in quite identical ways. The principal emphasis will be placed upon one aspect of the head teacher's work: the management of teaching and non-teaching staff in a school and particularly on the increasing impact of trade union activities upon the conduct of the head teacher's staff management responsibilities. The evidence about the head teacher's management of staff is derived from a field survey conducted by Lyons, Stenning and McQueeney (1985).

The management of staff represents perhaps the most intractable problem currently faced by head teachers. Let us first, therefore, show some of the difficulties and complexity inherent in this aspect of the head's task by presenting an instance reported in an interview with a male head teacher. This illustrates how, in the stream of events which come to or are brought to his attention, he has first to identify the event with which he is confronted for what it is and not for what it appears to be, subsequently to determine whether or not to act, and if to act to determine the mode and timing of any action.

> A senior member of staff of a school with responsibility for pupil welfare of third- and fourth-year pupils (a scale 4 Head of Third and Fourth Years) chose to spend each lunch time with colleagues in the staff room playing cards. The school draws both pupils and staff from a widely dispersed rural catchment area. Along with other members of staff the teacher concerned shares car journeys (a car pool) to school with three other colleagues and consequently it was rare for this teacher to be present much later than ten minutes after the close of afternoon school since one of the 'pool' always seemed to have an engagement necessitating an early departure. The Head is privately convinced that this behaviour is not acceptable on the part of a senior member of staff, and particularly for one holding Head of Year responsibilities which the Head feels in these circumstances are not being properly discharged.

What in this instance should this head do? Is there a problem whereby action can or ought to be taken? The head teacher's overriding concern must be the education offered to the pupils and the effectiveness with which the school provides this service to both pupils and community. Here are some examples of the issues which the head may rehearse in his mind before deciding on any course of action. He may feel that the senior member of staff concerned should be capable of judging for himself exactly what constitutes reasonable professional behaviour and thus be disinclined to approach a fellow professional on grounds which may ultimately lead to disciplinary action. If, however, the head wished to proceed systematically against the Head of Year, then action has to be demonstrably defensible and documented, and follow the procedure agreed between unions and employers. In these circumstances the head must ask himself whether his sole judgement of an 'acceptable level' of performance is sufficient; if not, should the professional judgements of others be sought? If this were done, and the teacher were asked to change his or her behaviour and given support to do this, one can ask what would be an acceptable time-scale for improvement to take place and whether this was a reasonable time span for the teacher to demonstrate genuine improvement. If disciplinary action were to result from the head's action, then he must be totally sure of his ground, must not unwittingly divide the staff over an issue involving the performance of a colleague's duties, and should ensure that were any action to be proposed against an individual member of staff, potential support of the staff for the action would have been previously tested. The head must also ensure full backing for any action from the employer (the local education authority — LEA) at both officer and elected representative level.

However, the head may be unwilling or unable to admit to his employer that he is faced with a problem that he does not know how to
handle. What does the teacher's contract say about his or her duties, and
does a job description exist which clarifies this? What has custom and
practice dictated in the school concerned regarding duties which are
performed by a Head of Year — and perhaps in the local education authority as well? Questions such as these are likely to be raised at an Industrial
Tribunal should the matter go that far, and any head teacher without
clear documentary evidence available to support his or her actions is
likely to experience considerable difficulty if cross-examined by Counsel.
Examples of head teachers losing cases and being pilloried in the press
are common enough.

This particular incident was further complicated by the Head of Year
being an active branch member of a teachers' union which was militant at
the local level in the pursuit of national policies. In the circumstances, the
head felt that extreme caution was necessary to avoid the school becoming
the focus of either an individual or collective dispute — with the ever-
present likelihood of damage occurring to the image of the school held by
the community when pupil enrolment was a key issue regarding the
school's future.

One further question for the head to consider was that, as he was
dissatisfied with the amount of time the Head of Year was spending on
pupil welfare duties, why had not more time been allocated within the
latter's timetable for these duties to be properly conducted? Where
resourcing becomes the issue, the dispute involves the employer. However,
the overriding problem for the head teacher to contend with remains the
impact of action on others. The head, through inaction or insensitive
action, must not allow any grounds for a legitimate grievance being
pursued by any individual or group.

Faced with such a complex situation, the head might be expected to
opt for inaction. However, it is likely that the experienced head teacher
will, through experience, recognize the critical issues on which to act,
and have a repertoire of skills and knowledge which will enable him or
her to proceed via short cuts to conventionally adopted responses, without
the clutter of a mass of unassimilated and unsorted information impeding
a decision to act. It is implicit in the work of Webb and Lyons that the
head would invariably perform his or her duties with a clear personal
signature or stamp to the action: an action which other actors in the role
set would recognize as belonging to that head teacher.

The type of issue and the possible courses of action illustrated in the
example above confront and increasingly engage the time of head teachers
in secondary schools in England and Wales. At this point we shall turn first
to the framework of *constraints* and *demands* set out by Stewart (1982)
and the areas of *knowledge* and *skill* identified by Webb and Lyons (1982)
in order to understand the context in which the head currently discharges
his or her managerial responsibilities for staff. Second, we shall look at the
issues of *choice*, *differentiation*, and *complexity* of *extended roles* (and

the skill in the appropriateness of their selection) as a way of understanding the *coping strategies* adopted by heads and as a way of identifying differences of observed head teacher action.

The context for the head's action: demands, constraints, knowledge and skills

In the last two decades considerable pressure has been imposed upon the
secondary education system in England and Wales. Initially that pressure
arose from the change to a non-selective secondary comprehensive system
with an associated increase in size of the schools, complexity of resourcing,
innovations of curriculum and pedagogy, and the inevitable bureaucratization of the system. These changes brought about corresponding changes
in organizational structures and staff relationships. Previous patterns of
headship which had sustained the head in his or her professional and
educative roles (see Bernbaum, 1986) had come under increasing pressure
for change and adaptation, and a movement towards a managerial style of
leadership by those holding senior responsibilities in schools was discernible (Lyons, 1984; 1976; Poster, 1976; Peters, 1976). However, these
changes were not always understood by those responsible for the governance of schools, by those holding executive responsibility within the
LEA, or by those in schools exercising day-to-day responsibility for
their management — head teachers, deputy heads, and particularly heads
of departments. A lukewarm response to the adoption of a management
system of relationships between senior and other staff has frequently
been noted.

Currently, the education system itself has come under increasing
scrutiny from central and local government, and from other well organized
external sources (Hart, 1983). These include pressure groups who aspire
to influence the content or structure of education, or to achieve a re-
distribution of scarce national resources away from the educational to
other sectors. The quality of State secondary education has increasingly
been questioned, and the supremacy of education as the biggest
autonomous spending sector within local government is being challenged
and its budgets and processes increasingly scrutinized. An unprecedented
movement towards accountability has arisen, and the performance of
schools increasingly subjected to public comment. Increased attempts to
control schooling have included the broadening of the base of membership of governing bodies, the legal requirement of publication of information by schools, including examination results, and the publication of
reports of school inspections by Her Majesty's Inspectors. A major change
is taking place in the distribution of the age of the population as the birth
rate decreases. This point is particularly important since the fall in the
level of live births, taken together with resource cutbacks and re-allocation,
has seen school closures, mergers, staff redundancies and redeployment
emerge as issues of substance in England and Wales. The morale of teaching

and non-teaching staff, staff promotion prospects, dissatisfaction with salary levels, uncertainties about security of tenure and terms and conditions of service in the present circumstances become central and dominant issues for the head teacher to handle. At the same time heads themselves personally experience these very problems regarding their own careers and future development. Many more heads are seeking early retirement than was previously the case (Hart, 1983). The support structure offered by LEAs in terms of the policies and procedures regarding management of staff vary considerably in their range and comprehensiveness, and at the moment there seems to be genuine confusion and ambivalence regarding the head's authority and responsibility, as evidenced by overlapping spheres of responsibility between governing bodies, officers and inspectors (advisers) of the LEA, the education committee and the head. Often the head has been uncertain whether he or she acts as agent, employer or employee.

The head's traditional freedom to manage is increasingly constrained by a movement towards a centralization of responsibilities, particularly on questions of finance and staffing, and by agreements negotiated centrally between the LEA as employer and unions on such matters as, for example, recruitment, redundancy and redeployment. The impact of labour law applying equally to schools as it does to employment in commerce, the civil service, industry, etc, is increasingly felt. The dramatic increase in organized trade union activity has, in the last few years, added a considerable extra dimension to the problems and difficulties heads have conventionally responded to, and which did not, by and large, previously form part of events occurring on a daily basis or of earlier models of headship. Schools currently display a high level of union membership and there is a proliferation of the number of unions representing both teaching and non-teaching staff. While the head him or herself is almost certainly a member of a professional association which restricts recruitment of membership to senior staff of a school, some heads deliberately choose to belong to that union numerically the strongest among their teaching staff. Union intervention in the affairs of schools is increasingly occurring. The withdrawal of goodwill, and the systematic application of sanctions by an increasingly disaffected staff, pose a fundamental and challenging problem to the exercise of the head's managerial skills and a challenge to his or her authority and responsibility. The unions with which the head is likely to deal are becoming increasingly sophisticated in exercising and applying their 'muscle', and while such union action is inevitably presented as being concerned to effect an improvement in the education service, unions nevertheless have as a fundamental concern the terms and conditions of service of their members. Thus union action could undermine the educational aims of the school when it takes the form of, for instance, staff refusal to cover for absent colleagues, leading to classes having to be sent home, refusal to undertake lunch-time supervision, even though the LEA may require of the head that the school is kept open, and refusal to attend parents' meetings, staff meetings, etc, held outside normal working hours. Strikes are also found to occur more frequently. The head may be a member of a union in dispute. When this is the case it is almost impossible for the head to simultaneously fulfil the expectations of colleagues in the union and those of the employer, and considerable confusion in relationships and in authority, and personal strain upon the head teacher, almost inevitably occur.

The terms and facilities provided in the school to unions are those negotiated and set out in national agreements, and few LEAs or schools would fail to fully implement such agreements. The workings of the unions at school level are generally carried out through elected school representatives. While many school representatives adopt a low key role, confining themselves to such matters as recruitment to the union, reception and display of information and the holding of meetings, this is by no means universally the case and some representatives adopt a confrontation stance in relation to the head. Where a matter of some importance concerning conditions of work has arisen, an official of the union with some overall or regional responsibility will most likely intervene and deal directly with the school and the LEA. Both regional officials and the school representatives are increasingly likely to have attended training schemes conducted by the unions for their membership, unlike the head who has probably received no training at all in relation to union matters. Heads may increasingly find their actions exposed, and themselves in increasingly isolated positions, with the assumptions which originally attracted them into teaching as a profession increasingly challenged and undermined. Individual and collective disputes appear to be increasing in number as unions seek to extend their influence, refine their ability to have an impact upon the educational sector, and increase their power to influence decision making about its future shape and direction. The manifestations of this and the outcomes upon the individual head teacher, some of which may be totally unexpected, occur in many different ways; some examples are as follows.

1. The head announcing the dates for the following year's school calendar is confronted by a union representative who says two of the dates are unsuitable and will have to be changed.
2. Teaching staff who are members of unions not involved in a proposed withdrawal of labour by another of the major teaching unions need to establish their own positions on their conduct during the strike.
3. The head consulting with all of the union representatives and the Chairman of Governors and the simplest solution appearing to be, with due warning to parents and pupils, to close school half an hour early. A local councillor witnessing the early departure of pupils asks the Chairman of the Education Committee to have the head reprimanded.
4. Union representatives asking to meet collectively with a head to raise that such matters as heating and physical conditions in the staff room, which previously appeared on the agenda of the Staff Association,

a non-union committee in the school, should in future be the exclusive province of the teachers' union.

A newly appointed head, in commenting upon his experiences in dealing
with non-teaching members of staff, observed:

> I had never been forewarned as to the problems I would have to deal with.
> I knew how to look after the curricular and pupil welfare sides of the school
> but this, besides the unbelievable amount of time it takes, was a total culture
> shock. The full-time manual workers' union officials came into the room and
> it was as though they were speaking a foreign language. The proceduralization
> of everything was beyond anything I had experienced before . . .
>
> I think one of the problems is that teachers never put themselves in the
> position of a caretaker or secretary or technician. They do not understand
> what their job is like, what their difficulties are. If [he or she] reports back, or
> the work is produced, then everything is as it should be. If, however, the
> work is not done then suddenly everything is in turmoil, and without a proper
> frame of reference to turn to it is very difficult for the new head to know
> how to begin to solve the problems. Knowledge of what policies and pro-
> cedures do or do not exist and what can and cannot properly occur, what the
> law says, what the head's own contract and conscience dictate he or she
> must do, all in one way or another considerably exercise the head teacher, for
> these simple examples raise many issues of strategy and tactics, of philosophy
> and attitudes as well as those matters directly relating to demands, knowledge
> and constraints. It is such factors as these and many others not reported here
> which provide the context of demands and constraints, the knowledge basis
> upon which the head teacher's actions are founded. It is on this basis that
> considerable differentiations of role and function and choice of behaviours
> begin to be apparent, and it is from the issues relating directly to demands,
> knowledge and constraints that we now turn to those issues involving choice,
> differentiation, and the role configurations adopted by the head, their coping
> strategies, that we now turn.

The impact of the head's action: choices, differentiation and role configurations

Heads have to make choices about which matters should be given prominence, which ignored, which given detailed attention, and which dealt
with superficially. The choices made are likely to give a personal and
identifiable signature to any head's actions. However, such choice and
differentiation as to the course of action the head chooses to follow,
or unwittingly follows, does not in itself imply appropriate or inappropriate behaviour: it is the purposeful choice and the desired impact
on others, the extended roles which are purposefully or unwittingly
enacted against which the head teacher's action should be assessed.

We can consider the following examples provided by two head teachers.
Both were faced with action mounted by trade unions against the school
but preferred to handle the situation they were faced with in quite
different ways. In this they reveal different philosophies and attitudes
and totally different uses of the organizational structures existing in their
schools and the interpersonal relationships which underpin them, and
choose to seek quite different impacts upon groups of individuals with
whom they regularly work.

Headteacher 1

The previous contract that existed between school and pupils is no longer valid. I am acutely aware of this. My job is to look at what this school should be doing in five years' time, to make sure that this school is still here in five years' time, and I am willing to be judged on these terms.

To do this I need to be in firm control; I need to make clear decisions, to act quickly and decisively. For example I removed economics from the curriculum and replaced it with BEC, informed staff of my intention through the departmental structure and asked for comment. By the same token I lean very hard on the weak teacher and particularly those who are holding a post which entails management responsibility.

The deputy head is very close to me; he is not an office boy; he can and does run the school in my absence. He is very accessible and staff often prefer to consult him rather than me. The other two deputies have assigned responsibilities and we meet as a senior management team. I have reduced other power bases by abolishing the post of head of Middle School and transferring the head of Lower School. I also scuppered the faculty system by making the departmental structure the key communication vehicle. It is used to pass information and policy down, and seek comment which is then passed back. Staff meetings are used to set out policy decisions and the staff handbook supplements these processes by documenting policy and practice.

External relationships are a crucial part of my job. I know exactly who to approach within the LEA and it is very important to be constantly aware of the working together of the executive and the political wings. I keep parents informed and governors at arm's length.

I joined the numerically strongest teachers' union in the school and attend all branch meetings. I would never meet union reps together — you do not teach teachers how to negotiate. I have a knowledge of employment law and know the union rule books better than the union representatives. The unions are concerned with terms and conditions of service for their members. I constantly point out to them that I am not the employer. When they proposed a withdrawal of goodwill I cancelled all meetings. I remember pointing out to one outraged union member that if they proposed withdrawing from the consultative process then they would have to accept arbitrary decisions.

This school was scheduled for closure 18 months ago but I managed to avert that.

Headteacher 2

I think one feels a very great sympathy for the plight of the young teacher just starting out on his or her career; teachers don't go on to the battlements without good cause. From the outset the strike had to be placed in its proper context and all actions had to be gauged against this long-term impact. You cannot afford to adopt a personal position — it wasn't, as some of my colleagues appeared to be saying by their actions, a personal insult to themselves.

A good school management structure and good communications are prerequisites. You have to develop anticipatory policies which are known and understood both by those who develop them and those to whom they are applied.

I maintained frequent and full contact with parents and with pupils — by circular letters and by regular meetings. The LEA directed me to keep the school open and a timetable running; meeting with the non-striking unions established what was acceptable. The real problem was the lack of uncertainty within the LEA and here the Chairman of Governors became my right arm.

I have for a long time adopted a policy of meeting regularly with union reps to exchange information so I was well briefed that the strike was coming off and what the attitude of the other unions was going to be.

During the weeks leading up to the strike I had numerous conversations with individuals, finding out what the issues were and how they felt about them, and when the strike was on I would spend up to one hour each day with the pickets. They were, after all, my staff and I felt loyalty and responsibility for them: the strike would come to an end one day and normal relationships would need to be re-established. When it was all over we were walking on egg shells for a couple of days. I had held a staff meeting and talked of looking to the future, re-establishing our standards and putting the past behind us. I patrolled the school all the time talking to pupils and staff, giving them as much support as was possible. Things settled down really remarkably quickly without tensions, animosity or recriminations.

You have to be a good listener, you do not commit yourself to a personal position (certainly not too early) and it was absolutely essential to have maintained those contacts and sense of trust and respect.

Both of these head teachers are known to be capable and experienced. However, in the circumstances which each judged to exist, and the outcomes which each had judged important to achieve, totally different approaches were adopted.

The period over which the issues and problems facing head teachers in relation to the management of increasingly disputatious staff has been relatively short. Many in the educational system were shown to lack knowledge and skills and even, in some cases, sympathy for new styles of professional relationships which were emerging. When matters relating to staff (including non-teaching staff) could be regulated by reference to shared professional norms (Lyons, 1976), the management of disputes was not a problem. Once, however, the basis of the head's authority and responsibility is challenged by reference to other sources of power, and to other sources of knowledge or expertise, etc, the legitimacy of the head's authority has necessarily to be restated. Those holding most rigidly to modes of behaviour previously acceptable and effective, or attitudinally opposed to the changes taking place, were likely to find their behaviour increasingly dysfunctional, and themselves becoming distanced from increasingly large numbers of their staff. The 'signature' which previously has served the head well subsequently becomes increasingly inappropriate. Additionally, if insufficient account is taken of the changes in demands, knowledge and constraints present in the situation, the head can enact totally inappropriate actions in relation to these actors who share the extended roles. However, the education system generally reacts slowly to change. Staff turnover in a particular school may be low and the staff body may have been together for many years. If parental expectations remain unchanged, in these circumstances, previously acceptable modes of behaviour, which in other schools are now proving dysfunctional, may still prove appropriate. Generally speaking, current issues relating to the management of staff in schools, particularly dealing with unions, have posed wholly new challenges to the educational sector. Consequently there is a need for new rules, new knowledge and more sophisticated behaviour.

Heads who cope, and are confident of their capacity to continue to cope, have this flexibility. Such heads have often acquired the new knowledge and skills or have repolished the old ones. They are attuned to the sources of staff discontent and conscious of the need to restate and restrengthen relationships with unions and staff. They recognize the importance of contingency planning, appropriate administrative systems and of helping staff to attune to new relationships between each other. As a matter of policy they have maintained and developed a network of communications outside the school and use this network adroitly and politically. There is, as a consequence, an erosion of previously existing relationships with the traditional support structures and helping agencies. This style of school management is still people orientated and accessibility is still the key-note. It is not that there is one pattern of behaviour or one response which is appropriate. There is a sophisticated armoury at the head teacher's disposal, the back-up of expertise from his or her own (and other) professional associations, and the context and the framework of policies and procedures set by the employer, which give the skilful head the basis for action. The experienced head is aware that he or she cannot simultaneously satisfy all the groups who have demands on him or her. The signature of the experienced head enables a shorthand to be used and he or she acts with long-term and short-term outcomes in mind. Compare the statement below, given by a sophisticated and experienced educationalist about the management of non-teaching staff, with the earlier statement by the new head:

By the nature of all the different jobs which exist in a school it seems inevitable that, at least sometimes, staff are likely to be at variance with each other. They have territorial rights and job boundaries which have to be respected, and the nature of these different jobs means that some issues should not be approached without recognizing that there are true interpersonal and job differences between them. Although all staff may have parity of esteem, invoking notions of parity is not the same as invoking notions of equivalence. The exercise

of overall responsibility and the coordination of activity to ensure standard-
ization of work-load, levels of work, produce job descriptions . . . etc, are of
fundamental importance.

Conclusion

It would appear that the perspectives of demands and constraints, allied
to the knowledge which the head has of the context in which he or she is
placed, provide a potentially substantial tool for analysis of head teachers'
managerial behaviour. Additionally, if this is also taken together with
Stewart's (1982; 1983) perspectives on 'choice' and 'differentiation', and
with the cognate work of Webb and Lyons (1982) dealing particularly
with the desired impact on others as forming part of the head teacher's
extended role network, then a practical tool for analysing head teacher
behaviour is available. The opportunity of 'choice' presents the possibility
of a more creative response than conventional responses may imply is
available. This, taken together with the likely impact on others who share
the head teacher's role network, points up the complexity and ambivalence
in extant roles, the breadth of repertoire and the real level of skill necessary for successful managerial performance in contemporary circumstances. For many, a failure to understand or come to terms with all the
factors present in contemporary staff management, a lack of flexibility to
produce new role configurations, allied to chance factors present in their
school circumstances, may dictate whether or not they cope successfully.
Previously, headship offered virtually a maximum opportunity of choice
and that may well have been one of its attractions. Constraints and
demands increasingly impinge. The constant need to acquire new knowledge is so exhausting that available behaviours are increasingly limited.
For some this now proves unacceptable and what previously gave
satisfaction as 'educators' is no longer available. Others can see a creative
response available to them and have the flexibility to adopt new roles;
these will almost certainly achieve the aims they have always striven to
achieve as educators.

The coping strategies adopted by those described to us as effective
head teachers clearly call for a sophisticated and flexible response and a
correspondingly comprehensive armoury of skills and knowledge. These
effective head teachers will also have adapted to the challenges present in
the contemporary context. Other head teachers have found in the new
modes of operation a substantial challenge and incompatibility with their
philosophies, and for many the present circumstances are proving extremely
exacting.

References

Allen, B ed (1968) Headship in the 1970s Basil Blackwell: Oxford
Bernbaum, G (1976) The role of the head in Peters (1976)

Gray, H L ed (1982) *The Management of Educational Institutions: Theory, Research and Consultancy* Falmer Press: Lewes, Sussex

Hart, D (1973) Head complaints *The Times Educational Supplement* (23 September)

Hughes, M G (1976) The professional as administrator: the case of the secondary school head *in* Peters (1976)

Lyons, G (1974) *The Administrative Tasks of Head and Senior Teachers in Large Secondary Schools* School of Education, University of Bristol: Bristol

Lyons, G (1976) *Heads' Tasks: A Handbook of Secondary Administration* National Foundation for Educational Research: Slough

Lyons, G, Stenning, R and McQueeney, J (1985) *Employment Relations in the Maintained Secondary Sector and the Training Needs of Headteachers* Report to the Department of Education and Science

Lyons, G and Stenning, R (1985) *Managing Staff in Schools: A Handbook* Hutchinson Educational: London

Mintzberg, H (1973) *The Nature of Managerial Work* Harper and Row: New York

Peters, R S ed (1976) *The Role of the Head* Routledge and Kegan Paul: London

Poster, C (1976) *School Decision Making* Heinemann: London

Stewart, R (1982) *Choices for the Manager: A Guide to Managerial Work and Behaviour* McGraw-Hill: New York

Stewart, R (1983) It's not what you do . . . it's the way that you do it *Personnel Management* (April)

Webb, P C and Lyons, G (1982) The nature of managerial activities in education *in* Gray (1982)

11. The selection and appointment of heads

Colin Morgan

Summary: This chapter discusses the selection and appointment of head teachers by reporting a major piece of research carried out in England and Wales between 1980 and 1983 on the selection of secondary heads (the 'POST' project), and some important research findings from the United States of America in the same period. An indication is also given of selection practice in Western Europe and Scandinavia. Exemplary practices for selecting senior leadership role holders are discussed, and their defining characteristics presented; in particular, the developmental *assessment-centre* work of the National Association of Secondary School Principals (USA) is summarized. It is argued that present practice, with its reliance on 'hunt the right personality' and cultural embodiment factors, raises important generic issues: the balance of assessment to be given to *technical*, ie job-related, abilities as distinct from *social* acceptability; and the type of contribution which should be made to the total selection procedure by the *professionals* — from whatever fields these should appropriately be drawn — and by the lay democratic controllers, that is, the local education authority (LEA) members and school governors.

Introduction

In 1985 the procedures for selecting and appointing head teachers in England and Wales were substantially unchanged from those established at the beginning of the century.

The main features of traditional British practice are that candidates are selected by a lay interview panel of local authority members and school governors which is advised 'professionally' by an education officer; successful candidates are given a tenured position in a specific school (rather than a school district as in some countries). Once appointed, head teachers can remain in post for the rest of their working life, unless they voluntarily move to another school or, in very rare cases, are dismissed.

However, this situation seems likely to change. In 1984 the Government, via the Secretary of State for Education, publicly called into question the viability of the selection procedures in current use and challenged the tenure appointment principle by suggesting a period of probation for newly appointed heads. This major concern with headship selection and appointment followed publication of the Open University research — the POST project — on the selection of secondary head teachers

(Morgan *et al*, 1983). This three-year project had itself originated in the debate about the overall importance of headship for school success initiated by the 'great debate' speech of Prime Minister James Callaghan at Ruskin College Oxford in 1977, which found formal statement in the Department of Education and Science (DES) publication *Ten Good Schools* (DES, 1977). 'Without exception, [these] heads have qualities of imagination and vision, tempered by realism, which have enabled them to sum up not only their present situation, but also attainable future goals.'

The POST project had been commissioned in 1979 to 'find out what currently happens in head teacher selection; to compare it with the methods used outside education; and to propose modifications and alternatives'. Head teacher selection and appointment, as well as curriculum appropriateness, the quality of classroom teaching and appraisal of teacher performance generally, emerged from the 'great debate' as major policy concerns of central government. This chapter will summarize some of the findings of the POST project, refer to relevant selection procedures elsewhere in the world, and indicate the emerging issues as they affect innovation.

The POST project

The POST project's brief was to evaluate the selection of *secondary school heads*, within England and Wales. However, from what is well known about procedures for selecting primary school heads, as well as the empirical findings of several unpublished dissertations, POST's findings are generalizable across all maintained schools. Also, informed commentators in Scotland, having read the research report, are clear that the ways the procedures operate in England and Wales are equally applicable there. As the methodology of this research is fully described elsewhere (Morgan *et al*, 1983), it is only pertinent to make clear the main basis which the research team adopted for evaluating the evidence. This was a *job analysis to procedures match*; that is, did selectors have a clear view of the job for which they were appointing, and did the procedures in use appear to measure those competencies which a job analysis of the secondary head's duties would indicate as necessary? Four of the main findings were:

(a) selectors had a meagre knowledge of the job and used undeclared criteria;
(b) the roles of the different groups of selectors were ambiguous;
(c) the selectors used a restricted selection technology;
(d) (of most significance) non job-related factors dominated the selection decision!

Absence of job analysis and declared criteria

Selectors were not helped in their task by the absence of a written description of headship duties. In fact, among the 59 local education authorities (LEAs) visited, only one was found where a written analysis of the secondary head's job had been made, and nowhere among the 26 LEAs where appointment stages were observed did selectors have a formal job description from which to work. This did not prevent selectors individually having their own ideas on what a head does, as will be seen below. Even these individual perceptions, though, were not shared; nor were selectors observed to brief or consult each other on criteria for selection or the appointment process. All selectors were observed to bring to bear their own variable and unstated criteria on their choice of candidate. It was not therefore surprising that candidates, unsuccessful at one final interview or failing to get through the first paper stage of eliminations in some places, continued until they successfully met the combination of individuals' undeclared criteria in another place.

Selector role ambiguity

Even within the distinctive 'province' of local government selection practice in England and Wales, the selection of head teachers presents a unique context because there are two lay groups — the LEA members and school governors — who participate as the ultimate decision makers. The members and governors are advised by a third selection group: the officers; though what the status or nature of their advice is to be is nowhere formally prescribed. Therefore it was little surprise for POST to find that current practice was characterized by considerable ambiguity of roles. There was even conflict between the participating groups on the fundamental issue of accommodating the necessary technical assessment and equity for candidates, with the local needs viewpoint expressed via school governors, and the LEA members' accountability for the final appointment decision. Often there was contention as to when in the procedure, with whom, and by what methods, 'tests' of *technical competence* as distinct from *social acceptability* were to be made. In fact, the whole notion of technical assessment in the job-related areas of educational leadership and management skills, as distinct from the more social concerns of the lay members, was sometimes lacking and generally undeveloped. Indeed, not everyone accepted that it was necessary. A need for an explicit definition of role duties was invariably apparent.

A restricted selection technology

The unsure status of technical assessment was reflected in the primitive selection methods used. For example it was found that, in one-third of LEAs, heads of even the largest secondary schools can be appointed on the basis of a two-stage procedure: just one formal meeting (averaging an hour) to consider the application form and references, and a final interview in which a candidate may be seen for as little as 20 minutes. Also, half of all LEAs did not have a preliminary interview stage. This not only ensures that candidates are seen twice on a formal basis, but also provides the opportunity for officers to examine in detail professional concerns of less interest to lay members. Even in those LEAs with a preliminary stage, selection methods were, however, restricted to interviewing, and this usually on a very ill planned and unstructured basis rather than in combination with the type of written and oral exercises which have been found to have such good predictive value in other occupational contexts (Anstey, 1971). Also, there was little tradition of using other types of selectors. External assessors — for example, officers from another authority — are unknown, though external assessors are, in fact, used in the health service in Britain. Only three LEAs involved experienced head teachers in the selection process. Technically, both preliminary interviews and the selection procedures as a whole were found to be entirely dependent on the interview, a tool repeatedly shown to have low or nil predictive value (Morgan, 1973; Tenopyr, 1981).

Decisive role of non job-related factors

The most striking finding of POST's research was what did and did not count among selection criteria. Fifty-two observations were made of LEA appointment stages by the researchers 'playing the fly on the wall' and writing down the criteria statements made by the selectors. Afterwards these statements were categorized according to the idea which all panel members, whether officers, governors, or LEA members, used as eliminating criteria, whether positively to commend that a candidate go forward or be appointed, or negatively to assert that a candidate should not be considered further. The categories constructed, and examples within each category, were as follows.

1. *The right career track record.* Selectors made positive or negative statements which encapsulated their idea of what was a correct or incorrect path, independent of the quality of performance on that path. They covered notions such as: the previous pattern of posts held, right age, right type of schools to have been in, the right pace of mobility etc. For example: '35 — the right age' (positive); 'A shade on the young side at 34' (negative). For this category, and the others which follow, many more examples are given in the book reporting the research (Morgan *et al*, 1983).

2. *Education and training.* Selectors used their own judgements about the value of a particular pattern of education and training, type of qualification, or about the place where the candidate received them, to make positive or negative recommendations. For example: 'I have a naive belief in the quality of a first class honours degree' (positive); 'Don't want anyone with a first as they are too clever to employ' (negative).

3. *Quality of experience and performance to date.* For example: 'Worked hard in a difficult school' (positive); 'Very narrow experience' (negative).

4 *Fitness for the particular type of school.* Selectors used a variety of comments to convey that a candidate was fitted or unfitted for the distinct circumstances, as they saw them, of the appointing school. For example: 'Comes from this part of the world and therefore has sympathy with the kind of children we have to educate' (positive); 'Comes from a progressive school and we are appointing to a traditional one' (negative).

5. *Seal of approval.* This term was used to include a range of statements, usually based on available documents, which indicated in the mind of the selectors that they conveyed a seal of approval or disapproval. For example: 'Excellent letter of application' (positive); 'Duplicated letter of application' (negative).

6. *Motivation.* Selectors inferred judgements about candidates' motivation from their autobiographies or statements. For example: 'Candidate wants to move — he's tired of commuting' (positive); 'Is it preparation for retirement?' (negative).

7. *Previous interview performance.* Selectors sometimes knew about candidates' previous interview performance. For example: 'Did well at last interview with us' (positive); 'Doesn't make a good impression at interview' (negative).

8. *Job related skills and knowledge.* For example: 'Very good ideas about the 14+ curriculum' (positive); 'Not demonstrated enough sensitivity or leadership in his current deputy's job' (negative).

9. *Personality/personal qualities.* Selectors made judgements about candidates' personalities, personal appearance and personal qualities and used them as evaluative criteria. These may have been perceptions either from information contained in the documents or generated by seeing the person. For example: 'Tall and physically distinguished' (positive); 'Hail-fellow-well-met type' (negative).

It is important to realize that the possession of quality encapsulated in a statement by one selector can be a positive recommendation for a candidate, whereas the same quality when expressed by a different selector can damn another candidate. Given the absence of explicitly agreed criteria by all selectors before the process of elimination begins, it is inevitable that the criteria constructed individually are as varied and idiosyncratic as the selectors' views of headship and its requirements. Among the nine categories described above, what counted most reveals why current procedures fail any *job analysis to procedures match.* Table 1 on p 157 shows which of these nine categories of criteria occupy the first three places in a ranking for each of the main elimination stages.

The picture presented by Table 1 speaks for itself; only three points need to be made. First, there is a low weighting given to job-related skills and knowledge, that is, the abilities that a job analysis would indicate were necessary. In the absence of any job analysis by the employers, or a statement of job-related criteria for selectors, this finding is hardly surprising. Second, the low weighting given to the category 'the quality

Rank of criterion category	Long and shortlistings	Preliminary interviews	Final interviews
1	Personality/ personal qualities 30%	Personality/ personal qualities 42%	Personality/ personal qualities 39%
2	Right career track record 17%	Interview performance 19%	Interview performance 17%
3	Experience and performance to date 14%	Fitness for this school 10% Specific job knowledge or skills 10%	Fitness for this school 13%

The percentage figures indicate the weight of usage of that category of criteria among the nine categories used at these elimination stages.

Table 1 *Secondary head teacher selection: main criteria used*

of experience and performance to date', seems surprising at the level of common sense expectation, until one recalls that the LEAs had no formal systematic performance appraisal policies to reveal such information. This absence was well illustrated by POST's analysis of the head teacher references, where mention of a candidate's experience and performance was made in only very general terms: 'sound organizing ability', 'respected by staff', etc. Third, the decisive weighting given to personality/personal qualities stages is both surprising and to be expected: surprising, because this category is predominant at the paper stages, the long and short listings, when no candidates were present in person. This is to be explained by the fact that selectors had to hand the references which POST found to contain 'personality' mentions as their major constituent. Also, selectors were observed to construe personal qualities by projecting from information in the documents on the basis of 'feel' and 'impression' generally. It does seem that, in the absence of the controls dictated by explicit job criteria and training, the human selector has a marked penchant for the personal traits he believes are job related. This weighting given in head teacher selection to 'hunt the right personality', rather than to measure the required competencies, is wholly consistent with all major research on interviewing. This has shown that panel selectors work from their own stereotypes. These are not shared; each individual selector works from his or her own notions of the image and values appropriate for the job. At final interviews for secondary comprehensive school headships, the POST researchers found the panel members' statements frequently revealed their preferred stereotypes: 'We need a character, someone like the heads of the other two schools, someone who can compete. They are over large characters who can speak' (LEA member); '[We need] someone like my headmaster when I was at school — I went to a boys' grammar school, we all knew he was the headmaster and respected him. I look for someone like him' (LEA member); 'He [the candidate who was appointed] will look like Mr X [a local head] in 15 years' time and be just as good' (LEA member).

Selection practice in Western Europe and Scandinavia

Interestingly, in the only other major research study of headship selection which the author can find, these same factors dominate the selection process. In the United States, Baltzell and Dentler, in their 1983 research report for the National Institute of Education, present findings which in two major ways are extraordinarily similar to those revealed for Britain by POST. First, there was found to be the same absence of explicit appointment criteria — what the authors termed *criterial* specificity: 'For instance, in one district the top decision makers all spoke with sincere intensity about the primacy of "finding the best educational leaders", yet, when pressed, none could specify precisely what basic training and experience requirements this need generated for candidates — rather the respondents argued that candidates' backgrounds had to be assessed on a "case-by-case" basis'. Second, and as their main conclusion, Baltzell and Dentler identify the same decisive reliance on the unstated notions of personality found by POST:

> This lack of criterial specificity opens the way for widespread reliance on localistic notions of 'fit' or 'image' which emerged as centrally important in almost every (school) district. Every district had a deeply held image of a 'good' principal . . . or 'just what we are looking for'. This image appeared to be widely shared by central administrators, parents and principals themselves. However, time and time again, this fit seemed to rest on personal perceptions of a candidate's physical presence, projections of a certain self confidence, and assertiveness and embodiment of community values and methods of operation (Baltzell and Dentler, 1983).

Whether the process of headship selection in Scandinavia and Western Europe also relies on these same notions is not known, as no published study of the selection *process* can be found. However, in a report on selection and preparation for headship, Esp described the formal procedures (Esp, 1980). Apart from Norway, where candidates for headship in the upper secondary school are, it seems, seldom interviewed, it is the interview panel that constitutes the ubiquitous tool of selection. In Germany candidates are additionally expected to conduct a lesson under observation and to chair a simulated conference. As in Britain, scepticism among the professional participants about the efficacy of the interview is expressed, as Esp reported of a Swedish county inspector, 'You cannot tell who will be best however careful the interview or the number of people'. It seems clear, though, that innovations to traditional practice in Western Europe and Scandinavia in recent years have not concerned themselves with technical adaptation; rather with increasing participation by parents, teachers, politicians and pupils in the selection process. If head teacher selection can be seen to involve in most educational systems two different, and sometimes competing, requirements — the assessment of technical or professional abilities (however difficult these are to define) and the assessment of social acceptability or fit by the lay controllers — it is the latter category that universally engages selectors' major concern. Almost everywhere, it seems, from the evidence reported, assessment of *acceptability* in a range of social criteria is emphasized at the expense of a rigorous attempt to assess technical competence in the job-related skills of headship.

It is important to realize that in Britain, at least, this emphasis does not distinguish education from the major part of industry or commerce, though there is a widespread belief that it does. A 1980 survey of the selection of managers for British industry makes this clear: 'Companies had not changed their approach to the selection process in any significant way in the last 10 years . . . (and) executives, particularly senior executives, are largely judged on a set of personal non-ability related criteria, and by a method which is ill-suited to the task of assessing such criteria' (Institute of Personnel Management/British Institute of Management, 1980). What, then, is the 'state of the art' in the occupational selection of top leaders, and to where does one look for exemplary practice that can guide innovation within education? The POST project studied a range of what it deemed exemplary practices, each of which was characterized by the following features: rigorous job analysis and stated selection criteria; a multiple-assessment approach, ie using more 'tools' than just the interview; and a policy of evaluating the validity of the procedures, ie measuring the extent to which a particular selection tool or set of procedures were good predictors of subsequent good performance in the job. In fact, it is this latter condition that is the essential feature of 'state of the art' status, because, unless alternative features can be demonstrated to give a significantly better prediction of on-the-job success than the miserable predictive record of the interview as a selection tool, the groups who at present hold the ultimate power in head teacher selection are unlikely to be impressed by exhortations to innovate. The exemplary procedures studied by POST were: the selection of two senior managers for industry by different private management consultancy firms, selection of administrative class and executive officer entrants in the British Civil Service, the selection of senior staff in the health service, police senior command selection, and the National Association of Secondary School Principals (NASSP) assessment centre policy in the USA. The findings of these studies of selection external to education are discussed elsewhere (Morgan *et al*, 1983), and here it is relevant only to consider the NASSP assessment centre policy which is remarkable for two reasons.

First, it is an assessment process which has been pioneered by the secondary heads themselves through their union. Second, it is an assessment process which concentrates heavily on specific skill dimensions of headship and places considerably less emphasis on experience or career track criteria *per se*. It aims to assess these skills by a battery of analogous tests, which are exercises designed to simulate real work demands, and structured interviews (Hersey, 1980).

The National Association of Secondary School Principals' exercises have been the subject of a validation study (Schmitt *et al*, 1982). Schmitt found that the exercises designed to provide information on the skill dimensions of headship met this purpose, and confirmed that the skills tested were relevant to headship. NASSP assessment centres are attended by 12 participants at a time, who have been identified according to specified criteria as eligible in each school district. Each centre has a team of six assessors, including principals and other administrators from school districts and the county office. All assessors have successfully completed 30 hours of residential training before undertaking assessor duties. They work to a detailed Manual for Assessors prepared by NASSP, in which every exercise, together with the criteria and behaviour to be observed and recorded, is set out. Marking schemes are provided, with 5-point rating scales of the behaviour to be sought and descriptions of what constitutes that behaviour.

The NASSP package came about because of the widespread belief that candidates in conventional selection procedures are rarely observed or evaluated with regard to their performance of skills needed on the job. Typically, appointments were made with little more than an educated guess of potential administrative abilities. In other words, the NASSP approach was tackling a selection process resembling the one that POST found operating in England and Wales. The purpose of the assessment centre approach was to ensure that elimination decisions would in future be based on the skills vital to good headship performance. Twelve skill dimensions to be assessed were derived by a job study that covered the tasks and responsibilities set out in the job descriptions and perform-ance appraisal instruments used by school districts, and as described in interviews with people with a thorough knowledge of the job.

In order to test these skills, NASSP has devised a variety of situational or analogous tests which allow an assessment to be made on the basis of each candidate's observed performance. In addition, personal interviews lasting two hours are held with each candidate. The final assessment report prepared on each participant is based on collation and discussion of individual assessors' scores and comments on each of the activities. Once the assessment programme is completed, each candidate receives a four-page assessment report. Although the NASSP assessment centres do not make decisions about selection for headship, the information generated about the participants' state of readiness for headship is available to school districts if they wish to use it when an appointment is to be made.

The significance of the NASSP methods is that, like the British Civil Service, police senior command selection, and (in part) the health service, they apply rigorous definitions of the job competences required, analogous tests, and in-depth structured interviews, all of which have been absent in educational circles and most of industry in the UK. In addition to observing and describing the existing practices the POST project carried out action research in 10 LEAs to test the feasibility of applying these three features in actual headship appointments. In devising their tests, POST drew extensively on NASSP and British Civil Service experience. POST found that many selectors expressed a greater sense of security about making decisions based on a wider variety of more systematically collected evidence using analogous tests and a better range of prepared interviews.

Conclusions

The POST research and its 50-plus recommendations have received unusual support by central government in the form of additional funding to prepare a handbook on selecting senior staff for schools (Morgan *et al*, 1984). In 1984, the Government called for a national conference representing LEAs, governors and teachers to discuss the issues. Recently, the White Paper, *Better Schools* (HMSO, 1985), drew the attention of LEAs and governors 'to the more detailed recommendations in the report of the Open University research'. The White Paper makes it clear that there will be legislation to establish the main features of the procedure for appointing a head teacher in maintained schools, but whether these will specify the nature of the technical assessments that should be carried out is not known. It does, however, indicate that the Government has dropped the idea of a probationary period for newly appointed heads — 'assessment of the suitability of newly appointed head teachers is best pursued as part of a general appraisal system embracing all teachers' (HMSO, 1985: 56). In the meantime, some LEAs have changed their selection procedures and are using some of the exemplary practices discussed above. For example, Table 2 on p 162 shows the preliminary 'interview' programme devised by a metropolitan borough authority to assess candidates for two secondary headships.

However, despite the public impact of the research report, in mid-1985 LEAs appeared to be changing their headship selection procedures only very slowly. In fact, the author has evidence that innovative head teachers in the selection of their teaching staff are more prepared than the LEAs to move into exemplary practices, especially with the application of oral and written analogous tests. The present slow pace of change within education authorities may be explained by the fact that the rigorous systematization of the selection process which innovation would bring at the same time would eliminate or considerably reduce officer patronage. This was a topic discussed in the research report, where a tradition of patronage was seen to be one of the greater blocks to reforming head teacher selection practices.

Whether the necessary changes are eventually achieved by legislation or, more likely, by a gradual dispersion of best practice, they will need to ensure the accommodation of two requirements which can be seen

Wednesday 4th May	
9.15 am	— Arrival
9.30 am – 10 am	— Introduction to programme (Committee Room 4, Council Suite)
10 am – 12 noon approx.	— Visit to school A
12.15 pm – 1.30 pm	— Lunch at teachers' centre
1.45 pm – 3 pm	— Visit to school B
Friday 6th May	
9.15 am	— Arrival reception office, education department
9.30 am – 9.45 am	— Introductory session (Committee Room 4, Council Suite)
9.45 am – 10.30 am	— Crisis management exercise Part 1 (Committee Rooms 1 and 4, Council Suite)
10.30 am – 11.30 am	— In-basket exercise
11.30 am – 1.00 pm	— Crisis management exercise part 2
2 pm onwards	— Individual interviews in the education department (Deputy Director and Chief Inspector)

Table 2 *The secondary headships preliminary programme of one LEA*

as conflicting: the need for impartial technical assessment methods to gather the evidence of candidate fitness for headship; and the need to satisfy demands for a visible democratic accountability and social legitimation by the local community.

References

Anstey, E (1971) The Civil Service administrative class: a follow up of post war entrants *Occupational Psychology* **45** 1: 27-43

Baltzell, C D and Dentler, R A (1983) *Selecting American School Principals: A Research Report* Abt Associates: Cambridge, Mass

Department of Education and Science (1977) *Ten Good Schools: A Secondary School Enquiry* Her Majesty's Stationery Office: London

Department of Education and Science (1985) *Better Schools* (Cmnd 9469) Her Majesty's Stationery Office: London

Esp, D (1980) Selection and training of secondary school senior staff: some European examples *Education* **156** 16: 1-4 (October)

Hersey, P (1980) NASSP's Assessment Center: practitioners speak out *National Association of Secondary School Principals Bulletin* **64** 439: 87-117

Institute of Personnel Management/British Institute of Management (1980) *Selecting Managers — How British Industry Recruits* IPM information report 34. BIM Management Survey Report: London

Morgan, C E, Hall, V and Mackay, H (1984) *The Selection of Secondary School Headteachers* The Open University Press: Milton Keynes

Morgan, C, Hall, V and Mackay, H (1984) *A Handbook on Selecting Senior Staff for Schools* The Open University Press: Milton Keynes

Morgan, T (1973) Recent insights into the selection interview *Personnel Review*:
    4-13
Schmitt, N *et al* (1982) *Criterion-Related and Content Validity of the NASSP Assess-
    ment Center* Research Report. Department of Psychology, Michigan State Uni-
    versity: East Lansing
Tenopyr, M L (1981) The realities of employment testing *American Psychologist*
    36 10: 1120-27

12. Linking school and community: some management issues

John Rennie

Summary: This chapter begins by looking at the historical antecedents in the community education field, particularly in the USA and UK, and goes on to point out some modern developments.

The chapter highlights six management issues for the community school which differ from those found in the 'ordinary' school. From these it draws attention to new challenges arising from changing societal factors.

Finally, the chapter examines likely future outcomes and recommends an approach from the UK which sees schools becoming 'neighbourhood learning centres'.

Introduction

'Comprehensivization' was the first great wave of change to hit education in the UK following the immediate post-war establishment of the tripartite system, which was a division of children, usually at age 11, purely on the grounds of academic ability. The transformation of separate and socially divisive schools into 'all-in' schools took a painful 20 years or so to implement, and even now is barely complete. Yet already a groundswell has built up for a second major shift, and this an even more significant one. In simple terms it is usually referred to as 'going community' — opening schools to all ages, with premises open throughout the year from early morning to late at night, and offering a much wider range of choice of activity than the narrowly academic or technical.

Worldwide, there are a number of antecedents for this latest and most radical of developments. Americans would point to the pioneering work of Frank Manley *et al* in Michigan (1961) and the flowering there of community schools — through what has become known as the 'Flint model' since it is in the city of Flint that the Manley principles have been most clearly accepted. Equally evident strands can be seen in schools influenced by John Dewey in the Phillipines; in community movements influenced by Ghandi in India; in Grundwig's folk high-schools in Scandinavia, in Australia, Eire, Trinidad, Israel and Colombia. In the UK, the seminal thinker was Henry Morris. This most unusual of education administrators was Chief Education Officer of Cambridgeshire, a rural English county, in the late 1920s when he first promoted the notion of 'village colleges' as educational and social magnets for people of all ages. His vision led to the building of imaginatively designed colleges which were aimed to look not like schools but rather the attractive centres of community life which they eventually became.

Morris's ideals and ideas were copied in very few places. Secondary education in the UK retained its traditional pattern until the late 1960s when two parallel influences came to bear. First, comprehensives were beginning to achieve a broader acceptance and with this came a growing awareness that expensive resources could not sensibly be made inaccessible to those who had paid for them through taxes. 'Dual-use' became a catch-phrase: schools in the day, evening centres at night — an echo of the 'night-schools' of an earlier generation. Second, a radical philosophy of parental and community involvement began to emerge in the primary sector of education, fuelled by the government-funded Education Priority Area Project (EPA) in five disadvantaged urban areas. The most radical thinker and energetic activist in this movement was Eric Midwinter (1972). He was also the most prolific writer to emerge from the movement and his many books provided a persuasive and analytical advocacy which is still drawn on and which influenced a new generation of teachers, community educators and government programmes.

Gradually, such thinking seeped into the secondary sector and the rural community school concept began to find urban expression in Coventry, Leicester, Walsall and elsewhere. Owing as much to Midwinter (1972) and the notion of 'positive discrimination' expounded in the Plowden Report (HMSO, 1972) as to Henry Morris and the 'dual-use' concept (Rée, 1985), these community schools are forging new roles for secondary schools which are increasingly seen as the natural and inevitable developments of the comprehensive school. Given that the primary schools in the UK are arguably even more community-orientated than the secondaries, there is now a broad platform on which community education is being built.

Management implications

In the train of such developments have come a host of management issues, most of them new to the field of education but all of them of a complexity and intensity which has begun to demand a thorough-going reappraisal of the whole concept of school management and the establishment of appropriate training strategies. The British head teacher, as the title implies, is a teacher; this means he or she is unlikely to have the background or training of, for example, the US school administrator. This may give the British principal an educational advantage over his or her American counterpart but, in theory at least, leaves him in a disadvantageous position in terms of management expertise. What follows is a closer look at six management issues faced by the head of a British community college.

First, how will the community dimension of the school be managed? Many of the original community secondaries simply appointed a 'head of community activities' — invariably a teacher but with the main task of establishing adult education classes, youth groups, pre-school groups and the like. At best, this led to nothing more than sophisticated 'dual-use' approaches. More adventurous places opted for a 'community deputy' — a model which is the most prevalent one nowadays — recognizing the importance of the community dimension in the management structure of the school, and placing the community deputy alongside the academic deputy and the pastoral deputy. Even more enlightened authorities encouraged all the members of school senior management teams to accept a community dimension to their role.

In this model, the community school is seen not as a separate entity, tacked on to the school and perhaps using the building at a different time of day; rather it is seen as a totality of school and community, together sharing resources and facilities, human and otherwise, across the board.

This points up a major difference between the UK system and the Flint model (Manley, 1961), for example. In the latter, the 'Director of Community School' is a combination of the old British 'Head of Evening Centre' and the still-existing 'Head of Community Activities'. It has led US community educators to talk of the need for links between the community school and the regular schools programme. The best of the British community schools would not understand the discussion — they see the two being inextricably joined as parts of the same process.

Second, how will the community participate in making decisions about the community college? Many European systems, centralized as they are, cannot begin to develop such notions which are essentially de-centralist in concept. The US Community Council model, on the other hand, is a democratic demonstration of the potential effectiveness of community participation — albeit for only a part (the 'Community School') of the total enterprise. The British 'managing and governing bodies', ranging as they do from narrowly politically sectarian bodies to others with varying degrees of democratic control and much wider representation, present a much cloudier picture. A decentralized education system, for all its strengths, is always likely to result in one of the hundred or so different systems operating in England and Wales. The Taylor Report (1977) recommended that there should be broader representation on governing bodies, and some authorities responded. Current government thinking seems to be that power will be wrenched from local politicians and handed over to parents — a simplistic exchange of control from one vested interest group to another and a denial of all the demands for genuine partnership which community educators have called for so often in recent years. It can only be stressed that community participation will flourish in direct proportion to the places available to the community on governing bodies, to management support for pro-active programmes encouraging and enabling such participation to flourish, to the devolution of power, whether from central or local government, and to governing bodies over issues concerned directly with the health of the institution.

Third, assuming that community participation will have been successful in identifying community needs, who will induct and support staff in the roles which are required to meet such needs?

It would not be unusual in community colleges to find staff organizing informal adult education groups in a variety of settings away from the school — 'outreach' in current parlance; to be offering training, on-site or off it, to leaders of local pre-school groups; to be organizing luncheon clubs for pensioners; to be arranging with local sports clubs new leisure opportunities for unemployed workers. These, and a host of other activities, demand far more than the traditional pedagogic skills of the teacher. They require skills more likely to be found in the adult educator, the youth worker, the social worker or community developer. The manager's task is not simply to encourage a generalist approach to such activities — this is always desirable but has palpable inherent dangers; it is also to identify skill requirements and sources of training and to ensure the deployment of appropriately trained and supported staff in using such skills. A far cry, indeed, from the old grammar school head timetabling the match of a given number of teachers to a limited range of academic subjects!

Fourth, what extra facilities will be provided and who will manage them? In the UK, there is no pattern of provision which could confidently be described as 'typical'. There are, though, certain basic facilities found almost always in a community school which appear much more rarely in ordinary schools. These are such things as floodlit all-weather playing surfaces, a sports hall, a swimming pool, a theatre, and a community lounge (a social area with a soft drinks bar). Other sites offer an increasingly wide range of provision and it is not uncommon to find squash courts, a ski slope or other more luxurious facilities. In at least two local authorities, community schools have a licensed bar, open only in the evenings.

All of these facilities create a dilemma for management. Are they to be strictly part of an *educational* provision — with the implication that they are provided for local people rather than on an open access basis? Are they to be used by adults as much as pupils during the day and vice versa in the evenings? Are they therefore to be a part of the mainstream responsibilities of the head teacher? Enlightened authorities have answered all these questions affirmatively. The Head is usually the licensee of the bar (though not the steward), and is responsible for the administration of the facilities during opening hours. No hint, then, of passing responsibility for evening use, say, to another person or another department. Of course, primary responsibility for any given facility rests with the specialist member of staff appointed — the head of PE often becomes the head of community sport and recreation, for example. But all of them answer managerially to the head teacher.

An alternative structure, fortunately much less common, treats additional facilities as a leisure outlet. They are then offered to allcomers on a commercial basis. No pretence is made of extending educational provision and no sense of ownership of the facilities on the part of the community can be felt. The structure's main aim is cost-effectiveness and does not take into account social and educational gains and losses.

An allied management issue is the whole question of financial control. It is not unusual in community secondary schools for as many as 8,000 people to come through the doors, each week, of a building with perhaps 1,200 full-time pupils. Spending money on courses, sports facilities, bars etc, they can generate as much as £200,000 per annum turnover. It would not be unusual for a community school to have eight or nine separate accounts to deal with such sums. At the very least, there is a clear need to strengthen the administrative back-up in the institution. One or two authorities have seen fit to appoint registrars in community schools — administrative officers responsible for all non-academic staff, financial control, etc who participate in the senior management of the school. Once again, the level and nature of the managerial control will be determined by the philosophical decisions taken about the purpose of the provision.

Fifth, once a school opens itself to its community it becomes, willy-nilly, part of a network of agencies meeting the needs of that community in a variety of ways. Put another way, once the gates of the citadel are open, a two-way street is created and the school cannot shirk the implications of that fact. Inter-agency collaboration becomes not merely a desirable goal, but an essential prerequisite for survival.

One of the major errors made by some newly established community schools has been to take over, in effect, other organizations, often voluntary ones, offering services to its community. An ailing youth club, perhaps existing in inadequate premises with volunteer leaders, may be easily seduced into using the plusher facilities of a newly-built community school. Existing pre-school groups, pensioners' clubs and the like are equally susceptible to such blandishments. This, of course, is the antithesis of community education. One can understand the pressure of an authority's expectations on a new school to 'deliver', but if the delivery is effected at the expense of existing provision it can effectively destroy the roots of community regeneration instead of nurturing them. Rather, schools should be seeking to support ongoing initiatives through outreach programmes and attempting to complement the services they provide by identifying, in conjunction with other agencies, unmet needs in the community. Coordinating the needs assessment process is itself a demanding management task. The ensuing problem of how to balance new provision with support for that already in existence can be even more demanding.

Machinery designed to facilitate such sensitive tasks is available. The US community schools' community council is, of course, one example. In the UK, the 'fieldwork forum' is a very commonly used strategy. Here, all the professionals and voluntary bodies who serve a particular neighbourhood will meet fairly informally on perhaps a monthly basis, often at lunchtime.

The forum is used as an exchange for news and information, a sounding board for new ideas, and a panel for assessing current programmes.

The prudent manager of a community school will need, though, to take account of community groups other than those which are likely to appear in the fieldwork forum. What are the local pressure groups and who are the influential leaders? Are their aims shared by the school or could they be in conflict? If such questions are not addressed by the school, the outcome might be, at best, a missed opportunity to share in meeting genuine need, at worst a clash between school and community which could damage the fabric of the whole community dimension of the school.

Similarly, the school might provide a focus for groups with shared interests working in the neighbourhood — for example all the early childhood initiatives. By making a specific contribution to such groups, whether it be by offering training facilities, coordinating fund-raising or simply providing an additional programme, the school can keep in touch with the needs and aspirations of any given set of interests and ensure its own integral role.

Finally, and perhaps crucially, what link into the local authority's own management structure is provided for the head of the institution? There seems to be a direct parallel between the senior management structure of a local authority's education department and that of a community school. Just as a school which sees the community dimension as being peripheral is likely to hive off responsibility for it to a relatively junior member of staff, so an authority with similar views might entrust its administrative role to, say, a fourth-tier officer.

It is no coincidence that those local authorities with proven track records in the field of community education are those led by chief officers with the foresight not only to give responsibility for administration to a senior member of the department, but also to ensure the integration of community education policies into the mainstream education service. Not surprisingly, these chief officers are themselves personally committed to the principles of community education. Though a local authority's structure cannot influence the head of an individual school, it can nevertheless have a profound effect on a head's capacity to manage the school.

Emerging challenges

Clearly, any community school, or even an 'ordinary' school seeking to operate with greater relevance within its community context, will find itself addressing the specific needs of its neighbourhood. There are, however, several sets of needs which transcend boundaries of country, social class or ethnic group, and all these have been growing more pressing over the last decade.

Of these, unemployment is at once the most damaging and, apparently, the most insoluble. Nobody doubts that there is sufficient work to be shared by all. Macro-economic decisions, however, seem to have forced people into responding to unemployment with palliatives and placebos on the one hand or complacency and 'victim-blaming' on the other. All the indicators are that the problem will worsen considerably over the next decade unless there is a fundamental change in approach to work-sharing and/or a basic change of attitude in society towards what constitutes work and leisure.

Community schools are on the receiving end of macro-economic decisions, just as much as any other organization. They cannot reverse major trends or shift government policies. They can, though, provide bases for experimental work in small businesses, youth enterprise, co-operatives, and alternative life styles which could influence decision makers in the wider community. Such developments would mean a further extension of the whole concept of education and would mean educationists entering into partnerships with businessmen, leisure industries, and government agencies. The few who have trodden this path so far have had encouraging signs of success.

Advances in medical care and in family planning techniques together have influenced the age profile of all Western societies. Ageing populations are now the norm and not only in advanced industrial nations. This is a situation which is changing the nature of demands being made upon community schools. In most parts of the UK, for example, there are more pensioners than children in schools. How long will it be before a school is closed in order to turn it into a 'senior centre'? How soon will the educational needs of retired people outweigh those of all the younger age groups? The development in France of universities of the 'Troisième Age', followed by Third Age education in Britain and 'Elderhostels' in the USA and elsewhere, are exciting indications of a practical recognition of a new situation. Managing a community school's response to educational needs of older people is a challenge which is clearly going to continue to grow.

Divorce and remarriage are social phenomena found in all Western countries on an increasing scale. One-parent families, seen only ten years ago as a problem, have had the social stigma removed and are now seen as but one, albeit important, strand in a changing pattern of family structures. Imaginative educationists are designing family education programmes which recognize the more fluid, ever-changing nature of the educational needs of such families. What has emerged is particularly interesting in that the style of such programmes has become at least as important as the content. Didactic teaching methods are increasingly seen as irrelevant, and participative modes, adopting a 'negotiated curriculum' approach, are proving much more effective. The challenge to management, then, exists to ensure appropriate styles of service delivery as much as to identify the required programmes.

Future conditional

If schools are to take the dramatic step of accepting the challenge of 'going community', there needs to be political support for them at both local and central government levels. The community school movement is as much in its infancy in the UK at present as were the comprehensives in the late 1950s. Its advocates find themselves cast in the same proselytizing role as their counterparts then. Once again, different models and different structures abound, but what are the over-arching ideals which bind them together as a recognizable whole?

Perhaps, above all, there is the belief that communities have within them the seeds of their own salvation, that their peoples can be helped to influence their own destinies. This is no naive failure to recognize the influence of the major factors mentioned in the last section, but a conviction that, whatever the circumstances, people eventually must join together to face their own problems and opportunities.

A concomitant thread is the recognition that educational needs exist and change throughout life. Community education should cater for everyone from the very young to the very old.

Equally important is the conviction that educational expertise is neither the sole preserve of professionals nor a fixed and rigid process inaccessible to all but a few. Open access is a by-word of community education. By the same token, 'each one teach one', coined for self-help programmes in Third World countries, has proved to be yet one more example of how those countries have so much to teach their supposedly more highly developed cousins.

A parallel belief is that education is a collaborative activity — that competition is inappropriate for true learning to take place. This is manifested in a number of ways. For example, the notion of inter-agency collaboration is an institutional indicator of it. Group projects in the classroom or community involvement in teaching are also pedagogic indicators.

How will the current disparate trends be welded into a more coherent whole in the future? A document recently produced by the Coventry local education authority in England called 'Comprehensive Education for Life' (1984) describes a future which its own schools are already beginning to forge. It sees schools not as teaching agencies for the young but as 'neighbourhood learning centres' for the whole of the community, throughout life. Further, the constitution of these centres is that of community centres, inside which exist schools. Such a radical proposal amounts to no less than a root and branch transformation of the school system and leaves such notions as 'linking school and community' far behind. It leads inevitably to a position where the boundaries between the two are virtually non-existent, where both are interdependent, and where power is shared. If these centres succeed, they will have implications for schools and their communities not only in the rest of the UK but in many other countries as well. Given the rate at which society is changing, it will surely be only through the establishment of flexible, responsive yet proactive institutions such as these that education will be able to play a full role in the total life of our communities.

References

Coventry Education Committee (1984) *Comprehensive Education for Life: A Consultative Document* Coventry Education Committee: Coventry

Department of Education and Science (1967) *Children and Their Primary Schools (The Plowden Report)* HMSO: London

Department of Education and Science (1977) *A New Partnership For Our Schools (The Taylor Report)* HMSO: London

Manley, F J, Reed, B W and Burns, R K (1961) *The Community School in Action: The Flint Program* Industrial Relations Center, Education-Industry Service, University of Chicago: Chicago

Midwinter, E C (1972) *Priority Education: An Account of the Liverpool Project* Penguin: Harmondsworth

Rée, H (1985) *Educator Extraordinary: The Life and Achievement of Henry Morris 1889-1961* Peter Owen: London

13. School management and administration: an analysis by gender

Patricia A Schmuck

Summary: In all Western countries women are a distinct minority in management and administrative positions in schools. They are most highly represented as teachers and managers in primary schools and their proportion decreases as one moves up the age-graded hierarchy of schools. In all cases, women's representation as managers is disproportionately lower than their representation as teachers. Three theoretical perspectives are discussed to explain this phenomenon: differences in socialization, the organizational constraints to women's mobility and gender-based career socialization. Two of the theories are criticized for their use of gender as explanatory rather than as problematic. Gender is an overlay for educational institutions; we must turn our attention to the subtle processes which influence gender segregation in the workplace.

Women constitute a majority of teachers and a minority of managers and administrators in schools in the Western world. These two facts emerge despite cultural differences in school organizational structure, educational roles, hiring practices, seniority systems, preparatory programmes, and educational opportunities. There are other relevant facts about women as educators in their roles as school managers and administrators which also transcend cultural and national boundaries, despite each country's unique configuration of schooling.

For instance, women's role as educational professionals is related to educational opportunity for girls. Women's entrance into the modern-day systems of education happened in most countries during the industrialization period and the pressure for common schools for all students, including girls (Van Essen, 1986; Schmuck, 1986; Brehmer, 1986; Sysiharju, 1986; Fenwick, 1986; Sampson, 1986).

The social ideology concerning women's place in the educational realm has changed over the years. In all countries, at some time, women have been excluded from the profession. It was not considered their proper place. This ideology changed, however, to the view that education was a proper role for women. Also, in all countries married women were, at some time, excluded from the profession. It was seen as detracting from their primary role as wife and mother; yet now it is seen as an ideal profession; the working hours and summer vacations allow women to contribute to the profession and fulfil their family obligations simultaneously

(Reynolds, 1986; 1986; Van Essen, 1986; Schmuck, 1986; Sysiharju, 1986; Fenwick, 1986; Sampson, 1986).

Women's presence as educators is also related to labour market trends; during war time or in affluent times women are more highly represented in education. Women's rate of participation in education decreases when there is a large supply of men available for the educational market (Spender, 1984; Enders-Dragasser, 1986).

Women's representation in education is also related to the access of other professional roles; today, in the United States, fewer women are seeking careers in education than previously (Adkinson, 1981; Shulman and Sykes, 1983).

Sex-segregated employment patterns are related to sex-segregated educational systems. In schools for girls only, women appear in a variety of roles: as teachers of various subject matter, as teachers of the elementary and secondary schools and as educational managers. In coeducational systems, however, women appear in more restricted roles; they are primarily the teachers of young children, their number decreases at the secondary level and they are segregated into certain subject matter areas (Schmuck, 1986; Sysiharju, 1986; Fenwick, 1986; Sampson, 1986).

In all educational systems, managers and administrators are drawn from the ranks of teachers. Yet in all coeducational systems, despite the greater proportion of women in the ranks of teachers, women are disproportionately under-represented in educational governance. They are in a minority among principals and district officers.

These macro-social patterns provide a gender overview of employment in educational systems and they are inextricably intertwined with women's lack of representation in school management and administration. But what are the processes at work which differentiate male and female employment in schools? That is the concern of this chapter. First, I will describe women's representation as school managers and administrators in some Western countries. Second, I will present three theories to explain women's absence as school managers and administrators and show how these theories have been applied in practice. Finally, I will show how two of these theories are faulty; they have used gender as an explanatory variable rather than as a manipulable variable in thinking about educational institutions and the roles women have performed. There is an exciting area of scholarship that has arisen in the last decade — one that enables us to look at educational institutions, as well as other instituions, without the blinding assumptions about gender that have guided research and theory in the past. It is hoped that this article will lay to rest some of these blinding assumptions.

Women's representation in educational management and administration

In all Western countries women are a distinct minority in management and administrative positions in schools. When they are represented they tend to be heads of schools at the primary level or provide support services to students. While this generalization holds true for all countries studied, some qualification is necessary about sources of data.

Qualifications about data

In the United States educational employment data have not always been gathered by sex for each specified role, and furthermore the categories of educational management often differ between districts and do not stay constant over time. The data are elusive and often incomplete (Jones and Montenegro, 1982). This problem is amplified when we consider cross-cultural comparisons. Different educational structures call for different role specifications. For instance, in Australia, New Zealand and Britain there are distinct divisions of teacher, head teacher, headships, senior headships which do not exist in other countries. In the Netherlands and Belgium there are different systems of free and 'public' schooling available and the data depend on which system has been studied. In the United States, with its local control of schools, the role of district superintendent is unique. Cross-cultural comparison of management or administration is difficult. In this chapter I have presented data about heads of schools or heads of districts. The data are for different times, so year by year comparisons are not possible. However, the pattern emerges clearly despite the flaws in the data: women are most highly represented in primary schools as teachers and managers and their proportion decreases as one moves up the age-graded hierarchy or the educational hierarchy. In all cases, women's representation as managers is disproportionately lower than their representation as teachers.

Women as managers of schools and administrators of districts

In the United States women comprise about 67 per cent of teachers and about 25 per cent of school administrators; there are about 20 per cent female elementary school principals and about 8 per cent female secondary school principals. As district superintendents they are less than 2 per cent (Schmuck, 1986). In Great Britain, in the primary schools women constitute 77 per cent of teachers and 43 per cent of headships; at the secondary level they are 43 per cent of teachers and 18 per cent of headships (Byrne, 1978: 218). In Finland, at the elementary level women are 62 per cent of the teachers and 6 per cent of the principals. At the secondary level they are 62 per cent of the teachers and 19 per cent of the heads (Sysiharju, 1986). In New Zealand they are 66 per cent of primary teachers and 13 per cent principals; at the secondary level they are 48 per cent female teachers and 15 per cent principals (Fenwick, 1986). In Canada, women are 65 per cent teachers and 8 per cent principals (Reynolds, 1986). In Australia, women constitute 71 per cent of the primary teachers and 25 per cent of primary principals; at the secondary level women are 49 per cent of the teachers and 13 per cent of the principals (Sampson, 1986).

Theories and critiques of the theories

In the following section I will review three theories used to explain women's skewed representation as managers and administrators in schools and their action applications. I will also present critiques of two of these theories which have arisen from the new understandings about gender issues in the workplace. The three theories are individual socialization processes, organizational constraints to women's mobility, and gender-based career socialization.

Socialization theories

In the educational hierarchy one becomes a manager or an administrator by being in the pool of qualified teachers and advancing 'up' the hierarchy. The question is, why do women, who comprise the majority of teachers, become fewer and fewer in number as one rises up the educational career ladder? There have been two standard approaches to answering this question. The first approach has been to look at the differences between men and women teachers — the qualified pool of applications — to determine their attributional differences. The second approach has been to study those women who have arrived in positions of management or administration and try to ferret out what makes their lives or careers similar and dissimilar to men who have followed such paths. These two approaches have dominated the educational literature from the 1950s until about the late 1970s.

The socialization studies have shown some differences between men and women in the teaching ranks. These studies support, in part, the portrait of the female school teachers drawn by earlier studies on the profession of teaching (Lortie, 1975). These earlier studies, however, were drawn more from the cultural assumptions about women's place in the educational workforce rather than on collected evidence (Acker, 1983; Biklen, 1985). Some of the socialization findings show that men entered education to enable them to have career mobility — women entered education to be of service to children; men entered education to earn the family income — women entered education to supplement the family income or to support themselves if they were not married; men tended to remain in education — women left for child bearing and rearing; men needed new challenges and were not satisfied with being classroom teachers — women were content to be classroom teachers. Differing personal ambitions, differing life responsibilities and differing orientations to work were offered as explanations for the few women in management positions (Adkinson, 1981; Havens, 1980; Schmuck, 1975).

And these socialization studies influenced the early research on women in educational administration. In the United States, with the impact of the women's movement, there was a plethora of research documenting the absence of women in educational management. Shakeshaft (1981) completed an analysis of 114 doctoral dissertations about women in educational administration completed in the United States between 1973 and 1979. About 25 per cent of these dissertations described the women who had achieved positions of leadership. By questionnaires and interviews, guided by the socialization literature, differences were found between men and women. By and large, women who achieved such positions were 'exceptions' to the normal rule. However, as Shakeshaft points out, the 'normal' rule is considered the male rule; the research presents men as the norm and women as deviations from the norm. Women who were administrators tended to be older, had had more teaching experience, were less often married, less often had children or had older children than their male counterparts. While the pre-socialization or pre-placement patterns of men and women were different, there were few or no differences found between men and women once they entered the career path of management, nor were there differences in their behaviour as managers or administrators (Paddock, 1981; Gross and Trask, 1976; Charters and Jovick, 1981).

Action applications of the socialization theories

This research has been helpful in substantiating the differences between males and females in education and has led to training and education for women to compensate for their perceived deficiencies in socialization. Implied throughout these programmes has been the use of the male as the model; women are perceived as the exceptions to the norm. Books such as *Women Getting Together and Getting Ahead*, conferences, workshops, meetings and newsletters on general topics such as 'institutional sexism' to more specific topics such as 'interviewing for a job' have been on the agenda of groups such as Northwest Women in Educational Administration, or the Northeast Coalition of Educational Leaders. These are established professional groups which continue to serve as advocates and supports for women teachers aspiring to educational management (Shakeshaft, 1981; Smith, Kalvelage and Schmuck, 1980).

Critique of the socialization theory approach

There are several problems to this approach. First, it embellishes the male definition of the 'appropriate' motivations and ambitions for advancement in education; the implication is that if one wants to be an educational leader one must follow the prescriptions based on male subjects. Thus, women are 'blamed' for not possessing the prerequisite motivation or ambition to enter administration. Second, this psychological orientation is simplistic; it does not account for the complex interactions between personal motives and the structure of institutions. It does not account for the influences that institutions have upon the career motives and aspirations of workers. Third, these studies imply a historical constancy when, in fact, the motives and ambitions of personnel in the education work force change over time. Indeed, in the United States at one time women held the majority of elementary principalships (Schmuck, 1986). While these studies may well represent women of a certain age cohort during the 1950s and 1960s, there is some evidence of change in attitudes and aspirations of the newer and younger cohort of women in schools (Edson, 1981; Havens, 1980). Finally, the most significant drawback of this approach is the treatment of these psychological variables as causes in the natural course of events. These 'facts' about sex differentiation in the personal motives of men and women personnel are treated as explanatory rather than as problematic. As Sandra Acker (1983: 132) says, 'The sequence of events and decisions may be more complex than is usually appreciated . . . the strong numerical presence of women in certain senior posts . . . suggests modifications need to be made to any generalized thesis about women's reluctance to seek promotion. Under what circumstances do women seek promotion? And under what circumstances are women actively sought or encouraged to apply for promotion? Researchers should ask these questions rather than simply repeat commonsense views about women.' These socialization arguments do not explain — they merely describe a state of affairs at a given time period and offer little explanatory power.

Organizational constraints to women's mobility

Since the 1970s, researchers have focused on the structure of educational institutions and the barriers confronting women in educational leadership. This more macro, sociological perspective has focused on institutions rather than on individuals. As one moves up the educational hierarchy there is a winnowing of women at each level. Why? The approach used to answer this question has been to identify the variables involved in promotion and advancement and to point out the structural factors that differentiate males and females each step of the way. Several variables have emerged; among them are the 'grooming' and recruitment of male teachers, sex-biased preparatory programmes in institutions of higher education, the preference for males in sponsoring and mentoring future administrators, the lack of female role models for women teachers, differential opportunities for male and females to exhibit leadership, and male domination on selection committees which leads to discrimination in hiring (Shakeshaft, 1981; Ortiz and Marshall, 1986; Ortiz, 1982). At each step of administrative preparation, job seeking and selection, there are organizational processes which clearly indicate a preference for males.

Action applications of the organizational constraints theory

The perspective on organizational constraints has been instrumental in guiding the formation of policy and law concerning sex discrimination in educational institutions. The equal opportunity legislation of Title IX (concerning educational institutions) and Title VII (concerning employment generally) specifically focuses on the structures and practices which result in the under-representation of women in certain positions. Affirmative action, procedures outlined for fair hiring practices, district policy statements on equal opportunity and grievance processes are examples of institutional procedures to break down the barriers of sex discriminatory practices. Federal, State and local policy and structures for implementation and enforcement designed to provide equal opportunity have met with some measure of success in some districts (Schmuck *et al*, 1985). But the fact remains that there is often a wide gap between policy and practice. And the national sentiment and current administrative practices in the United States are seriously eroding the positive gains made from such legislation.

Critique of the organizational constraint perspective

Despite specific regulations prohibiting sex discrimination in educational institutions, the portrait of the school as a sex-segregated institution remains unaltered. The number of women in educational management and administration in the United States has not significantly altered. For instance, in the state of Oregon in 1977-78 all administrative openings were followed through from their advertised openings to the final selection. There were approximately 300 different openings in 129 different school districts. Women comprised about 19 per cent of the applicant pool. Women also comprised 22 per cent of those hired, but the portrait of Oregon public schools remained unchanged. Women remained represented in those jobs previously primarily held by women; men remained represented in those jobs previously primarily held by men (Schmuck and Wyant, 1981). How is it that organizations reproduce themselves despite changes in personnel and despite laws prohibiting sex discrimination?

This perspective identifies the structural variables which tend to sort out men and women in career mobility. It does not, however, explain the processes at work; it does not explain how, what Dale Spender refers to as, 'gender codes' operate within institutions. It does not account for the overarching tenet in all the facts about educational institutions — their androcentrism. In theory and in practice, the image of the school leader is male.

In practice, men hold the primary positions of responsibility and authority; they are the 'gatekeepers' to the profession. When faced with choosing another person to fill their ranks, their propensity is to choose another person like themselves. People tend to hire others like themselves. For instance, the odds ratio of a woman being hired when there are no women on a selection committee was found to be 20 per cent; when there was at least one woman on a screening committee the odds rose to 35 per cent (Schmuck and Wyant, 1981). Through all the stages of preparation — from encouraging teachers to seek administrative positions to final selection of administrative candidates — the chances are that a man will be preferred to a woman. The exclusion of women is self-perpetuating, despite active efforts to change institutional practices.

In theory, the male image of the leader permeates the literature. Men are the objects and the subjects of study. Only recently have we begun to investigate leadership concepts without such an androcentric bias — to include concepts that describe the population of those who are in leadership positions, not merely samples of males. Shakeshaft and Nowell (1984) have described several leadership studies that have influenced our views about educational leadership; the samples chosen for studying leadership are often drawn from the corporate and military world and definitions of leadership emerge from studying only male behaviour. On the occasions when females have been included as subjects for study, and differences noted in their behaviour, they are seen as 'deviant' or discrepant from the male norm.

This line of thinking does not suggest that leadership behaviour is differently executed by males or females; in fact the research on the behaviours of males and females as elementary school principals shows only minor variations (Gross and Trask, 1976). It suggests, however, that the concepts for study have been selective. To understand the phenomenon of leadership we need concepts that do not presume the male experience is universal and speaks to all of humanity. Women need to be included as objects and subjects of study in leadership and we need to investigate how our concepts of leadership have been formed by the blinding assumption that leader means male. Fortunately, there is some preparatory work in the area defined as 'feminist scholarship' or the 'new scholarship on women' (Acker, 1983; Biklen and Shakeshaft, 1985; Tetreault, 1985).

Gender-based career socialization theories

The literature on career socialization documents a rich interplay between personal orientations and environmental supports and incentives. A person incrementally learns the skills, attitudes and orientations of his or her workplace. In turn, one is given information, support and opportunities to develop further. This concept, of intimate interaction between individuals and their organizations, I believe offers the most fruitful ground for study. It moves us beyond the simplistic orientation of explaining women's absence in administration because of their individual deficiencies or the more macro pictures of schools as discriminatory. It shows, instead, the complex picture of interacting individuals within organizational structures and identifies the subtle gender-based practices in operation.

Women and men teachers bring different aspirations and hopes to their role as teachers and the organization provides differential information, support and opportunities to them. Many administrators report that the active encouragement of their principal was the first step in aspiring towards an administrative position and there are some data to suggest that women receive their encouragement from different sources from men (Duke, Isaacson, Sagor and Schmuck, 1983). In one small study of two male and two female principals, Gilbertson (1981) showed that these principals, regardless of sex, tended to interact more with male teachers than with female teachers regarding school-wide matters. A male high school principal described how he consciously encouraged women and men teachers who had leadership potential. Upon further consideration, however, he said, 'But you know, I take "no" more quickly from a female. With a male I just keep persisting.' Thus, at this very first stage of socialization, there is gender differentiation and a preference for males.

Wheatley (1981), using the arguments of Kanter, demonstrates the interplay between personal orientations and job incentives. She presents a case of 'opportunity' differences: there are jobs with high opportunity and low opportunity. Presumably all teachers have the same opportunities but there are clear sex differentials. Men more often are given extra responsibilities; they are assigned to committees; they more frequently become chairs of departments and these are high opportunity positions. Thus, given roles with high opportunity, one behaves appropriately with authority and responsibility. And the organization rewards such behaviour. Those with low opportunity positions tend to take fewer risks and do not demonstrate their leadership, thus fitting the organizational portrait of the deferential and directionless person. Teaching, where most women remain, is low in opportunity and power in the educational hierarchy. Thus, even in the ranks of teaching, the preference for males begins to dominate.

But there are women who aspire 'upwards' and achieve positions of authority and power. Although there do not appear to be any sex differences in how leaders perform their roles, there do appear to be differential expectations from others depending on whether a leader is a male or a female. Fennell et al (1978) calls it a 'legitimation gap' and points out that institutional authorities are often less likely to back up the authority of a female than they would be to support a male. Women's devalued status in the society transcends to the workplace. The double standard exists: if a woman has achieved a position of power and responsibility she is supposed to be exceptional and must 'prove' her worth, whereas the male is not expected to perform in such an exemplary manner. And in meetings with peers the 'lone' woman is clearly at a disadvantage; the dynamics of the group changes with its sex composition; whereas in sex-segregated groups there is an even division of task and social-emotional roles played out by the members, in mixed sex groups men tend to exhibit the task roles and women the social-emotional roles. Thus in work groups men display their task-initiating behaviour and women display their concerns for people, despite the fact that men and women are capable of both kinds of behaviour (Lockhead and Hall, 1976).

These kinds of studies I find to be illuminating because they describe how gender, as a variable, permeates institutional life. This perspective moves us beyond the simplistic orientation of sex differences socialization research or the more structural view which identifies the organizational constraints to women but does not explain how the processes work. Educational institutions have a gender overlay; we need to focus on those subtle and often unintentional behaviours and practices which perpetuate gender-based employment patterns and which result in a minority of women exercising leadership in schools.

References

Acker, S (1983) Women and teaching: a semi-detached sociology of a semi-profession in Walker and Barton (1983)

Adkison, J A (1981) Women in school administration: a review of the research Review of Educational Research 51 3: 311-43

Biklen, S K (1985) Teaching as an occupation for women: a case study of an elementary school. NIE Grant G-81-007. Unpublished paper Syracuse: New York

Biklen, S K and Shakeshaft, C (1985) The new scholarship on women in Klein (1985)

Boyan, N J ed (1986) The Handbook of Research on Educational Administration American Educational Research Association: Washington, DC (forthcoming)

Brehmer, I (1986) Women as educators in Germany: a history in Schmuck (1986) (forthcoming)

Byrne, E (1978) Women and Education Tavistock Publications: London

Charters, W W, Jr and Jovick, T (1981) The gender of principals and principal teacher relations in elementary school in Schmuck et al (1981)

Duke, D L, Isaacson, N, Sagor, R and Schmuck, P (1983) The socialization of administrators. American Educational Research Association Annual Meeting Paper: Chicago

Edson, S (1981) If they can, I can: women aspirants to administrative positions in public schools in Schmuck et al (1981)

Enders-Dragasser, U (1986) The privatization of school: women's unpaid work in Schmuck (1986) (forthcoming)

Fennell, M L, Barchas, P, Cohen, E, McMahon, A and Hildebrand, F (1978) An informative perspective on sex differences in organizational settings: the process of legitimation Sex Roles 4: 598-604

Fenwick, P (1986) Women as educators in New Zealand in Schmuck (1986) (forthcoming)

Gilbertson, M (1981) The influence of gender on the verbal interactions among principals and staff members: an exploratory study in Schmuck et al (1981)

Gross, N and Trask, E (1976) The Sex Factor and the Management of Schools John Wiley: New York

Havens, E (1980) Women in Educational Administration: The Principalship National Institute of Education: Washington, D C

Jones, E and Montenegro, X (1982) Recent Trends in the Representation of Women and Minorities in School Administration and Problems in Documentation American Association of School Administrators: Arlington, Va

Klein, S P ed (1985) Handbook for Achieving Equity Through Education John Hopkins University Press: Baltimore

Lockheed, M E and Hall, K P (1976) Conceptualizing sex as a status characteristic: applications leading to leadership training strategies Journal of Social Issues 32 3: 111-24

Lortie, D C (1975) School Teacher University of Chicago Press: Chicago

Ortiz, F (1982) Career Patterns in Education: Women, Men and Minorities in Public School Administration Praeger Press: New York

Ortiz, F and Marshall, C (1986) Women in educational administration in Boyan (1986) (forthcoming)

Paddock, S (1981) Male and female career paths in school administration in Schmuck et al (1981)

Reynolds, C (1986) Too limiting a liberation: a case study on married women as teachers in Schmuck (1986) (forthcoming)

Sampson, S (1986) Teachers' careers and promotion in Australia in Schmuck (1986) (forthcoming)

Schmuck, P (1975) *Sex Differentiation in Public School Administration* National Council of Administrative Women in Education: Arlington, Va

Schmuck, P ed (1986) *Women as Educators in the Western World* SUNY Press: New York (forthcoming)

Schmuck, P, Charters, W W Jr and Carlson, R eds (1981) *Educational Policy and Management: Sex Differentials* Academic Press: New York

Schmuck, P and Wyant, S (1981) Clues to sex bias in the selection of school administrators: a report from the Oregon network *in* Schmuck *et al* (1981)

Schmuck, P, Adkison, J, Peterson, B, Bailey, S, Glick, G, Klein, S, McDonald, S, Schubert, J and Tarason, S (1985) Administrative strategies for institutionalizing sex equality in education and the role of government *in* Klein (1985)

Shakeshaft, C (1981) Women in educational administration: a descriptive analysis of dissertation research and paradigm for future research *in* Schmuck *et al* (1981)

Shakeshaft, C and Nowell, I (1984) Research on theories, concepts and models of organizational behavior: the influence of gender *Issues in Education* 2 3: 186-203

Shulman, L and Sykes, G eds (1983) *Handbook of Teaching and Policy* Longman: New York

Smith, M, Kalvelage, J and Schmuck, P (1980) *Sex Equality in Educational Leadership: Women Getting Together and Getting Ahead* Education Development Center, Mass

Spender, D (1984) Women as educational employees: a brief consideration of the principles and trends in Britain at a time of economic change. Paper presented at the Second International Interdisciplinary Congress on Women. Groningen, The Netherlands

Sysiharju, A L (1986) Women as educators in Finland *in* Schmuck (1986) (forthcoming)

Tetreault, M K (1985) Stages of thinking about women: an experience derived evaluation model *Journal of Higher Education* (summer)

Van Essen, M (1986) Female teachers in the Netherlands, 1800-1865 *in* Schmuck (1986) (forthcoming)

Walker, S and Barton, L eds (1983) *Gender, Class and Education* The Falmer Press: Lewes, Sussex

Wheatley, M (1981) The impact of organizational structures and issues of sex equality *in* Schmuck *et al* (1981)

14. The school and occupational stress

A Ross Thomas

Summary: The purpose of this chapter is to introduce the reader to the concept of stress. Although much of the literature equates stress with particular experiences or 'life events', there has developed an increasing concern about stress in the workplace. Schools are, of course, the workplaces for teachers and principals and they too may become the victims of stressors unique to that particular form of organization. The bulk of research that has been undertaken so far has focused on teachers. A great deal of this unfortunately lacks any database. Of the publications based on collected data, virtually all have been dependent on self-report questionnaires. This serves to emphasize the methodological problems that are associated with stress studies. However, more objective, physiological methods are now being used and it is hoped that the future will see more combined methodological approaches adopted in the study of stress in teachers and principals. The author indicates the urgency for such studies, particularly to provide a more definite basis on which one can assess the prevalence and intensity of stress among teachers and principals as compared with that characteristic of other occupations.

Introduction

Within this chapter it is intended to undertake several tasks. First, the concept of stress will be discussed, and occupational stress — stress generated by and in the workplace as distinct from that attributable to 'life events' — will then be considered. Methodological problems encountered in measuring stress will be mentioned, followed by a brief review of the literature on teacher stress. This will lead on to a consideration of several studies that investigate stress and the school principal. In the final section of the chapter some of the implications of stress research will be considered.

The concept of stress

Notwithstanding the first appearance of the phenomenon in the psychological literature of the 1940s, the identification of stress is generally attributable to Hans Selye (1956) who, it should be noted, observed the loose and often contradictory use of the term and thus was obliged frequently to emphasize the essence of his definition (Selye, 1981; 1983). Stress is the *non-specific* response of the body to any demand made upon it. Exposure of the body to heat causes the *specific* response of perspiring, and the evaporation of perspiration has a cooling effect. Similarly, running causes the blood pressure to rise and the heart to beat more rapidly in order to speed the delivery of blood to the hard-working muscles. The increases in blood pressure and heart beat are also *specific* responses.

> But heat, running, exposure to cold, one drug or another − all, in addition to eliciting specific responses, produce as well a non-specific response − a non-specific increase in need for the body to perform *adaptive functions* and then to re-establish normalcy. This non-specific demand is the essence of stress. (Selye, 1983: 4)

Severe disturbances in the adaptive functions in people are what are commonly accepted as indicators of serious stress. From his extensive survey of field observations and clinical studies, Lazarus (1966: 4) concludes that:

> The stress reactions appear to be the result of conditions that disrupt or endanger well-established personal and social values of the people exposed to them.

Accordingly, in terms of human responses, Lazarus (1966: 6-7) outlines four main classes of reaction which may be used to 'index' stress. These are:

1. Reports of disturbed effects such as fear, anxiety, anger, depression, guilt.
2. Changes in motor behaviours such as increased muscle-tension, speech disturbances, and particular facial expressions.
3. Changes in the adequacy of cognitive functioning such as perception, thought, judgement, problem-solving and motor skills.
4. Physiological changes as shown in reactions of both the autonomic nervous system (the heart, respiratory organs, sweat glands) and the adrenal glands and the secretion of various hormones under stress.

The nature of the preceding responses points to several other aspects of stress which are of importance. For example, stress − or, more accurately, one's adaptation to stressful circumstances or *stressors* − is an individualistic phenomenon. It may thus be conceptualized along a continuum (Lazarus, 1966: 5) and should not be seen only as a negative or destructive factor. It may be positive or constructive. As Selye (1983: 5) repeatedly observed:

> Stress is the spice of life. Being associated with all types of activity we could avoid it only by never doing anything. Who would enjoy a life of 'no runs, no hits, no errors'?

Finally, there is perhaps the need to draw attention to the concept of *distress*, ie the negative extreme of the stress continuum. Although the evidence is not conclusive, stress appears to be linked to diseases such as ulcers, arthritis, heart disease, and other circulatory disturbances. Selye (1983) insists that it is not stress which is the cause of such; it is the reaction to stress when the reaction becomes *distress*. Ellis (1978) has argued strongly for the need to distinguish between stress and distress. It is, he maintains, appropriate to develop feelings of concern, frustration or sorrow when confronted by situations which are threatening, frustrating or upsetting. It is not appropriate, however, for people to *distress* themselves by feeling anxious, hostile, or depressed. These 'extremities' of affective behaviour impede people's abilities to find solutions to their problems. Although 'distress' may therefore be more appropriate, hereafter the more comprehensive term 'stress' will be used. The context of its use will normally suggest the degree of intensity of such.

What then are the causes of stress — the stressors — that have been identified as posing extraordinary demands on the adaptive mechanisms of individuals? There is little doubt that for many the Social Readjustment Scale (SRS) developed by Holmes and Rahe (1967) has tended to restrict the perceived range of stressors that may impinge upon individuals. The SRS ranks several 'life events' in terms of 'life change units', ie the scale of impact each is likely to have on an individual. Some of these life events, eg being fired from work, a change to a different line of work, and trouble with one's boss, presage what has become in more recent years an increased awareness of stressors that are located in the individual's occupation or work environment. The two definitions that follow highlight the nature of *occupational stress*. To Farkas (1982: 1) it is:

> an experience arising from a perceived imbalance between work-related demands and an individual's capability, power and motivation to meet these demands, when failure to respond to them is seen as having important consequences.

while to Levi (1979: 27) occupational stress is experienced:

> where discrepancies exist between occupational demands and opportunities on the one hand and the workers' capacities, needs and expectations on the other.

That the workplace constitutes a 'harbour' for stressors should not come as a surprise. Organization theory has for many years directed attention to such, particularly with its focus on conflict. There is, arguably, no clearer example than the Argyris (1960) thesis which states that the demands of an organization and the needs of its members are in fundamental conflict. Drawing on the work of psychologists such as Erikson (1950), Bronfenbrenner (1951) and Lewin (1935), Argyris (1960: 8-94) categorizes the stages through which 'human beings in our culture' develop. For example, from infancy to adulthood individuals tend to move from passivity to increased activity, from dependence to relative independence, from restricted behaviour to multiple ways of acting, from subordinate to superordinate position in the family setting. Admission to an (employing) organization subjects the individual to a situation that emphasizes rationality, specialization of task, power and conformity, and loyalty to company objectives.

Argyris claims that the effects of such principles are to be seen in the placement of employees in work situations where (i) they have 'minimal control' over their work, (ii) they are expected to be 'passive, dependent and subordinate', (iii) they are expected to make frequent use of their 'skin-surface shallow abilities', and (iv) they are expected to produce under conditions that lead to psychological failure. Another theme associated with stress is developed by Crane (1980: 211) who examines the concept of anxiety in organizations and concludes that:

> strategies and tactics of impression management aimed at reducing the anxiety level of each individual are the hidden agenda of every encounter between members of an organization.

Hoy and Miskel (1978) examine the place of professional autonomy in the operation of bureaucracies. The authors point to the dysfunctional or negative consequences stemming from the conflicts between professional autonomy and bureaucratic formalization. The theme of stress in organizations is developed in considerable depth and 'legitimated' by Cooper and Payne (1978) in their important contribution *Stress at Work*.

Schools are, of course, organizations. They display most of the structural characteristics of organizations so frequently described in the literature. Hence, they too may readily be identified as harbouring stressors. There are also particular characteristics of schools *qua* organizations that may be viewed as contributing to the development of stress in their members. Jury, Willower and De Lacy (1975: 299) point to some of these features:

> Schools are characterized by vague and diverse goals, ambiguous criteria of success, lack of a widely accepted technology of teaching, a mandated relationship with clients who may or may not be willing participants, high population density, stimulus overload especially for teachers, a host of logistical problems, and political vulnerability.

The measurement of stress

Although the concept of stress is generally understood, there remain many problems in its operational definiton. As Hosking and Reid (1985: 3) ask:

> How does one measure experimentally when a worker is stressed? How do you define in a way which can be measured the difference between stress due to work and personal factors? This is probably the single most important reason why the literature on occupational stress and its management is so varied and reflects in many instances the bias of the researcher.

The measurement of stress has, in fact, been bedevilled by methodological problems, a review of which has been compiled by Cooper and Marshall (1978).

The questionnaire-survey has been by far the most widely used approach to the measurement of occupational stress. Many of those have been concerned largely with job satisfaction. Spillane (1983: 6-7) is most critical of this approach, arguing that:

> job satisfaction questionnaires often invite cautious, stoical responses which reflect resignation and adaption to work environments. When general questions

are raised, responses are largely conservative — a mixture of resignation and accommodation.

He adds:

> Many researchers and practitioners have accepted survey results at face value and have not concerned themselves with the psychological processes which underpin questionnaire responses.

One must also exercise caution in the selection and interpretation of articles on stress. This is the clear warning that emerges from the survey of the literature on teacher stress completed by Hiebert and Farber (1984). These authors found four distinct categories of paper which they called Types 1, 2, 3 and review articles. Type 1 articles have no database and are essentially statements of opinion about stress and teaching. Both Type 2 and Type 3 articles include data in support of their claims — in the former these are derived from self-report questionnaires; in the latter, data are provided by third-party sources. Review articles are summaries and/or syntheses of extant publications. Of their sample of 71 papers there were 50 Type 1 (70.4 per cent), 15 Type 2 (21.2 per cent), four Type 3 (5.6 per cent) and two (2.8 per cent) review articles. (It should be noted, however, that the number of Type 1 articles is artificially low. So vast were the numbers and sources of Type 1 articles that the authors stopped the tabulation of such!)

Similarly, publications which report associations between stress and life events (similar to those identified by Holmes and Rahe) should be read with caution. Brown (1974), for example, is most critical of this approach and points to the possibility of direct and indirect *contamination* of life event stress measures. He also warns of the possibility of *spurious* conclusions linking a life event and stress, when both may in fact result from a third factor. Brown also claims that schedules of recent life events are too vague in their description of situations and thus open to widespread variations on interpretation.

Nevertheless, the questionnaire approach continues to be widely used in research on occupational stress. A noteworthy multivariate attempt to develop a reliable and valid instrument to measure teacher stress was undertaken by Pettegrew and Wolf (1982). However, the authors admit to some weaknesses in the instrument. For example, data on stress are accumulated at a particular moment and not on a longitudinal basis. The information is thus not obtained on teacher stress for longer periods of time, for example a term or a year. Jick (1979) identifies a further limitation:

> Pencil-and-paper instruments providing self-report data are only one of many useful tools in social/psychological measurement. The use of these measures should be accompanied by interview data, school absenteeism and turnover records, medical histories, and the like. It is likely that job-related stress can be measured more effectively with a variety of data originating from multiple sources, or method triangulation.

Strong opposition to the use of questionnaires in stress research has been recorded by Spillane (1983: 8) who has embarked on studies of various occupations using hormone analysis as an objective, physiological measure of stress in individuals. (Data are often supplemented by information gathered by questionnaires, however.) Although several occupations have been studied, it appears that those employed within the education sector, such as teachers and principals, have yet to be examined.

Teachers and stress

Most stress research on educationists has resulted in the Type 2 publication defined above by Hiebert and Farber (1984: 15). Of these articles the great majority focus on stress in teachers. To attempt to acknowledge all these publications is a task well beyond the ambit of this chapter. There are, however, some aspects of this research which have implications for (or certainly should be of concern to) educational administrators.

It has almost become conventional wisdom in educational circles to regard teaching as a high-stress occupation. Although this belief may be the outcome mainly of the large number of Type 1 publications (eg opinions lacking databases) that address the topic, there are Type 2 articles that support this relationship. One of the most widely quoted of these is by Kyriacou and Sutcliffe (1978) who conclude that teachers find teaching stressful. Hiebert and Farber (1984) are critical of this finding as it is based on responses to but one question. Kyriacou and Sutcliffe's questionnaire is also characteristic of those criticized by Keavney and Sinclair (1978) for being too speculative and for failing to distinguish between the conditions that produce 'concern' or 'problems' and those that produce 'anxiety'. Also, a dearth of comparative studies equating stress levels in teaching with those associated with other occupations suggests that one should exercise considerable caution in designating teaching either as an inherently high-stress role or as an occupation whose level of stress exceeds that of others. Bentz *et al* (1971), for example, suggest that there is no difference between teachers and other professional groups.

In his survey of the literature, Leach (1984) points to the findings of studies conducted in the UK by Andrews (1971), Dunham (1976), Kyriacou and Sutcliffe (1978), and Pratt (1978). The last two mentioned suggest that approximately 20 per cent of teachers in comprehensive and primary schools rated teaching as either very stressful or extremely stressful. In a study conducted by the State School Teachers' Union of Western Australia (1982), 40 per cent of teachers reported they were working under 'considerable stress'. However, in surveys conducted in the USA in 1938, 1951 and 1967, 37.5 per cent, 43 per cent and 16 per cent respectively of teachers indicated they were working under stressful conditions of one kind or another. From his summary of the preceding figures Leach (1984: 158) concludes:

> that fairly widespread teacher stress is not a new phenomenon nor, assuming some comparability between socio-cultural factors and institutional development, is it necessarily on the increase in Anglo-American educational systems.

Much of the survey research has been concerned with identifying the sources of stress — the *stressors* that impinge on teachers. From his review of the literature, Leach (1984: 158) identifies six 'clusters of stressors' noting that:

> On the whole, the similarity of findings is impressive despite differences in samples of teachers, varieties of definitions and methods used in obtaining the data.

The categories of stressors, together with reference to some of the studies characteristic of each, are listed below.

1. Pupil misbehaviour and its effective management (Coughlin [1970]; Kyriacou and Sutcliffe [1978]; Pratt [1978]; Dunham [1977; 1981]).
2. Concern for pupils' learning and the effectiveness of the teaching programme in reaching desired or personally satisfied standards (Coughlin [1970]; Kyriacou and Sutcliffe [1978]; Pratt [1978]).
3. Poor personal relationships with colleagues and principal (Coughlin [1970]; Kyriacou and Sutcliffe [1978]; Pratt [1978]; Dunham [1977; 1981]).
4. Too severe time pressures and workload to complete perceived demands satisfactorily (Pratt [1978]; Kyriacou and Sutcliffe [1978]; Dunham [1980]).
5. Inadequate resources and facilities for teaching effectively (Olander and Farrell [1970]; Kyriacou and Sutcliffe [1978]; Pratt [1978]).
6. Poor personnel management (especially lack of consultation) and inadequate administrative policies and procedures (Coughlin [1970]; Dunham [1976]).

Leach's categories of stressor have much in common with the six groups identified by Hiebert and Farber (1984: 16-17), namely:

1. Teacher-student conflict and discipline-related problems (Carter [1979]; Cichon and Koff [1978; 1980]; Feshback and Campbell [1978]; Kyriacou and Sutcliffe [1978]; Pratt [1978]).
2. Staff interpersonal interactions (Feshback and Campbell [1978]; Pratt [1978]).
3. Working conditions, including such things as inadequate resources, overcrowded classrooms (Cichon and Koff [1978]; Feshback and Campbell [1978]; Kyriacou and Sutcliffe [1978]).
4. Time pressures, including too much to do and too little preparation time (Feshback and Campbell [1978]; Kyriacou and Sutcliffe [1978]; Carter [1979]).
5. Role ambiguity and perceived role conflict (Bensky *et al* [1980]; Schwab and Iwanicki [1982]).
6. Inadequate teacher preparation including lack of skills, and poor problem-solving and decision-making strategies (Pratt [1978]; Carter [1979]).

Hiebert and Farber (1984: 22) also offer criticisms of many of the foregoing types of publication, particularly those that use 'homemade' questionnaires which do not describe procedures for developing such, or report reliability or validity estimates. Seldom is the questionnaire included in the article and quite often there are no examples of items. Perhaps of even greater importance is the tendency of many writers to assume that 'pressure' and 'stress' are synonymous and thus all situations that produce pressures must result in stressful reactions. This assumption overlooks what other writers (eg Albrecht [1979] ; Hiebert [1983]) have pointed out — individuals may encounter pressures, cope with such, and experience little stress in so doing!

This observation highlights another 'popular' concern of the writers on stress and teaching, namely, how *do* teachers cope; or, expressed another way, what mechanisms enable some teachers to combat and survive the stressors of their work while others fail to cope and become victims of 'burnout'? Again, the publications addressing this question are largely of the Type 1 category and, as Hiebert and Farber (1984: 16) summarize, they:

> establish that teaching is stressful usually by giving examples of stressed teachers; indicate the working conditions creating the stress; identify some ways of coping with the stress.

Personal opinion is thus the basis for these articles; in general their authors appear unaware of the research that has been carried out on the control of stress.

A most recent summary of some of the stress control literature has been prepared by Blase (1984: 174) who expresses surprise 'that so little attention has been given to the precise ways in which teachers cope with job-related stress'. In the absence of such, 'general coping models' — developed from studies of other occupations — are often used to describe teachers' reactions. Kyriacou (1980) and Needle *et al* (1981) have investigated coping behaviours in teachers. Kyriacou, for example, suggests that teachers may cope with the stress of work in three ways — by expressing feelings and seeking support; taking considered actions to deal with sources of stress; and focusing away from stress and towards other things.

A most comprehensive review of the literature on teachers' coping beahviour has been completed by Cairns (1984) who identified three major areas of 'intervention' — individual, school-based, and management-based.

1. Advice on individual coping mechanisms may be found in a plethora of sources across the range of popular academic literature. Suggestions directed specifically at teachers have been made by Styles and Cavanagh (1977), Hendrickson (1979), and Adams (1982).

2. School-based interventions such as those the principal may manipulate are described by Reed (1979) and Blase (1982), and those involving the whole staff and executive by Iwanicki (1983).

3. The concern of employing agencies is reflected in articles dealing primarily with management practices (Cichon and Koff [1978] ; Schwab [1983] ;and Iwanicki [1983]), design of school environments

Connors [1983]), school stress management and training (Friedman [1978]), and teacher training (Coates and Thoresen [1976] ; and Edgerton [1977]).

Although the three areas of intervention identified by Cairns are relevant, comprehensive, and supported elsewhere (Leach, 1984), Pettegrew and Wolf (1982: 390) argue very forcefully the importance of the second of these factors, namely the school administration.

> As such, management/school administration appears to be both the most logical and cost-effective point of intervention into teacher stress . . . As with organizations in general, public school systems and the teachers they employ would stand to benefit most in regard to stress intervention through the improvement of management practices . . . The locus of teacher stress prevention/intervention most clearly rests with school administration.

Elsewhere (NAS/UWT, 1976: 39), three types of principal have been identified — the ambiguous head, the non-consulting head, and the unpredictable head — each 'guilty' of contributing in one way or another to the development of stress in teachers.

Principals and stress

The preceding comments relating to the linkage between teacher stress and the management of schools place considerable emphasis on the role of the principal in mitigating stress. What this literature overlooks, of course, is that principals themselves experience stress and may suffer as a consequence.

Research on stress and the principalship has not been as extensive as that directed at teachers. Although undoubtedly stimulated by genuine cases of harmful stress among their membership, teachers' unions continue to see and to use stress altruistically and pragmatically as grounds for securing improved conditions. This, no doubt, is sustained by the far greater number of teachers as compared to principals. Perhaps the 'blame' ascribed to them as stressors discourages research among principals. One must query the adverse influence of such, however; after all, principals, almost without exception, were formerly teachers and could thus be expected to understand and empathize with teachers. Spillane (1983: 17), although not referring to teachers in his observation, suggests a further reason why studies of stress among principals are relatively few:

> To date all Australian studies of work stress which used hormonal analysis have been commissioned by trade unions. Management has retreated behind a wall of defence in the hope that stress research will not alter present attitudes to workers' compensation, work value cases, job design, industrial health and safety legislation.

The literature on stress in principals, albeit much reduced in frequency, would appear to approximate to the distribution of that relating to teachers in terms of the Hiebert and Farber (1984) classification referred to earlier. In the following sections some of the more significant Type 2 (self-report questionnaire) and Type 3 (third-party report) papers are discussed.

The objectives of a study conducted by Koff et al (1980) included an assessment of the relative magnitude of stress that appeared to be induced by various events associated with the administration of elementary and secondary schools in the United States. Data were collected through the completion of the Administrators' Events Stress Inventory (AESI) in which 48 administrative activities were rated in terms of the amount of stress induced. Respondents were drawn from the membership of the National Associations for Elementary and Secondary School Principals. Factor analysis of the 1291 responses suggested four underlying themes relevant to the stress experienced by principals — (i) helplessness/security, (ii) management tasks/problem solving, (iii) teacher conflict, and (iv) student conflict.

The rankings of the four factors were compared in terms of three categories of principal — elementary, middle/junior high, and high school. Administrative events that related to administrator-teacher conflict were perceived by principals in each category to be *most* stressful. These events related to a threat to one's job/physical security and status were perceived uniformly as next most highly stressful. The routine, expected, accepted tasks of school administration were associated with low amounts of stress. The mean score for only one factor (student conflict) was ranked highest by high school principals.

Koff et al (1980: 3) also analysed the many comments made on their survey forms by the respondents. Respondents believed a definition of the cause of stress in administration should make provision for:

> constant demands of the job, lack of sufficient time, threat of the unexpected, management of conflicts among school and non-school personnel, strikes and the processes and occurrences accompanying strikes.

Conversely, 'low-stress' schools were thought to be small or private, affluent, non-urban, and well supported by the community.

No support for the preceding supposition was found in a study completed by Farkas (1982) in which 198 elementary and secondary public school principals in the State of New York completed three self-report questionnaires — the I-P-C Scale (measuring locus of control) (Levenson, 1972), Index of Hierarchy of Authority (measuring powerlessness) (Aiken and Hage, 1966), and the Index of Job-Related Tension (measuring perceived occupational stresss) (Kahn et al, 1964). No evidence was found to support the 'conventional view', that urban schools are inherently more stressful than non-urban schools; nor did secondary principals perceive more stress than did their elementary counterparts.

While acknowledging that secondary schools are more complex and bureaucratic, and hence offer greater potential for conditions of alienation, isolation, and stress, Farkas speculates that the very nature of the bureaucratic structure of a secondary school with its assistant principals and departmental heads may actually help to 'buffer' the principal from many potential sources of stress.

Farkas's study also revealed that principals, as a group, display a high locus of control and generally perceive themselves to be in control of future events. The principals also expressed the belief that they were afforded sufficient decision-making power to enable them satisfactorily to discharge the responsibilities of their position. Consequently, contrary to what much of the popular literature may suggest, principals reported a low level of stress in their jobs, a finding consistent with that of Gorton (1982).

In another study conducted in the State of Oregon, Tung and Koch (1980) applied the Administrative Stress Index (ASI) to a sample of 1156 vice principals, principals, and superintendents. Factor analysis of the ASI also revealed four dimensions of stress — role-based, task-based, conflict-mediating, and boundary-spanning. Tung and Koch observed that superintendents experienced a greater degree of boundary-spanning stress, probably a reflection of their greater concern with coordinating the activities of several schools and/or relating their schools to the community. Principals, on the other hand, appeared more affected by role-based, task-based, and conflict-mediating stress, all conceivably the outcome of dealing with problems that arise in their particular schools. The respondents also reported on the state of their physical health, thus revealing that each stress dimension was strongly and significantly associated with reports of current physical health, ie the higher the level of experienced stress, the poorer the physical health.

The study by Tung and Koch was apparently based on the analysis of data gathered in the first instance by Gmelch and Swent in 1977 and reported by them in 1984. Gmelch and Swent's study approached the data differently, placing greater emphasis on the responses to each of the 35 items in the Administrative Stress Index. The researchers reported a few differences between the categories of respondents and the degree of stress associated with various items. Substantial agreement existed, however, on the major three stressors. Compliance with State, federal and organizational rules and policies was seen as the most bothersome, followed by attendance at meetings and the completion of reports on time.

In their recent survey of 197 principals and deputy principals in Government primary and secondary schools in the State of Western Australia, Hill and Schoubroeck (1984) used the 30-item version of the General Health Questionnaire (GHQ). (This was the same instrument used in studies of teacher stress by Pratt [1978] and Mykletun [1984].) Responses were scored in order to classify each respondent as a 'case' or a 'non-case'. 'For individuals classified as cases there is the distinct probability that such people suffer levels of tension, anxiety and depression sufficiently high as to have an adverse effect on their physical and mental well being.' The cases among the respondents were compared with normative data for the general population of Perth. The male case rate was two and a half times that of the general population, and three and a half times that for males of the same social class. Case rates were the same for principals and deputy principals but administrators in the primary sector had a case rate twice that of their secondary counterparts.

Elsewhere in Australia, using a significant departure from the 'standard' questionnaire approach, Phillipps and Thomas (1983) observed five principals in public primary schools in New South Wales. Each principal (having previously been observed for three consecutive weeks [Phillipps and Thomas, 1982]) was subjected to five days' observation during which evidence of stress was recorded *inter alia*, eg changes in behaviour patterns and speech habits. Throughout the period of observation, each principal wore a light, battery-operated electrocardiogram. By matching observed activities in which the principals engaged, with recorded fluctuations in heart rate, Phillipps and Thomas were able to confirm certain behaviours as stressful episodes. But on numerous occasions the evidence of stress recorded on the ECG was not identified in the principal's behaviour by the observer, thus confirming that stress may be an 'invisible' phenomenon.

In their detailed profile of one of the principals, Phillipps and Thomas report that their physiological measure revealed that stress was omnipresent. For example, throughout the period of observation the principal was interrupted on 91 occasions. Twelve of these were associated with rapid fluctuations in heart rate. Similarly, stress was present during several decision-making activities, during a sequence of events relating to a scurrilous letter written by a parent, and during several of the multifarious tasks performed by the principal.

Conclusion

The intentions of this chapter have been to discuss the concept of stress and, in particular, to acquaint the reader with the problem of stress in the educational workplace. The stresses of organizational life can prove overwhelming to some. The school administrators surveyed in the Tung and Koch (1980) and Gmelch and Swent (1984) studies, for example, ascribed 75 per cent of total stress experienced to the rigours of their occupation; a not-inconsiderable number of principals and superintendents throughout the United States acknowledged their use of drugs of one form or another (Youngs, 1984). There is little doubt that the problem should be confronted, since the damage induced may be significant. As Hill and Schoubroeck (1984) point out, this may be reflected in three ways. First, there is the personal cost to physical and mental well-being. Second, those personal costs are translated into public costs of various kinds. Third, there is the longer-term damage to teaching as a career. A better understanding of occupational stress — and hence improved therapies for its remediation — are largely dependent on appropriate methods of identifying and/or measuring the phenomenon. From the extensive literature on occupational stress that has now accumulated, those studies that report data of some kind have mainly relied on the application of self-report questionnaires. But, as this chapter acknowledges, more objective methods are being applied. The complexity of stress, however, presents a most difficult methodological problem to any researcher. Future developments in the field may require a *combination* of measures (such as those used by Phillipps and Thomas [1983]) to cater simultaneously for the physiological, psychological and sociological manifestations of stress as it affects the individual in the workplace.

Within the boundaries of that unique workplace called a school, stress research has reflected closely the models and methods used in other organizations. The bulk of this research has been concerned with teachers; a little has involved principals; and, as far as can be ascertained, none has yet focused on the children.

In spite of the prolificacy of publications dealing with the theme, uncertainty still exists with regard to the severity of stress among teachers and principals and also with regard to the incidence of such as compared with other occupations. Perhaps it is timely, therefore, to encourage and support further studies (using broader methodological approaches) directed at these issues. Prompt answers to these questions may prevent reachers (in particular) and principals from building stress into a self-fulfilling concern.

References

Adams, B (1982) The staff burn-out syndrome: by way of a review *The North West Counsellors' Association Newsletter* 6 1: 37-41

Aiken, M and Hage, J (1966) Organizational alienation: a comparative analysis *American Sociological Review* 31: 497-507

Albrecht, K (1979) *Stress and the Manager* Prentice Hall: New Jersey

American Psychological Association (1972) *Proceedings of the 80th Annual Convention*

Andrews, A G (1971) Ground rules for the great debate *Cambridge Journal of Education* 7: 90-94

Argyris, C (1960) *Understanding Organizational Behavior* Dorsey: Homewood, Ill

Bensky, J M, Shaw, S F, Grouse, A S, Bates, H, Dixson, B and Beane, W E (1980) Public law 94-142 and stress: a problem for educators *Exceptional Children* 47 1: 24-29

Bentz, W K, Hollister, W G and Edgerston, J W (1971) An assessment of the mental health of teachers: a comparative analysis *Psychology in the Schools* 8 1: 72-76

Blake, R R and Ramsey, G B (1951) *Perception* Ronald: New York

Blase, J J (1982) A social-psychological grounded theory of teacher stress and burn-out *Educational Administration Quarterly* 18 4: 93-113

Blase, J J (1984) A data based model of how teachers cope with work stress *Journal of Educational Administration* 22 2: 173-91

Bronfenbrenner, U (1951) Toward an integrated theory of personality *in* Blake and Ramsey (1951)

Brown, G W (1974) Meaning, measurement and stress of life events *in* Dohrenwend and Dohrenwend (1974)

Cairns, G E (1984) Teacher burnout in New South Wales secondary schools: a review of the literature on occupational stress, the nature of teacher burnout and preventive measures in relation to teachers in New South Wales secondary schools. Unpublished MEd Admin dissertation, University of New England

Carter, P H (1979) Teacher stress: discipline, paperwork top the list of causes *Massachusetts Teacher* 59: 7-11

Cichon, D J and Koff, R H (1978) The teaching events stress inventory. ERIC Document ED 160 662

Cichon, D J and Koff, R H (1980) Stress and teaching *National Association of Secondary Principals' Bulletin* 64 34: 91-104

Coates, T J and Thoresen, C E (1976) Teacher anxiety: a review with recommendations *Review of Educational Research* 46 2: 159-84

Connors, D A (1983) The school environment: a link to understanding stress *Theory into Practice* 22 1: 15-20

Cooper, C L and Marshall, J (1978) *Understanding Executive Stress* Macmillan: London

Cooper, C L and Marshall, J (1980) *White Collar and Professional Stress* Wiley: Chichester

Cooper, C L and Payne, R (1978) *Stress at Work* Wiley: Chichester

Coughlin, R J (1970) Dimensions of teacher morale *American Educational Research Journal* 1: 221-34

Crane, A R (1980) Anxiety in organizations: explorations of an idea *Journal of Educational Administration* 18 2: 202-12

Dohrenwend, B S and Dohrenwend, B P (1974) *Stressful Life Events: Their Nature and Effects* John Wiley: New York

Dunham, J (1976) Stress situations and responses *in* National Association of Schoolmasters/Union of Women Teachers (1976)

Dunham, J (1977) The effects of disruptive behaviour on teachers *Educational Review* 29 3: 181-87

Dunham, J (1981) Disruptive pupils and teacher stress *Educational Research* 23 3: 205-13

Edgerton, S K (1977) Teachers in role conflict: the hidden dilemma *Phi Delta Kappan* 59 2: 120-22

Ellis, A (1978) What people can do for themselves to cope with stress *in* Cooper and Payne (1978)

Erikson, E H (1950) *Childhood and Society* Norton: New York

Farkas, J P (1982) Stress and the school principal: old myths and new findings *Administrator's Notebook* 30 8: 1-4

Feshback, N and Campbell, M (1978) Teacher stress and disciplinary practices in schools: a preliminary report. ERIC Document ED 162 228

Friedman, M H (1978) School stress management training: an integrated approach. Unpublished paper presented at the Annual Meeting of the American Education Research Association

Gmelch, W H and Swent, B (1984) Management team stressors and their impact on administrators' health *Journal of Educational Administration* 22 2: 192-205

Gorton, D (1982) Administrator stress: some surprising research findings *Planning and Changing* 12 4: 195-99

Hendrickson, B (1979) Is 'exhausted' an apt description of your present state of mind? *Learning* 1: 37-39

Hiebert, B A (1983) A framework for planning stress control interventions *The Canadian Counsellor* 17 2: 51-61

Hiebart, B and Farber, I (1984) Teacher stress: a literature survey with a few surprises *Canadian Journal of Education* 9 1: 14-27

Hill, P and Schoubroeck, L V (1984) Stress and the school administrator: a survey of principals and deputy principals in government schools in Western Australia. Unpublished paper, Education Department of Western Australia: Perth

Holmes, T and Rahe, R (1967) The social readjustment rating scale *Journal of Psychosomatic Research* 11: 213-18

Hosking, S and Reid, M (1985) Teacher stress — an organisational perspective. Unpublished paper, Victorian Teachers' Union: Camberwell

Hoy, W K and Miskel, C G (1978) *Educational Administration: Theory, Research, and Practice* Random House: New York

Iwanicki, E F (1983) Towards understanding and alleviating teacher burnout *Theory into Practice* 22 1: 27-32

Jick, T D (1979) Mixing quantitative and qualitative methods: triangulation in action *Administrative Science Quarterly* 24 4: 602-11

Jury, L E, Willower, D J and De Lacy, W J (1975) Teacher self-actualization and pupil control ideology *Alberta Journal of Educational Research* **81** 4: 295-301

Kahn, R, Wolfe, D, Quinn, R, Snoek, J and Rosenthal, R (1964) *Organizational Stress: Studies in Role Conflict and Ambiguity* John Wiley: New York

Keavney, G and Sinclair, K E (1978) Teacher concerns and teacher anxiety: a neglected topic of classroom research *Review of Educational Research* **48**: 2: 273-90

Koff, R, Laffey, J, Olson, G and Cichon, D (1980) Stress and the school administrator *Administrator's Notebook* **28** 9: 1-4

Kyriacou, C (1980) Coping actions and occupational stress among school teachers *Research in Education* **24**: 57-61

Kyriacou, C and Sutcliffe, J (1978) Teacher stress and satisfaction *Educational Research* **21** 2: 89-96

Lazarus, R S (1966) *Psychological Stress and the Coping Process* McGraw-Hill: New York

Leach, D J (1984) A model of teacher stress and its implications for management *Journal of Educational Administration* **22** 2: 157-72

Levenson, H (1972) Distinctions within the concept of internal-external control: development of a new scale *in* American Psychological Association (1972)

Levi, L (1979) Occupational mental health: its monitoring, protection and promotion *Journal of Occupational Medicine* **21**: 26-32

Lewin, K (1935) *A Dynamic Theory of Personality* McGraw-Hill: New York

Mykletun, R J (1984) Teacher stress: perceived and objective sources, and quality of life *Scandinavian Journal of Educational Research* **28** 1: 17-45

National Association of Schoolmasters/Union of Women Teachers (1976) *Stress in Schools* Hemel Hempstead

Needle, R H, Griffin, T and Svedsen, R (1981) Occupational stress: coping and health problems of teachers *The Journal of School Health* **51** 3: 175-81

Olander, H T and Farrell, M E (1970) Professional problems of elementary teachers *Journal of Teacher Education* **21**: 276-80

Pettegrew, L S and Wolf, G E (1982) Validating measures of teacher stress *American Educational Research Journal* **19** 3: 372-96

Phillipps, D and Thomas, A R (1982) Principals' decision making: some observations *in* Simpkins *et al* (1982)

Phillipps, D and Thomas, A R (1983) Profile of a principal under stress *Primary Education* **14** 6: 6-8, 31

Pratt, J (1978) Perceived stress among teachers: the effect of age and background of children taught *Education Review* **30** 1: 3-14

Reed, S (1979) What you can do to prevent teacher burnout *National Elementary Principal* **58** 3: 67-70

Schwab, R L (1983) Teacher burnout: moving beyond 'psychobabble' *Theory into Practice* **22** 1: 21-26

Schwab, R L and Iwanicki, E F (1982) Perceived role conflict, role ambiguity, and teacher burnout *Educational Administration Quarterly* **18** 1: 60-74

Selye, H (1956) *The Stress of Life* McGraw-Hill: New York

Selye, H (1981) On executive stress *Executive Health* **18** 1: 1-6

Selye, H (1983) It's not the amount of stress you have, it's how you respond to it *Executive Health* **19** 5: 1-6

Simpkins, W S, Thomas, A R and Thomas, E B eds (1982) *Principal and Task: An Australian Perspective* University of New England: Armidale, Australia

Spillane, R (1983) Occupational stress and organisation development: a new research strategy. Unpublished paper presented at Seminar '83, Melbourne Organisation Development Network: Melbourne

State School Teachers' Union of Western Australia (1982) Teaching and stress. Position paper, Perth

Styles, K and Cavanagh, G (1977) Stress in teaching and how to handle it *English Journal* **66**: 76-79

Tung, R L and Koch, J L (1980) School administrators: sources of stress and ways of coping with it *in* Cooper and Marshall (1980)

Youngs, B B (1984) Drug use in the leadership area *The Canadian Administrator* **24** 1: 1-6

15. School management and nation building in a newly independent state

O E Maravanyika

Summary: Newly independent states generally regarded the systems of education they inherited from the colonial powers as designed to serve colonial
commercial and political interests. At independence, efforts were made to
transform the post-colonial societies so that their economic, social and political
institutions would reflect local rather than foreign values. Education was seen
as being at the centre of this transformation. Zimbabwe shared this faith in
the potency of education to transform the inherited colonial capitalist state to
a post-colonial socialist egalitarian state. However, it inherited an education
system which was racially divided with the European division designed to
produce high-level manpower in government, commerce and industry, and the
African division designed largely to produce African teachers and a large pool
of semi-skilled and unskilled labourers. The two divisions were administered
differently, with the former being more decentralized and headmasters and
parent-teacher associations having more autonomy than the latter, which was
highly centralized and controlled. Attempts to unite the two systems at
independence created problems not only in terms of lack of management skills
from the African division, but also in terms of reconciling the inherited
ideologies of school management. Meanwhile, varying and sometimes conflicting expectations and aspirations as to the benefits to be derived from
independence by parents and pupils made school management for nation
building more difficult as there was sometimes disagreement on the ideological
basis on which national development should be based. As a result, more was
achieved in quantitative than in qualitative changes.

Introduction

Newly independent states generally inherited systems of education which
were invariably regarded as serving the political, economic and commercial
interests of the colonial powers. As Beeby (1967: 19) states, 'any good
educational plan will be firmly based on certain broad political and social
principles that have either been formally propounded by the government
or are taken for granted in the society.'

Thus Nyerere (1967) saw colonial education as motivated by a desire
to inculcate values of the colonial society and to train individuals for the
service of the colonial powers. Although, on the whole, missionaries rather
than the colonial administrators were in the forefront of the provision of

African education, in some cases they were only able to carry out their evangelization by means of starting schools, in order to attract the young after the powers of the local chiefs had been destroyed by the colonial authorities. Missionaries thus owed a debt of gratitude to the colonial powers for creating conditions which enabled them to carry on with their evangelical work without fear of expulsion by local chiefs. This does not mean that all the values and attitudes inculcated by missionaries as proxies of colonial governments were wrong and inappropriate; what it means is that education was modelled on foreign systems and, at independence, efforts were made to redress the situation in the hope that it would reflect nationalist rather than colonial ideologies. For example, the racially segregated school systems were integrated and more primary and secondary schools were built in an effort to equalize opportunities of access to schools. In some cases, policies advocating universal primary education were enunciated, for example, in Tanzania and in Nigeria (Omari *et al*, 1983). In other cases, attempts were made to revamp the content of education and the curriculum so that they would reflect the new post-colonial economic, social and political order. The school was thus seen as playing a central role in the expected transformation.

In Rhodesia (now Zimbabwe), education under colonial rule was designed to serve a racially divided society based on a dual-society philosophy where no 'African was expected to aspire to live in the manner of a European and vice versa'. Through various forms of legislation, the economy, including mining, farming, commerce and industry, was entrenched in white control. The blacks were expected to provide cheap labour and when there was a shortage of labour, especially on farms and in mines, the government, as Van Onselen (1976) notes, not only introduced forced labour organized by the Rhodesia Native Labour Board, but also introduced taxation on African huts, dogs, individual males and live-stock in order to create a need for cash earnings among the peasants. Thus there were two separate divisions of European and African education, designed deliberately to serve different purposes. All European education (except for a few independent schools) was state responsibility and was compulsory for all children up to the age of 15. Only about 10 per cent of African schools were under government control and African education was not compulsory. The rest of African education was under various local authorities and organizations, the majority of whom were missionaries who had started schools as a means of attracting young people for purposes of evangelization.

Colonial government policy on African education did not change significantly over the period of colonial rule. Its main thrust was to provide some kind of vocational education suited to rural trades which would not raise African aspirations to compete with European artisans. It was argued that, for purposes of employment, academic education for blacks had no purpose in the white economy. European employers did not want to emply 'a jumped-up mission native with the gratuitous insolence acquired to perfection from no more than two years of mission training' (*Rhodesia*

Herald, 5 April 1906). Such Africans were considered a bad influence on the rest of the labour force. However, for various reasons, academic education found its way into African missionary primary schools and, by 1939, the Anglican Church had started an academic secondary school for Africans. Other denominations followed and, in order to halt further expansion of academic secondary education, the government introduced legislation in 1966 which, among other things, ruled that only 12½ per cent of African primary school leavers would get places for academic secondary education, 37½ per cent would go into vocational, largely rural, secondary schools, and 50 per cent would not be provided for in the formal school system. However, at independence in 1980 only about 18 per cent of African primary school leavers were in both the vocational and the academic secondary schools.

Management as social control in the colonial era

The management of schools in the pre-independence era thus depended not only on the various factors peculiar to a particular community and school, but also on whether the school was for whites or blacks. White education was intended to provide manpower requirements in nation building in government, commerce and industry by providing skilled labour, whereas black education was intended to provide unskilled and semi-skilled labourers. White education was regarded as a part of the colonial system, whereas there were fears that black education could, if not controlled, encourage African nationalism and provoke civil unrest. Part of the control was in the allocation of resources. For example, a European child received 13 times more than the African child from the government in per capita grant. Colonial authorities also insisted that teachers in European schools had to have formal teaching qualifications before they could be employed and yet, in African schools, there were invariably more unqualified teachers than qualified ones. The quality of teachers in African education tended to depend on the ability of a particular denomination to marshal resources at its disposal to improve teacher education. Some denominations were renowned for employing underqualified teachers. The Dutch Reformed Church missionaries in the early days of their work were particularly notorious for employing evangelist teachers, who in some cases had no formal qualifications other than their ability to read the New Testament (Department of Native Education Director's Report, 1928). The employment of underqualified teachers meant easier control in terms of what was taught and in terms of monitoring general school management. Although various local authorities ran their own schools, the system as a whole was highly controlled as a means of checking what went on in the schools. For example, for some time the Chief Native Commissioner and his assistants were authorized to inspect any African school at any time without prior notice to check whether subversive propaganda was being taught or if pupils were being taught 'to disturb the peace' (Synod Minutes, 1923; quoted in Zvobgo, 1980).

African schools were managed according to specific instructions given to head teachers by the missionary superintendents and occasionally by the government schools' inspectors. Schools were separate institutions, deliberately divorced from the life and culture of the local African people they were intended to serve. This was so because some missionaries regarded African culture as 'working so powerfully for evil' that it had to be destroyed root and branch. Boarding schools were sometimes encouraged as a means of separating the newly converted pupils from the 'corruping influences of their homes'. Local black parents had little say in the running of the schools in terms of policy or curriculum content, though they did provide cheap labour for the construction of buildings. In the colonial economic and socio-political milieu, where the aim was to squeeze Africans out of the reservations so that they could provide the cheap labour required by new industries, black parents saw in missionary education a way of enabling their children to escape from the deliberately engineered rural poverty, as those who succeeded in missionary education obtained jobs in mission service as teachers, messengers or evangelists, or joined colonial government service, commerce and industry as clerks and messengers. Towards the end of colonial rule some of those who had managed to get secondary education, and more, had obtained jobs in middle management in African affairs. The parents thus tended to accept the provision and management of schools more or less on missionary terms. In the majority of cases this meant that they, too, had to be 'converted' if their children had to have priority of acceptance especially in the upper primary and in secondary schools where there were relatively fewer places. Local school committees were formed largely to provide a forum for marshalling local material and human resources in the construction of schools.

The missionary-appointed headmaster, receiving instructions from the missionary superintendent and assisted by local Church elders, was a key functionary on the school committee and in the management of the school. The teachers, who in the majority of cases were underqualified and in a situation where the content of the curriculum was prescribed and packaged in detailed schemes of work, scheduled in some cases on a period-by-period basis, were simply purveyors of other people's ideas. Extra-curricular activities tended to be confined to soccer for boys and netball for girls and Church-related activities with pupils and parents during weekends. Teachers also supervised pupils during general work to keep the schools clean and occasionally went out to work for money with pupils to raise money to buy school equipment. Matters related to nation building were beyond the conscious grasp of most of the head teachers. Missionaries and district commissioners were supposed to represent their interests. Thus the African missionary-run school in the colonial period contributed towards nation building to the extent that missionary activities in general consolidated colonial government activities.

Indeed, Rhodes, the founder of Rhodesia, went on record as encouraging missionary activities on the grounds that they were 'more effective and cheaper than policemen' in maintaining law and order.

The management of the European school was necessarily different from that of the African school. In the racially segregated suburbs and avenues in the city centres, the school was seen as a part of the local community with the local parent-teacher association involved in its day-to-day activities. White parents, who generally shared similar political and educational values with colonial administrators, were better educated and articulate. They were regarded by the colonial authorities as part of the system and therefore did not pose any threat to colonial government interests. Since white parents had the franchise and therefore were directly involved in national affairs, they directed the school activities along lines best suited to develop the kind of person who would provide the kind of leadership needed to perpetuate colonial ideology. The white school headmaster had more autonomy than his black counterpart. He and his teachers were given freedom and authority to decide on curriculum issues and to decide on which board of examinations to use to meet the different needs of different pupils. They would also arrange that pupils sat for examinations when they were deemed ready. Such choices were not extended to the African education division where everyone sat for the Cambridge School Examination in November each year. White schools were organized along the prefect system with school and house prefects assisting in the maintenance of discipline. Inter-house and inter-school competitions were encouraged with a view to promoting leadership training and encouraging group cohesion, especially among pupils of English and Afrikaner extraction. There was an emphasis on character training and, as a result, outdoor activities like camping in wild game parks and mountaineering were encouraged. This was crowned with military training (National Service) just before the individual went on to higher education or into the world of work. The role of the school in nation building was seen as one of providing young men and women with a liberal education that emphasized character training enabling them to take positions of leadership in government, commerce and industry. The schools supported and serviced existing structures and institutions — they did not initiate them.

This background information to school management in the colonial period is necessary if we are better to appreciate the problems of school management and nation building in the post-independence era. The problems in question were, however, not peculiar to Zimbabwe alone. We might, with profit, briefly examine the experiences of other African countries at analogous periods and then look at Zimbabwe specifically later on.

Changing educational values after independence

At independence, most former African colonies tried to introduce new political philosophies which were generally inspired by an egalitarianism which was the very antithesis of the colonial, racially divided societies. Some of these ideologies and philosophies were justified on the grounds that they were closer to African traditional culture. In cases where independence had been won after a war of liberation, as in Zimbabwe, the ideology might be borrowed from the countries that provided arms as a gesture of consolidating friendship or just as a way of thwarting the former colonial power. Whatever the reasons, the problems as perceived by the new 'philosopher presidents' were those of transforming various institutions in their societies so that they could reflect indigenous, as opposed to foreign, values. The school was seen as being at the centre of this national transformation in terms of providing not only manpower and leadership training, but also in terms of transforming itself so that it would produce young men and women prepared to make a living out of the land rather than look for non-existent jobs in urban centres. It would also help train those who 'missed out' during the colonial era in order to sensitize them to the demands of the new political dispensation, so that they would play their rightful role as citizens aware of their political rights and responsibilities. Just as the colonial administrators used products of European schools for their interests, the new independent states looked to African schools to produce the kind of manpower that would help in nation building. This was mostly so because they derived their political support and power from the predominantly rural communities.

A few African examples quoted in Hawes (1979) will suffice to show this trend. In Tanzania, Nyerere's socialism based on self-reliance expected schools to be self-supporting productive units that would also provide adult literacy programmes which were seen as necessary for development. In Zambia, schools were encouraged to become production units under humanism. Kenya's brief flirtation with African socialism encouraged Harambee schools which were community supported schools. Similar ideals inspired the Imbokodvo Movement in Swaziland which challenged citizens to meet the needs of society by changing the curriculum to develop local human resources and Botswana's 'education for a nation' where schools were expected to contribute to social and economic development. Zimbabwe's mode of education for self-reliance developed under the banner of 'education with production'.

Such ideals derived moral support, justification and legitimacy from external bodies such as the United Nations, the Organization of African Unity, the International Labour Organization and the World Bank as indicated in Omari *et al* (1983). The United Nations Declaration on Human Rights encouraged, among other things, equity and justice in social and economic development as fundamental human rights. Although the colonial powers as signatories to the declaration generally accorded human rights to their citizens in the metropolis, they did not always extend them to their colonies so this was attempted at independence. The 1961 Addis Ababa Declaration by the Organization of African Unity Ministers of Education encouraged universal primary education on both moral and economic grounds. The International Labour Organization, on the same theme, stressed that all development required participation and that education was a driving force in human participation in economic, social and political transformation. Lastly, the World Bank in 1974 in its Education Sector Policy Report, stated that the provision of a minimum education was an essential condition for the effective participation of the masses in the development process that ensured better use of human resources. In its 1980 Education Sector Report, it saw education not only as a means of meeting labour needs, but also as a means of responding to the dynamics of a changing world, ensuring civic participation and making use of other human inputs such as nutrition, health, drinking water and housing.

Thus, in declaring universal primary education, Omari *et al* (1983) noted that Tanzania justified this by stating that education was a human birth-right for every citizen which would promote equality among members of its society. It saw education as a weapon for the eradication of ignorance and disease. It further stated that education would help develop national identity and unity which were necessary for meaningful political participation. Whether these assumptions were realistic or not is not the issue; what is important is that they inspired and influenced decisions made which were generally published as development plans.

At independence, Zimbabwe shared a similar faith in the potency of education and the school in spearheading nation building through social, economic and political transformation from a colonial capitalist society to a socialist independent state. However, unlike other black states, Zimbabwe had a sizeable white settler community after independence, and hence social transformation included encouraging racial harmony through the policy of national reconciliation — especially after the seven-year guerilla war that preceded independence and 90 years of legislated racial separation. The role of the schools in nation building was seen not only in terms of providing education for as many people as possible, but also in terms of teaching a socialist ideology through the curriculum and in creating racial harmony between blacks and whites. The small white settler communtiy, however, controlled the highly sophisticated capitalist economy (by African standards) and did not necessarily share the government's socialist and egalitarian ideology. This deprived the government of a strong economic base to effect its social and economic policies. Unlike Cuba and China, which at similar periods revolutionized their countries' institutions in line with their new ideologies, Zimbabwe could not do so without infringing on the Lancaster House Constitutional Agreement, on the basis of which elections leading to independence were held. The constitution enshrines, among other issues, individual rights to land and property, freedom of worship and freedom of political affiliation. This did put some limit on the extent to which the government could take arbitrary action to implement its policies. The government might also have been cautious in rushing change in the light of experiences elsewhere in Africa, where 20 years after independence ideological changes had not always meant economic and social development for the majority of the people. Destroying a sound economic base without a viable alternative might have been foolhardy.

However, the new government integrated the formerly segregated school system. It declared all primary education free and ruled that no child would be barred from entering a secondary school because of lack of school fees. The number of secondary schools increased from about 200 at independence in 1980 to about 1200 in 1984. School enrolment in both primary and secondary schools increased from about 800,000 in 1980 to 2¼ million in 1984 (Government of Zimbabwe, 1983). This put a lot of strain on both human and material resources and, as a result, too many untrained and underqualified teachers had to be employed. Some teachers had to be recruited from outside the country. Changes in curriculum included the introduction of 'education with production', where schools were encouraged to teach both academic and practical subjects with a view to marrying theory with practice. Former refugee schools in Zambia and Mozambique were repatriated into the country and sited on recently bought commercial farms. They were expected to pilot the scheme as they themselves had depended on self-reliance in exile during the war. The schools were expected to inculcate in the young habits of self-reliance on the land, as land and untrained manpower were seen as the biggest resources the country had. As a matter of policy the government stated that local authorities would be responsible for all primary education building, while it would pay teachers' salaries. Secondary education would remain its responsibility.

The management of change: dilemmas for head teachers

Such a massive expansion in schools, and the anticipated ideological transformation, called for a singleness of purpose among central government, local authorities, communities, schools and teachers for which the heritage of Rhodesia afforded little opportunity. We have noted the differences in school management between European and African schools prior to independence. These differences were removed at independence with the integration of the systems although in reality integration meant African pupils moving into former white schools in former white areas and not the other way round. White headmasters, teachers and pupils initially resented this influx of black pupils into 'their' schools. One Chief Education Officer in the Harare region commented, at a conference held in 1981, that the 'pupils who moved into former white schools were fighting a war worse than the liberation war in these schools.' In the black areas, the headmasters who had to manage the change process had no experience in taking independent decisions or in being innovative. They had been schooled in taking specific instructions from school superintendents and carrying them out. Whereas in the past instructions and directives came in the form of circulars, the expected reforms were generally announced at political rallies by politicians and reached some of the teachers through radio, television or the press. The newly appointed black educational administrators, recruited from the rank and file of teachers and college lecturers, were inexperienced in translating policy for purposes of implementation in schools. Moreover, the policy of Africanization of the civil service and other sectors of the economy through a presidential directive resulted in the movement of experienced secondary school teachers from the schools into these other sectors. At the same time, there was a massive expansion of education but because of this movement of teachers out of the system there were not enough managers left to manage the change process. Primary school teachers and untrained teachers were recruited into the new secondary schools while primary schools recruited largely from the pool of unemployed school leavers. They had enough problems in trying to settle down in their new jobs, let alone in managing change as envisaged by the politicians. In some cases the new administrators, teachers and parents did not always understand or even agree with the new ideology. Although, as elsewhere in Africa, the new ideology expounded by the political leaders was generally regarded, both internally and externally, as representing the views of the majority of the people in the country, there was a sense in which some administrators, teachers and parents saw the advantages of independence not in terms of fundamental ideological and qualitative changes (to the extent that they were aware of them) but rather in quantitative terms. They welcomed the expansion in secondary and primary schools but did not necessarily want a change in the curriculum, especially the academic secondary curriculum. Independence to them meant having access to those institutions and facilities that they had been denied. Education had always been seen as means of escaping from rural poverty; therefore any educational plan that was seen as purporting to keep the young on the land was likely to meet with resistance. Such a plan smacked of vocationalism which had been rejected during the colonial era. To some headmasters, independence did not necessarily mean learning new ways of doing things, but freedom from what was seen as the repressive authority of education officers under colonial rule. Some saw independence as giving them an opportunity to start small rural enterprises to augment their small salaries.

If some blacks resisted the suggested ideological changes, it was worse with the white community who regarded such changes as communist inspired. The movement of blacks into former white areas in itself was a traumatic experience. A year before independence, legislation had been passed through the 1979 Education Act which enabled local communities to buy government schools and run them as community schools. The local community was then to decide on who was to be admitted into the schools and who was not. To anticipate any possibilities of bussing pupils from the crowded African schools in the townships into the European dominated suburbs, zoning regulations were instituted which were intended to control the movement of pupils from one zone to another.

Both these pieces of legislation had been intended to keep black children out of white schools, except for those whose parents could buy or rent property in white areas. The new government, however, instructed the headmasters to ignore both the zoning regulations and the community schools concept. Some white parents threatened to take the new black Minister of Education to court, but to no avail. Others formed what was tantamount to a laager to control local parent-teacher associations which virtually ran their schools. They successfully applied for Management Agreements from government which enabled them legally to levy parental fees which would enable their school to employ additional teachers, as they believed that the new government teacher/pupil ratio of 1 to 40 in the primary schools was too high. Government, however, insisted that no pupil would be expelled from school because the parents had failed to pay the levy. The parent-teacher association could sue the parent but could not expel the child from school. Voting in some parent-teacher association meetings tended to go along racial lines, and where the blacks were in a minority they tried to invoke their newly acquired political power to influence events, which did not help in creating racial harmony as had been intended. In staff rooms, black and white teachers kept apart and so did the pupils during break times. The teaching of the new ideology was virtually ignored in both white and black schools, especially in the urban areas. Former white schools resisted the teaching of African languages — which was intended to facilitate racial understanding. 'Education with production' as a curriculum innovation became an empty slogan, with the former refugee schools gradually becoming more and more like ordinary schools as the pupils and teachers who had been in Zambia and Mozambique left the schools and were replaced by those who had no experience of the war.

The various authorities which ran schools during the pre-independence era, most of which comprised missionaries, continued to do so after independence. They did not necessarily share the new Government's socialist ideology. Thus, some headmasters found themselves caught between the conflicting demands of their local authority and those of national government. For example, when Government declared all primary education free, and that no pupil would be expelled from school because he or she did not have proper school uniform, some local authorities insisted on uniforms and charged a building fee to maintain old classrooms and build new ones. Some parents, mostly blacks, saw the charging of a levy or insistence on uniforms as a way of flouting government authority.

In some rural areas, in an effort to bring the school to the village, the school became a centre for local party political activities. The Chairman of the Education Committee of the local branch of the Party might want to inspect the teachers' books to show his authority. This sometimes resulted in the headmaster losing confidence as the line of authority became more and more diffuse. The headmaster had hoped that independence would allow him to enjoy the kind of autonomy his white counterpart had enjoyed under colonial rule. In some cases his ability to influence events in the community depended on his political party affiliation. Indeed, there was a tendency to use the political party machinery as a means of bringing parents together. In some cases this tended to isolate teachers and made them strangers in their schools.

In the area of curriculum, changes were generally enunciated from the top and new materials developed by central government through the Curriculum Development Unit. The extent to which the curriculum material writers themselves were ideologically in line with the proposed changes is difficult to assess, but they were generally recruited from the pool of experienced school teachers, and consequently there did not seem to be significant changes in orientation in the new materials they produced. The conceptual scaffolding of the materials remained basically Western-oriented, in line with the teachers' own training — except that in subjects like history, African heroes replaced colonial heroes and in social studies emphasis was now on local rather than foreign experiences. There were few in-service courses on how headmasters and teachers could use the new materials to reflect the new orientation within the context of their local communities. For example, when 'education with production' was introduced, there was little support given to schools on how this could be applied under various conditions obtaining in the country. Most head-masters interpreted 'education with production' as raising chickens and rabbits or growing vegetables. As the majority of schools were in communal lands where there was little arable land around the schools, very little was done to implement the policy. Some schools in rich commercial farming areas hired labourers to look after school fields, thus defeating the whole philosophy of the innovation where pupils were expected to respect manual work and relate it to theory.

A more insidious issue which confronted the innovators was one of societal attitudes towards what was considered worthwhile education and what was regarded as the good life. Although the policies put forward appeared plausible and realistic, set against the background of predomin-antly impoverished rural communities, society's view generally was that vocationally-oriented education was second rate, an option for academic failures. Worthwhile education was still seen in terms of obtaining good O levels. Good headmasters and teachers were those who produced good results. The Governor of the Midlands Province appeared on national television addressing headmasters and he promised a prize of Z$1500 out of his own pocket to the school that had the best O level results in 1985. Moreover, the children of politicians and senior civil servants were still sent to prestigious former white schools and independent schools, where the emphasis was still largely on the liberal curriculum and character training. The very maintenance of such schools after independence tended to undermine the newly enunciated policies. These schools continued to produce élites, albeit black élites, who would continue to take over roles of leadership in all sectors of Zimbabwean life. Indeed, it was the educated blacks, together with the remaining whites, who formed the new reference groups against which African aspirations were set. At independence, the educated Africans took over European jobs and moved into former European residential areas. This, to the ordinary parent, epitomized what a good education could do to change one's life style. Parents wanted this kind of education for their children, and not an education that would confine them to the land.

Thus, the kind of post-independence changes envisaged in Zimbabwe, and in other African states, required new types of schools, new roles for parents and teachers, and probably new profiles of teaching, which called for material and human resources and skills not available at the time of independence. Yet it appears that the authorities, spurred on by pre-independence rhetoric intended to mobilize the masses, were sometimes too impatient to allow resources to build up and institutions to evolve that would facilitate the change processes. To its credit, Zimbabwe, it appears, has not forced qualitative changes. These are allowed to evolve as opportunities present themselves.

On the whole, it is doubtful whether schools on their own can spear-head nation building through social and economic transformation. Schools, it appears, can only change at a pace dictated by other supportive dominant social, economic and political institutions.

References

Beeby, C E (1967) *Planning and the Educational Administrator* United Nations Educational Scientific and Cultural Organization (UNESCO): Paris

Department of Native Education (1928) Director's Report, Southern Rhodesia

Government of Zimbabwe (1983) *Annual Report of the Secretary for Education and Culture for the year ended 31 December 1982:* Government of Zimbabwe

Hawes, H W R (1979) *Curriculum and Reality in African Primary Schools* Longman: London

Nyerere, J K (1967) *Education for Self Reliance* Ministry of Information and Tourism: Dar-es-Salaam

Omari, I M, Mbise, A S, Mahenge, S T, Malekela, G A and Mbesha, M P (1983) *Universal Primary Education in Tanzania* International Development Research Centre (IDRC): Ottawa, Canada

Rhodesia Herald (1906) Rhodesia Herald (5 April)

Van Onselen, C (1976) *Chibaro: African Mine Labour in Southern Rhodesia 1900-1933* Pluto Press: London

Zvobgo, R J (1980) Government missionary policies on African secondary education in Southern Rhodesia with special reference to the Anglican and Wesleyan Methodist churches. Unpublished PhD thesis. University of Edinburgh: Edinburgh

Part 5: Management Training

16. Recent trends in management training for head teachers: a European perspective

Tony Bailey

Summary: In Europe over the past 15 years serious efforts have been made, despite difficulties, to launch major training schemes for head teachers. Much has been learnt from the experience: the increase in professional dialogue at the international level, facilitated by such bodies as the Organization for Economic Co-operation and Development (OECD), the Council of Europe and the European Economic Community (EEC), has made a significant impact upon development, particularly among latecomers to the field.

However, claims that training programmes are successful are advanced only with great caution. Where detailed and systematic evaluation of effectiveness has been undertaken, it has confirmed the complexity of the problem. Nevertheless, the field is not static. Training is developing in both concept and practice. There is a clearly discernible trend away from traditional, modular 'knowledge-input' courses towards personal development programmes, which help heads improve their ability to learn from experience. Other innovations are seeking to integrate training within broader programmes of policy development.

Introduction

School management training in Europe is in a phase of rapid development, with training strategies being increasingly influenced by international dialogue. In the early 1980s several international organizations (OECD, Council of Europe, Association of European Education) sponsored workshops, conferences and development programmes. These in turn have led to an exchange of written papers and a lively debate on policy and practice, which has yielded a growing body of literature. From these exchanges I wish to select four general areas of concern in an attempt to demonstrate that there is, amidst all the debate, a general trend among the major programmes to integrate management training in broader regional or national policies of educational development and school improvement. These four areas of concern are:

1. applying the concept of management to schools and its implications for training;
2. emerging questions of theory and method in school management training;

3. the problem of effective training;
4. the links between management training and policy development.

Applying the concept of management to schools and its implications for training

The first and most obvious point to note is the increasing interest in school management training in recent years. Training opportunities for heads and senior teachers have been available in most countries for many years, but there was little systematic provision until the 1970s. Over the past 15 years, several European States have launched national training initiatives — especially for head teachers. France (1971), Sweden (1974) and the Netherlands (1976) were the early developers, and still are considered to be the leaders in systematic training provision. However, other countries have followed suit. Norway in particular has, since 1981, developed an imaginative national programme. In 1983 the United Kingdom launched a major national initiative which is yielding some interesting developments in training at regional level, and the newly established National Development Centre for School Management Training is conducting a pilot scheme with local authorities in management development.

It is clear from the various descriptions of these initiatives that they have been taken as a result of changing views of the functions of the school and its provision of educational services. In Sweden, for example, the national training programme arose in response to the move to decentralize educational decision making. In Britain, it is closely connected with demands for a more effective response from State education to changing social and economic circumstances.

There is a general consensus that these changes in the school place a heavy burden on the head teacher in particular, requiring the job to be reconceptualized. In some cases, especially in the United Kingdom, attempts have been made to construe the role by reference to industrial and commercial management. Thus Hughes (1983: 24) reports 'Head teachers in the 1970s advocated a more managerial approach to their role', and academic writers 'drawing on the literature of industrial management'. Although there are still strong reservations about the industrial management analogy in its more simplistic form, its influence is considerable in the United Kingdom. The recent national training initiative has been accompanied by a strong industrial influence, with several industrial training modules being offered to head teachers and to school management trainers as examples of good practice.

This direct transposition of industrial management concepts is not so apparent in other European training programmes. There is a clear recognition of the need for schools to adopt more effective methods of planning and organizing their affairs, and there is evidence of the influence of the 'human relations' and 'scientific management' traditions of management development. But training strategies would appear to have been developed as a direct response to the perceived needs of heads, teachers and schools rather than being imported from other fields of management. Thus, for example, Ekholm (1981: 25), writing on the Swedish national programme which he co-directs:

> A headmaster is expected to work with others (adults and young people) in a truly democratic fashion. Democracy in each and every school should, if possible, serve as a model for and make a lasting impression on the young pupils, so that they wish to continue it and, where necessary, introduce it at various phases of and situations in their lives.

Soubry (1978: 18), in explaining the impact and consequences of the student riots of 1968 on French educational policy, emphasizes the key concept of 'la vie scolaire' (school life) in the national head teacher training programme:

> What is apparent in these definitions is the idea that the French educational establishments are something other than places of teaching — where pupils were to learn and the teachers give lessons — that they are also places where pupils and teachers live together outside the classroom, where relationships are formed amongst them and with others . . .'

Bailey and Renner (1980: 4) record clear statements from British, Danish and German head teachers on the educational imperatives which shape and condition management practice in schools within pluralist democracies:

> Schools must create a cooperative and tolerant community atmosphere creating a climate within which the spirit of democracy and respect for individuals can be inculcated in students . . . If schools are seen to be controlled democratically with a constitution which directly involves parents, teachers and community representatives this provides a working example for the student which will be significant in his own development.

This requirement of schools to reflect a broad range of social and cultural values in the quality of their internal relationships is not in itself contrary or alien to the experience of industrial management, but it provides a particular bias or emphasis both to the job itself and to the training experience. Similarly, the common British image of the head as the leading professional provides its own point of emphasis as Hughes (1983: 36) observes: 'In particular the professional-as-administrator construct provides a conceptual basis for the consideration of matters such as staff participation and development, school evaluation and accountability at various levels'.

In the United Kingdom, the demand to inject industrial management practice and training into schools has been over-simplified. As long ago as the mid-1970s, empirical analysis of managers in industry and commerce indicated that there was no single pattern of managerial action. Stewart (1976) clearly demonstrates the very wide range of conditions which the modern manager faces in terms of the pattern of working contacts or relationships and the nature of the tasks undertaken. Some managers spend most of their working life in contact with subordinates; some are themselves closely supervised; some need the social skills to secure the cooperation of peers; some have a hectic life, facing new tasks, telephone calls or face-to-face contact every few minutes; while some regularly engage in tasks with longer time spans.

Stewart's analysis raises a major question for industrial management trainers: how can the training experience be made relevant to the needs of managers, each of whom may have to cope with very different working conditions?

There is scope for the transfer of training practice between different sectors of management training and there is much potential for head teachers gaining insights into the working conditions of industry and commerce. But there is no case, even within industrial management, for a universal pattern of training. Consequently, simplistic analogy and the wholesale importation of training models from one management situation to another is not a serious option.

Emerging questions of theory and method in school management training

Stewart's insight into the variety of experience which managers face is of considerable importance to school management trainers and is at the heart of this second issue.

Accusations of irrelevance are frequently levelled at professional in-service training courses and school management training has not escaped criticism. The point was put quite forcefully by one speaker at the Association for Teacher Education in Europe (ATEE) conference at Gatwick, England in May, 1982: 'Trainers with strongly favoured ideas of their own can have a ball and can manipulate the training scheme to fit their own needs'.

One of the main areas of irritation is in the apparently irrelevant presentation of 'theory' and its constant companion – the lecture. Hopes, representing a German perspective at the Gatwick conference, demonstrated the two-sided nature of this problem:

> Trainers experience a strong resistance to theoretical concepts by the practice-orientated participant. Trainers are obliged to use material from commerce and industry, and from countries where training in educational administration has a long tradition, yet the trainees often have difficulty in relating the 'foreign' theory to their own practical situation (ATEE/NAHT 1982: 17).

Attempts to remedy this situation have frequently involved an emphasis on practical management issues through simulations, role plays and specially created case studies. These activities have considerable merit. They can generate enthusiasm and provide the participants with a range of personal insights into situations closely resembling their own working experience. However, the experiences and insights yielded by the game need to be analysed purposefully and their implications for school management or personal professional development considered in depth. Without this, games and case studies are just as susceptible to irrelevance as lectures; the fact that they engender interest rather than boredom is in itself of little significance. To the trainer, case studies and simulations, once developed, have the same appeal as the lecture; they are easy to organize and to repeat in subsequent courses since they do not require any adjustment to accommodate the experiences of individual participants. But herein lies the limitation.

To overcome this problem, course designers have tended to incorporate project work and practical school-based exercises. The term 'exercise' is used here to indicate that the work is undertaken for training purposes and not necessarily for practical implementation. Thus, for example, it is possible to engage in strategic planning exercises based in a school in order to gain insight into the process without any commitment to implementing the outcomes. But again, without subsequent analysis of the experience, the exercise has only limited value.

This issue was taken further in Sweden in the early 1970s by the PLUS Commission (Plan for the Training of School Leaders). Ekholm (1979: 22) reports that the Commission in the end came down in favour of 'concrete and immediate experiences that each participant brought from his own everyday situation'. The Swedes were prepared to take the bull by the horns and accept that vicarious experience is second best. More significantly, they were raising a much bigger question which trainers all too often avoid: what assumptions can be made about the way in which head teachers as mid-career professionals and managers learn and develop?

The Swedes were, in effect, challenging the model implicit in most training programmes of the time – the 'technical deficit' model (Figure 1).

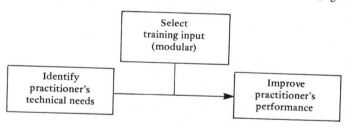

Figure 1 *Technical deficit model*

The design of training courses frequently begins with a generalized review of head teachers' needs, often conducted by exerienced heads who are considered able to speak for their colleagues. Usually courses are designed in modular form to meet these needs. The PLUS Commission rejected this approach and sought a training programme which required the participants to focus on their own experiences and their own definitions of need.

Looked at another way, the call for *experiential* learning enables us to place training in its proper context. Any discussion of training programmes must recognize that some head teachers have achieved success without any mid-career training at all. Senior people in all walks of life have successfully responded to new challenges and generally improved their performance as they *learn from experience*. The starting point, therefore, is to consider how these people achieve their success: how they manage their own development. It may be that we can provide more effective training experiences if, from the outset, they are perceived as an aid and adjunct to this common human intellectual process of coping with life and not as an independent external initiative.

Two main approaches have been advocated in response to the call for experiential learning which might, for convenience, be labelled the *problem-solving* and *learning-plan* approaches. These two approaches are not incompatible; indeed they both owe their intellectual origins to the social psychology of Kurt Lewin in the 1940s and they can be brought together with considerable effect. But it is useful to present them here separately, partly because they are often to be found in courses as quite separate entities.

Problem solving has close links with planned change and innovation theory. It came to prominence in the education world through the work of R G Havelock (1973) concerning guidelines for change agents, although the concept was already well established (see, for example, Lippitt *et al*, 1958). Several training programmes now require participants to spend time on an institutional problem of their own choice. Perhaps the most single-minded example is contained in the types of action learning workshop advocated by Revans (1971) and more lately Braddick and Casey (1981). Braddick and Casey describe how practitioners meet for whole-day sessions at three- or four-week intervals over a period of a year or so to help each other resolve institutional problems. A set adviser helps with the process of problem solving, but not with solutions. Several of the new regional school management courses in England (Bristol, for example) have attempted to incorporate action learning sets within broader, modular training programmes.

Proposals to design school management training around the concept of a personal learning plan were advanced by members of the Swedish and Dutch training teams at an OECD conference held in Dillingen, West Germany, in October 1984. This reflected developments in their own thinking and planning which had been considerably influenced by North American research on mid-career professional learning styles (Kolb *et al*, 1974). The basic assumption is that people benefit from systematic reflection on their experiences in formulating, reformulating or consolidating what they do and how they work. Kolb advances a model of experiential learning (Figure 2 on p 219) to clarify this process.

The following extract elaborates the model:

> Learning is conceived of as a four-stage cycle. Immediate, concrete experience is the basis for observation and reflection. These observations are assimilated into a 'theory' from which new implications for action can be deduced. These implications or hypotheses then serve as guides in acting to create new experiences. The learner, if he is to be effective, needs four different kinds of abilities — *concrete experience* abilities (CE), *reflective observation* abilities (RO), *abstract conceptualization* abilities (AC), and *active experimentation* abilities (AE). That is, he must be able to involve himself fully, openly, and without bias in new experiences (CE), he must be able to reflect on and

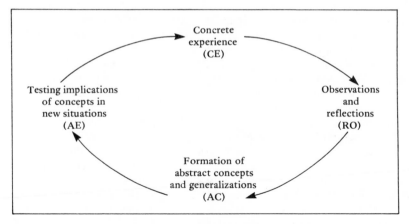

Figure 2 *The experiential learning model*

observe these experiences from many perspectives (RO), he must be able to create concepts that integrate his observations into logically sound theories (AC), and he must be able to use these theories to make decisions and solve problems (AE). Yet how difficult this ideal is to achieve! Can anyone become highly skilled in all of these abilities or are they necessarily in conflict? How can one act and reflect at the same time? How can one be concrete and immediate and still be theoretical? Indeed a closer examination of the four-stage learning model reveals that learning requires abilities that are polar opposites and that the learner, as a result, must continually choose which set of learning abilities he will bring to bear in any specific learning situation. More specifically, there are two primary dimensions to the learning process. The first dimension represents the concrete experiencing of events at one end and abstract conceptualization at the other. The other dimension has active experimentation at one extreme and reflective observation at the other. Thus, in the process of learning one moves in varying degrees from actor to observer, from specific involvement to general analytic detachment (Kolb, 1974: 28).

Kolb then examines the different learning styles which people develop in their attempt to reconcile these polar opposites of learning. For Kolb, a main purpose of training is to help people be more aware of their learning style and improve it.

In Kolb one can identify a constructive response to the theory/practice debate raised earlier. For he focuses firmly on the function of experience in achieving learning and development. In this he is not alone. But his major contribution is in demonstrating that it is the use made of experience that matters; that the crucial question is the process of learning *from* experience, not *about* it. He reveals the connections between action and reflection; he establishes the significance of the ability to externalize experience in order to consider which patterns of action are appropriate to the future.

The OECD conference in Dillingen was addressed to these issues and attempted to formulate training procedures which were consistent with this view of professional development. Gonzalez-Tirados (1983), reporting on school management training in Spain, gives another example of the use of Kolb's learning cycle within a modular course. These closely parallel current experiments in industrial training (eg Richardson and Bennett, 1984). Other work, drawing on the same conceptual background, includes the development of learning materials to support management self-development (Boydell and Pedler, 1981; MSC, no date; Francis and Woodcock, 1982; and the Local Government Training Board, 1984).

However, while both the problem-solving and learning-plan approaches show much promise, difficulties are still found in gaining a transfer of new learning skills to life in school. Even when a training programme focuses on working experience, participants still find difficulties in connecting the training experience in any lasting way. Somehow, with the best will in the world, the new approaches to personal development are lost in the pressure of daily work; the sharing of thought and experiences is not quite so easy with colleagues in school as it was on the course. This leads on to the third issue: the problem of effective training.

The problem of effective training

Even with the adoption of an experiential approach to school management training, course designers are still faced with difficulties in helping heads make good practical use of their training. All courses provide access to new ideas, skills and knowledge and a chance to share experiences with other heads. But this alone is no guarantee of effectiveness. Effective training relates to *subsequent actions*: actions in terms of both personal development and school improvement. However interesting a course may be, however well presented, it will have no lasting effect for the course members unless they are able to make use of the experience in practical terms. Ideas without action atrophy.

In terms of personal development, the process of experiential learning can be greatly enhanced by the range and quality of personal contacts available to discuss ideas and issues which arise, and the most important source of support lies within the school community. Head teachers must find ways of sharing thought and perspectives on personal development with some senior colleagues. Their common understanding of the school and its purposes, their perceptions of the head at work, and their availability for discussion and joint action, make them an invaluable resource. The head's perception of school management as a collective professional enterprise or team effort will have considerable bearing on the degree of support available. If headship is seen as authority in isolation, then personal development will be a lonely affair and the poorer for it.

If one is looking for subsequent action in terms of its effect upon the school then it must be recognized that schools do not develop simply by the efforts of one person, however talented or influential. School improvement is the result of a collective effort by the whole of its community.

This principle of collective action is echoed in much of the work on organizational development (Schmuck and Miles, 1971); in the United Kingdom, The Schools Council Guidelines for Review and Internal Development in Schools (McMahon *et al*, 1984) insist that the essential first step is to secure collective support for action. Kolb (1974) also stresses the potential of organizational members with different learning styles cooperating to solve organizational problems.

The process of school improvement, therefore, cannot be seen simply as a definition of new policies and programmes, or problem solving within the school's organizational system. It must take into account the efforts of the teachers to respond collectively to the challenge of new policies and operational problems by helping each other to learn from experience. If heads are to harness their training to the cause of school improvement they must be prepared to share the experience with other members of the school. In turn, they should accept a responsibility to support colleagues in their own development, since this is just as important to the school. Personal development is an essential ingredient in school improvement, provided it is seen as an open and interactive process.

There are quite basic steps to be taken which will increase the chances of effective training. For example, heads can attend courses 'ready for action'; that is, having prepared themselves and their colleagues back at school for subsequent action. Unless from the beginning they are expecting to act, they are unlikely to develop a positive orientation later. Trainers and local authority inspectors can also help in this briefing process and can indicate what resources are available to the school in support of subsequent action. The question of resources is crucial. Without support of this kind, even the best training experience is of limited value. Esp (1980: 15) regards the Arnhem courses in the Netherlands as being 'in the premier league of head teacher initiatives'. But their effect is limited: 'The basic problem is that this course stops at the critical stage where heads are ready to continue development in their own schools of skills gained on the course. Because of staff shortages the Arnhem team are unable to act as consultants for this work'. (Esp, 1980: 14).

The Norwegians would appear to be taking the question of systematic, post-course support more seriously than most others, creating a structure of consultancy and a system of 'schools in contact' (Kvist, 1982: 8). Seljelid (1982: 47-55) also gives details of the steps taken to provide financial support for this period of action. But in other cases attempts to support subsequent actions have had disappointing results.

This may be a question of time scale. Ekholm (1981: 24) comments from the Swedish experience: 'We assume that significant improvements in individual schools will take an appropriate period of time. A change in procedures and relationships at a school seems to need about five to seven years, otherwise there is no real chance of achieving lasting effects'.

The Swedish and Norwegian courses are spread over a period of two to three years in an attempt to foster effective training. The French are building a three-tier system of training which may have similar effects.

Once management training is seen in terms of support for a process of reflection and action, the question of time scale becomes crucial and Ekholm's estimate might seem quite credible. But the speed of externally imposed change might require a more urgent response.

Management training and policy development

We have seen how the perception of management training has ranged from notions of the technical skill needs of individuals to support for the process of school improvement. In situations where a major policy change is being imposed upon schools it is necessary to go further to design management training programmes as an integral part of the developmental support for the policy change. In essence, this is the approach adopted in both Sweden and France where the training programmes emerged as part of a national policy of decentralization.

A further example is provided by the Hordaland experiment in Norway which began in 1978. New legislation, giving employees greater influence over their working climate, had clear significance for teachers and for the style of leadership in schools. From the outset, management training was seen as a response to this policy and incorporated the following principles: (Kvist, 1982: 2)

1. Leadership is a comprehensive concept. School administrators, headmasters and teachers are all leaders and need leadership training. Headmasters are key figures in schools and therefore strategies for change and innovation should take particular care to secure their full involvement and cooperation.
2. The training should be organized in such a way that leadership, change and innovation are continually subject to discussion in the school society.
3. There should be widespread participation by the people involved in all phases of the project. The responsibility for progress is *in* the school, not outside.
4. The innovation process should start on a basis of a self-analytic diagnosis.

In the United Kingdom, the national training initiative of 1983 was initially conceived in much more individualistic terms. The need for schools to respond positively to the demands of the times was at the heart of the initiative, but there was no clearly expressed connection. Nevertheless, some of the regional initiatives are beginning to experiment in more direct links between policy development and training.

The City of Liverpool has recently reorganized all its secondary schools as a result of a declining school population and migration away from the city centre to the suburbs. Some schools have been closed, others amalgamated. The resources available to the City for management training under the national initiative are being deployed in collaboration with the

North West Regional Management Centre and integrated into programmes of support to enable the reorganized schools to respond positively to their new circumstances. As with the Hordaland experiment, personal and organizational development are brought together at the school level.

There are also strong external pressures on British schools to make radical changes to the curriculum to provide more effective technical and vocational education for young people. At the same time schools are being asked to institute procedures for self-evaluation and accountability. These types of change, coupled with the uncertainties of school reorganization of the type experienced in Liverpool, require quite major changes in management practice. School management implies flexible teamwork with head and teachers being prepared continuously to re-assess the changing situation; to reform into appropriate task groups for the development of new school policies and programmes; to be reorganized into new teaching teams as the curriculum changes. It is 20 years since Burns and Stalker (1966) argued the need for organismic structures within organizations if they were to cope with conditions of environmental uncertainty. The situation which schools now face matches their analysis.

But schools cannot be left to face the problems alone. The need for flexible teamwork spreads beyond the school to involve the local authority support teams of officers and advisers. They, too, must become involved in integrated training programmes. This has been recognized by the London Borough of Merton in a programme developed in collaboration with the University of Sussex. The following extract from an internal planning document makes the point:

> Education generally, and especially secondary schools, face new challenges in the next few years. The autonomy of heads and the separate specialisms of inspectors are a potential handicap in developing strategies for the implementation of LEA policies and Government initiatives. Clearly, neither group can ignore what is happening and it is vital that all learn to work together so that, through corporate action:
>
> (a) specific issues are taken up properly and professionally; and
> (b) policies and plans are implemented as effectively and efficiently as possible.
>
> Hence a major objective of the course must be to improve and develop the skills of working together on issues of common concern. The course will provide opportunities for heads and inspectors to work together on joint tasks of educational planning, development and evaluation. It will encourage them to reflect on this experience and to formulate plans for further joint action after the course ends. Participants will be expected to have regular contact during the course with a senior officer of the LEA who will be involved in the discussion of future action.

Thus there are signs in the United Kingdom, as well as in the Netherlands and Scandinavia, that a structure of training is evolving in response to a reassessment of the support needs of head teachers. Glatter (1983) urges a broadening of concept from 'training' to 'planned development'. He reports on the work of Burgoyne (1976) and Houle (1981) which draws attention to the development potential of other activities such as participation in policy-forming committees.

Such approaches remind us that much professional learning and development occurs in an unplanned, spontaneous way; and that planned development need by no means be restricted to formal instruction, which often seems to be the sole connotation of the term 'training' (Glatter, 1982: 102).

Moreover, training provision is now being perceived within the broader framework of management development. In the UK, the National Development Centre for School Management Training is engaged with eight local education authorities to design systematic programmes of management development which will relate the provision of training experiences and other support for personal development to the broader issues of school improvement and regional educational policy. Training programmes must not be seen in isolation, but as an integral part of a developing education service.

References

Association for Teacher Education in Europe and National Association of Head-teachers (1982) *Training for Heads (School Leaders) in Europe.* Report of conference 12-14 March at Gatwick, ATEE: Brussels; NAHT: Haywards Heath, West Sussex

Bailey, A J and Renner, G (1980) *Education for Democracy* Report of a conference 7-12 July 1980 organized by the European Academy, Berlin, in association with the University of Sussex: University of Sussex

Boydell, T and Pedler, M eds (1981) *Management Self-development: Concepts and Practices* Gower Press: Aldershot

Braddick, B and Casey, D (1981) Developing the forgotten army — learning and the top manager *Education and Development* **12** 3: 169-80

Burgoyne, J G (1976) Learning processes in the acquisition of management skills and qualities *Management, Education and Development* **7** 3: 205-08

Burns, T and Stalker, G M (1966) *The Management Innovation* Tavistock Publications: London (second edition)

Council of Europe: Council for Cultural Cooperation (1983) *School Management Training in Europe* Report of the 12th Council of Europe Teachers' Seminar, 21-26 September 1981, Donaueschingen. DECS/EGT(81)3-E Council of Europe, Council for Cultural Cooperation: Strasbourg

Ekholm, M (1979) *Research in Education — Does it Matter?* Report No 3 from School Leader Education, University of Linkoping: Linkoping, Sweden

Ekholm, M (1981) How does the headmaster put what he has learnt into practice? Experiences with the Swedish training programme for headteachers *in* Council of Europe: Council for Cultural Cooperation (1983)

Esp, G D (1980) *Selection and Training of Secondary School Headteachers in the Netherlands* Report on the author's AEC Trust Fellowship study visit ERIC/ED209179 Somerset Education Committee: Taunton

Francis, D and Woodcock, M (1982) *Fifty Activities for Self-development* A companion volume to Woodcock and Francis (1982) Gower Press: Aldershot

Glatter, R (1983) Implications of research for policy on school management training *in* Hegarty (1983)

Gonzalez-Tirados, R M (1983) A programme for the training of school directors at the Polytechnic University of Madrid *in* Hegarty (1983)

Havelock, R G (1973) *The Change Agent's Guide to Innovation in Education* Educational Technology Publications: New Jersey

*Hegarty, S ed (1983) Training for management in schools. Papers from an educational workshop organized by the National Foundation for Educational Research (NFER) at Windsor, 14-17 September 1982, under the auspices of the

Council for Cultural Cooperation of the Council of Europe. NFER-Nelson for the Council of Europe: Windsor, Berks

Houle, C (1981) *Continuing Learning in the Professions* Adult Education Association of the USA: Washington, DC

Hughes, M G (1983) The role and tasks of heads of schools in England and Wales: research studies and professional development provision *in* Hegarty (1983)

Kolb, D (1974) On management and the learning process *in* Kolb, Rubin and McIntyre (1974)

Kolb, D, Rubin, I and McIntyre, J (1974) *Organizational Psychology: An Experiential Approach to Organizational Behaviour* Prentice Hall: New Jersey (second edition)

Kvist, P (1982) Leadership in schools: a Norwegian programme for improvement. Sheffield Papers in Educational Management No 27 Sheffield City Polytechnic: Sheffield

Lewin, K (1943) Forces behind food habits and methods of change. National Research Council Bulletin CVIII: Washington, DC

Lippitt, R, Watson, J and Westley, B (1958) *The Dynamics of Planned Change: A Comparative Study of Principles and Techniques* Harcourt, Brace & World Inc: New York

Local Government Training Board (1984) *The Effective Manager: A Resource Handbook* EMAS Publishing: Budleigh Salterton, England

McMahon, A, Bolam, R, Abbott, R and Holly, P (1984) *Guidelines for Review and Internal Development in Schools (GRIDS): Secondary School Handbook* Longman for the Schools Council: York

Manpower Services Commission (no date) *Management Self-Development: A Practical Manual for Trainers* MSC Training Division: Sheffield

Revans, R (1971) *Action Learning in Hospitals* McGraw-Hill: Maidenhead, Berks

Richardson, J and Bennett, B (1984) Applying learning techniques to on-the-job development Parts I, II and III *Journal of European Industrial Training* **8** 1: 3-7, 3: 5-7 and 4: 3-7

Schmuck, R A and Miles, M (1971) *Organization Development in Schools* National Press Books: Palo Alto, Cal

Seljelid, T (1982) *Handbook for the Working Environment and the Running of the School (AMS) Project* Ministry of Cultural and Scientific Affairs: Oslo

Soubry, G (1978) France: the training of headmasters *Educational Administration* **7** 1: 15-32

Stewart, R (1976) *Contrasts in Management* McGraw-Hill: Maidenhead, Berks

Woodcock, M and Francis D (1982) *The Unblocked Manager: A Practical Guide to Self-development* Gower Press: Aldershot

17. Can educational management learn from industry?

Elisabeth Al-Khalifa

Summary: Research into school improvement has encouraged interest in the training of principals as a means of increasing effectiveness. In Britain, industrial management training has been invoked as a model for the training of head teachers. The application of such a model of management to schools is questioned. Generalizations about managerial work are criticized for ignoring significant variations in behaviour and in work contexts. It is argued that comparisons between school and industrial management, despite similarities on the surface, are unsatisfactory because of organizational differences. A classification of these is developed focusing on organizational boundaries, accountability and control relations, goals and organizational functions, and the allocation of resources. Furthermore, the management function in schools is significantly different from industrial management in both its non-specialist character and the ambiguity of its status. The conclusion reached is that industrial models can have some usefulness in developing an understanding of school management but that schools require context-related management models and training practices.

Background: school management training and the influence of industrial training

A feature of much recent research into school improvement internationally has been a focus on the role of the principal and the provision of training to increase the principal's effectiveness. In England and Wales this same concern has led to a growing investigation into the concept of school management, and the development of school management training. The latter has been accelerated by central government allocating funds to support a range of regional and local training initiatives intended to train those teachers identified as 'managers', especially the head teacher and deputy head teacher, but also teachers with curricular or pastoral posts of responsibility, none of whom necessarily receive training before taking up managerial posts.

The concept of management and management training has been taken from industrial sources, especially from private sector profit-making organizations, and has influenced perspectives on theory and training within the State school system. School management training has been perceived as novel for the education system, and disastisfaction with traditional approaches to in-service training, as well as a view that industrial management training is well established, has encouraged those responsible for funding and policy to search for models and strategies for educational management training within industry. The appearance of publications on educational management strongly influenced by industrial management or written by industrial trainers, such as Handy (1984) or Everard (1982), and the use of industrial trainers in an advisory capacity in current management training initiatives in education, reflect the underlying assumption that there are parallels between industrial and educational management and therefore between the training needs and methods of such. However, if industrial training methods are introduced into educational management training it is important to establish more clearly in what respects there are similarities between educational and industrial management and, where there are differences, what the significance of these might be for thinking about school management and training.

One approach to this problem is to consider what managers actually do. Key studies investigating this, using diary and observation methods (Stewart, 1967; Mintzberg, 1973), reach similar conclusions about the character of management work which, they claim, is marked by the manager's preference for live action rather than planning, for face-to-face contact rather than solitary activity.

> In contrast to activities performed by most nonmanagers, those of the manager are characterized by brevity, variety, and fragmentation. The vast majority are of brief duration, in the order of seconds for foremen and minutes for chief executives . . . The manager actually appears to prefer brevity and interruption in his work. . . Superficiality is an occupational hazard of the manager's job. The manager gravitates to the more active elements of his work − the current, the specific, the well defined, the non-routine activities (Mintzberg, 1973).

Mintzberg's work is of particular interest, not only because he is much quoted in the management literature, but also because his research provided a model for research into school managerial work conducted by Webb and Lyons (1982) in British schools. They arrived at similar findings, thus apparently confirming the appropriateness of comparing school and industrial management.

Mintzberg maintains that all managerial work is similar: 'managers' jobs are remarkably alike. The foremen, presidents, government administrators, and other managers can be described in terms of ten basic roles and six sets of working characteristics'. The ten roles he formulates are classified into three groups − interpersonal, informational, and decisional − and within these groups are: figurehead, leader, liaison; mentor, disseminator and spokesman; entrepreneur, disturbance handler, resource-allocator and negotiator. He argues that any managerial job will include all ten roles, and these can serve as the basis of training, as a role is a 'categorization of what the manager does'. Mintzberg goes on to assert the possibility of scientifically constructing programmes which can be associated with each role.

> From production work to clerical work to the complex information-processing activities of the specialist, the power of management science has been demonstrated. As he achieves more and more success in reprogramming the complex tasks of the specialist, it is inevitable that the management scientist will turn his attention to the job of the senior manager, the last and the greatest of his challenges (Mintzberg, 1973: 134).

It would appear that Mintzberg was committed to establishing generalizations about management in order to develop standardized training procedures for all managers (especially in view of his later claim that the findings of his research demonstrate the need to use management scientists in order to make management more effective). Since his role categories are frequently referred to, and have been used to describe the work of heads and deputies in secondary schools by Webb and Lyons to their satisfaction, it is necessary to examine these more closely.

First, Mintzberg's claim for having established some general findings are qualified by the point he makes himself that there are variables which account for variations in observed managerial behaviour, namely, variations in job levels and function, the manager's personality, and environmental and situational factors such as seasonal variation. In his own group of five managers he points out that the hospital manager is divergent from the others. It would appear from this that the generalizations are not as comprehensive as he initially claims.

Second, Mintzberg quotes an example of a manager who realizes nine out of ten of the roles, and refers to the study of a production line superintendent whose work includes checking daily machine-load charts, checking up on machine failures, tracing the faults and bringing in the mechanics. It is clear from this example that, although a manager may perform the ten roles, the role classification does not provide a description of managerial behaviour in a way which is likely to illuminate the essential character of the work. In what sense can it be seen as meaningful to argue that the work done in the case of the line superintendent is similar to that of a head teacher, of a managing director or of an accounts manager? Indeed, most of Mintzberg's roles could equally well be used to describe the work of mother and housewife, but such a description would tell us little about the meaning and the skills involved in such work. Mintzberg's account of managerial work does not, therefore, offer either a reliable or useful basis for comparing industrial and school management because of the level of abstraction of his generalizations, and his interest in demonstrating regularity because of his conception of management as a science.

Stewart's research (1967; 1976; and 1982), although including a set of role classifications, has been engaged in pursuing the differences between managers. Significantly, in her first study (1967) she draws attention to the divergence between managers in their work and concludes that it is impossible to talk about 'managers' as an undifferentiated group. She argues the need for a more selective approach to description and training. Her subsequent studies have addressed the question of difference and seek explanations for such differences and a means of classifying these in order to improve selection, effectiveness and training. Her research was motivated by three main gaps:

> The first, and most important, is our ignorance of the differences between managers' jobs. The second is that we still know little about what the manager has to do, apart from the specialist aspects of his work. The third gap, which stems from the first two, is the paucity of the tools available for those who need to analyse managers' jobs for selection, identification of training needs, or for evaluation (Stewart, 1976).

Using a sample of 250 managers, Stewart develops a typology of managerial work based on different work contact and work activity patterns, analysing the differences she maintains exist among managers beyond the functional differences of their work. These are differences not only of individual style but also of constraints operating in different contexts, which in turn require variations in skills and experience.

In her most recent book on managerial work, Stewart (1982) re-emphasizes the unsatisfactory nature of knowledge about managerial work, and therefore of the training offered. The theme of her previous studies of difference in managerial work is reiterated and developed here, together with her focus on demands, constraints and choices in management. Management is too often described in terms of function (specialism) and level.

> Management training rarely takes account of other variations between jobs, yet the identification of training needs requires a good understanding of the characteristics of individual jobs, and of the abilities and skills that they require. Those involved in training managers from different organizations also need some understanding of the variations in jobs caused by organizational differences (Stewart, 1982).

Problems of using industrial management models in school management studies

Stewart's analysis raises considerable problems about comparisons between industrial and school management, because of the weak knowledge base she identifies in the field of industrial management. On the one hand it is possible to make comparisons, if the focus of the comparison is on what can be observed of managerial behaviour in daily routine tasks. Thus, on the evidence of diary studies, we know that senior staff in schools engage in their work in the same fragmented manner as their counterparts in industry, that they prefer live action to long-term planning, that they spend most of their time in contact with other people, and that the head in particular engages in external contacts (Webb and Lyons, 1982).

However, these analyses reveal little about the meaning of such activities in the life of the different organizations, or their appropriateness and effectiveness in relation to the overall purposes of the organizations concerned. Stewart's interest in examining the demands, constraints and choices in management jobs requires a much more specific and context-dependent analysis of managerial work, and moves away from the notion of broad comparison and broad generalization which characterizes most thinking about management and management training. Moreover, her criticisms of management research suggest the need for caution when drawing on industrial models of management as a reference point for school management.

Stewart touches on the issue of organizational differences and the effect of these on managerial work, but there is little evidence of this being developed by those who have written on school and industrial management, with the exception of Handy (1984). Some of the analyses which compare industrial and school management take up the issue of organizational differences, but in ways which obscure or avoid the implications. Jenkins (1983), for example, in a study comparing industrial managers and school head teachers in England and Wales, contrasts the leadership styles of the two groups in his sample, and concludes that these differ. Using the two dimensions 'initiating structure' and 'consideration' taken from leadership theory, he argues that school heads and deputies were more preoccupied with a people-centred approach to management, and were 'high in consideration', whereas the industrial chief executives were concerned with task completion and were 'high in initiating structure'. As evidence for this he uses self-perception measures and cites the extensive contact of heads with pupils, parents and staff, and concern with pupil control. In contrast, he suggests that industrial managers were concerned with people only insofar as they needed to solve problems such as work stoppages and ensuring continuing production.

However, this type of comparison is not especially helpful because what constitutes 'initiating structure' in schools is not examined and so the basis for making comparisons from this perspective of leadership is not clarified. What is missing is whether, when comparisons are made, the organizations under discussion have enough in common to make comparison worthwhile, and whether the measures of managerial work used are appropriate and can allow action which will improve management of the organizations concerned. These factors do not appear to have been considered.

This question can be examined further by other examples of comparisons made between school and industrial management. Everard, writing on what can be learned from industry, argues that comparisons can be made and makes his case by referring first to role similarities using Mintzberg's classification, and second listing skills which are held in common, including such items as 'bureaucratic and clerical skills, resource planning, and decision-making skills' (Everard, 1982). These lists, while they are superficially recognizable ways of describing work, carry little information about the demands, constraints and choices affecting management work that Stewart sees as important. Nor are we able to derive any information about the content or situations in which such skills have to be operated. Everard argues the case for making comparisons and stresses the similarities, but then goes on to point out that there are, of course, some differences:

> the *raisons d'être* are different, the culture and the norms are different, the outlooks and aptitudes of the staff are different, the structures are

different, and the environments are different in some respects (Everard, 1982).

This list of differences is far from trivial but is passed over without further comment. Later, Everard (1982: 35-41) goes on to outline a collection of training techniques which could be useful in school management training, but without any reference to organizational context or work types. What is missing from these comparisons is an account of the organizational life of the school and the significance of this for managerial work.

A classification of organizational contexts for industrial and school management work

The following discussion is intended as an exploratory classification contrasting the organizational contexts of managerial work in schools and industry (summarized in Figure 1 on p 232) and may help to pinpoint some general and more specific features of the two. Is it possible to conceive of the two types of organization as entities, with definite boundaries, thus delimiting the scope of management? In the case of industrial organizations the boundaries are clear, and it is easy to identify those features which are internal to the organization and those which are external, even if the latter influence or affect the business of the organization.

Although schools can be located in a set of buildings, and could be narrowly defined as composed of teachers and pupils, this definition of the organization becomes problematic when the relationship of others to the school is considered. For example, in British schools, what is the status of ancillary staff, or of advisers, school governors, the national inspectorate, local elected members, officers, and parents? Handy (1984) points out how, even in teachers' minds, there is uncertainty about the membership of the school as an organization, since teachers apparently do not consider pupils part of the organization. If the limits of the school as an organization are defined as a membership of pupils and teachers, there is still the problem of explaining the organizational relationship between the employers, that is, the local education authority (LEA) and the school. If the school is seen as part of a larger organization — the local education system — an account still has to be provided of the relationship between the LEA and the Department of Education and Science (DES) and others. Such broader definitions of organization become distanced from the concept in the industrial context and, furthermore, they fail to reflect the perceptions of individual school staff and pupils of school membership. It is probably necessary to see schools as organizations with rather fluctuating boundaries.

The source of such ambiguity can be traced to the kind of power and accountability relations which exist in the education system, and which differ from the industrial situation. In industrial organizations, power is located within the organization, and is linked to the hierarchy of authority. Although there is some degree of external control through shareholders,

Industry	Schools
Organizational boundaries	
Clear — easy to distinguish between internal and external relations.	Unclear.
Accountability and control	
Internal system, based on formal hierarchy within the company. Specific criteria for evaluating managerial effectiveness.	Complex process, with internal and external referents. Lack of specific criteria for staff effectiveness.
Goals and functions of the organization	
Determined within organization. Specificity possible at the discretion of individual manager, unit, or for whole organization.	Determined internally, externally. Fluctuating participant groups. Goals multiple, diffuse, conflicting, rapidly changing.
Individual values marginal to goals.	Personal values and ideologies form basis of goals. Legitimate concern of managers.
Management function	
Managers form a distinctive section of workforce. Specialize in managerial work. Differentiated pay and status. Career commitment to management.	Managerial work distributed widely among staff. Overlap of professional role. Orientation to teaching.
Resources	
Internally determined. Dependant on market performance. Clear criteria for allocation.	External allocation by budget decision, as a result of political processes.
Management continuity	
Control of personnel and succession internal to company reflecting goals or policy.	Control of appointments divided between a variety of external interests.

Figure 1 *Organizational differences in industry and schools which affect managerial work*

and constraints on some aspects of company functioning because of government legislation (for example, on safety or pay), these controls are limited in impact on the overall policies and functioning of the company, and do not in themselves constitute an accountability system for evaluating managerial effectiveness, or criteria for managers to operate with in supervising other staff. Control of organizational members is embodied in the organization's structure and accountability is channelled through this, using job-specific criteria for evaluating effectiveness. Managers know their location within the power hierarchy and chain of command,

and their job specifications define as much what they cannot do as what they can do. These relationships are often reinforced in visible aspects of the working environment, a feature of industrial and commercial organizations examined in Kanter's study of a multinational corporation (Kanter, 1977). Thus the hierarchy of control is maintained simultaneously through formal structures and task definitions and through informal but visible signs of status and stratification.

In schools, the ambiguity of boundaries is related to the existence of a complex system of control and accountability and several referent groups holding power. The head teacher has responsibility for the school and has legally constituted authority to direct staff and to determine policy within the school; in turn, he or she is responsible to the Chief Education Officer, and therefore to the elected members of the Education Committee. Nevertheless, various groups have the power to intervene or attempt to influence the school. This hierarchy of authority is therefore misleading, and the division of funding between local and central government compounds this problem. Evaluating managerial effectiveness is made more difficult in the absence of clear criteria for this. The differences that exist between the structures of control in industrial organizations and in education are not simply a matter of form and procedure but reflect a complex of philosophical, political and economic issues which divide the two. Such differences are evident in discussions of accountability within the British education system, for example, the three-fold classification used by Barton *et al* (1980) of strict accountability, responsibility and answerability.

A key feature, or characteristic, of organizations is the existence of goals, and such goals are articulated in industrial management by the statement of company business plans. Targets and tasks can be defined both for the whole and individual units. Although such goals can be disputed they are defined within the organization, by criteria and preferences found therein. There are constraints operating, notably the markets available, and legislation which may affect the means of achieving such goals, but even though these limits exist on industrial management, the nature and scope of the business is essentially an internal matter. Mergers, sackings, redundancies, product changes and new subsidiaries are manifestations of changing goals, but all these will be the result of management choices within an organization and be relatively specific and open to clarification. As well as overall goals related to profitability, all the different levels of management and the sections they are responsible for can operate with targets and programmes amenable to evaluation and success/failure measures.

In schools, the concept of goals is less satisfactory at both theoretical and practical levels and, indeed, the term itself has little acceptance. Even the more conventional terms, 'aims and objectives' are resisted by teachers when describing their work. School heads can, and do, decide policy to some extent and conventionally are considered to exercise considerable autonomy in this along with their teachers. There are also, however, a number of interest groups which have both the authority and influence to shape and direct school policy. While the purposes of an individual school are open to the direction of the head, direction is also a process which teachers expect to engage in as professionals — not only in their own subject area but also in relation to issues concerning the whole school curriculum and ethos. In contrast to industry there is a large area of discretion for individual initiative. The formal goals are partly a product of political processes within the school, and dependent on changing power relations and interest networks within the school staff rather than the result of processes undergone within management alone. (This is not to deny that in both industry and schools, participants can have personal or alternative goals which are pursued at the expense of the managerial goals; what is under discussion are the organizational goals which are essentially managerial.) In industry the goals are formally the product of managerial decision, although the extent to which different levels of management participate in decision making will vary. In schools, all teachers expect to participate, and because of the system of control and accountability all goals depend on teachers' commitment for their legitimacy and realization.

Another distinctive feature of school goals is that they do, in fact, originate from sources other than the head and the staff. Goals may emerge through what Eric Hoyle has described as a 'dialectic' between what is imposed and what is actually done, and schools thus operate with a succession of goals, with certain issues paramount at a given time. External bodies, including the DES, the LEA advisers, the local education committee, the university examination boards, parent groups, teacher unions, and so on, may have their own agendas for the school concerned, which they can pursue with varying degrees of success depending on circumstances and their power base. Particularly evident is the ability of central government to redefine the goals of schools in radical ways, so that not only do goals change rapidly, but they can also involve a substantial reorientation of function and purpose. So, for example, schools can change from selective to comprehensive, or from age range 11-18 to 11-16 in a short period with consequences for their goals and organization. When schools are credited with substantial autonomy, this ignores the limits to this which actually exist. It is possible for a head and staff to change what is taught within subject areas, and often the styles of teaching, but it is extremely difficult for more radical change to be undertaken except when a school is newly created. The limits to school-based control of goals are heavily circumscribed.

A further dimension of difference in goals is the problem of arriving at overall goals which are both meaningful and can be agreed, an almost impossible state given the number of stakeholders in education and the uncertainty of educational technology. The key is, of course, the nature of the educational process itself, concerned as it is with growth and change in children, as contrasted with the product orientation of industrial organizations. This management problem is made more complicated by the way in which personal values and ideologies of teachers have the potential to define organizational purposes and that these are considered to be legitimate aspects of school life. Thus a head's personal values may become the dominant values to be pursued in the school, and parents may well search for one school whose ethos reflects a given set of values in preference to another. However, consensus on values and norms in a school is unlikely and it follows that the centrality of personal values in formulating a school's purposes carries with it the major problem of how such differences can be resolved and what constitutes the basis for such solutions.

The problematic nature of the issue of goals is summed up by Handy (1984) when he points out that schools have too many purposes:

> Organizations that have clear-cut tasks to do are easy to run. A one-product business may be financially risky but it is not organizationally complicated. All its energies and resources go in one direction, success is clearly measured and failure is obvious. Schools are not so fortunate. Education is an envelope word — we can make it include almost anything we want, and school can end up as the melting-pot of society's expectations. Success in education is elusive, hard to measure and, maybe, not evident until many years have passed.

Handy concludes that such features of schools create a major management problem, and the measurement of progress necessarily becomes highly subjective.

The difficulties of conceptualizing schools as organizations in the same way as industrial organizations is demonstrated by the difficulties in describing what are considered key components of organizations, that is, the boundaries and goals. This difficulty is dealt with at a theoretical level by the description of schools as loosely coupled systems (Weick, 1976), but at the level of management practice this suggests significant differences between schools and industry. At a very concrete level, the most striking structural difference is the distribution of the management function. In industry, there exists a distinctive group of personnel who specialize in management, whatever their previous expertise. This group is identifiable even in small companies with as few as 20 employees, and managers are distinguished by differences of status and pay, with managerial work seen as a legitimate full-time activity. For many managers, the job represents a career commitment which they entered into when first employed, or early in their careers after working in a specialist function. In British schools, however, only the head is a full-time manager, and even then, in some cases, still teaches. Jenkins comments on the continuing orientation of even the head teachers towards teaching, a feature even more pronounced among the deputies who had a considerable teaching timetable (Jenkins, 1983) and the same points are made by Webb and Lyons in their 1982 study.

Handy (1984) observes that school management is also characterized by an absence of 'managerial' space, since head teachers, deputy heads and heads of department do not have offices or adequate resources and time for meeting. Managerial work is distributed widely among staff and there is therefore considerable overlap of 'professional' and 'managerial' responsibilities. (This is a point reflected in the small degree of differentiated allocation

of space and with the absence of a clearly stratified distribution of
facilities and equipment, as compared with the arrangements in industrial
settings.) The status of school management is therefore not clear, and
certainly teachers' attitudes towards it are ambiguous, with a noticeable
orientation and commitment to classroom teaching persisting even when
teachers are in fact appointed to posts which are seen as managerial,
such as those of deputy head and headship itself.

Such ambiguity has immediate as well as long-term implications for
school management and the role of management in school improvement.
Teachers who move into managerial work, especially as deputies or head
teachers, often find it difficult to reorient themselves from a style of
working as classroom teachers — which is concerned with direct face-to-
face activity with children — to managerial work, which embodies a
dependence on others working through teachers to achieve effects and
change.

The weakly developed management function in schools is emphasized
by other factors which are typical of schools but not of industry. First,
resources in schools are allocated by externally devised budget arrangements, and so school management is deprived of one of the major tools
for planning and the means of determining and realizing its aims. Second,
the managers' scope is also restricted by the system of what in industry
would be conceived of as planned succession and development in management. In schools, appointments are controlled by various interests, and the
head does not necessarily have much influence on senior appointments.
The criteria for appointments at senior level are haphazard and may bear
little relationship to school aims, or even overall LEA aims, as Morgan
et al (1983) have shown in their study of appointment processes. Third,
although in-service training provides a means of developing staff, it rarely
can realize organizational aims, and does not provide the change of experience that can be achieved within industrial organizations — by job moves
as well as in-company training. Most striking is the fact that a typical head
will have had only one experience of senior management before appointment, that is, as deputy head in one other school, whereas in the industrial
context, especially in larger companies, it is possible for managers to be
given a range of experience at a similar level, either within one company
or through job changes. There is also the possibility for particular managers
to be given new projects which they are especially suited for. School
managers are constrained in the choices to be made regarding staff
appointments and, therefore, in building up a preferred team, and also in
their own preparation and experience, in contrast to the potential for
development and wide experience that exists in the industrial context.

Schools would be wise to be different

The differences outlined here between schools and industry as organizations indicate the contrast that exists between the task of management

in each case. The problems of comparing organizations which exhibit such differences of structure and function may make the attempt to compare the two misconceived. The unease that school teachers feel about the terms used, such as 'manager', 'middle manager', 'performance appraisal', 'managerial effectiveness' and so on can be interpreted as fear or distrust both of non-educational experience and the introduction of such models into their professional sphere of influence. The unease can also be seen as a manifestation of the significant differences between schools and industrial organizations in meanings and purposes. That there is reason to doubt the validity of over-extended comparisons is apparent in the writing of some commentators on management.

The treatment of non-educational management as generic is in itself unsatisfactory when it is recalled that a variety of organizations are included in this — manufacturing and service industries, public and private sector, profit and non-profit making — with any number of employees, ranging in size from small businesses to multinational corporations. The Director of the British Institute of Management has pointed out that the management of public services appears to be very different from that of industry and the private sector, indicating structural and functional reasons for this, and thereby identified problems for training and effectiveness which were distinctive. If comparison between public and private sector services is seen to be difficult then arguably it must be even more so in the case of schools.

Handy's (1984) discussion of school management demonstrates how experience of management and organization processes in industry can illuminate our understanding of schools and their management and change assumptions about their organization and leadership. Generalized comparisons between industrial management and school management should be treated with caution, however, not only because of the major organizational differences but also because industrial organizations themselves are diverse. This does not mean that comparisons are not possible, as Handy demonstrates. Rather, following Stewart, that insight into managerial work and its effectiveness can be achieved by considering the context, and the requirements arising from that context. It follows that training for management should not be regarded as a matter of direct transfer from one situation to another, but instead reflect similar contexts of use and need.

Although an attempt has been made here to clarify organizational features of schools and industrial concerns, there is no reason to suppose that these are static and not amenable to change. It is often assumed in discussions of industrial management that, at its best, it can provide a model for schools. It is arguable that the changes needed in schools to improve educational provision may require structures and practices which would actually distance schools further from the mainstream of industrial organizations. As Handy (1984) comments: 'Schools would be wise to be different'.

References

Barton, J, Becher, T, Cannng, T and Eraut, E (1980) Accountability and Education in Bush *et al* (1980)

Bush, T, Glatter, R, Goodey, J and Riches, C eds (1980) *Approaches to School Management* Harper and Row/The Open University: London

Everard, K B (1982) *Management in Comprehensive Schools: What Can Be Learned from Industry?* Centre for the Study of Comprehensive Schools: York

Gray, H L ed (1982) *The Management of Educational Institutions: Theory, Research and Consultancy* Falmer Press: Lewes, Sussex

Handy, C (1984) *Taken for Granted? Understanding Schools as Organizations* Longman for the Schools Council: York

Jenkins, H O (1983) *Job Perceptions of Senior Managers in Schools and Manufacturing Industry* Unpublished PhD Thesis University of Birmingham

Kanter, R M (1977) *Men and Women of the Corporation* Basic Books: New York

Mintzberg, H (1973) *The Nature of Managerial Work* Harper and Row: New York

Morgan, C, Hall, V and Mackay, H (1984) *The Selection of Secondary School Headteachers* The Open University Press: Milton Keynes

Stewart, R (1967) *Managers and their Jobs* Macmillan: London

Stewart, R (1976) *Contrasts in Management* McGraw-Hill: Maidenhead

Stewart, R (1982) *Choices for the Manager: A Guide to Managerial Work and Behaviour* McGraw-Hill: New York

Webb, P C and Lyons, G (1982) The nature of managerial activities in education in Gray, H L ed (1982)

Weick, K E (1976) Educational organizations as loosely coupled systems *Administrative Science Quarterly* **12** 1: 1-19

18. Training for school management in the Third World: patterns and problems of provision

Paul Hurst and Susie Rodwell

Summary: This chapter presents an overview of the patterns and problems of educational administrator training in the Third World, drawing on the authors' experience and observations of a range of training initiatives and on some of the pertinent literature.

The current emphasis on training educational administrators is discussed in relation to earlier educational preoccupations and trends in developing countries, and the danger that administrator training will become another in the list of transient fads is noted. The chapter identifies five principal patterns of current provision, briefly highlighting some of the issues and problems associated with each.

The nature of this provision is examined further. Until now greater emphasis has been given to quantitative questions than to questions of quality. It is suggested that the latter needs to be more carefully addressed and that course design and training methodology are key problem areas; a brief overview is given of developments in the use of a variety of methods and materials. The challenges faced by Third World trainers are, it would seem, remarkably similar to those faced by trainers in industrialized countries, namely, how best to solve the problems of what training schemes to adopt, what content to cover, what learning experiences to provide and what methods to employ. However, these issues are particularly critical in the Third World because of the shortage of trained trainers.

The chapter concludes by suggesting that if the initiatives in the Third World are to have significant impact in the future there are five key problem areas that will need to be tackled. These are: inadequate budgets, undertrained trainers, lack of suitable materials, neglect of research into training needs and the impact of training, and the lack of a coherent national training policy.

Introduction

Education in the developing world, as in industrialized countries, is rather prone to waves of enthusiasm for some particular aspect of activity, which is ultimately supplanted by another. Right now, training educational administrators seems to be an area of intensifying interests, at least in quite a few different parts of the world.

There has been a succession of different educational preoccupations in the Third World since the days of newly achieved independence in the early 1960s.

1. The build-up of secondary and higher education to meet shortfalls in well-qualified manpower.
2. The generation of many curriculum development projects aimed at making the content of education more relevant, and less influenced by colonial perceptions of what was appropriate.
3. The disappointing love affair with educational technology, which promised to make education more effective, cheaper and more widely disseminated, and which largely failed to deliver these promises.
4. Educational planning and the push to increase enrolments rapidly. There were massive achievements in enrolments but, against a background of rising population figures and falling economic growth figures, the anticipations of universal primary education in many developing countries by 1980 proved a cruel disappointment. Educational planning has come under heavy attack, since it is widely perceived to be unduly centralist and undemocratic, as well as prone to margins of error in guessing the future. These margins of error are so substantial as to put the utility of the planning exercise in considerable doubt.
5. Non-formal education as the life-raft on which optimistic pundits seek to escape from the sinking ship of formal educational systems which are said to be irrelevant, ineffective and inefficient. (De-schooling — the extreme reaction — never caught on in the Third World, thank goodness.)

So now the training of educational administrators/managers (call them what you will) seems to be one of the current and growing enthusiasms. Curiously this preoccupation is as equally visible in industrialized countries as in the Third World. For some reason, Australia, Canada and some (but by no means most) parts of the USA have given administrator training priority and emphasis for a good few years now. Indeed, a small number of institutions in the USA have a track record going back decades, although their work was often heavily oriented to research and theory-building as opposed to training. Elsewhere the emphasis is fairly new. Britain, for example, has just launched a national scheme for the training of head teachers, with a centre currently located at Bristol University, and there are some parallels in other Organization for Economic Co-operation and Development (OECD) countries.

Many of these new developments are clearly based on dissatisfaction with prior arrangements. Four questions immediately post themselves.

1. Why this new preoccupation with training educational administrators?
2. What patterns of provision exist in Third World countries?
3. What is the nature of current training provision?
4. Is present provision having a significant effect, or is it likely to?

These are questions we shall address in the rest of this chapter.

Training — the new emphasis

The new emphasis on training educational administrators has its roots in the experiences of the 1960s and 1970s. As remarked earlier, these decades saw a succession of attempts to extend the provision of education in developing countries, to define more relevant goals and contents, to improve effectiveness and raise the quality of education, and to make it more efficient, thereby increasing quantity and quality without escalating costs. In broad terms, the achievements in extending access to education have been impressive, even if they fell short of the early optimistic targets. But a considerable price has been paid. Many would argue that standards have fallen (albeit compared to earlier systems that were much more élitist) and costs have not been significantly reduced. Perhaps most significantly, the belief that the models of education which the Third World inherited from the West are irrelevant is still widespread. Yet efforts to reform education have made relatively little progress (at least in relation to the early expectations of what would be accomplished). Hence the current diagnosis that it is the implementation of these reforms that is the weak link in the chain. If education is managed at the middle and lower levels by people who have had no training, then (the argument runs) it is not surprising to find that they are not particularly effective, efficient or responsive to change.

One of the principal agencies to espouse this view is the World Bank, and it is no coincidence that several of the national institutes being established in Third World countries were set up with World Bank funds. However, the Bank does not dictate to borrowers what they must borrow for, although it wields considerable influence, and there is no doubt that this analysis is as widely shared in ministries of education as it is in other agencies such as UNESCO. It is hard to disagree with this consensus, although there are several dangers inherent in it. One is that training administrators will become another on the list of transient fads or gimmicks to which education is prone, to be replaced by something else as soon as it appears that results will be hard to come by and will not be achieved overnight. Another is that commitment will be rhetorical rather than real, and that token efforts will merely scratch the surface of the problem. A third is that the training programmes are likely to succeed in training people in systems maintenance but not in innovation and reform.

Current provision — principal patterns

In developing countries, attention to the training of administrators is by no means evenly distributed. Some countries give it much more weight than others. We can distinguish five principal forms of provision:

1. *Ad hoc* one-off courses or conferences, organized by departments of the Ministry of Education or local authorities (this term is used

to denote any regional, provincial, district or local authority charged
with providing educational services).

2. Courses organized by university departments of education.
3. On-the-job training.
4. Training abroad.
5. Specialized Ministry-sponsored institutes for the training of educational administrators.

In the first form of provision, we find ministries laying on courses or
conferences within the Ministry itself as a rule. These are provided for the
planners, the curriculum developers, the inspectorate, office managers and
local directors of education, but usually on an occasional basis. There is
not normally any sequential basis to this provision — it attempts to deal
with specific problems as they occur — and it rarely attempts to cover the
mass of principals and deputy principals who are usually too numerous
to be catered for in a provision like this. The weaknesses of this provision
are numerous. There is usually little or no investigation into the real
training needs of the participants, and very often the courses are mainly
intended to inform participants of some new initiative rather than equip
them to carry it out. The 'trainers' are often carrying out a propaganda
role; they may have little training skill or ability; not infrequently they are
ignorant of education and will have been brought in temporarily from a
national institute of public administration or some university equivalent.
There is also often little follow-up in terms of supporting the participants
in their subsequent work or evaluating the impact of the original input.

The second form of provision — by university departments of education — has also been exposed to a considerable volume of criticism.
The courses usually lead to an academic award, and this may mean that
they are too long and too preoccupied with the acquisition of academic
knowledge and skills which are different from those needed by the
administrator. A frequent complaint is that these courses are too 'theoretical' and insufficiently 'practical'. This distinction is really a naive one;
the problem is more that such courses tend to stress acquisition of knowledge (of facts and theories) rather than acquisition of skills or
competencies. Of course, in reality one needs the most appropriate
mixture of both, and ultimately the distinction between 'theory' and
'practice' breaks down; 'there is nothing so practical as a good theory',
and it has often been said that the problem is to know what theories are
good ones and to discern their practical implications. Also, academic
courses do entail the acquisition of skills — taking notes, writing succinct
presentations, listening and exposition, gutting texts for their essential
significance under pressure, and others which are very much germane to
the administrator's task. Nevertheless, many administrative skills, particularly in the human relations domain, are given little airing in these courses
other than by exposure to such theoretical fields as organizational
sociology, industrial psychology, systems theory, and development
economics. The chances of administrators being able to improve the
morale of their subordinates as a result remain doubtful. Even much more

mundane ideas, such as how to run a staff meeting, or a parent-teacher association, or how to do the accounts, tend to receive scant attention. Further, university-sponsored courses often apply excessively stringent admissions and assessment criteria in relation to the employer's and the employee's needs in terms of job performance.

On-the-job training, our third category, is rarely practised in any systematic way. School principals are often expected to make the transition from classroom teacher to head teacher on the basis of classroom experience alone. A fortunate few will have served a period as deputy principal under the watchful eye of an experienced and helpful head, or a novice inspector may be teamed with a more experienced one, but whether any formal training other than 'sitting with Nellie' or 'learning by doing' takes place is unlikely. One of the few countries anywhere to have a formal scheme where principals train their deputies is Japan. Another form of on-the-job training is in the use of distance teaching materials — self-instructional manuals or correspondence courses. These are not widespread at the moment but there is growing interest in the techniques. The Alama Iqbal Open University of Pakistan provides correspondence courses for educational administrators, for instance. However, doubts have been expressed about whether distance teaching can effectively improve skills, although its scope in improving the knowledge base of trainees is not questioned.

The fourth form of provision, training abroad — most frequently on academic award-bearing courses in foreign universities — has usually been reserved for higher-level administrators and planners. It is, of course, very expensive and in most countries it depends on the supply of aid-funded scholarships from foreign donors. (One curious omission in the past, which is now beginning to receive some attention, is courses for the training of trainers.) The same kind of criticisms of university-type courses reported earlier are levelled at this form of training and, in some instances, such courses may be even more irrelevant. It is not unknown for administrators to attend courses in industrialized countries which are intended purely for nationals of those countries. In Britain, for example, trainees from Third World countries may find themselves on courses which demand a detailed knowledge of the workings of British local government and the Department of Education and Science, and which rarely contain even an element of comparative study of administration in other European countries. Indeed, our observation is that educational administration training in many parts of the world is very parochial; we have known trainers to maintain that they have nothing to learn from other countries.

This raises a very important question, to which we shall return later, concerning the relevance of training aims, contents and methods developed in any one context to any other. Interestingly, one form of foreign training which is developing and increasing is for groups of trainees from one Third World country to go to another.

The fifth form of provision, that of national institutes for training educational administrators, normally sponsored by or part of the Ministry, is a more recent phenomenon. There are several of these new institutions — particularly around the rim (and in the middle) of the Indian Ocean and the South China Sea.

In order to draw some tentative conclusions about the effectiveness of this new emphasis on educational administrator training in the Third World, it is pertinent to examine further the nature of this provision. We will do this by drawing on some of the relevant literature and on our own observations and experiences.

The nature of the provision

Training is only one of a number of solutions that can be adopted to equip the administration with the managerial and technical know-how it requires. There is growing recognition in the West that formal training has not lived up to its promise in terms of improved performance. This has led to some disenchantment with training itself and consideration of alternative approaches to professional development and organizational development. It has also stimulated a search for conditions under which training might be more effective and the closer examination of strategies and methods to identify those which might better promote the transfer of learning to the job. Are there parallel concerns in the Third World concerning the quality and impact of provision?

Many of the recent initiatives in training educational administrators in the Third World have tended to focus on meeting the immediate quantitative requirements for training rather than in addressing qualitative questions. There has been little exploration of alternative approaches to professional development and, given the implications of these in terms of resources and expertise, it is most likely that the main option in developing countries will probably continue to be some form of formal training, at least in the foreseeable future.

A few countries which have a longer record of administrator training are, however, now paying attention to the quality of present provision. This is particularly so in the Far East region where the UNESCO Regional Office has been instrumental in enhancing the capability of national training centres in carrying out their training programmes, through training and materials development workshops and inter-country study programmes. A key focus of such activities has been the recognition of the need to explore the use of a wider variety of training methods and improve materials (UNESCO, Roeap, 1983). Poor course design and inappropriate training methodology appear to be the major problems of present provision and it will be useful, therefore, to take a closer look at these, focusing in particular on methods and materials.

An overview of methods used in training administrators

The descriptive literature on teaching methods and materials used in preparing educational administrators is extensive, particularly as it pertains to the West. The methods of instruction range from traditional lectures to case studies and modern instructional technology, such as the use of computer simulations. Many of the non-traditional methods now used derive from the experience in fields other than education (eg military and business training), but there has been an increasing tendency to explore the potential of approaches such as case studies, in-basket exercises, simulations, and so forth, in educational administration training, and to shift the emphasis in training courses from learning through theoretical and knowledge-packed lectures to learning and developing administrative skills through practice, experience and less traditional methods (Wynn, 1972; Rost, 1980).

Reports and observations of methods used in the Third World have indicated that there is also a trend towards greater use of non-traditional methods. Thus, a review of programmes for training school adminsitrators and supervisors in the Far East (UNESCO, Roeap, 1981) revealed that methods used included lecture-type sessions, panel discussions, viewing of films, in-basket training, group dynamics, simulated games, and role playing.

Training methods — key issues

The case for non-traditional approaches to training is based on a number of arguments. A key feature of these is the view that experience is all-important in the learning process. One of the major proponents of learning through experience is Kolb *et al* (1979); training, it is argued, needs to be experiential and directly related to the reality of administration, in order to help promote the transfer of learning to the job. While one approach is to take the classroom 'into reality' through attachments, non-traditional training methods are designed to help bring reality into the classroom; often they are the only substitute available for supervised field attachments.

The case for non-traditional methods is supported by what is known of how adults learn. There must be a clear distinction between andragogy and pedagogy (Knowles, 1973); the former is described as process model, where the teacher (trainer) acts as a facilitator and creates a mechanism for mutual learning with suitable techniques and materials. This is contrasted with the pedagogical method where the teacher decides the knowledge or skills to be transmitted, and 'teaches' using lectures, readings, discussions and other expositive methods.

There are, however, many factors which militate against the wider use of non-traditional methods. One problem is that the development of materials in support of methods, such as in-basket exercises, and simulations is time-consuming and demands expertise which is often not available. The methods have implications in terms of space — depending as they frequently do on intensive small group work and/or large areas for simulation situations — and time; human relations techniques achieve best results through a series of events over a period of time. Such methods can also prove threatening to both participants and the trainer. The former are confronted with difficult situations, in which their responses and behaviours are exposed and challenged; the latter can no longer depend on being the teacher and the font of wisdom, but becomes a facilitator of unique learning experiences.

Factors such as these are very critical in Third World countries where all too frequently the availability of trained trainers is a severe limitation to more widespread use of non-traditional methods. Moreover, concern is sometimes expressed about the appropriateness and acceptability of methods developed in a different (Western/business) context. It is certainly important to consider the possible cultural bias of the assumptions of learner-centred participatory training. Discussions in the literature about the appropriateness of Western methods in developing countries is, however, not very widespread, although in recent years increasing attention has been given to the suitability of transferring Western models of professional preparation and development of educational administration, and to the relevance of theories of school administration (Marshall, 1983; Lungu, 1983).

One writer, Thiagarajan (Thiagarajan and Prahalad, 1969), highlights a number of problems involved in running behavioural science-oriented management training programmes in developing countries. He questions the relevance of the human relations methods as they are based on alien assumptions about student-teacher roles, and suggests that while there are some universally related and unique areas of behaviour, there is 'little systematic evidence as to where and to what extent cross-national differences exist and what environmental factors explain these differences'.

A contrasting view is given by Kindervatter (1983), a non-formal adult educator, who suggests that the hierarchical patterns of dominance and deference evident in Asian cultures, which some see as conflicting with the active participation fundamental to a learner-centred approach, are only evident in certain relations and certain contexts. In rural areas a picture emerges of informal learning through peer interaction and group discussion. Thus, if the teacher acts in a formal classroom manner, the learners will assume formal roles but, if the teacher acts as facilitator, the group will behave more similarly to the informal discussion patterns; a learner-centred approach may actually reinforce rather than conflict with traditional values.

In discussing the question of cultural appropriateness we are faced with a paucity of research. However, it also seems that there is very little more general research concerning the effectiveness or otherwise of non-lecture methods in administrator training. Much of the evidence regarding the benefits of the various participatory methods is subjective, random and derived from the opinion of participants and trainers. Very little detailed or rigorous evaluation has been carried out, particularly with regard to the transferability of learning to the work situation. There has been some research on methods used in management training but most of this focuses on human relations methods, and in reviewing research Burgoyne (1976) found no 'pure' research studies on case study methods, for example.

Despite the lack of empirical evidence, attempts have been made to produce 'models' for selecting 'appropriate' methods for training administrators which identify the relationship between various training methods and a range of variables (eg Pfeiffer and Jones, 1977; Laird, 1978; Hawrylyshyn, 1975; McCleary and McIntyre, 1974; Pareek and Rao, 1918). Most such models highlight the fact that, since there are so many complex interactions between the various decisions on methods, it is difficult, indeed undesirable, to stick doggedly to the use of one particular method. All training methods have some comparative advantages and disadvantages which are contingent upon the context, and there is no such thing as *the* training method; often a combination of methods may be the most appropriate choice. In the final analysis, a decision to adopt a particular training method may well be influenced by the availability of 'materials', however undesirable this may be.

Materials for training educational administrators

In the last few years there have been a number of initiatives to promote the use of participatory training methods and stimulate the production of materials for use in training Third World educational administrators. Particularly notable are the activities of UNESCO (the Division of Educational Policy and Planning in Paris, and the Regional Office for Asia in Bangkok), the Commonwealth Secretariat and the Commonwealth Council for Educational Administration (CCEA).

The CCEA, for example, has recently produced *The Commonwealth Casebook for School Administrators* (Commonwealth Secretariat, 1983), which is a useful collection of case studies drawn from Commonwealth countries. The Secretariat has also published *Leadership in the Management of Education: A Handbook for Educational Supervisors* (Hughes, 1981). A further valuable handbook, published by UNESCO's Bangkok office, is the *Handbook for Trainers in Educational Management* (Pareek and Rao, 1981), which gives examples of training materials.

A range of self-instructional print-based materials for training educational planners is being produced by UNESCO's Division of Educational Policy and Planning (eg UNESCO, 1980 and ongoing) and UNESCO's Regional Office in Asia at Bangkok has produced basic modular materials in educational planning and management (eg UNESCO, Roeap, 1979; 1980; 1983), which have been widely used and adapted by other Asian countries (eg Sri Lanka, Nepal, and the Philippines).

Our own project at the University of London Institute of Education, 'Training Third World Educational Administrators — Methods and Materials', is funded by the Overseas Development Administration for a period of four years. The project originated out of a concern for the shortage of appropriate materials for use in the training of Third World educational administrators, and we have collaborated closely with Third

World trainers in developing and field testing modular print-based materials and training guides.

The aim of the project is, however, not to disseminate packages of materials to serve as recipes or standard models to be applied indifferently in various contexts, but rather to present prototypes for local modification and elaboration. This is also the intention with the UNESCO Educational Policy and Planning (EPP) training materials project which aims 'to present materials which can be applied to different situations after local experimentation and adaptation to local needs' (Renon, 1981). Certainly some materials can be relatively easily adapted and it is often surprising how similar the day-to-day problems can be in different countries and continents.

The need to develop national training materials and to reproduce existing ones for wider distribution is keenly felt. Ideally, material should be produced by local trainers and lecturers, for use within their own very specific contexts, and to meet clearly identified learning objectives. The problem here is resource constraints and lack of expertise, although undoubtedly the next few years will see an increasing range of locally produced materials. Indeed, a number of national training agencies such as the Institute for the Development of Educational Administrators (IDEA) in the Philippines and the National Institute of Educational Planning and Administration (NIEPA) in India have already produced a range of case study materials, simulation exercises and role plays (eg Virmani, 1980).

To sum up then, in considering the nature of present educational administrator training in Third World countries, it is evident that there are still many unresolved questions concerning how best to go about improving the quality of provision. The challenge, and one faced by trainers worldwide, is to solve the problem of what pattern of training schemes to provide, to decide the precise content of courses and the learning objectives, and to select the appropriate methodology and materials to achieve transfer of learning. It would seem that, as with so many of the past preoccupations and fads, not enough support is being given to those involved in implementation, both in terms of resources and training, and in this context we refer to the training of the trainers. The final part of this chapter summarizes some of our conclusions on the effects of the new emphasis on educational administrator training in the Third World.

Conclusions — the effects of the new emphasis

It is too early to say whether the new emphasis being given to training administrators is having a significant qualitative impact. Most of the new institutes have not been in existence long enough to have done more than begin to address the needs. Even in countries like India and Malaysia, where the training programmes have been in operation for a number of years, the numbers of personnel requiring training are very large.

If the new initiatives are to have a significant impact in the future there are a number of problem areas that will need to be tackled. The following *problematique* is, of course, a general one, based on our experience of a wide variety of institutions. Not every problem afflicts every institution, though many experience most of them.

(i) Inadequate budgets

Some of the new institutes are run on a shoe-string. They are housed in poor accommodation, often premises that have been vacated or abandoned by someone else. There is insufficient equipment, especially transport. There are not enough ancillary personnel — in one place a trainer with UNESCO experience and a master's degree does all the photocopying. Very few institutes have a research/evaluation officer, or spend significant sums on these crucial activities. It is essential to impress on administrative trainees that the training institute is itself a model of efficient organization; otherwise they are likely to be unmoved by the rhetoric of the trainers.

(ii) Undertrained trainers

The trainers themselves sometimes lack sufficient knowledge of their own subject matter, especially in regard to having a critical approach to it. Planning techniques, for example, are often taught without any discussion of their limitations. The trainers, in some instances, have inadequate knowledge and experience of alternative training methods and techniques; their style and approach are frequently that of the teacher rather than the trainer. In general, though, this problem of undertrained trainers is being tackled because it is an area where aid agencies can fairly easily supply technical assistance (although one wonders sometimes about the appropriateness of some of this assistance).

(iii) Shortage of suitable training materials

Materials production is a very time-consuming exercise which requires a good deal of special skills. Indeed, being a good trainer and being a good materials designer are by no means identical. Trainers often have timetables that leave insufficient time for generating materials, and this increases the pressure on them to use traditional methods, particularly the lecture.

(iv) Neglect of research into training needs and impact of training

Research is a greatly neglected area. Very little systematic study of the training needs of the clientele is carried out. When there is some effort it is usually done by the trainers, who frequently have little or no research background. Gross sampling errors, ambiguous questionnaires, prejudged conclusions, invalid inferences and other weaknesses are common. The results often indicate broad vague topic areas without specifying the skills or competencies that are needed to perform a particular job in a particular context — similarly with impact studies. Evaluation consists all too frequently of finding out whether trainees found the course useful, and which bits they found most useful. Whether training actually improves job performance is a very difficult question to answer, and it is significant that the few studies which make a serious attempt to answer it usually find little evidence in favour. This may, of course, be due to the methodological problem.

(v) Lack of a coherent national training policy

A fifth problem area, and one which to a great extent contributes to those institutional problems we have already mentioned, is the lack, in some countries, of any coherent training policy on educational administrator improvement and poor coordination and integration of training provision. It seems that many of the questions covering the status and priority to be given to training, trainee selection and incentives for training, personnel policies, and so on, are insufficiently explored for the new initiatives to achieve maximum impact.

References

Burgoyne, J G (1976) *A Classified Bibliography of Some Research on Teaching Methods in Management Education and Some Inferences about the State of the Art* Management Teacher Development Unit Paper: University of Lancaster, UK

Commonwealth Secretariat (1983) *The Commonwealth Casebook for School Administrators* Commonwealth Secretariat: London

Hawrylyshyn, B (1975) Management education — a conceptual framework *in* Taylor and Lippitt (1975)

*Hughes, M G (1981) *Leadership in the Management of Education: A Handbook for Educational Supervisors* Commonwealth Secretariat: London

Kindervatter, S (1983) *Learner-Centered Training for Learner-Centered Programmes* Training Notes Series No 1. Centre for International Education: University of Massachusetts

Knowles, M (1973) *The Adult Learner: A Neglected Species* Gulf: Houston, Tex

Kolb, D, Rubin, I and McIntyre, J (1979) *Organizational Psychology — An Experiential Approach to Organizational Behaviour* Prentice Hall: London (second edition)

Laird, D (1978) *Approaches to Training and Development* Addison-Wesley: Reading, Mass

Lungu, G F (1983) Some critical issues in the training of educational administrators for developing countries of Africa *International Journal of Educational Development* 3 1: 85-96

McLeary, L and McIntyre, K (1974) Competency development and methodologies of college teaching *in Principal In-Service: Where Will They Find It?* NASSP: Reston, Va

Marshall, D (1983) *Critical Decisions in the Professional Preparation and Development of School Administrators in Developing Areas* A discussion paper prepared for the CASEA section of the Canadian Society for the Study of Education

*Pareek, U and Rao, T V (1981) *Handbook for Trainers in Educational Management: With Special Reference to Countries in Asia and the Pacific* UNESCO, Roeap: Bangkok

Pfeiffer, J N and Jones, J F (1977) An introduction to structured experiences *in* Pfeiffer and Jones (1977)

Pfeiffer, J N and Jones, J F (1977) *Annual Handbook for Group Facilitators* University Associates: La Jolla, Cal

Renon, A G (1981) *The Functions of Education Administrators and the Training of Education Administrators* UNESCO EPP Report Studies TM/D2/2.1 UNESCO: Paris

Rost, J C (1980) Human relations training in educational administration programs: a study based on a national survey *Group and Organization Studies* **5** 1: 80-95

Taylor, B and Lippitt, G (1975) *Management Education and Training Handbook* McGraw-Hill: Maidenhead, Berks

Thiagarajan, K M and Prahalad, C K (1969) *Some Problems in the Behavioural Science Education of Managers and Management Instructors in Developing Nations* Management Research Center: Rochester University, New York

UNESCO, EPP (1980) *The Co-ordination of Training Activities (Training Materials) in the Field of Educational Planning, Administration and Facilities* Workshop Report Division of Educational Policy and Planning, UNESCO: Paris

UNESCO, Roeap (1979) *The Training of Educational Personnel* Report of a regional seminar, Thailand October 1978. Regional Office for Education in Asia and Oceania, UNESCO: Bangkok

UNESCO, Roeap (1980) *Development and Testing of National Training Materials in Educational Planning and Management* Report of a consultative meeting. UNESCO: Bangkok

UNESCO, Roeap (1981) *Supporting Innovations in Education: Preparing Administrators, Supervisors and Other Key Personnel* Report of a technical working group meeting 29 September–11 October. UNESCO: Bangkok

UNESCO, Roeap (1983) *Training Education Personnel in Planning and Management Using Distance Teaching and Other Techniques* Report on an evaluation workshop. UNESCO: Bangkok

Virmani, K G (1980) Training for educational managers in India: a case for experiential learning methods *EPA Bulletin* **3** 2: 38-52

Wynn, R (1972) *Unconventional Methods and Materials for Preparing Educational Administrators* UCEA: Columbus, Ohio

19. The National Development Centre for School Management Training

Ray Bolam

Summary: Many governments have set up some form of central school management training support agency. This paper presents a descriptive case study of a national centre which was established by the UK Government as one means of promoting its policy for improving the quality of schooling. In 1983 specific funds were made available for two new types of management course which the National Development Centre (NDC) was asked to monitor and support. These courses have been successful in stimulating awareness and increased support throughout the country for school management training but they have been less successful in having an impact upon the practice of school management and the improvement of schools. Better preparation and support would strengthen this impact, but experience in industry and education indicates that real improvements will only come about when each local education authority (LEA) roots such courses in an overall management development policy and programme. The NDC has mounted a development project with eight authorities to explore these ideas in practice. It also acts as a national clearinghouse and support agency for good practice in school management development and training. The chapter concludes by arguing that the knowledge base for school management development and training is inadequate and calls for more research and development work.

The national context

The purpose of this chapter is to present a case study of the National Development Centre for School Management Training. All governments, sooner or later, have to face the policy issue as to how they equip school head teachers and principals with the knowledge, skills and attitudes required for the successful management of their institution. This is an account of how the Government in England and Wales (*not* Scotland and Northern Ireland) is tackling this issue. It is mainly a descriptive case study of policy and practice as it has occurred. The final section does, however, offer some preliminary conclusions and raises some theoretical and research issues.

Developments in school management training have to be seen in the context of a government's education policy. The present UK Government is widely regarded in the education profession as the most interventionist, and by many as the most radical, since the Second World War. Key elements in the Government's overall education policy proposals were summarized by the Secretary of State for Education, Sir Keith Joseph, at the November 1984 meeting of the Organization for Economic Co-operation and Development (OECD) Education ministers concerned with the quality of education, as including an agreed curriculum for primary and secondary schools, a single system of examinations, new methods of student assessment, effective management of schools and of the teaching force, and more parental involvement in schools. The main aim of the policy was said to be: '. . . to see 80 to 90 per cent of all pupils reaching and surpassing at age 16 the standards now associated with the average.' These policy initiatives must also be seen in a wider national context which includes: extremely high unemployment; severe public expenditure cuts; declining student numbers; school closures and amalgamations; a reduction in teachers' salaries, both in real terms and relative to other public servants; the publication of hitherto confidential school inspection reports by Her Majesty's Inspectorate; proposals from the teachers' employers (the 104 LEAs) for a radical restructuring of the profession which includes performance appraisal linked to 'merit' increases in salary; the introduction of numerous and varied innovations, by both national and local agencies, with profound implications for school organization, curriculum and teaching methods; widespread disruption of schools due to sustained industrial action by teacher unions over a pay dispute with their LEA employers and the national Government; and considerable political and professional controversy about the Government's interventionist stance.

It is against this background that the Government has expressed its commitment to improving the quality of the teaching force. In a major statement of policy (Department of Education and Science, 1983, para 1) it was argued:

> In the schools the teacher force, some 440,000 strong in England and Wales, is the major single determinant of the quality of education. The supply, initial training, appointment and subsequent career development and deployment of school teachers are of vital concern to the Government and to the nation.

Accordingly, the Government has promoted a number of radical initiatives and changes to initial and in-service education.

With respect to school management, the same policy statement asserted:

> Head teachers, and other senior staff with management responsibilities within the schools, are of crucial importance. Only if they are effective managers of their teaching staffs and the material resources available to them, as well as possessing the qualities needed for educational leadership, can schools offer their pupils the quality of education which they have a right to expect. This is why the Government attaches . . . importance . . . to in-service training for senior staff in schools (Department of Education and Science, 1983, para 83).

In pursuing this policy, the Government has funded research into the selection and appointment of head teachers and into performance appraisal. It has also initiated consultations on the desirability and feasibility of introducing a compulsory probationary period for all newly-appointed heads. Finally and, as far as this paper is concerned, most relevantly, it has promoted a major national initiative in the training of heads and senior staff.

The present UK Government has thus developed a set of coherent and radical, though extremely controversial, policies on school improvement and is implementing them via mechanisms which are themselves innovative and controversial. The Government's ultimate goals are framed in terms of student learning and, because it regards those responsible for school management as having a crucial role in the achievement of these goals, it has accorded high priority to funding school management training for head teachers and senior staff.

For some time it has been widely accepted in the UK that certain teachers have a management function. (The term 'management' is commonly used in preference to 'administration', although this usage is by no means uncontroversial.) The key person with school management responsibilities is the head teacher; others include the deputy heads, heads of department in secondary schools and certain teachers with specific responsibilities (known as scale post-holders) in primary schools. All such people, including the head teacher, have a classroom teaching function. Hence what distinguishes them from ordinary classroom teachers is that they are responsible for a management function *outside* the class-room which will normally have implications for other *teachers* in the school. Thus, they have some managerial responsibility for one or more of the following task areas: the school's overall policy and aims; the school's decision making and communication procedures; the curriculum; the staff; the pupils; materials resources; external relations; and the processes of maintaining and evaluating the work of the school.

On this working definition, there are at least 130,000 staff with a management function in primary, middle, secondary and special schools in England and Wales. They include approximately 30,000 head teachers, 25,000 deputy head teachers, and 70,000 department or section heads. Any national policy for improving the effectiveness of this school manage-ment function must recognize the sheer scale of the task.

Four further background features of the situation in England and Wales are worth highlighting. First, appointments to headships and deputy headships are made by school governors, some of whom represent local political parties, following a process of advertising in professional journals and press. Second, applicants for such posts are not required to have completed an accredited course in school management and administration (since accredited courses, as such, do not exist), but are judged on the basis of their previous experience and performance in a selection inter-view. Third, there is a trend towards management by teams of senior staff, including the head, particularly in secondary schools, which affects job specifications and training needs. Fourth, women are significantly under-represented in senior positions in all types of school.

Until 1983 the main types of school management training were short, practical, non award-bearing courses (provided mainly by LEAs and institutions of higher education, including some universities), diploma courses with an industrial management flavour (provided mainly by polytechnics) and advanced academic award-bearing courses (provided mainly by universities). A major survey (Hughes *et al*, 1981) revealed that, in any one year, approximately 1 per cent of heads and senior staff were involved in approximately 90 award-bearing courses with a significant management component and that approximately 14 per cent were involved in 430 practical, non award-bearing courses of from one to 20 days in length.

The following features of this pre-1983 provision are worthy of note. First, the university-based, award-bearing courses, mainly at masters and PhD levels, dealt mainly with issues in the education administration or theoretical knowledge tradition and, as such, were frequently criticized as being insufficiently relevant and practical. Second, many of the short practical courses were staffed by practising head teachers and senior teachers. Third, this provision was geographically 'patchy' so that in some areas there was an abundance of courses on offer and in other areas very few. (The Open University has begun to alleviate this problem through its distance learning courses which are of both an academic and practical kind.) Fourth, very little systematic evaluation has so far been made of these courses.

The 3/83 initiative

The Government's 1983 initiative (conventionally called 3/83 after the circular of that number) was designed to rationalize this patchy provision and to stimulate providing agencies and LEAs to offer high quality training. The initiative had three components:

1. Direct Government funding to LEAs.
2. Designated courses provided by regional institutions.
3. It was supported by a small National Development Centre (NDC) for School Management Training.

Direct funding

The Government's use of the specific grant as a funding mechanism for designated courses was itself a significant policy development in the relationship between central and local government. In earlier years LEAs had discretion over whether such money was spent on in-service training, education in general or some entirely different local service. A note-worthy feature of the present Government's strategy is that the money goes to the LEAs and not to the institutions providing the training. Hence the LEAs can choose among several providers, depending on the kind of training or service they wish to 'purchase', and the providers are placed in a 'market' relationship with the LEAs.

The 3/83 management training courses

Two types of course were designated as being eligible for the specific grant: first, a 'basic' course for less experienced heads and senior staff, lasting a minimum of 20 school days; second, a so-called One Term Training Opportunity (OTTO) for those with more experience, lasting 10 to 12 weeks or 150 to 160 school days. Both programmes were intended to improve the participants' management performance and, in addition, the OTTO programmes were intended to equip participants to contribute to 20-day courses, thus having a 'training the trainers' function.

In 1983-84, according to an NDC survey, 20 institutions (universities, polytechnics and colleges) ran 21 basic courses with 588 participants, and 27 OTTO programmes with 224 participants. Primary and secondary courses attracted roughly equal numbers. Of the 48 courses run, 15 were for head teachers only, seven were for deputy heads only and 26 were for both — with heads attending the latter in much greater numbers. There were no courses specifically for middle management (for example, department heads) though some are now planned. More men than women attended, partly because only 44 per cent of primary and 16 per cent of secondary head teachers are women. During 1984-85 approximately 1600 heads and senior staff attended 81 such courses — about double the first year's figures.

The NDC survey identified a variety of structures for the basic courses, ranging from 20 single days spread over several months to a four-week continuous block. These differences reflected the particular circumstances of each area, which also gave rise to a wide variety of content and methods in both the basic courses and OTTO programmes. Decisions about such matters rest with the regional consultative committees and programme steering committees in each area. Representatives of the LEAs, the providing agencies and the head teachers normally sit on these committees, and they advise the course directors on the needs of both potential participants and the LEAs. However, the effectiveness of these arrangements varies a great deal around the country.

One (typical) 20-day basic course was aimed at 25 secondary head teachers from four LEAs, and had a pattern of 11 single days and three blocks of three-day residential sessions. The two tutors were experienced head teachers and were supplemented by occasional guest lecturers. Major topics included the management of the curriculum, staff development, decision making and leadership. The methods used included action learning, whereby participants brought their own real-life problems to the group who together acted as a problem-solving resource; participants then tried out potential solutions in their own schools and brought back the results to the group for further discussion and advice. One Term Training Opportunity programmes typically had fewer participants (normally ranging from 8 to 10) and, although sometimes covering similar topics, also included a component on 'training the trainers'. Perhaps more important, most OTTO students have produced a short individual study on a topic of current practical concern.

The National Development Centre for school management training

The idea of a national centre was not new. The report by Hughes *et al*, 1981 had recommended establishing a school management unit based in the Schools Council for Curriculum and Examinations, but the latter was abolished. One of the national head teacher associations had argued for many years that a staff college for secondary head teachers should be established at national level on the model of the Civil Service Staff College. This approach was not adopted for at least two reasons: first, a single staff college could not cater for both primary and secondary heads (30,000 approximately), let alone the 100,000 or so other teachers with a management function; second, it made economic, logistic and professional sense to root the initiative in those regional institutions which already had experience and expertise in school management training.

The NDC was funded by the Department of Education and Science (DES) and the Welsh Office for three years (1983-86) in September 1983, following competitive bidding from 13 institutions of higher education. It became fully operational in January 1984 when the core team of six professional staff (three working full time and three part time) were established in the School of Education, Bristol University. Overall responsibility for the direction, policy formulation and management of the project rests with the DES Steering Committee chaired by Dr William Stubbs, the Education Officer for the Inner London Education Authority (ILEA), and the membership is drawn from LEAs, teachers, industry and providing institutions. The NDC is a joint activity of the School of Education, Bristol University and the South West Regional Management Centre at Bristol Polytechnic, and a small university/polytechnic management group regularly reviews progress.

The NDC's mission is to promote the provision of high quality school management development and training for head teachers and senior staff in maintained primary, middle, secondary and special schools throughout England and Wales (*not* Scotland and Northern Ireland) in order to improve their capacity to manage schools for more effective teaching and learning.

The NDC does not itself provide management training for heads and senior staff, nor does it carry out large-scale research. It has five principal functions (see Figure 1 on p 258). First, it acts as a clearinghouse by collecting information and ideas about good practice in school management and in school management development and training. The main mechanism for this is the resource bank which contains an information and training materials databank, a 'people' databank and examples of audio-visual training materials. Second, it promotes rigorous evaluation of school management training provision by advising on new courses as they are proposed for DES recognition, via survey research through intensive case studies and by the promotion of course self-evaluation guidelines. Third, it promotes the development of good training materials, courses and programmes by NDC staff, by consultants and fellows on attachment to the

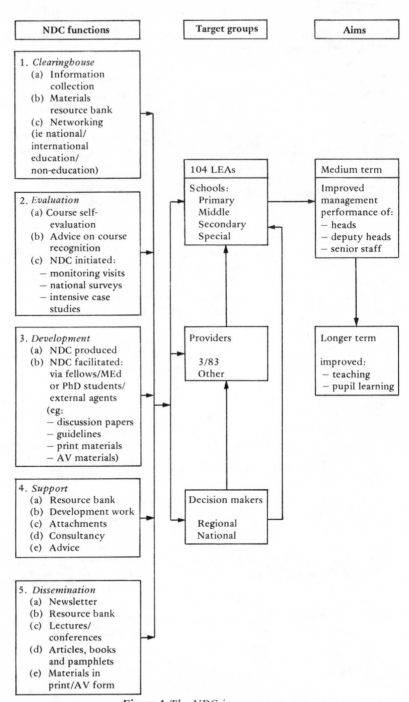

Figure 1 *The NDC in summary*

NDC and by facilitating and collaborating with the work of other developers (such as the Open University). Fourth, it supports the adoption and implementation of school management development and training policies, programmes, courses and activities via workshops, direct advice, a limited amount of consultancy work and through a number of NDC fellowships and attachments. Finally, it disseminates its ideas and materials via a termly newsletter, resource bank news-sheets, conferences and publications.

The NDC's main clients and target group are the 104 LEAs in England and Wales, together with their heads and senior staff. The second target group consists of all those providing agencies (including the 3/83 and non 3/83 providers, LEA advisers, teachers' centres and those agencies outside education) which offer various forms of support and training. The third target group consists of key national and regional decision makers, together with those who influence them. The broad goal of the NDC's work with these three target groups is to enable LEAs, together with their heads and senior staffs, to implement effective management development (MD) programmes, with appropriate support from external providers and within an overall framework that recognizes the importance of MD and allocates resources to it on a cost-effective basis. The five functions of the NDC — clearinghouse, evaluation, development, support and dissemination — are all focused on the achievement of this broad goal and directed at the three target groups.

From management training to management development

In its first year, the NDC concentrated much of its attention upon promoting the improvement of the 3/83 courses. A great deal of money, time and effort were, and are, being expended on school management training and it was important for the NDC to try to identify the conditions necessary for such training to be effective in terms of its impact upon the school management performance of course participants. It did this first by engaging in the 'advice on course recognition' process. Potential providers of courses are required to submit their course proposals to the DES and, simultaneously, to the NDC and to Her Majesty's Inspectorate (HMI). The NDC then advises the provider on the content and methods of the course and also advises the DES as to the suitability of the proposal. The DES decides on whether the course should be recognized on the basis of advice received from the NDC and from HMI. The NDC thus intervenes at a strategically important stage in the course design process. In addition, the NDC has promoted rigorous self-evaluation by publishing evaluation reports and by producing, in collaboration with providers, advice on good practice in course evaluation. Finally, the NDC has organized, again in collaboration with providers, a series of training the trainers workshops on good practice in course organization and implementation.

In considering how effective the 3/83 courses were, a number of factors have to be borne in mind. First, a distinction has to be made between the 20-day basic course and the OTTO programme, because of the latter's 'training the trainers' component. Second, the number of people involved annually from any single LEA was small: typically up to four heads (two primary and two secondary) allocated the OTTO programme and up to six heads (three primary and three secondary) allocated the 20-day courses. Third, partly as a result of the hurried start to the initiative, the LEAs were unclear about the aims of the courses and participants frequently stated that they did not know why they were on the course. At the first NDC national conference for providing institutions there was widespread agreement that, unless LEAs had a clear policy for selecting, preparing and providing follow-up support for course participants, the impact of the courses would be seriously impaired. More generally, it was clearly essential to understand the policy context within which LEAs were operating before any final judgements and recommendations could be made about the impact of the 3/83 initiative.

Accordingly, early in 1984 the NDC surveyed all LEAs in England and Wales requesting information about their policy on school management training for senior staff in primary, secondary and special schools. Sixty-one responses were received from 104 LEAs. All responding LEAs indicated their general commitment to school management training for heads and senior staff. The majority defined this commitment in terms of support for such staff to attend off-the-job courses, either run by polytechnics, colleges and universities (sometimes in collaboration with the LEA) or organized by the LEA. Over half the responding LEAs described their own in-house programmes of courses, some of which were very comprehensive. Not infrequently, however, it seemed that there was a more systematic provision of courses for senior staff in secondary schools than in primary schools. Only one LEA made reference to specific provision for senior staff in special schools. No LEA referred to or submitted a written statement of its policies related to school management training, though half a dozen did send a variety of papers which could be said to form the basis for such a written policy.

A small number of LEAs mentioned comprehensive programmes and approaches which went far beyond the notion of courses. For example, one LEA in the north of England has, over the years, developed a thorough and extensive programme of external and on-the-job support for heads using a range of agencies including trainers from local industry. In this LEA training the trainers courses have also been provided for the heads and LEA advisers who act as course tutors. A Midlands LEA is in the process of developing a systematic policy in which individual performance appraisal plays a central role. A few of the LEAs implementing course-based programmes over a period of years have trained a large proportion of their senior staff.

One LEA had carried out a systematic recent survey of training needs, but most LEAs appeared to have relied on their local advisers or inspectors, in consultation with heads and local in-service training committees, to identify needs. Most LEAs also confirmed that there was a lack of understanding and clarity about the purpose of the 20-day courses and OTTO programmes, and also that in many cases this led to recruitment difficulties. LEAs were unclear about the selection criteria they should apply for the OTTO courses, and heads were sometimes reluctant to attend such a programme if they were uncertain about its purpose. Two authorities were critical of the emphasis upon courses and the inflexibility of the funding arrangements being confined to 20-day courses and OTTO programmes. They saw this concentration upon the external course as unduly emphasizing only one among many techniques, and argued that there should be greater flexibility of provision and wider discretion to individual LEAs.

Towards the end of 1984 a survey of LEAs was carried out to establish to what extent OTTO programme 'graduates' were being used as trainers. A sample of 12 LEAs produced data on 72 'graduates' or 32 per cent of the national total. Of these, 12 (17 per cent) were acting as tutors on the second round of 20-day courses, as originally intended in the DES 3/83 circular; seven were not being used and one had been judged to be 'unsuitable'. By far the majority (42: 58 per cent) were said to be contributing in a variety of ways to their LEAs' evolving management development programmes. It seemed reasonable to conclude that this evidence was encouraging, since it indicated that LEAs were frequently using the experience gained by OTTO programme 'graduates'.

The NDC's first year's experience also led to a recognition of the importance of management development as the key underlying concept. The reasons for this growth in awareness were broadly twofold. First, there were lessons to be learnt from the non-education sector. It was a central part of the NDC's brief from the DES to explore the relevance of management training ideas and methods in industry, commerce and the non-education sector in general. A small-scale NDC study and an invitation conference for industrial trainers and senior educationists led to the conclusion that effective management training had to be rooted in a wider policy of management development. Second, there were the lessons from experience within education. There is now a well established tradition in the UK of school-focused in-service training (see Bolam, 1982) and it is widely accepted that both schools and LEAs should have staff development and, therefore, management development, policies and programmes.

Thus, as a result of reflecting on the 3/83 course, on the reaction of LEAs and on non-education sector practices, the NDC broadened its mission to embrace management development as the major concept underlying its work. The NDC's working definition is that management development refers to the process whereby the management function of an organization becomes performed with increased effectiveness. An alternative definition, which teachers find acceptable, is that MD is staff development for those staff who have school management responsibilities. The rationale for the NDC's approach to MD is as follows:

(a) The *ultimate aim* of MD is to improve the quality of teaching and learning in schools. The *immediate aim* is to improve the management performance of those with school management responsibilities.

(b) At *school level* this requires a policy and programme within which the *professional development needs* of the individual manager are balanced with the *institutional development needs* of the school. This, in turn, requires the school to use some form of systematic diagnostic process for individual needs (eg appraisal) and for school needs (eg self-evaluation in relation to the school's development plan).

(c) At *LEA level* this requires a policy and programme within which the following four sets of needs are balanced:

> the needs of individual heads and senior staff;
> the needs arising from school development plans;
> the needs of groups across an LEA (eg new heads);
> the needs arising from an LEA's policies (eg vocational training, school reorganizations).

This, in turn, requires that each LEA has the senior staff and procedures to coordinate and implement this process of needs assessment across the LEA. For example, it may involve setting up a database on the MD needs of individuals and groups in the LEA.

(d) At both school and LEA level it needs to be recognized that the MD requirements of *individuals and groups of individuals* may well vary significantly according to:

> their age;
> their gender;
> school type (ie primary, secondary, etc);
> their job stage, ie:
> — the preparatory stage (as they wish to apply for a new job);
> — the appointment stage (as they are selected or rejected);
> — the induction stage (eg the first two years in post);
> — the in-service stage (ie 3-5 years, 6-10 years, 11 years in post);
> — the transitional stage (ie promotion, redeployment, retirement).

(e) Once needs have been identified, each school and each LEA has to plan, implement, and evaluate *a programme of MD activities*. This will include activities which take place:

> — on the job (eg job enhancement, job rotation, performance review, planned succession);
> — close to the job (eg self-development, team building, consultant support);
> — off the job (eg external training courses, secondments).

(f) Management development should not be equated solely with attendance at external courses, since this is only one, albeit important,

MD activity. Each LEA and school should see its MD policy and programme as part of its overall human resource strategy. Such a strategy should include its management recruitment and appointment procedures, its personnel system, its appraisal system and, finally, it should be rooted in the LEAs' and schools' organizational structures and should be designed to meet their policy needs.

To explore the feasibility of these ideas, the NDC has collaborated on a major development project with eight LEAs: Cambridgeshire, Cleveland, Dorset, Gwent, Northamptonshire, South Glamorgan, Birmingham and Leeds. The ILEA is involved in an associate capacity.

At LEA level, all eight LEAs have designated two senior staff (eg at Chief Education Officer (CEO), Chief Inspector and Senior Inspector levels) to coordinate the management development scheme. Five LEAs have established LEA steering committees for management development and training. All eight are drawing upon industrial training expertise and also reviewing management development needs across the LEA concerned. Four LEAs are also working on management development for officers and inspectors, some in collaboration with their own authority staff and some with external support.

At school level, 53 schools (primary, middle, secondary and special), with their head teacher as coordinator, have embarked upon the management development process. Most of them began with an analysis of their management development needs. Priority topics selected for further work include:

1. Drawing up agreed job descriptions.
2. Individual staff development review interviews.
3. Managing external relations.
4. Managing communications within the school.
5. Management of time by head and senior staff.
6. Managing the curriculum.

The NDC has supported this work by producing practical guidelines and advice on management development for schools and LEAs. These are being trialled and will be available nationally by late 1986. It has also organized five two-day workshop conferences for participating LEAs.

Emerging conclusions and issues

Given the complexity, scope and time scale of the innovation represented by the 3/83 initiative, only interim conclusions are possible. Before presenting them it is important to re-state the professional values which underlie such conclusions. National Development Centre team members are in agreement about their broad long-term goals for school management development and training in England and Wales. In their view, the ultimate goal of school management development and training should be to improve the quality of teaching and learning in the country's classrooms and schools. They therefore believe that the immediate goal of school management development and training should be to improve the management knowledge and skills of heads and senior staff so that they can more effectively influence the improvement of the quality of teaching and learning. They are also agreed about the broad structure and nature of the system which would be most likely to promote the achievement of these policy goals. Ideally, each school and each LEA should have a coherent and systematic policy of management development which balances the professional needs of individual heads and senior staff with the requirements of school and LEA policies in order to achieve more effective teaching and learning. Such management development policies would include, as one important component, the active involvement of the training course providers in meeting the identified needs of individuals, schools and LEAs.

If such statements are to be more than rhetorical, they must be applied to the concrete, practical realities of existing arrangements, policies, courses and activities and the means of their improvement. Although a remarkable amount of progress has taken place since 1983, these goals will only be achieved through the consistent implementation of a clear concept of management development and this will take a long time to carry through effectively. In practice, management development will involve a clear explanation and demonstration of the desirability and feasibility of the concept and the long-term implementation strategy, together with a recognition that any process of improvement must start from the position as it is now.

External course provision

To begin with the position now: present practice and thinking at all levels are dominated by the idea that external training courses are the best way to improve school management. That, therefore, must be *one* starting point, and the NDC is accordingly committed to the goal of improving the quality of external courses.

Moreover, it is reasonably clear what this would require. A good course is one which is designed to meet the needs of a specified target group. Potential participants, their schools, and their LEAs should have an accurate understanding of its aims and scope and the course should be selected because all three perceive it as relevant, and because all three wish to use the knowledge gained to promote more effective school management. In certain cases, this requires thorough and specific preparation prior to the course, and in all cases it requires thorough and specific follow-up, sometimes by the course organizers but always by the participants themselves, their schools and their LEAs. Available evidence shows that this fundamental process rarely occurs at present. A basic condition for effective school management training is that this situation should improve and this is, therefore, a priority focus for the

NDC, through the 'advice on course recognition' process.

In the meantime, it is also possible to achieve significant, though possibly marginal, improvement in the quality of the external courses themselves. Hence, the NDC is committed, through its resource bank, its workshops, its publications and its support function, to the promotion of such approaches as action learning, team building, and other experiential methods which strengthen the likelihood of effective learning.

It is also important that, as well as targeting on generic management skills and the training needed to teach them, external courses should equip participants to manage the many tasks — existing and new — which confront them every day. Hence the NDC is also committed to the promotion of high quality courses on, for example, the school management implications of curriculum change, of changes in examinations, of the transition from school to adult and working life, of the school in the community, and of children with special needs.

Impact of the 3/83 courses

In assessing the impact of the OTTO and 20-day courses, it must be recalled that they were partly designed to act as a pump-priming stimulus to LEAs. On this 'pump-priming' criterion, the initiative has been successful. There has undoubtedly been an upsurge of activity and interest in management development and training. Profitable interchanges have taken place with industry and the non-education sector generally. The nine regional conferences organized in 1985 by the NDC revealed a degree of enthusiasm for, and commitment to, managerial development and training, auguring well for the long-term future. Nevertheless, there are still some LEAs making minimal use of the provision of these courses. The reasons for this and ways of dealing with them are being investigated.

One Term Training Opportunity programmes are now contributing a great deal to LEAs' training programmes. Increasingly, head teachers and senior staff, LEA officers and advisers are playing key roles in management training. Whereas formerly they were being involved in one-off lectures or, at best, in self-contained units, they are now contributing as course directors, associate directors and tutors. This role involves them in course planning and, even more significantly, in course follow-up.

The impact of OTTO and basic courses upon the managerial effectiveness of individual heads and senior staff is much more problematic. An interim NDC (Ballinger, 1985) analysis of available evaluation reports is instructive in this context: most of them use participant satisfaction rather than effective learning as their criterion for judging success. So, although the evaluators report that many participants thought their courses were relevant, had improved their self-confidence and had stimulated them to plan specific changes in their schools, there is little evidence of *actual* changes, even of a self-reported kind.

The reasons for this, not unexpected, outcome are fairly familiar.

Evaluating the impact of in-service courses on teacher (or manager) effectiveness is difficult for several reasons. One difficulty relates to logistics and resources: it is expensive and time-consuming to interview participants after the course; even a follow-up questionnaire of a self-report kind can only be administered and analysed by a researcher or by an institution with a continuing staff commitment to the programme (since course teams normally disband at the conclusion of the course). It is also technically and professionally difficult to obtain reliable independent information about changes in performance: this would require pre-course and post-course performance data from, for example, an inspector or school colleagues. Moreover, even if evidence of changes could be obtained, it could not be positively attributed to course attendance, even on a correlational basis, given the small number (eg eight) of participants on any one course. The most fundamental difficulty of all, however, is that there is no agreement about the precise behavioural features displayed by heads and senior staff who do successfully promote effective classroom teaching and learning.

Diagnosing training needs

It is evident that, at present, the ways in which training needs are identified are unsatisfactory. The methods used vary between and within LEAs, and can best be labelled *ad hoc*. They include self-diagnosis (eg where OTTO or 20-day courses are advertised throughout the LEA and applications are invited), questionnaire surveys of group needs, surveys by a seconded head using interviews, working party reports, and (the most common method) the collective judgements of advisers. There is little evidence of staff development interviews being used to diagnose individual needs. There is some, limited, evidence of advisory teams systematically appraising group needs (eg of *new* heads) but no evidence of the use of an LEA database to identify priority groups and their needs.

The NDC is accordingly committed to the systematic exploration of several practical approaches to the identification of training and development needs. At school level these will include the use of job descriptions and staff development interviews to identify individual needs and the use of school self-reviews to identify needs arising from group and school policies and tasks. At LEA level these will include the use of procedures and methods to identify the needs of groups of staff across the LEA (eg newly appointed heads), to identify the management training implications of existing and new policies and for dealing with the needs of individuals and schools identified at school level. These priorities will be tackled in cooperation with the eight pilot LEAs and incorporated into individual LEA and school guidelines.

The transition to management development

The management development approach represents a major innovation for

Stage	Main observable features*	No of LEAs
1	The LEA makes little management training provision of any kind for heads and senior staff. Its use of external courses, including 3/83, is small.	A diminishing minority
2	The LEA makes considerable use of internal and external courses but on an *ad hoc* basis and without any clear policy framework. This includes its use of 3/83 provision. It is only just becoming aware of the 'development' approach.	The majority
3	The LEA has been working for several years on the evolution of a management training policy related to school improvement.** The pattern of activities is varied, vigorous and well established but still consists mainly of courses. Most heads and senior staff have experienced them and, occasionally, so too have officers and advisers. In consequence, there is a reasonably common understanding in the LEA of the possibilities and limitations of training, including 3/83 provision and, accordingly, of the need to adopt a 'development' approach.	A growing minority
4	The LEA has a coherent and explicit policy for management development aimed at school improvement. Procedures and staff exist for implementing the policy in the form of a regular programme. The programme includes the use of job descriptions, development interviews and other methods of diagnosing needs at individual, school and LEA levels, and a varied range of on-the-job, close-to-the-job and off-the-job activities. Off-the-job courses, including 3/83 provision, are one component in the programme and the LEA has an infrastructure and personnel capable of supporting course participants during the preparatory and following stages, and of relating such courses to the identified needs of the LEA and its schools. Heads, senior staff, advisers and officers regularly engage in the programme which is systematically monitored and evaluated in terms of school improvement.	None at present

Notes

*   One important complicating feature is that each LEA has to consult and collaborate with several providers and with other LEAs, and that each provider has to work with several LEAs which are located in more than one sub-region.

**   LEAs at stage 3 have emphasized the importance of having a shared understanding and a clear vision of what kind of school the management development strategy is designed to achieve.

*** Comparable tables could be produced for schools and providers, both of which display analogous features at roughly similar stages.

Table 1 *Possible stages in the adoption of a management development approach by LEAs****

LEAs, schools, providers, heads and senior staff. The somewhat simplistic typology presented in Table 1 on p 267 is helpful in clarifying the possible stages involved for LEAs in adopting it. The evidence from the pilot LEAs and the regional conferences indicates that a quantitative move from stage 1 to stage 2 can be achieved relatively quickly, but that the qualitative move to stage 3 takes several years, since it depends upon the creation of a climate of opinion, practice and understanding which can only come about as a result of sustained and positive experiences.

The transition from stages 3 to 4 raises quite different issues. The basic barrier is one of a lack of familiarity and understanding: many education-ists are simply not aware of the non-course techniques of MD, nor do they understand the underlying concept of MD and its practical implications. The NDC is tackling these issues in collaboration with representatives of industry and the non-education sector generally but the adaptation of such exogenous ideas has to be handled carefully. It has to be recognized that MD is the product of a culture (industry) which differs in certain essentials from the culture of the education system.

Three examples of these differences are worth citing. First, 'best practice' indicates that in industry, in-company trainers are drawn from middle managers who subsequently move back into management: yet it is rarely the case that, for example, LEA advisers or teachers' centre leaders move back into headships. Second, industry appears to be prepared to spend proportionately more per manager on MD than is true of LEAs. Third, and perhaps most important of all, LEAs and schools are finally the responsibility of elected members and governors. One important consequence is that decisions on management appointments are taken by lay rather than professional people. Thus, LEA officers cannot at present operate a system of planned management succession, as is the case in industry.

The need for research

This paper has presented primarily a descriptive account of the NDC in the context of the 3/83 initiative, and has only occasionally raised issues of a fundamental kind. The main reason is that the Centre is a *develop-ment* agency and does not have a major research function. However, in this final section, certain theoretical and conceptual questions are out-lined within a research framework.

First, it must be recognized that the 3/83 initiative does not rest upon a solid base of research knowledge. Although industry has been cited as a source of experience, at least one recent researcher has seriously questioned the validity of doing so (Handy, 1984) and, in any case, industrial training practice itself rests upon a shaky research knowledge base (see Stewart, 1984). Although the ultimate aim of training is said to be improved school manager effectiveness, there is no conceptual clarity about how this might be judged (see Murphy *et al*, 1983) — even in the USA, where the issue has been most thoroughly addressed. Although the initiative is a major organizational innovation, it is being pursued, as are other comparable innovations in the UK, without apparent reference to existing knowledge of the change process (see Fullan, 1982) and without apparent acknowledgement of the complexities of schools and LEAS as organizations (see Herriott and Firestone, 1984, for one perspective on this issue).

Moreover, valuable as recent research in the UK undoubtedly has been, it does not directly illuminate these issues. Hughes (1983) provides a good summary of recent work which reveals that secondary heads have received most attention and that role theory has been the main theoretical orientation. The tasks of heads have been studied directly or indirectly by several researchers (eg Lyons, 1976; Webb and Lyons, 1982; Morgan *et al*, 1984; Jenkins, 1983; Hall and Mckay, 1983; Weindling and Earley, 1983). Some of these studies have also addressed training needs but the training structure and process has only recently become the focus of attention (Hughes *et al*, 1981; Bailey, 1985; Glatter, 1983).

The implicit framework within which this research appears to have been conducted is represented in Figure 2.

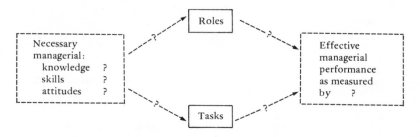

Figure 2 *The present state of research knowledge on school management in England and Wales*

Its main purpose seems to have been to deepen and extend our understanding of school management roles and tasks and, as a result, we can now make certain statements with some confidence, particularly about the roles and tasks of secondary head teachers: hence the two boxes in unbroken lines. However, the rest of the field is riddled with unanswered (and often unasked) questions: hence the broken lines and question marks. Thus, the articulation between the work done on roles and that on tasks is unclear. Moreover, although a secondary purpose of the research has often been to inform management training, the relationship between, for instance, management tasks and the knowledge, skills and attitudes needed to carry them out has usually been assumed rather than investigated. Finally, this research has either not addressed the issue of managerial effectiveness or has been vague regarding criteria and dependent variables. It is worth noting that the knowledge base about other school management roles (eg deputy heads and department heads) is even sparser.

One responsibility of the NDC is to highlight issues of this kind in order that the Government and researchers can take appropriate action. Regrettably, whatever concern there is about the many gaps which exist in our knowledge, that concern is not being met with the necessary resources. At present, research in the UK (and indeed in Europe as a whole) falls far short of that being funded in the USA (see Mulhauser, 1983). Until more resources and energy are directed towards such research, the valuable efforts of management developers and trainers in education will continue to rest on a very shaky foundation.

References

Bailey, A J (1985) *Support for School Management: Project Report* School of Education, University of Sussex: Sussex

Ballinger, E A (1985) *An Interim Analysis of Available Evaluation Reports on Basic and OTTO Programmes* National Development Centre for School Management Training, School of Education: University of Bristol (mimeo)

Bolam, R ed (1982) *School-Focussed In-Service Training* Heinemann Educational: London

Department of Education and Science (1983) *Teaching Quality* Cmnd 8836. HMSO: London

Fullan, M (1982) *The Meaning of Educational Change* Teachers College Press, Columbia University: New York

Glatter, R (1983) Implications of research for policy on school management training *in* Hegarty (1983)

Gray, H L ed (1982) *The Management of Educational Institutions: Theory Research and Consultancy* Falmer Press: Lewes, Sussex

Hall, V and Mackay, H (1983) *The Changing Role of the Secondary Headteacher: Project Outline* The Open University School of Education: The Open University

Handy, C (1984) *Taken for Granted? Understanding Schools as Organisations* Longman for the Schools Council: York

*Hegarty, S ed (1983) *Training for Management in Schools* Papers from an Educational Workshop organized by the National Foundation for Educational Research at Windsor, 14-17 September 1982, under the auspices of the Council for Cultural Cooperation of the Council of Europe. NFER-Nelson for the Council of Europe: Windsor, Berks

Herriott, R E and Firestone, W A (1984) Two images of schools as organizations: a refinement and elaboration *Educational Administration Quarterly* 20 4: 41-57

Hord, S ed (1983) *A US Strategy for Research and Development Concerning the Principalship* OECD: Paris (mimeo: CERI/SI/83.03)

Hughes, M G (1983) The role and tasks of heads of schools in England and Wales: research studies and professional development provision *in* Hegarty (1983)

Hughes, M G, Carter, J and Fidler, B (1981) *Professional Development Provision for Senior Staff in Schools and Colleges* Faculty of Education, University of Birmingham: Birmingham

Jenkins, H O (1983) *Job Perceptions of Senior Managers in Schools and Manufacturing Industry* PhD Thesis. Faculty of Education, University of Birmingham: Birmingham (unpublished)

Lyons, G (1976) *Heads' Tasks: A Handbook of Secondary Administration* National Foundation for Educational Research: Slough, Berks

Morgan, C, Hall, V and Mackay, H (1984) *The Selection of Secondary School Headteachers* Open University Press: Milton Keynes

Mulhauser, F (1983) Recent research on the principalship: a view from the National Institute of Education *in* Hord (1983)

Murphy, J, Hallinger, P and Mitman, A (1983) Problems with research on educational leadership: issues to be addressed *Educational Evaluation and Policy Analysis* **5** 3: 297-305

Stewart, R (1984) The nature of management: a problem for management education *Journal of Management Studies* **21** 3: 323-30

Webb, P C and Lyons, G (1982) The nature of managerial activities in education *in* Gray (1982)

Weindling, R and Earley, P (1983) *The First Years of Headship in the Secondary School: Project Outline* National Foundation for Educational Research: Slough, Berks

20. Interstudie SO: school management development in the Netherlands

Kees J M Gielen

Summary: *Interstudie SO* is the only institute in the Netherlands which provides in-service courses in the management of secondary schools. It has 18 members and, during 1984-85, 1400 participants took part in eight kinds of programme. It functions in a context of a multi-track system of secondary education which is constantly undergoing reorganization. Each secondary school has a principal (*directeur*) and one or more deputees (*adjuncten*). There is currently much interest in school management training in the Netherlands. *Interstudie SO* provides a package of in-service training with two components. One is a structural training project for school leaders; the other consists of a set of separate project programmes.

The main features of *Interstudie SO* programmes are: a pattern whereby participants alternate between course-based tasks and school-based tasks, a rhythmic structure of conferences and working meetings over a period of nine months, compulsory enrolment of at least two members of the school management team, and the fostering of a back-up team at the participants' own schools. Participants undertake both short and long assignments. Future plans include the establishment of a network of school management consultants and an improvement in training methods. *Interstudie SO* is evolving from a training institute to a centre for school management development.

Introduction

In the Netherlands, school management development is a field which is rapidly attracting the attention of teachers, experts and policy makers. In this article we shall concentrate on one of the parties involved in this field: *Interstudie SO*. Briefly, *Interstudie SO* provides in-service school management training courses at all levels of the education system, ranging from basic education (4- to 12- year-olds) to university education. It is the only institute in the Netherlands which has school management training as its chief activity. Following a rapid period of growth in recent years, it now has 14 full-time staff members/course leaders and four ancillary employees. Staff members are purposely drawn from different fields of experience (school managers, school consultants, policy makers, personnel managers, information experts, management trainers and management advisers) and from varying disciplines (educational science, labour and organization psychology, economics and sociology).

Staff members are grouped into three teams. Each of the teams is responsible for the part of the training programmes (development, implementation and evaluation, plus the policy preparation for the programmes as a whole). The team members consult with one another, exchange ideas and together study certain themes. Each of the three teams is represented by the team leader in the coordination group, and the director of the institute is chairman. The director and the team leaders are each responsible for part of the institute's policy (training policy, management, personnel, etc). Together, as the coordination group, they prepare what is known as the 'package policy': this is the way in which individual programmes or groups of programmes are interrelated and coordinated. The policy-making organ is the full policy meeting, which is held once every four to five weeks. The institute has its own board. This board is represented by its chairman on the board of the *Interstudie* Foundation. This foundation is made up of a total of seven educational institutes (*Interstudie SO* is one of these seven). It is a private foundation.

Interstudie SO is 100 per cent subsidized by the State. It has an annual budget of around $680,000. The main cost items are the personnel costs for the 18 employees. The course participants pay about $40 per person per year. The remaining costs (primarily the costs of conferences lasting several days) are paid by *Interstudie SO* (and therefore indirectly by the State). In 1984-85 about 1400 participants (mainly school leaders and their deputies) took part in eight different in-service training programmes. There were over 120 conferences, each lasting several days.

The remainder of this article is arranged as follows. First we shall deal with the context or work environment of *Interstudie SO*; we shall say a little about the school system, about school management and about school management development; then, for the remainder of the article, we shall confine ourselves to *Interstudie SO*, describing the package of in-service training courses and their characteristic features; finally, some information will be provided about policy in the immediate future.

The context

School and administrative system

The Netherlands is a small country; it has a population of 14,000,000 in an area of 41,000 square kilometres: about 340 inhabitants per km². From the centre of the country (40 km south-east of Amsterdam) every corner of the country can be reached in two to three hours by train or car.

The school system is multi-track. This is particularly true of secondary education, *Interstudie SO*'s field. Secondary education comprises pre-university education, general secondary education and vocational training at all levels, taking place in over 20 different types of schools and school-groups.

For years now, attempts have been made to reconstruct this patchwork quilt of educational facilities, partly for pedagogical reasons and partly for demographic and economic reasons — eg, the large increase in the number of students and increased funds in the 1960s and 1970s, drastic fall-off in student numbers and sharp cut-back of funds in the 1980s which is predicted to last until the 1990s. The restructuring of the first phase of secondary education (13- to 16-year-olds) has now reached a dead end after a public debate lasting over ten years, experiments and *ad hoc* legislative amendments.

The large-scale reconstruction of secondary education is taking place in the context of an administrative system which has typically Dutch characteristics. One of these is 'pillarization'. 'Pillars' are separate communities, formed around different religious and secular beliefs: Catholic, Protestant, private (*Interstudie*'s domain) and, in some sectors of community service such as education, the State and the local community. Some 2000 school boards administer approximately 2900 secondary schools; in addition, several hundred local authorities and the State are competent authorities for about 600 State secondary schools. State and private schools are put on the same financial footing. All private schools are eligible for maintenance from State funds, provided they comply with certain statutory conditions.

The administrative system as a whole is a rare mixture of a high degree of decentralization and a large number of strict directives from the State. The legal and operational balance between board and State power differs according to the particular field concerned. Because the requirements of good quality which the legislature can stipulate are not definitively laid down in the constitution, the discretion of boards and State is periodically at issue in political discussions. In practice, school boards are seldom active in policy and decision making. They seldom act as executives. Most board activities are confined to monitoring, leaving almost all policy and decision making to the school management, which mainly comprises the principal school leader and his deputies.

Management of secondary schools

The Secondary Education Act (the 'mammoth' act) is a legal status directive which defines the formal functions of the principal school leader (called *rector* or *directeur* in Dutch). These definitions are brief and succinct:

'The *directeur*, under the responsibility of the competent authorities, is charged with:

1. providing the school with leadership;
2. teaching and carrying out a proportionate part of the teachers' duties — to the extent that the nature and size of the school warrant it;
3. doing everything necessary to ensure the smooth running of the school, within the reasonable limits of a *directeur*'s normal duties.'

The function of the deputy comprises:

'1. supporting the *directeur* in his duties and if necessary standing in for him in the event of his being absent;

2. if his duties include teaching, carrying out teachers' duties.'

No further explanation is given of the definition of these formal and legal functions. The *directeur* or *rector* of a secondary school is not required to teach provided the school has more than about 300 pupils; one deputy is completely exempt from teaching duties when there are approximately 500 to 550 students. Besides the principal school leader and his deputies, secondary schools also have heads of department. Formally and legally there are no stipulations for this function. Heads of department are teachers from a group of teachers in one or several related subjects who, in consultation with the other teachers, arrange meetings and implement decisions taken at those meetings.

Finally, large secondary schools have heads of year. These teachers have various titles and their function is to coordinate the assistance given to individual pupils and groups of pupils and, sometimes, to shape school policy with respect to year groups.

The work of school managers of secondary schools in the Netherlands conforms to the characteristics of management given by Mintzberg in that it is hectic and highly unpredictable. It consists of a large number of activities and events varying from short to very long duration. Information exchange is mainly done informally: orally and by way of individual contacts. There is little priority setting. Abrupt changes from one activity to another occur throughout the day.

The daily work of the effective secondary school principals can be summarized as follows:

(a) making sure the school is running smoothly (administering the building and materials, book-keeping);

(b) induction and instruction of staff, allocation of duties amongst the staff;

(c) attracting and allocating new students;

(d) maintaining contact with individual students to monitor their adjustment to school, keeping in touch with the students' world, and demonstrating to the students the team spirit amongst the teaching staff;

(e) developing and maintaining a working team;

(f) introducing and implementing, or helping to implement, new concepts and ideas;

(g) trying to ensure that the school and other educators of the child are pedagogically coordinated; and

(h) arranging and coordinating contact with other institutions important for the students.

The work of these more effective principals is hindered by the following problems:

(a) the teaching task dominates the management task; principals are

ambivalent about this, because they like to teach;
(b) the lack of explicit policy: the boards only monitor;
(c) team building in secondary schools is far from optimal; urgent matters have priority;
(d) too many and too divergent expectations: teachers, parents, boards and many others expect the principal to fulfil their very different, sometimes opposing, expectations;
(e) insufficient team building; an innovative school is an intensively communicating school; but there is a great lack of communication within the team on important school matters;
(f) insufficient cooperation between schools, so there is a waste of time, money and opportunities to buy more advanced facilities, or to buy at least something.

School management development

The Netherlands is not a country in which management is likely to flourish. The Dutch manager traditionally maintains a low profile. This is particularly true in education. And yet in recent years school management and its development has rapidly become a field which has attracted a great deal of attention, as we stated at the start of this article. An increase in scale, division of labour, concentration, disappointment about large-scale innovation, etc, have played a part in this.

There are at least three important factors involved:

1. educational administration, or school management, is currently emerging as a scientific discipline and field of research; promising starts have been made, but very little research data is actually available;
2. an extensive support system surrounds schools with guidance, advice, training and information; unfortunately, from a professional point of view, this system is 'pillarized', so that cooperation between researchers, consultants and trainers occurs only occasionally and takes a great deal of energy;
3. principals are organized; most principals and some deputies are members of two school leaders' associations. Until recently the promotion of interests was the most important policy; there now appears to be a shift towards professional development.

These three factors, along with the existence of a large number of small school boards, make school management development an as yet scarcely developed area in which it is difficult to gain an overall impression or to set in motion coordinated activities.

Just how the career of a school manager actually develops is unclear. A simple survey carried out by *Interstudie SO* suggests that a third of the principals and deputies in secondary education have worked outside education; that, in addition to being teachers, they tend to have held three or more other functions at school (eg form teacher, careers adviser, head of department); that over 50 per cent of principal school leaders are recruited from outside the school; and that virtually all deputies are recruited internally. A striking feature is the fact that women are occupying a decreasing number of management positions. The percentage of female principals fell from 11 per cent in 1978 to 8 per cent in 1982; and during the same period the percentage of female deputies dropped from 10 per cent to 9 per cent.

As regards the formal education of school leaders, it should be mentioned that pre-service training of any kind is completely non-existent in the Netherlands. On the other hand, the number of in-service training courses is on the increase. Most of these are developed, organized and evaluated by *Interstudie SO*. Besides these programmes, occasional courses are provided for school leaders in secondary education by teacher training institutes and national educational centres as part of the support system. In the area of innovation projects in particular, these centres are becoming increasingly involved in the development of the management function in schools.

Interstudie SO

Some basic information about *Interstudie SO* was given at the beginning of this article. There now follows a description of the package of training courses, of the external and internal structure of these courses, and the developments expected in the near future.

A package of training programmes

Interstudie SO's package of training programmes consists of two parts: one part is meant to provide a programme of structured training for principal school leaders and their deputies; the other contains a number of separate project programmes. The part of the package that provides *structured in-service training* for school leaders contains four programmes:

(a) A starting course for newly appointed principals; over a period of one year about 30 newly appointed principals take part in a programme consisting of an opening day, a three-day conference and two conferences lasting two-and-a-half days; in between the conferences and after the last one there are several one-day meetings. This programme was first implemented in 1985-85.

(b) A basic course for two or more members of the same school management team, preferably the principal and at least one of the deputies; over a period of about nine months this basic programme has two four-day conferences with, in between and afterwards, several one-day working meetings at the principals' schools. Seventeen groups of 27 school leaders took part in this programme in 1984-85; up to and including 1984-85, a total of over 4000 people had taken part in this programme.

(c) Two follow-up programmes. The first is a personnel policy programme, having roughly the same structure as the basic course
(over 100 participants in 1984-85); and the second is a system
course for entire management teams from the same school or
several full teams from different schools. Following some intake
contacts there are usually two two-and-a-half-day residential conferences over a period of nine months, again with one day of half-
day meetings taking place in between or afterwards at the participants' schools (with over 130 participants in 1984-85).

The ideal situation would be for the newly appointed principal to take
part in the initial course during his or her first year; he or she would
then join the basic course during the third year, along with one or two
deputies; then go on the personnel policy course in the fifth year, again
with one or two deputies; and finally complete this stage of his or her
professional training with a system course together with the entire
management team. This would, as has been said, be an ideal training.
However, for the most part, we have not yet reached this situation.

The second part of the package consists of a number of *project
programmes.* In 1984-85 these were:

(a) An orientation programme about school management for female
teachers (two three-day conferences with 162 participants in
1984-85).
(b) A programme for the full complement of larger management
teams from the newly formed teacher training colleges for primary
education (54 participants in 1984-85).
(c) An introductory management programme for heads of department
of higher vocational training institutes (30 participants in 1984-85).
(d) A merger skills course for key figures involved in the merging of
secondary schools (with almost 500 participants in 1984-85).

External structural features

As regards external form the following features are characteristic of
Interstudie SO's programmes:

Spatial location and degree of social isolation. The structure of most of
Interstudie SO's programmes involves alternating locations between
residential conferences in hotels and working meetings at participants'
schools. The residential conferences provide optimum screening from the
outside world, so that a cultural island is created as a context for new
learning. The working meetings at schools make for direct confrontation
between learning and reality, between reflection and action. Alternating
the spatial location, and hence the degree of social isolation, brings a
certain rhythm to the learning conditions.

Duration and schedule. Almost all the programmes last from 10 to 13
days; in many cases an additional five days are added to this for private

study, conducting interviews and surveys, dossier research, etc. *Inter-studie SO* views this period of time as being somewhat brief. However, the spread over a period of nine to 12 months, combined with the altern-ation in degree of social isolation mentioned earlier, makes for good learning conditions, and particularly so for school managers who are thereby given the opportunity of learning how to combine their busy, hectic style of working with longer and shorter moments of reflection and observation.

Composition of the course members. Another typical characteristic of *Interstudie SO*'s programme is that one teacher only from a school is not allowed to participate in most of the programmes; instead there has to be two or three members from the same school management team or the entire management team together. This means that the reality content of the learning process, and the proximity to the real-life situation, are provided with a natural medium in which to grow. This creates the potential for intensive learning moments, not only during the programme, but also afterwards.

Another aspect of the composition of the participants is the way they are grouped; usually a course group is made up of a maximum of 25 to 30 participants with two course leaders; as far as possible the pairs and trios come from schools of the same size (ie participants from small schools with others from small schools; those from very large institutions with others from very large institutions, etc). Two subgroups are formed within the course group; these subgroups ('working groups') are selected to be as homogeneous as possible according to the type of school. The idea behind these selection criteria is that this enables the degree of heterogeneity in management situations to be reduced somewhat, so that the range of content-related learning aspects is not too great.

The third and final aspect regarding the composition of the course members is their relationship with non-participating colleagues or non-teaching staff at their own school. During the basic course the pair or trio from the same school are encouraged to make arrangements with a 'back-up team' which comprises three to five colleagues or non-teaching staff at their own school who are prepared to support the course participants during the programme period. The function of this back-up team might be: to be available for interviews and surveys, to act as a sounding-board for what the participants believe they have learned about themselves or their school, and to help conceive and design plans of action for learning. During the personnel policy follow-up course, the formation of a back up team is compulsory before enrolment; during this course the back-up team forms a project group which helps to analyse the personnel policy at their own school and helps to select, design and implement an innovation in at least one small part of the policy.

The content of the course. In the final analysis the theme is the most important aspect. Obviously there is a wide degree of variation in the different topics, the result of both the differing nature of the courses and the selection, which is partly based on the work problems and learning requirements of the participants; nevertheless, the theme of *Interstudie SO*'s programmes can, generally speaking, be characterized by key words such as: diagnosis, design, implementation, and evaluation of innovation, as well as policy making with regard to the school's organizational sub-system (designing and changing the organizational structure and culture), and the school leaders' own contributions to, and roles within, a systematic school development.

Internal structural features

The more or less passive variables linked to the extenal form of *Interstudie SO* programmes have important learning potential because of their specific combination. Thus, ways of influencing the participants are selected even before they start the courses. *Interstudie SO* programmes are also actively arranged and used to enable the participants to learn and to give direction to their learning. Besides the architectural features of the external form there are also the choreographic features of the internal form (van der Vegt, 1974). Let us look at a few of these:

(a) *Information.* The programmes make for an informative climate, not by means of 'lessons' on particular topics (there are only a few of these), but by regularly providing small cognitive inputs from a series of prepared information modules at suitable moments during the learning process, with the content of these inputs also being relevant at that point. Intensive exchange of information between the participants is also encouraged by means of purposeful questioning by the course leaders, the learning tasks set during the programme and the 'lobby discussions'. (These lobby discussions are often the result of critical incidents during the meetings or else they provide material for the meetings because the course leaders make specific use of them.) Information is also generated by the participants themselves who constantly reflect upon one another's experiences; this reflection gives rise to new ideas and new concepts, which are then tried out. In this way a cycle of experience-reflection-analysis-design is regularly completed.

(b) *Social interaction.* Right from the beginning of the programme interaction within groups is encouraged and interaction between the two or three participants from the same school is also constantly called upon. The participants are challenged to help create their own learning process within the contours of the programme. Regular short progress discussions and evaluations of the conference are used to encourage participants to provide feedback for one another and for the course leaders.

(c) *Assignments.* Each programme is actually a succession of learning assignments for individual participants, for the two or three participants from one school, for the subgroup, and for the entire conference group. For example, at the start of a programme the participants are asked to give some relevant information about their school by drawing up a systematic school description, but they are also asked to give a critical appraisal of a school description from a different pair or trio of course members. Then the subgroup as a whole examines the school descriptions critically and compares them in terms of description categories, planning and relevance; also with regard to their thoughts on their own learning process. The participants may have, for example, an assignment to keep a learning logbook and to draw conclusions from it for future learning purposes.

In conjunction with the external structural features, these internal ones are illustrative of the particular nature and character of *Interstudie SO*'s in-service training programmes.

Future developments

We have been describing *Interstudie SO*'s present activities. It started in 1976 as a single course. A programmes commission, consisting of representatives of school leaders' organizations and the national education centres plus several experts, had been working for several years to achieve this. After 1976, six staff members/course leaders and two other employees worked intensively to develop, implement, evaluate, adjust, etc, this commission's proposals. This was the single-course phase (1976-80).

After 1980, the expansion and differentiation phase began. The system course and the personnel policy course were created at the request of former course members. At the same time individual requests from school leaders for advice in special situations began to come in regularly. Intensive contacts were also established with policy makers in the Ministry of Education. This second phase led up to the present situation, consisting of a package of in-service training courses pus a small amount of occasional consultancy work and intensive policy advice to the Ministry of Education (1980-85).

Interstudie SO is now in a transitional phase. A number of new developments have either actually started or are due to start in 1985-86.

1. For 1985-86 a course in distance-learning programmes is being developed for the middle managers of the new large multisectoral institutes for higher voactional training; components of this are to be: an individual learning workbook, a series of group meetings and a laboratory for management skills.
2. The period 1985-86 will probably see the first stages in the setting up of a network of school management consultants; the provisional idea is for 12 to 15 school leaders to be released from some of their duties in order to be trained and supervised, and eventually become available for management consultancy and interim management duties.
3. In 1985-86 a preliminary recommendation will be made to the

Ministry of Education regarding a structured training traject for school leaders; *Interstudie SO*'s present package will form the basis for this; improvements in cohesion, the inclusion of educational and management science as subjects, an extension of the total duration of the learning traject, sharpening admission policy, etc, will, in the long run, result in improved opportunities for professionalization among school leaders.

Interstudie SO's policy is, in the long term, also directed towards careers advice for individual future school managers. This advice will be related to an advisory function in connection with school boards as the bodies which select and appoint school managers. Other future policy relates to the continuing formation of a documentation bank, which may come to function as a clearing-house in the field of school management. A factor which will affect policy is that in the near future it will prove desirable to develop a training course for school management trainers.

How *Interstudie SO* will actually develop in the next few years, only time will tell. The institute's policies are aimed towards the long-term creation of a differentiated system of services concerned with school management development in the Netherlands. In this sense the title of this article is a label for the strategic mission which *Interstudie SO* envisages for itself in the Netherlands: not only as an in-service training institute, but also as a centre for school management development.

Reference

van der Vegt, R (1974) *Opleiden en evalueren (Training and Evaluation)* Boom Uitgeverij: Meppel, The Netherlands

21. The National Institute of Educational Management, Malaysia

Chew Tow Yow

Summary: The National Institute of Educational Management is an administrative division of the Ministry of Education, Malaysia. It was established in 1979 in response to the need to advance the professional growth and development of educational administrators and to improve educational planning and management practices. Its first five-year training programme (1979-84) priority was on the training of primary and secondary school principals. However, the Institute is responsible for conducting training in educational planning and management and general administration for almost 25,000 educational administrators and administrative support staff at the central, State, district and school levels of educational administration. Training programmes vary in duration from four days to several weeks and are generally undertaken after the assessment of training needs. The Institute has training facilities for 400 fully residential participants at any one time. Besides conducting training, the Institute is attempting to increase its role in organizational renewal through collaborative efforts with other agencies within the educational system.

Introduction

Training in educational planning and management on a large scale was not given priority in educational development in Malaysia till the more urgent tasks of providing adequate places in schools had been undertaken successfully. Major resources were directed toward school building construction, curricular reforms, pre- and in-service teacher training. Having to fulfil the immediate needs of providing basic education for the masses, even if the methods of educational planning and management are not sophisticated, is a reality and a paradox of educational development. Educational planning and management practices evolve concurrently with the practicalities of setting up organizational mechanisms to deliver mass education. Malaysia's experience reflects such a trend.

The first educational report (the Razak Report, 1956) addressed itself to the issue of evolving a national system of education that would meet the demands of nation building and the tasks of building a united and progressive society. It only dealt with educational administration in very broad terms. When Malaysia achieved nationhood in 1957, the then existing form of educational administration was adopted, and over the years this

educational administrative system underwent gradual changes to meet
with the imperatives of rapid quantitative expansion of education. This is
much to the credit of the early educational administrators, men of vision
with practical knowledge and wisdom who, while they were dealing with
the more immediate task of quantitative expansion of education, began
to lay the foundation for the qualitative improvement of education and
educational planning and management. Though the number of educational
administrators trained through specific programmes was small, a beginning
was made. The establishment, in early 1979, of the Malaysian Educational
Staff Training Institute — renamed in 1984 the National Institute of Educational Management (NIEM) — was the culmination of successive efforts
made to improve the efficiency and effectiveness of educational planning
and management. Resting on a 120-acre highland site the Institute became
fully operational in May 1985 with a training capacity for 400 people at
any one time, and a potential clinetele of 25,000 educational administrators and administrative support staff.

Institutional role and goals

The Institute is a division of the Ministry of Education, a division being
a major constituent of the organizational infrastructure of the Ministry.
The conceptualization of the role of the Institute has moved away from
the initial dichotomy of regarding the Institute either as a division of
the Ministry with total responsibility for all aspects of professional staff
development or as a purely training institute, conducting short courses
for school principals and other management staff. The Institute is now
seen as having a role reflecting a judicious balance between the maintenance and development concerns of staff development: the maintenance
concern views training as fitting people into existing jobs to carry out
existing tasks in accordance with existing procedures, while the developmental concern views the Institute as playing a definite role in promoting
reforms in educational and management practices.

    The developmental role of the Institute would require the Institute to
be highly innovative, with in-house staff competence higher than is
generally found in the field. The Institute would also have to be actively
involved in organizational development and renewal at all levels of the
national educational administrative system, in addition to undertaking
developmental studies to promote more efficient and effective models
and procedures in educational planning and management. Currently, it
is felt that the maintenance function of the Institute should not use more
than 70 per cent of its resources. The developmental function should
increase as the demands for basic training in educational planning and
management are being met and as the Institute develops its own staff
competence.

    The Institute, as one of several educational programme activity centres
of the Ministry of Education, has specific responsibilities for educational

leadership and management training. Conceptually, the rationale for the Institute's role may be illustrated as in Figure 1.

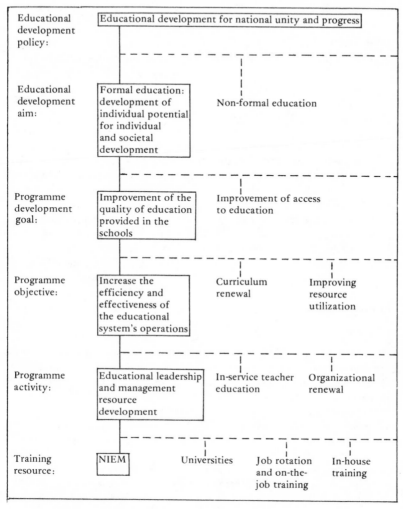

Figure 1 *Rationale for the establishment of the Institute*

Therefore, as a training resource within the educational programme activity of increasing the efficiency and effectiveness of the national educational enterprise in delivering quality education through the nation's school, the goals of the Institute are:

1. to advance the *professional growth and development* of the educational service personnel as educators, educationists, administrators, and as agents of change within the nation's educational strategy; and

2. to promote the development of *educational planning and manage-ment practices* relevant to the nation's goal of planned social change through education.

In the light of the above institutional goals, the Institute's short- and long-term programme objectives are:

1. to conduct *evaluative studies* to monitor the efficiency and efficacy of organizational and management systems operating within the nation's educational enterprise;
2. to undertake *intervention studies* to develop viable alternatives in educational planning and management;
3. to maintain an ongoing system of *training needs assessment* within the context of continual development of educators, educationists, administrators and administrative support staff;
4. to plan and implement *training programmes* relevant to the demands of educational development on the competence of the educational service personnel at all levels of educational administration;
5. to evaluate the *effectiveness of training strategies and programmes*;
6. to provide *consultancy services* to educational organizations and institutions for in-house training and organizational development; and
7. to improve *training technology* in educational management.

Programme and activities

Programme priority

The Institute's first five-year programme priority was concerned with the training of school principals. The need to focus training resources on school heads/principals arose because school principals were rarely and specifically prepared for the job. While they may be regarded as being at the lower end of the hierarchy of the national educational administrative system, school principals, however, play the most crucial role in making the school, and thus the broader national educational programme, a success.

Working on irregular schedules in borrowed premises, the Institute was able to reach approximately 20 per cent of the school principals through the three-/four-week Basic School Principal Course during its first five years of operation. The School Principal's Training Programme has been developed as a three-stage training programme: the basic, inter-mediate and advanced stage/course; these run separately for primary and secondary school principals. The Basic School Principal's Course prepares a principal for the fundamental tasks of leading and administering the school.

During the next five-year period (1985-89) the Institute proposes to upgrade the training of school principals through the Intermediate and Advanced School Principal's Courses. The Intermediate Course, lasting seven weeks, was tested in 1984. The overall aim of the course is to increase the school principal's capability of solving problems creatively as well as to develop sound project planning and implementation practices. By the end of 1985 it is hoped that the sequence of training programme development for school principals will continue with the try-out of the Advanced School Principal's Course which aims at enhancing the capability of school principals as local agents of social change, curriculum innovators and institutional managers.

Recent developments within the country call for new emphasis in the principal's role. The school is now seen as having to play a more dynamic role as a catalyst for local community development. School principals and teachers are also expected to deal effectively with such social issues and problems as drug addiction, religious extremism and racial polarization within the schools. These developments have implications for personnel training right across the spectrum of the national educational administrative system. The effort to remove the social distance, which has imperceptibly separated the school from the local community as educational administration became increasingly centralized during the last two decades, has led to the need to re-emphasize the value of close parent-teacher cooperation and to promote dynamic school-community relations. Increasingly, private individuals and organizations are encouraged to participate with schools in joint ventures that will benefit both the school and the community.

Training mode

The Institute uses two training modes:

   (a) serial training programme mode with either a horizontal or a vertical/hierarchical content/competence increment at each succeeding training course; and
   (b) *ad hoc* training to meet specific training needs.

Training is fully residential, lasting from a few days to several weeks. The practicum as post-residential training reinforcement, and distance teaching as a training activity, have yet to be tried out. Figure 2 on p 288 summarizes the types and duration of representative training courses undertaken to date.

Training needs assessment

Mapping the educational planning and management personnel profile of the Malaysian educational system was the first task undertaken by the Institute in 1979. The strategy adopted was to have an initial bird's eye-view of the personnel profile of the national educational administrative system, while concentrating on developing more detailed personnel inventory and assessing the training needs of the priority training clientele, the school principals. In identifying the training needs of school principals, the Institute began with the task of identifying the existing perceptions of

Clientele in the educational service	Total clients to be reached	Duration (days) of training programme							
		Multi-level programme				Series programme		Ad hoc courses	
		Basic	Intermediate	Advance		Regular	Irregular	Irregular	
School heads	7335	21	49						
Deputy heads	2655	21							
District officers	388	12				10			
State officers	2100	6						4	
Ministry officers	2500							4	
Teacher educators	1600	10						10	
College principals	26						4		
Deputy principals	26						4		
School inspectors	310	10					5		
School clerks	8000	21							

Figure 2 Duration (number of days) of training programme

experienced school principals concerning their roles, responsibilities and tasks. A total of 270 school principals of diverse experience and background were involved in diagnostic workshop sessions lasting two to three days. The opinions collected were then reviewed in similar workshop sessions involving a total of 150 school supervisors, inspectors of schools and previous school principal course organizers. The outcomes were:

1. a comprehensive listing of the school principal's tasks and responsibilities;
2. indicative norms of desirable performance of school principals;
3. a breakdown of competences needed to carry out specific tasks;
4. indicators concerning areas of training most needed; and
5. nine major areas of school principal responsibilities, viz

   (a) curriculum leadership and instructional supervision;
   (b) management of services to pupils;
   (c) management of the teaching staff;
   (d) management of the non-teaching staff;
   (e) management of the school plant and facilities;
   (f) financial management and accounting;
   (g) administration of the school office;
   (h) promoting school-community relations; and
   (i) management of school hostel.

Within the nine areas of school principal's responsibilities, it was discovered that there were no fewer than 240 specific tasks that a school principal has to perform in any one school year. Each of these tasks was analysed in terms of the knowledge, attitude and skills that would be needed to perform it.

Training needs assessment is a continuing activity of the Institute. To date, similar efforts have been directed to determine the personnel training needs of:

   (a) deputy school principals;
   (b) district educational officers;
   (c) State Department Educational Officers and Supervisors; and
   (d) members of the educational clerical service.

Two other areas in which more explicit work needs to be done are:

1. the personnel profiles of classroom teachers and teachers who assume a variety of additional tasks related to improving the teaching-learning environment such as student counselling service and school-community relations; and
2. educational administrators who are positioned at the Ministry of Education and who undertake a great variety of independent and inter-related tasks of planning, implementing and evaluating educational programmes and projects.

A preliminary diagnostic study of educational management practices at the State Department of Education and at the Ministry of Education was completed in 1984. It is proposed that further in-depth studies be made in the near future to determine measures to increase productivity in view of current and anticipated future resources constraints. In the light of these demands, the Institute is endeavouring to improve its data sources in the following areas:

1. current knowledge about educational planning and management;
2. client characteristics, such as previous training and job experiences; and
3. nature of organizations, eg the school as an organization, with its variants in terms of size of pupil enrolment, location, standard of facilities, pupil and teacher characteristics.

Process for programme development and implementation

The *modus operandi* adopted by the Institute for training programme development and implementation is summarized and illustrated in the development of the Basic Principal Course (see Figure 3 on p 291).

Besides developing its own training programmes using only the Institute's staff, the Institute collaborates with other divisions of the Ministry of Education, State Departments of Education and agencies outside the Ministry to develop joint training programmes. The Institute also makes available its training facilities to agencies in the educational system to conduct training courses, seminars and workshops.

Evaluation of training programme

A deliberate effort has been made to treat evaluation as an integral part of programme development and implementation. The purposes of programme development evaluation are:

1. to determine the degree of effectiveness of the training programme in achieving the anticipated training outcomes that are consonant with the findings of training needs assessmet; and
2. to assess the efficiency of the administration of the training programme.

At the course development stage, evaluation is aimed at assessing the 'plan worthiness' of the training curriculum. Formative evaluation is scheduled as a continuing activity of training programme development since the structure and organization of a training programme has to respond to changing needs.

In determining the training outcomes accrued from participation at a course, the immediate outcomes measures include periodic tests during the course, end-of-course tests and project assignment. In some courses, face-to-face evaluation, using schedules of competences, is used before the course participant proceeds to the next stage in the course. The Institute is continuing its efforts to improve the reliability and validity of its testing procedures as it officially certifies participants' attendance and performance at training courses. The Institute has yet to develop a satisfactory strategy

Process	Basic School Principal's Course

1. Training needs assessment:
  – identification of the tasks and responsibilities of the target client
  – determination of norms of performance
  – analysis of competences for tasks by norms of performance
  – assessment of discrepancies between observed level of performance *vis-à-vis* norms of performance
	16 workshop sessions, lasting 2 to 3 days, involving 270 principals of diverse experience and background and 150 supervisors and inspectors of schools and previous course organizers, were conducted to obtain:
	(a) comprehensive listing of principal's tasks and responsibilities;
	(b) desirable norms of job performance;
	(c) breakdown of competences needed for carrying out identified tasks;
	(d) areas in which training is needed.

2. Determination of training outcomes/course objectives	Institute's staff reviewed training needs and formulated course objectives based on findings in 1 above.
3. Structuring of course content and training techniques	The 10 general objectives of the course were translated into specific objectives in 6 major content areas. Specific topics in each major content area were identified in collaboration with experienced supervisors, inspectors and lecturers from teachers' colleges and local universities.
4. Development of training materials	Trainers' and trainees' materials were developed by the Institute's staff, supervisor, inspectors, and lecturers.
5. Try-out	30 primary and 30 secondary school principals participated in a trial course which was evaluated session by session (two-hourly) and day by day. The course was tried out in its totality.
6. Revision and rewriting	Trainers' manuals and trainees' materials were rewritten following try-out feedback. Additional materials were produced.
7. Dry-run of implementation plan	It was not necessary in this instance to dry-run the implementation plan of the Basic Course which is to be conducted for all newly appointed principals and existing principals whom the State Directors of Education felt needed to attend the course.
8. Implementation	The revised packages of the training programme were used in subsequent years with modifications where deemed necessary. The training programme is now available according to the need to provide basic training to newly appointed principals.

Figure 3 *Organizational structure*

for assessing the impact of training in the work environment. Measures under consideration include seeking the participation of supervisors at various levels of administration to undertake periodic diagnostic personnel performance audit of course participants.

It has been the experience of the Institute that training in educational planning and management cannot be undertaken without some form of involvement in organizational renewal either directly or indirectly. Consequently, the Institute is attempting to incorporate in its training programmes some aspects of organizational renewal assignments to be attempted by course participants on return to their working environment.

Organizational structure

The development of the Institute's organizational structure has been based on an analysis of the Institute's goal and programme objectives. A schema of the Institute's operational structure is given in Figure 4.

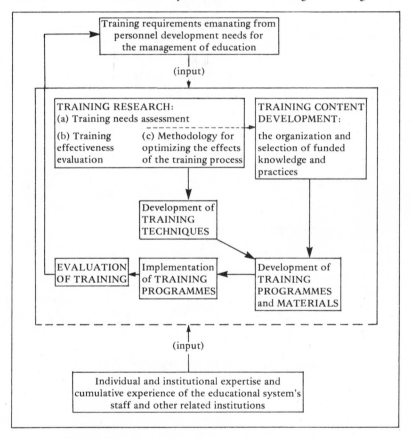

Figure 4 *Schema of the Institute's operational structure*

It is hoped that the organizational structure will facilitate the recruitment and deployment of trained personnel for the research, programme development and training functions of the Institute.

At present, the Institute has five academic departments, five service centres and an administrative unit.

The five academic departments which bear the burden of developing the substantive content for training are:

1. Department of Educational Development.
2. Department of Curriculum and Pedagogy Leadership.
3. Department of Educational Management.
4. Department of School Management.
5. Department of Educational Research and Evaluation.

The five service centres and their respective functions are as follows:

1. *Training Research and Evaluation Centre*, which conducts the identification and analysis of training needs and monitors and evaluates the short- and long-term effects of training.
2. *Training Technology Centre*, which is responsible for research and development of training methodologies.
3. *Training Resource Centre*, which serves as a depository and clearing house for reference and training materials.
4. *Administrative Support Services Centre*, which provides training in office administration, accounting and book-keeping, the maintenance of the school plant, and the management of supplies and auxiliary services.
5. *Course Administration Centre*, which attends to all aspects of training programme implementation and the day-to-day administration of training courses conducted at the Institute.

The General Administrative Unit looks after the daily house-keeping functions and activities of the Institute.

The Institute's organizational structure is reflective of the bureaucratic model of administration. However, in terms of carrying out the Institute's training functions, a matrix structure has been employed in which staff members from various departments and centres work together in various project teams and assume leadership and subordinate roles at different times. While collegial responsibility is an attractive management concept, it is hard at times to sustain enthusiasm and a high level of cooperation and mutual support, especially when 'territorial jealousy', breakdown in communications, uneven workload, overlapping interests and lack of coordination are such common human and management weaknesses.

Future growth and development

With the establishment of the Institute in 1979, a definite attempt has been made to systematize the hitherto *ad hoc* and piecemeal attempts at personnel development. The setting-up of the Institute has focused the Ministry's attention on the need for an overall strategy for the continuous training of the total educational service personnel, including classroom teachers numbering 120,000. In attempting to resolve this massive problem, the Institute will continue to take the initiative to work with relevant agencies in the educational administrative system to develop the following:

1. a system for the ongoing monitoring and analysis of the training needs for all categories of the educational service personnel *vis-à-vis* social and technological changes;
2. realistic and practical personnel performance appraisal;
3. temporary and permanent systems to meet increasing training needs;
4. a greater variety of, and more effective, training programmes, techniques and materials; and
5. a strategy for the continuous assessment of the effects of training on job performance and organizational productivity.

The Institute is well placed to promote the vertical articulation of ideals and ideas across the bureaucratic levels of the educational administrative system as well as the horizontal integration of the multifarious concerns of educational planning and management. More than any organization within the national educational system, the Institite can help to ensure the cross fertilization of experiences and practices directed at improving the delivery of quality education to pupils in schools. However, the effectiveness of the Institute is dependent upon the vitality and vigour of its individual staff members. Young officers may be enthusiastic. But enthusiasm alone is not enough. Experience and knowledge in substantive areas of educational planning and management, the knack and capability of training and inspiring others, and the competence to undertake developmental research are important personal attributes of trainers. Establishing and maintaining a high calibre staff is and will remain a major developmental task of the Institute. The trainers or professional staff positions for 1985 number 60, of which only 38 positions were filled half-way through the year.

Reference

Malaysia, Government of (1956) *Report of the Education Committee (The Razak Report)* Government Printers: Kuala Lumpur

Part 6: Reflections

22. From leadership training to educational development: IMTEC as an international experience

Per Dalin

Summary: Per Dalin is Director of the International Movement Towards Educational Change (IMTEC) and in this chapter offers a frank, personal reflection on the 15-year history of the institution. This reflection focuses particularly on some of the ironies entailed when an institution is evolving a strategy for the improvement of schooling through leadership training and organizational development while at the same time the institution itself, and particularly its Director, is mobilizing support, competing for resources, negotiating with government and international agencies, developing and modifying a strategy of change, establishing legitimacy, and developing its own pattern of internal management. The Director now feels that he could have benefited from the training which IMTEC was offering to others. IMTEC was itself coping with becoming the kind of learning system which it was urging on clients. The chapter concludes that IMTEC, and associated and related projects, has developed a valuable knowledge base for the process of institutional change but ends with the question of whether this knowledge is being fully utilized by the institution and associated projects.

Introduction

The International Movement Towards Educational Change (IMTEC) is now 15 years of age. It is time to look back. This could be done in several ways. We have sufficient evaluation data to reflect on the IMTEC experience in some objective format. That would not be my task. As the one who initiated IMTEC, and has directed the organization over these 15 years, I could at the most present a *subjective viewpoint*. I am fully aware that some of my colleagues over these years may look at our experience differently. This is my story.

Since my entire professional career has been spent studying change, in particular in educational organizations, I will attempt to use the very same theories on my own management experience — it is to be hoped in a critical and constructive way. In a sense, I hope this story will be about learning at different levels; about our emerging understanding of how educational systems can be improved and about the relevance of our own theories on our life experience.

I should also say what this chapter is *not*: it is not an objective history of IMTEC. It does not reflect a comprehensive view of the dynamics of this rather unique international development programme. It does not attempt to analyse the context (eg the Organization for Economic Co-operation and Development — OECD) in any comprehensive way. In any case, if I do reflect on the context of IMTEC it is *my subjective perspective* and nothing else. What I do hope is that I will be able to relate my own management dilemmas in a rapidly changing project to my own and others' theories about change.

The background

Some 50 selected educational administrators, educational developers, and researchers studying educational change met in the summer of 1969 at Cambridge at an OECD conference on the 'Management of Educational Innovations'. The newly started Centre for Educational Research and Innovation (CERI), under the directorship of Ron Gass, had embarked on a very ambitious international programme.

It had become fairly clear in most OECD countries that the sweeping proposals for reform of the 1960s were having little impact in the schools. Most systems had experienced major difficulties *implementing* school reforms. The general idea behind the Cambridge conference was to alert key decision makers in the OECD countries to the fact that there was something called the *process* of educational reform, as well as the ideas, or objectives, of educational reform. The assumption was that process knowledge could have a direct impact on the *management process* — which again would lead to more efficient management of educational reform. Even in 1969 we knew that it could not be that simple. However, the optimism was clearly there.

I was asked to join the CERI staff, and became the coordinator of the Research and Development Program of the Centre. I was quick to follow up one of the key recommendations of the Cambridge conference: to organize a research programme studying the change process in member countries. A major educational research programme called the CERI Case Study Program of Educational Innovations was created. It provided studies of internal school processes, the change process at the local and regional levels, and at the central level. A series of publications was produced, including a volume analysing existing theories of educational change. That volume also generated a number of new hypotheses related to educational reform based on the 17 case studies of the research programme. A number of researchers who later became well known internationally were involved, such as Matthew Miles, Michael Fullan, Ron Havelock (who was already involved in Cambridge), Francis Chase, John Nisbet, Brian Holmes, to mention a few. It was the first attempt internationally to cope with the topic.

My analysis of these studies (Dalin, 1973) made it fairly clear that:

(a) our theories of educational change were insufficient to explain the process;

(b) we needed theories grounded in practice that could take the many unique conditions into account (phenomenological perspective);

(c) we needed to understand *the systemic implications* of educational change (some theories were too general, others were too narrow in looking at the school as an isolated community);

(d) 'resistance to change' was not necessarily negative — in fact it could reflect important value conflicts, power conflicts, and a number of other 'signals' to reformers;

(e) the R and D strategy, so popular in the 1960s, had major problems within the educational system — since most innovations were not 'adopted' but 'adapted';

(f) the question of centralization versus decentralization was not the issue but rather to develop an *innovation policy* that was based on an understanding of the school as an organization and the system implications of the large educational bureaucracies.

The Cambridge conference had also recommended that the OECD initiate a programme providing training for 'Managers of Educational Change'. The planning of this programme started a year after the case study programme was launched, and IMTEC — then known as the International Management Training for Educational Change — was started in mid-1972, supported by 17 governments, with the Ford Foundation providing the first major grant.

As for most programmes — in particular international programmes — objectives were general, and the individuals representing their governments often had quite different ideas about what such a programme should do. In many cases they were simply individuals with their own ideas; sometimes they had support from a few individuals in their own ministries, and in a handful of cases their ideas represented some decision previously taken within the relevant educational bureaucracy. I doubt that any decision was based on needs assessment. As so often the case, the international bureaucrats ·(myself included) had most of the decision-making power.

There were clearly differences among country representatives. The Swedes were of the opinion that a training programme for educational managers should basically aim at providing them with the tools to implement the Ministry's reform decisions. The purpose would certainly be to give the managers a better understanding of the reforms and provide them with effective management tools.

At the other extreme, the British saw management training as something basically for the head teacher. He or she should be given a better understanding of the school as an organization and assistance in how to draw more effectively on his or her staff. The Americans had a different perspective: it was the time of leadership development in America, in contrast to the training of administrators or managers. In fact the American Governing Board member was the Director of the Educational Leadership Development Program that recruited talented persons from fields other than education, the assumption being: if we could only draw on some outstanding individual talents, we would be able to fix it!

There were many other assumptions. Most board members were very unclear about their assumptions — and so were the staff. We experienced what most project managers experience: lack of clarity about mission, lack of common agreements among board members, a lack of understanding of how the project would actually influence the target population, and uncertainties about the basic theories underlying the programme. We just had to accept uncertainties — and live with the unfinished — for a long time.

As a manager I was faced with some very basic dilemmas:

(a) to sell a project to get the necessary resources — without promising too much;

(b) to involve as many countries as possible (a typical OECD trait) with quite different agendas, without losing all control;

(c) to give the staff and myself sufficient room for experimentation without upsetting influential members (and we certainly needed to experiment to 'test the water');

(d) to involve participating countries as much as possible in project developments (to create ownership of the programme), without losing necessary control;

(e) to identify what we considered the best theoreticians and practitioners and involve them in the programme — without going through the traditional OECD procedures (which in some cases involved clearance by national ministries — places where our persons either were not known or not accepted);

(f) to show results quickly (we were operating under heavy time constraints) — without compromising on quality, and hoping to draw on the best expertise within the Western hemisphere.

The *politics of educational innovation*, so well described by Ernest House (House, 1974), became quite evident during the first years of IMTEC. While the formal agenda was to develop a programme for management training, the project found itself in the middle of organizational conflicts and country politics. Again a beautiful illustration of what many educational managers experience facing demands for change:

1. Conflicts over control and influence.
2. Institutional and personal rivalries.
3. Manipulations and backroom politics.
4. Discrepancies between project aspirations and project resources.

Management training courses

At the same time, the *knowledge base* of management training was uncertain — to put it mildly. No one really said that. It was taken for granted that we knew what the technology actually would be and that we would know what to teach. In general terms we knew. We saw the content of management training being a mixture of:

Perspectives: meaning presentations of a variety of philosophies and theories about education, discussions of schools as organizations, perspectives on learning and curriculum, and theories about the process of change.

Human relations training: basically skills-oriented sessions providing participants with the opportunities for self-study, experimenting with different roles and approaches to problem solving, conflict resolution, and spending considerable time in 'process training' (with an emphasis on communication and group dynamics).

Management techniques: giving participants the opportunities to become acquainted with practical tools to be used in planning, implementation, and evaluation. Since the IMTEC mandate was management training for *educational change*, the emphasis was *innovation management techniques.*

We had access to the very best resource centres and resource people in the Western hemisphere. Indeed, we also recruited some excellent consultants and we organized some exciting seminars. We pioneered new training designs, using case studies as the main vehicle. We also used participant projects as a major input, and organized seminars around the ideas of small stable work units ('family groups'), with daily feedback to the seminar management — which again provided the input for decisions about changes in the seminar programme. IMTEC seminars have always been flexible, providing ample opportunities for participants to live through some major changes — and to feel the frustrations and anxieties about living with uncertainties. The seminars have been laboratories for change analysis.

I believe IMTEC seminars are known to provide exciting opportunities. They have also been useful laboratories for management training development work. We were still concerned with the following aspects of our work:

Relevance: What is relevant management training for educational change? In the early 1970s when IMTEC started we had only a fairly general knowledge about the process of educational change. Did we know something that was worth telling?

Training and development: Increasingly we began to see that the idea of management training as a prime condition for successful educational change might be questioned. What evidence did we have that participants in our management courses actually had a better chance of managing the complexities of educational change? In other words, what did we know about management training?

Change strategy: We talked about the need to have a clear strategy, to understand who your client or your target population is, and how your efforts could be seen in a total concept of change. Now, what was IMTEC's own change strategy? What was our target population? How would our management training courses at the international level be linked to national developments?

Internal dynamics

We were certainly unclear. We had used so much energy to get some programme going — visible to everyone — that we had forgotten our own change strategy. How could that have happened? Let me reflect on what I now see as our main concern at that time:

1. We were *development* oriented and not change oriented. That was exactly what we tried to convince our course participants was the major problem of the R and D strategy of the 1960s! We were trying to invent and produce — and to prove that IMTEC certainly was the best management training programme around (and it was!).

2. We were also *competition* oriented. We lived within a competitive climate. We wanted to prove that we could get an excellent programme off the ground. Since the criteria was 'successful courses', who cared about the long-term change effects? (Whoever thought in those terms?)

3. Our goals were spelled out — but were nevertheless still quite ambiguous. Therefore we became more occupied with the short-term internal dynamics, to get access to necessary resources, to manage conflicts within a large bureaucracy, to try to develop some territory and independence — rather than look for *goal clarification*.

At a deeper organizational level, what was going on? I am pretty sure that none of us was clear about it, but the lack of clarity about goals was probably quite necessary. The first few years of the IMTEC project (and most development projects) were used to get the project accepted, or adopted, by member governments. We were more politicians than managers.

At the same time, we needed acceptance in the intellectual circles of the OECD countries in terms of management training. No doubt, the USA and possibly Canada and the United Kingdom at that time were important to us. *Legitimizing* became an important management activity.

What was important to me as a manager at that time? First I was overwhelmed by the enormous task. We were understaffed. We knew too little about our task. No one had actually done this before. My perspective was limited, I now feel, mainly due to my own definition and perceptions. Important things were not seen. We had set up our headquarters in Oslo. A good idea from an 'independence point of view'; a bad idea from the point of 'perception check'. Any organization needs ways of breaking its psychological set — to question whether it is open to other perspectives. That can best be done in an open dialogue. I should have spent much more time simply listening and trying to find out the needs of the system I was trying to serve.

Instead I was deeply involved in developmental work. And I loved it! I became an expert, a trainer, a 'modeller', and a developer. I was also a manager, soon becoming an advocate of our own ideas and products. And we did have a good product. Also, indeed, it seemed as though we were succeeding.

Let us assume that I had received an invitation to participate in a management training course at that time (I probably received several such invitations). I did not know about any course at the time that I felt was attractive. It may be that I was not fully aware of my needs. I guess that is true for most of us. How do we actually define our needs? Also, it could be that the courses had little relevance to my work situation. What courses were actually offered that would deal with the kind of dilemmas I was involved in?

Looking back at that stage of my management career, I feel that I could have benefited from training, for example to participate in sessions that would explore my own perceptions of reality and provide alternatives, sessions questioning our own change strategy, sessions analysing the internal dynamics of our organization and sessions helping me to clarify my own role. Yes, indeed, management training could have been useful. The questions remain though: How would I have known? How would I have understood my needs at the time — and would I have taken the time and energy to do it?

Critical processes in educational change

Already in 1973, however, we were quite convinced that management training for educational decision makers alone would not do much good. We knew we had to understand the school as an organization better — and understand the dynamics of educational change at a much deeper level than we did. We came up with the idea of having an international meeting of the best people we could identify to discuss the theme 'Critical processes in educational change'.

That was a very hard idea to sell, in particular to the IMTEC Board who rightly felt that its brief was to supervise a management training programme! I saw quite early that IMTEC had been given too narrow a mandate, mostly due to internal politics. We needed a wider platform, more room for experimentation and research, and possibilities to test out ways in which organizational development could be used as part of management training.

The 'Critical process' seminar took place in the mountains of Norway in December 1974. It was fantastic. We had gathered together some of the most creative, development-oriented educators, and we produced a lot.

The conclusions were fairly clear: IMTEC should embark on a development course leading towards an integration of management training and organizational development. I was impressed and influenced by the work of Seamour Sarason, and felt that his thinking had opened up an entirely new dimension for me (Sarason, 1971). IMTEC had a very influential network of researchers studying change, and this seminar was very much influenced by people such as Matthew Miles, Milbrey McLaughlin, Michael Fullan, Harry Gray, and Richard Williams.

Now, we were in the middle of a major change effort. We had successful management training courses behind us, and we had several proposals for more of the same! Why change to something clearly different — and very ambiguous? That was difficult to sell. We also had quite limited resources; we knew our mandate would be up for discussion in a year's time; and a large number of ideas were generated to launch IMTEC on a sounder economic base.

To launch a highly innovative and debatable new programme in the middle of a fight for survival by an organization, with a Board representing some 17 governments with only lukewarm support, in an organization that had many competing demands, was probably quite stupid. We did, because we were professionally convinced that it was right. We were *professionals* and development oriented, and we looked for legitimacy in the professional community of educators, not among ministry bureaucrats and others more concerned with the politics of change.

One factor that was quite crucial: IMTEC's headquarters had moved to Oslo. We had little opportunity for informal chats and face-to-face problem solving. We started to resolve conflicts using internal memoranda! It was not easy.

School organizational diagnosis

Over the next year we developed what I still consider to be one of the most important IMTEC programmes: the 'Institutional Development Programme'. In the early phases it was simply a diagnostic instrument ('guide to institutional learning' — GIL) that was tested out for the first time in 1975 in 18 teacher training institutions in five countries. It was clearly a success. We were fortunate to have an excellent international team to work on the GIL, among whom Larry Krafft made a very substantial intellectual contribution.

The idea was simple: we needed to know more about the organization and how members of that organization looked upon leadership within the organization before it made any sense to provide manager training. Our perspective was 'situational leadership', and our organizational philosophy was 'contingency oriented'. GIL, therefore, did not intend to provide answers, but rather to provide members of the school with an opportunity to understand themselves and their organization better. Most of the instrument measured the 'real' situation, as understood by its members, as well as the 'ideal' situation. It gave a unique opportunity to discuss potential needs for change. And it provided the manager with a knowledge base for action.

With this programme IMTEC's management training programme became heavily influenced by organizational development (Dalin and Rust, 1983). We also found ourselves with a new clientele — an International Network of Teacher Training Institutions (INTTI). Teacher training institutions became important partners for several years to come.

I reflected my growing pessimism about educational change in a book published at the time: *Limits to Educational Change* (Dalin, 1978).

I became convinced that we had to understand the school as an organization before we could draw up any useful change and management
strategy — and were not to talk about a management training scheme.
I developed a systemic theory of educational change, presented a theoretical model of schools as organizations, argued for the usefulness of
resistance to change (I analysed it as barriers, that is, value barriers, power
barriers, practical barriers, and psychological barriers), and argued for
for change as 'mutual adaption and development'.

IMTEC was in the middle of a major change. It had considerable
support from the professional community. That community had no
resources. Our mandate with the OECD came to an end. And we really
had no business plan!

I feel that this situation is typical of many well intended educational
development projects. They are usually headed up by teachers, as most of
us are. We are usually interested in *the message*. We are content oriented
and we do not sufficiently understand the *process of change*. It is so hard
to grasp. Not so much in theory, but in our own lives.

In some way we are like engineers: we think that if we only have a
good product it will automatically sell! Educational administrators plan
as if dissemination and implementation of reforms can be taken for
granted. This does not work. The first major study that told us this loud
and clear was the 'Change agent study' of the RAND Corporation
(Berman and McLaughlin, 1974; 1977). Innovations are not 'spread'
or adopted, they are adapted. More important than the innovation itself
is the organizational dynamics and the politics of change.

Let me reflect on my own situation in 1975-76. It was quite clear
that IMTEC as an isolated innovative project based in Norway could not
survive within the OECD context. The choices were fairly clear: to go back
to Paris, 'integrate' (and thereby continue as an OECD diplomat), or to
discontinue the activities within the OECD.

I chose the uncertainties. I stayed in Norway (I was too close to the
Norwegian way of living, the outdoor life, skiing, and friends to do anything
else). I had made decisions about my career that did not work for the
organization I was a part of. I am not suggesting that this was in any way un-
reasonable as seen from the OECD, but I use this situation to reflect on a
common problem in organizations: what do we do with the innovator?

Brooke Derr, in a study soon to be published, has analysed different
career patterns and management options and it has given me new insights
about the management of change (Derr, 1986). He talks about five
different career patterns and the dynamics between careers and organizational cultures; the 'getting ahead' people who seek managerial positions;
the 'getting secure' people who look for job security; the 'getting free'
people who look for space and independence (and who are often very
innovative); the 'getting high' people who are driven by the need for
excitement, challenge and the engaging process of work; and the 'getting
balanced' people who strive for a balance between personal growth,
family interests, and work.

I did not find the space I needed. How many teachers and managers in our educational bureaucracies have ideas and energy but do not find the space necessary for innovative work? What do we do as managers to facilitate innovations within our organizations and to manage diverse career patterns? How can bureaucracies change their own behaviours? I feel quite convinced that educational change to a large extent is dependent on an organizational reward structure and its ability to provide people with different career orientation rewards that are satisfying to them. There is no doubt in my mind that there is untapped energy in our schools that we do not even know and understand the potential of, and we therefore do not know how to use.

The creation of a new setting

In January 1977 I was faced with a new challenge: to build an independent IMTEC. I was given the opportunity to do so by the IMTEC Board. In discussions with colleagues around the world we decided to create an independent, non-profit making educational foundation. We had no money, no mandate from anyone, and no clients — and IMTEC became International Movement Towards Educational Change.

It was a challenge — and a very rewarding task. This is not the place to analyse the process of creating a new organization. What I would rather do is look at the consequences of going from a fairly sheltered position to a free market situation as far as our services were concerned. The OECD umbrella gave us a number of advantages: a secure market, access to the highest decision makers, and legitimacy. At that time we did not have to ask the really hard questions. We were sheltered. Would we be able to survive without the OECD support, to get the necessary resources to grow, and to provide useful services?

We could no longer offer management training courses at an international level. The market would not pay for that. What was needed? We had to find out. Quickly! We continued our international network seminars (in particular for teacher training institutions). These seminars, however, were actually money losers. We found several other areas within the general area of the management of change where our knowledge was needed:

1. We moved close to schools. We saw management development as part of organizational and educational development. If schools were to be able to improve their practices, a number of conditions needed to be fulfilled. Management training might just be one small piece that could have an impact. We worked with the schools on strategies such as: school assessment (often using the GIL and similar diagnostic tools), development of operational plans, securing staff development programmes, strengthening management capability (see below), and bringing schools in contact with other institutions

they could learn from and where they could share their own experiences.

2. We developed a school based management development programme. Our approach was to work with the *management team.* Clarity regarding mission, roles and role relationships and division of labour are typical areas of work within this programme. Our philosophy is that leadership takes place at all levels of the organization, that the various functions of leadership need to be shared, and that the optimal solution must be found in an open and cooperative climate. A precondition, therefore, is often to work with the climate of the management team and the school as a whole.

3. Increasingly we also found that schools are very different, and that they need all kinds of 'entry strategies'. There is no one way. All strategies have some value and some costs. We are phenomenological in our approach, and have developed a series of programmes dealing with different types of organizations. Our 'bank' of materials includes a number of evaluations, readings, exercises, mini-lectures and a variety of 'designs' to enable us to be as flexible as possible when we work with organizations and managers.

We also found that IMTEC has an unusual international resource. A network of professionals in more than 40 countries has evolved over the years. We were able to provide knowledge about the change process and its management at different levels of policy and management and at different phases of developments. We have developed programmes for governments, managers and developers. Examples of such programmes are:

1. International leadership development programmes, where we usually train a *leadership team* from a country the members of which have been designated to develop a major reform programme. The programme includes knowledge and skills in diagnosis, planning, staff development, training designs, curriculum development, monitoring and evaluation. At the same time it is practical: we provide internships placed in relevant institutions in other countries, mini-seminars bringing experts from different countries together, and follow-up coaching with each manager upon his or her return.

2. Technical assistance programmes, where IMTEC provides a government with consultants, materials, programmes and institutions that may be of assistance to a project. Over the past nine years we have subcontracted with 55 universities and other resource institutions for these kinds of contract. These are usually World Bank-financed programmes implemented in less developed countries. We are particularly concerned about *the process of change* and do our best to provide diagnostic capability, management support, and evaluation to assist our clients. Again, we have learned the lesson: most managers are 'process blind'.

3. International management support programmes. These programmes range from consultancy help in developing a change programme,

to organizational development efforts within large organizations, to major evaluation programmes of educational reforms. Most managers involved in large-scale development work benefit from some outside assistance, sometimes because outsiders bring in new perspectives, sometimes because internal dynamics make an outsider the right choice. In most of these programmes we learn a great deal about the management of change — and we develop organizational based management development schemes, as well as external training programmes.

4. International network seminars. The traditional IMTEC seminars on educational change continue at a somewhat irregular pace. They provide a forum for educational developers and researchers, and educational managers. These seminars are 'theme-oriented' (eg 'The quality of teaching in lesser developed countries', Bali, Indonesia, October 1986).

Over the last year IMTEC has developed a series of new programmes for managers, including 'leadership laboratories' combined with school-based development work. We invite managers from different kinds of organization within a geographical region to work together in a 'laboratory' one day each month over one year. They will all develop improvement schemes for their organization. The laboratory is the place where they share their process experiences and get feedback and support. We are developing the same model for change agents. The strategy is: educational change is a process over time where a number of critical resources must be integrated in a unique way for each institution. The manager becomes the person who understands the strengths and weaknesses of his organization — and can skilfully draw upon the untapped energies for change.

IMTEC has been a very important learning opportunity. Many other projects have been generated over the last few years, some of them spin-offs from IMTEC, and other new international, national, or local programmes (see, for example, Goodlad, 1982; Huberman and Miles, 1984; Crandall *et al*, 1982; Fullan, 1982; van Velzen *et al*, 1985). They all make contributions to our understanding of educational change.

We do have a fairly good knowledge base at this stage. Do we use it? In our own lives? As managers? As researchers? As developers? As teachers?

References

Berman, P and McLaughlin, M W (1974) *Federal Programs Supporting Educational Change* I: *A Model of Educational Change* Rand Corporation: Santa Monica, Cal

Berman, P and McLaughlin, M W (1977) *Federal Programs Supporting Educational Change* VII: *Factors Affecting Implementation and Continuation* Rand Corporation: Santa Monica, Cal

Crandall, D P *et al* (1982) *People Policies and Practices: Examining the Chain of School Improvement* I-IX The Network: Andover, Mass

Dalin, P (1973) *Case Studies of Educational Innovation* IV: *Strategies for Educational Innovation* OECD/CERI: Paris

Dalin, P (1978) *Limits to Educational Change* Macmillan in association with the International Movement Towards Educational Change: London

Dalin, P and Rust, V D (1983) *Can Schools Learn?* NFER-Nelson: Windsor, Berks

Derr, B C (1986) *Managing The New Careerists: How to Direct Career Politics* Jossey-Bass: San Francisco, Cal

Fullan, M (1982) *The Meaning of Educational Change* Teachers College Press, Columbia University: New York

Goodlad, J A (1982) *A Place Called School — Prospects for the Future* McGraw-Hill: New York

House, E R (1974) *The Politics of Educational Innovation* McCutchan: Berkeley, Cal

*Huberman, A M and Miles, M B (1984) *Innovation Up Close: How School Improvement Works* Plenum: New York

Sarason, S (1971) *The Culture of the School and the Problem of Change* Allyn and Bacon: Boston, Mass

*van Velzen, W G, Miles, M B, Ekholm, M, Hameyer, U and Robin, D (1985) *Making School Improvement Work — A Conceptual Guide to Practice* International School Improvement Project Acco Pub: Leuven, Belgium

23. IIP 66: source of an operating manual for educational administration on spaceship earth?

William G Walker

Summary: The publication *Educational Administration: International Perspectives*, which emerged from the first International Intervisitation Program held in the USA and Canada during 1966, reflected the same enthusiasm and confidence in the future as did R Buckminster Fuller's contemporary paper *An Operating Manual for Spaceship Earth* (1968).

The first international conference was deliberately designed to bring together practising senior educational administrators, researchers and theorists in the field; it resulted in 16 papers by authors from the USA, Canada, the UK, Australia and New Zealand. In a real sense these papers were scenarios for the future of educational administration around the world.

The three main expectations which emerged from the papers appeared to assume that in the future the practice of educational administration would be illuminated by:

1. The social sciences, in much the same way as the practice of medicine is illuminated by the natural sciences.
2. The widespread adoption of both traditional and alternative training modes for administrators.
3. The adoption of an international perspective by both scholars and practitioners.

In the course of the two decades since 1966 there have been considerable achievements in these three areas in many parts of the world, and less developed, as well as developed, nations have benefited profoundly from them. While by no means all schools and school administrators have been touched by these developments there is good reason to be optimistic regarding achievements arising from future International Intervisitation Programs and similar gatherings.

Introduction

It is nearly two decades since R Buckminster Fuller (1968) wrote his seminal paper, 'An operating manual for spaceship earth', which represented the Utopian climate of the 1960s. The paper reflected Fuller's hopes for an Earth-planet-based humanity which would be physically and economically successful and individually free in the important sense of not having to struggle for survival. Man, as he put it, would be free 'to cooperate in spontaneous and logical ways'.

A product of the same era and the same optimism was the International Intervisitation Program, the first international meeting designed deliberately to bring together senior educational administrators and distinguished academics interested in research and theorizing about educational administration. It is fortuitous that about the time this present paper is published it will be just 20 years since the IIP 66 was held at the University of Michigan, the University of Alberta and at numerous institutions in between, during the autumn of 1966.

As one who played a major part in planning and organizing the peripatetic programme and in editing, together with George Baron and Dan Cooper, the publication which emerged from it (1969), I intend here briefly to attempt an overview and analysis of some developments in the study and practice of educational administration since that time. My comments will necessarily be personal. They will be based heavily on my own impressions and observations as both a senior academic and practising administrator, as founding editor of *The Journal of Educational Administration* and as founding President of the Commonwealth Council for Educational Administration. It may be of interest to note that I recently adopted a somewhat similar approach in looking at the decline and fall of administrative narcissism among US professors of educational administration during roughly the same period (1984).

There had, of course, been many earlier international meetings of educators, such as those which occurred at UNESCO in Paris and numerous international gatherings of practising educational administrators in a variety of centres. The IIP, however, as pointed out above, was different from previous gatherings in that it brought together simply and deliberately not only those who practised educational administration, but those who thought systematically about it, wrote about it, researched it and theorized about it.

Born out of the enthusiasm of the key members of the comparatively newly-formed University Council for Educational Administration (UCEA), with its headquarters at Ohio State University, the IIP was funded by the Kellogg Foundation. It was the combination of this enthusiasm and funding which brought together for the first time practitioners and scholars in the field from the USA, Canada, Britain, New Zealand and Australia.

The effect was almost magical: inexorably during the 1960s and 1970s the interest and enthusiasm emanating from the IIP spread throughout many of the universities and departments of education of the Commonwealth of Nations and later to those of Europe, South America and beyond. In several countries professional associations of school administrators and university lecturers and professors were established. I have described elsewhere (1972) the birth of the Commonwealth-wide Commonwealth Council for Educational Administration and that Council's debt to its US forebears.

So widespread was interest in the area that further International Intervisitation Programs have been held — in Australia (1970), Britain (1974), Canada (1978), Nigeria (1982), and future events will be held in Hawaii,

Fiji and New Zealand in 1986. Moreover, numerous journals, magazines and newsletters were established to provide outlets for those who wished to have their say on issues close to the hearts of scholars and practitioners alike.

It is hardly necessary to point out that the 1960s' developments described above took place in an atmosphere of excitement and optimism, especially in the USA. Anyone who was fortunate enough to attend the annual convention of UCEA or the rather less formal meetings of the National Council of Professors of Educational Administration came away stimulated by the level of debate and the energetic search for 'The Truth'. Regrettably, there was no equivalent meeting in Britain, for example, until nearly a decade later.

The expectations of many who attended those early meetings were wide-ranging. As one present at several such gatherings in the USA during the mid-1960s I recall vividly the expectations and ambitions of those who were on the cutting edge of thinking about the administrative process at that time.

Clearly, the papers delivered in 1966 reflected the hopes and aspirations of the contemporary leaders in the field. Invited from all the major English-speaking nations, in effect these men (there were no women speakers) were writing their individual scenarios for the future of educational administration on Spaceship Earth.

As pointed out above, following IIP 66 the major papers were published by Rand McNally under the title *Educational Administration: International Perspectives*. It is my intention here to attempt to capture the main thrusts of those papers and to ask where we are 20 years on.

I can find three chief sets of hopes and aspirations represented in the 16 major contributors presented at Ann Arbor and Edmonton. These three 'sets', as I saw them, are:

1. That the practice of educational administration will, in the future, be illuminated by the social sciences in much the same way as the practice of medicine is illuminated by the natural sciences.
2. That the practice of educational administration will, in the future, be illuminated by the widespread adoption both of additional traditional university preparation programmes and by a range of alternative training modes.
3. That the practice of educational administration will, in the future, be illuminated by the adoption of an international perspective by both scholars and practitioners.

It is important to note that there were expressed many more aspirations tied to the needs of individual countries and the structures of school systems. I have selected here only those with over-arching, international implications for practice.

Recognizing this, it is appropriate now to look at each of the above 'sets' from the perspective of two decades on.

Educational administration and the social sciences

The IIP gathering reflected clearly the hopes and aspirations of the early theory movement which had evolved in the budding departments of educational administration in the US universities during the 1950s and 1960s and which was reflected in the remarkable 1964 *Yearbook* of the National Society for the Study of Education (1964). The birth, infancy, childhood and adolescence of this movement is very well documented. Underlying the movement was the growing acceptance of Dewey's dictum that theory was, in the end, the most practical of all things and the belief that the proper role of theory was both to explain and predict administrative phenomena (Walker, 1970).

Enmeshed with this movement were scholars of the standing of Dan Griffiths at New York University, Andrew Halpin of the University of Chicago, Dick Lonsdale of the University of Syracuse, the late Van Miller of the University of Illinois, and a score of others. The university departments which employed these men had, for the most part, joined the newly-formed University Council for Educational Administration by the early 1960s and the encouragement given to the study of educational administration by this body, led by the indefatigable Jack Culbertson, was extraordinary. There was an urgency and enthusiasm running through these departments which was infectious to those who, like myself, were fortunate enough to be involved in them.

Significantly, Culbertson was a major mover in launching the IIP, while Griffiths and several other key professors, including Reller of Berkeley and Miklos of Alberta, made major presentations.

Although both Griffiths and Miklos were careful not to be too optimistic in their predictions (Griffiths felt that the theory movement had peaked in the 1950s) Miklos summed up the feeling of the gathering when he wrote: 'Although no strong evidence has been presented here, there is little doubt that the behavioural sciences have a significant contribution to make in furthering the study of educational administration'.

From the perspective of two decades on he was certainly right. Indeed, by the mid 1970s the contribution was widely acknowledged, as guides to action, by sciences such as psychology, social psychology, sociology, anthropology, economics, politics and philosophy (Walker and Crane, 1973; Crane and Walker, 1976). Moreover, just as medicine reaches beyond the natural sciences, administration reaches beyond the social sciences. In addition to the 'core disciplines' outlined above, there are other areas of inquiry which help scholars and practitioners alike to understand the dynamics of that particular aspect of organizational behaviour which is described as 'administration'. These include history, finance, cybernetics and the law, to say nothing of biology, genetics and engineering (Walker, 1978).

Looking back over two decades one notes the work of writers far too numerous to mention. On a purely subjective level I mention only a few of those whose work has assisted me with my own administrative insights.

I shall forever be grateful to, *inter alia*, Ordway Tead (1951), 'The administrator as educator'; Halpin (1957), 'Initiating structure in interaction: consideration'; Getzels and Guba (1957), 'Role theory'; Presthus (1962), 'Upward mobiles, ambivalents and indifferents'; Weick (1976), 'Loose coupling'; Cohen *et al* (1972), 'Garbage can model' and Carlson (1964), 'Wild and domesticated organizations'.

I think it is important to note that, as I have grown older, become more experienced and have accepted greater organizational responsibilities, these and other theories and concepts have become more and more useful in helping me both to lead and to understand the enterprises for which I have been responsible. As suggested earlier, beyond the social sciences I have personally found the geneticist Schwab's description of the organization as an animal and the engineer Von Bertalanffy's view of the organization as a system to be most helpful in explaining why organizations and their populations act as they do.

It is true, of course, that the information provided by each of these constructs is inexact, when compared with much data available to doctors from the natural sciences. Nevertheless, it *is* information and its ingelligent use *does* assist in producing sensitivity to the organizational environment, diagnosing the nature of problems, picking up messages from a variety of directions and through numerous filters, choosing among alternatives and making decisions.

Putting all of this together, it can confidently be said that from my perspective educational administrators do indeed have available to them a much richer and more powerful range of data, constructs and theories than was available to their predecessors 20 years ago. It can also confidently be said that both the number and proportion of administrators and tyro administrators being exposed to this material through reading, taking part in short courses and undertaking disciplined systematic study in higher educational institutions is growing exponentially.

In short, Miklos's guarded optimism of 1966 has been more than justified.

Modes of training and education

It was stated or implied by several speakers at IIP that the practice of educational administration will be illuminated by the adoption of both more 'traditional' university preparation programmes and innovative and alternative training modes. The latter included such innovations as the use of simulations and the mixing together of administrators from a wide range of occupations. Thus, Alan Crane of Australia presented a strategy of change based on university programmes for the education of administrators in his country. Luvern Cunningham of the USA and Bill Taylor of Britain described the possibilities of simulations as a means of training and Richard Snyder wrote about an experimental cross-vocational graduate programme at the Irvine Campus of the University of California.

There has certainly been a marked growth in training and education programmes in the two decades under review. While in some countries the growth has been more noticeable than in others a glance through the Commonwealth Council for Educational Administration's (CCEA's) *Directory of Qualifications and Courses in Educational Administration* (1980) will show vividly how the picture today differs from the virtual void of the 1960s in countries outside the USA. The institutions listed include universities, colleges, institutes and polytechnics in great variety. Of some interest, too, are the newly established institutions in Australia, Malaysia, Thailand and, more recently, England, designed solely for the training of educational administrators.

It is fair to say that the development of simulations for use in such institutions has been much less dramatic than has the expansion of the programmes in which simulations might be used. The early flurry, which followed the UCEA's Whitman and Britain's Fox Green Schools, produced only a few publications, including those by Walker (1965) in Australia, Taylor (1969) in Britain, and Webb and Webb (1967) in the USA.

In fact, there has been comparatively little done outside the USA and then only in a limited range, when compared with the sophisticated management games, many of them computer based, employed in business schools throughout the world. However, case studies have been extensively used in conference settings, good examples being at the regional symposia held in Western Samoa, Malaysia and Vanuatu in recent years. Moreover, the CCEA has produced a Commonwealth Case Book edited by the late Harry Harris (1982).

There has not been any noteworthy growth in the number and variety of institutions which train educational administrators, together with managers and administrators, from other spheres. This has long been the tradition at staff colleges such as Henley and Ashridge in England, Mount Eliza in Australia and Tatum Park in New Zealand, but comparatively few colleges have followed the example of Snyder at the University of California or Willis at the Royal Melbourne Institute of Technology.

The international perspective

A major implication of the IIP papers is that the practice of educational administration will be illuminated by the adoption of an international perspective.

This is an area in which there has been a considerable development since 1966, as the successive International Intervisitation Programs, innumerable UNESCO activities and large number of Commonwealth symposia have demonstrated. The present author, for example, has in that period attended The Conference on the World Crisis in Education, called by the US Government at Williamsburg, Commonwealth conferences held in Canberra and Kingston, Jamaica, regional Commonwealth symposia held in Darwin, Malaysia, Fiji, Western Samoa and Vanuatu, UNESCO activities in Bangkok and Hamburg, East-West Centre-sponsored programmes in Honolulu and Alaska, CCEA activities in Penang, Wellington and Singapore, and others too numerous to mention.

A current activity which highlights the new internationalism is the Congress on Technology and Education, to be held in Vancouver in May 1986 in association with Expo '86. The sponsors of this event, the British Columbia School Boards Association, ensured that the Planning Council included members not only from Canada, but from the USA, Britain and Australia, and went to special lengths to interest scholars and practitioners in Europe, Asia and Oceania in participating in the dialogue. Further, there have developed increasingly strong links among associations of educational administrators, including the members of the University Council for Educational Administration, the Commonwealth Council, the Inter-American Council and the European Forum. Moreover, at the time of writing there is a plan for an Asian Council or other form of grouping in the Orient.

Indubitably, in educational terms the world is much more a global village than it was in 1966 and modern international direct dialling telephones and both satellite-based and terrestrial television have undoubtedly contributed to this, as has jet air travel. Indeed, in many countries, from Sweden to Papua New Guinea, the new technology has been used to instruct school students, teachers and even administrators in novel educational modes.

It has been inevitable that the decreasing distances of the global village and the increasing travel by administrators have led to the more ready availability of knowledge across national boundaries. The travelling scholar sees his or her books in use in far distant countries and is asked questions about procedures in his or her country which only a few years ago would have gone unnoticed. For example, the present author has heard arguments about the well-known Griffiths versus Greenfield controversy of a few years ago discussed in a dozen countries and in as many more has been asked to explain the administrative structures of the Australian Schools of the Air.

The present

All of these developments since 1966 are of more than passing interest, for on the whole they display a remarkable zeal and reflect the expenditure of a great deal of energy, time and money on the part of professors, policy makers and, indubitably, politicians. The real question to be asked is, 'has it all been worth it?'

On balance, I am sure that it has been. Whenever I visit schools in both the developed and less developed countries I am struck by the improvement on similar institutions of two decades ago. While this is by no means universally true, I believe that there are clear signs of the impact which the starry-eyed optimists of 1966 hoped for.

They sought a more systematic, 'scientific' approach to the theory and practice of educational administration: the contemporary plethora of publications, programmes and research activities surely continues to reflect the continuing dynamics of this area. They sought more and varied programmes for administrator preparation. Both have obviously been achieved, though the sphere of simulations is less developed than might have been hoped for. They sought a new international perspective and, as this present publication in part demonstrates, they were successful beyond the expectations of many who participated. In an important sense the IIP 66 did, therefore, provide an operating manual for educational administrators on spaceship earth.

There remain, of course, areas of great concern for educational administrators, especially in terms of structure, centralization and decentralization, funding and political control. These, and many other topics, remain challenges to the participants in IIP 86 — and in the many other IIPs to come.

References

Baron, G, Cooper, D H and Walker, W G eds (1969) *Educational Administration: International Perspectives* Rand McNally: Chicago

Carlson, R O (1964) Environmental constraints and organizational consequences: the public school and its clients *in* Griffiths (1964)

Cohen, M D, March, J D and Olsen, J P (1972) A garbage can model of organizational choice *Administrative Science Quarterly* **17** 1: 1-25

Commonwealth Council for Educational Administration (1980) *Commonwealth Directory of Qualifications and Courses in Educational Administration* Commonwealth Secretariat: London

Crane, A R and Walker, W G (1976) Theory in the real world of the educational administrator *UCEA Review* **17** 3: 1-40

Culbertson, J et al (1973) *Social Science Content for Preparing Educational Leaders* Merrill: Columbus, Ohio

Ewald, W R ed (1968) *Environment and Change: The Next Fifty Years* Indiana University Press: Bloomington, Ind

Fuller, R, Buckminster (1968) An operating manual for spaceship earth *in* Ewald (1968)

Getzels, J W and Guba, E G (1957) Social behaviour and the administrative process *School Review* **65**: 423-41

*Griffiths, D E ed (1964) *Behavioural Science and Educational Administration: The Sixty-third Yearbook of the National Society for the Study of Education* Chicago University Press: Chicago

Halpin, A W ed (1957) *Administrative Theory in Education* Midwest Administration Centre, University of Chicago: Chicago

Harris, H T B ed (1982) *The Commonwealth Case Book for School Administrators* Commonwealth Secretariat: London

Presthus, R (1962) *The Organizational Society* Knopf: New York

Taylor, W (1969) *Heading for Change: The Management of Innovation in the Large Secondary School* Routledge and Kegan Paul: London

Tead, O (1965) *The Art of Administration* McGraw-Hill: New York

Walker, W G (1965) *The Principal at Work: Case Studies in School Administration* University of Queensland Press: St Lucia, Queensland

Walker, W G (1970) *Theory and Practice in Educational Administration* University of Queensland Press: St Lucia, Queensland

Walker, W G (1972) UCEA's bright son at morning: the Commonwealth Council for Educational Administration *Educational Administration Quarterly* **8** 2: 16-25

Walker, W G (1978) Values, unorthodoxy and the 'unscientific' in educational administration research *Educational Administration* **6** 2: 94-106

Walker, W G (1984) Administrative narcissism and the tyranny of isolation: its decline and fall, 1954-1984 *Educational Administration Quarterly* **20** 4: 6-24

Walker, W G and Crane, A R (1973) The selection of content for a theory-based perspective *in* Culbertson *et al* (1973)

Webb, H and Webb, D J (1967) *School Administration: A Casebook* International Textbook: Scranton, Pa

Weick, K E (1976) Educational organizations as loosely coupled systems *Administrative Science Quarterly* **12** 1: 1-19

Part 7: Bibliography and Biographical Notes

Bibliography

Mike Wallace and Biddy Niblett

The bibliography is divided into four sections. The first covers published books and pamphlets by individual authors, the second lists publications (books and documents) issued by official bodies, and the third includes articles, periodicals and working papers. These three sections include all the references cited in individual chapters.

In section IV a number of key references from sections I, II and III listed in the various chapters have been annotated. An asterisk (*) beside a particular entry in the main part of the bibliography indicates that it has been annotated in section IV.

Section I: Published books and pamphlets

Abbott, R (1985) *An Introduction to GRIDS* School Curriculum Development Committee: London

Abramowitz, S and Tenenbaum, E (1978) *High School '77* National Institute of Education: Washington, DC

Acker, S (1983) Women and teaching: a semi-detached sociology of a semi-profession *in* Walker and Barton (1983)

Albrecht, K (1979) *Stress and the Manager* Prentice Hall: New Jersey

Allen, B ed (1968) *Headship in the 1970s* Basil Blackwell: Oxford

Allison, G T (1971) *Essence of Decision: Explaining the Cuban Missile Crisis* Little, Brown: Boston, Mass

Apple, M (1979) *Ideology and Curriculum* Routledge and Kegan Paul: London

Argyris, C (1960) *Understanding Organizational Behavior* Dorsey: Homewood, Ill

Bacharach, S B ed (1981) *Organizational Behavior in Schools and School Districts* Praeger: New York

Bachrach, P and Baratz, M S (1970) *Power and Poverty: Theory and Practice* Oxford University Press: New York

Bailey, A J and Renner, G (1980) *Education for Democracy* Report of a conference 7-12 July 1980 organized by the European Academy, Berlin, in association with the University of Sussex: University of Sussex

Bailey, A J (1985) *Support for School Management: Project Report* School of Education, University of Sussex: Sussex

Bailey, F G (1965) Decisions by consensus in councils and committees, with special reference to village and local government in India *in* Banton (1965)

Bailey, F G ed (1971) *Gifts and Poisons* Basil Blackwell: Oxford

Bailey, F G (1971) Gifts and poisons *in* Bailey (1971)

*Bailey, F G (1977) *Morality and Expediency: The Folklore of Academic Politics* Basil Blackwell: Oxford

Ball, S J (1983) *Beachside Comprehensive: A Study of Comprehensive Schooling* Cambridge University Press: Cambridge

Baltzell, C D and Dentler, R A (1983) *Selecting American School Principals: A Research Report* Abt Associates: Cambridge, Mass

Banton, M ed (1965) *Political Systems and the Distribution of Power* Tavistock: London

Baron, G, Cooper, D H and Walker, W G eds (1969) *Educational Administration: International Perspectives* Rand McNally: Chicago

Barr, R and Dreeben, R (1977) Instruction in classrooms *in* Schulman (1977)

*Barr, R and Dreeben, R (1983) *How Schools Work* University of Chicago Press: Chicago

Barton, J, Becher, T, Canning, T and Eraut, E (1980) Accountability and education *in* Bush *et al* (1980)

Beeby, C E (1967) *Planning and the Educational Administrator* UNESCO: Paris

Benson, J K ed (1977) *Organizational Analysis: Critique and Innovation* Sage: Beverley Hills, Cal

Berliner, D C ed (1981) *Review of Research in Education* American Educational Research Association: Washington, DC

Berman, P (1981) Educational change: an implementation paradigm *in* Lehming and Kane (1981)

Berman, P (1981) Toward an implementation paradigm *in* Lehming and Kane (1981)

Berman, P and Gjelten, T (1982) *Improvement Maintenance and Decline: A Progress Report* Berman, Weiler Associates: Berkeley, Cal

Berman, P and McLaughlin, M W (1974) *Federal Programs Supporting Educational Change* I: *A Model of Educational Change*

Berman, P and McLaughlin, M W (1977) *Federal Programs Supporting Educational Change* VII: *Factors Affecting Implementation and Continuation* Rand Corporation: Santa Monica, Cal

Bernstein, B (1975) *Class, Codes and Control 3: Towards a Theory of Educational Transmissions* Routledge and Kegan Paul: London

Bidwell, C E (1965) The school as a formal organization *in* March (1965)

Biklen, S K and Shakeshaft, C (1985) The new scholarship on women *in* Klein (1985)

Birchenough, M (1985) *Making School Based Review Work* National Development Centre for School Management Training: Bristol

Birnbaum, G (1976) The role of the head *in* Peters (1976)

Blake, R R and Ramsey, G B (1951) *Perception* Ronald: New York

Block, J H and Burns, B (1977) Mastery learning *in* Schulman (1977)

Blumberg, A (1985) *The School Superintendency: Living with Conflict* Teachers College Press, Columbia University: New York

Blumberg, A and Greenfield, W (1980) *The Effective Principal: Perspectives in School Leadership* Allyn and Bacon: Boston, Mass

Bolam, R ed (1982) *School-Focused In-Service Training* Heinemann: London

*Borich, G D ed (1977) *The Appraisal of Teaching: Concepts and Process* Addison-Wesley: Reading, Mass

Borich, G D and Madden, S K (1977) *Evaluating Classroom Instruction: A Sourcebook of Instruments* Addison-Wesley: Reading, Mass

Bossert, S T (1979) *Tasks and Social Relationships in Classrooms: A Study of Instructional Organization and its Consequences* Cambridge University Press: New York

Bossert, S T (1985) Effective schools — the elementary level *in* Kyle (1985)

Bowles, S and Gintis, H (1976) *Schooling in Capitalist America: Educational Reform and the Contradictions of Economic Life* Routledge and Kegan Paul: London, and Basic Books: New York

Boyan, N J (1951) *A Study of the Formal and Informal Organization of a School Faculty* Doctoral dissertation. Harvard University: Cambridge, Mass

Boyan, N J (1982) Administration of educational institutions *in* Mitzel (1982)

Boyan, N J ed (1986) *The Handbook of Research on Educational Administration* American Educational Research Association: Washington, DC (forthcoming)

Boyd, W L (1982) Local influences on education *in* Mitzel (1982)

Boyd, W L and Crowson, R L (1981) The changing conception and practice of public school administration *in* Berliner (1981)

Boyd-Barrett, O, Bush, T, Goodey, J, McNay, I and Preedy, M *eds* (1983) *Approaches to Post-School Management* Harper and Row/The Open University: London

Boydell, T and Pedler, M *eds* (1981) *Management Self-Development: Concepts and Practices* Gower Press: Aldershot

Brehmer, I (1986) Women as educators in Germany: a history *in* Schmuck (1986) (forthcoming)

Bronfenbrenner, U (1951) Toward an integrated theory of personality *in* Blake and Ramsey (1951)

Brookover, W, Deady, C, Flood, P, Schweitzer, J and Wisenbaker, J (1979) *School Social Systems and Student Achievement: Schools Can Make a Difference* Praeger: New York

Brophy, J E and Everston, C M (1974) *Process-Product Correlations in the Texas Teacher Effectiveness Study: Final Report* University of Texas at Austin: Austin, Texas

Brophy, J E and Everston, C M (1977) Teacher behavior and student learning in the second and third grades *in* Borich (1977)

Brown, G W (1974) Meaning, measurement and stress of life events *in* Dohrenwend and Dohrenwend (1974)

*Buckley, J (1985) *The Training of Secondary School Heads in Western Europe* NFER-Nelson for The Council of Europe: Windsor, Berks

Burford, C T (1985) The Relationship of Principals' Sense of Humor and Job Robustness to School Environment. Doctoral Dissertation, Pennsylvania State University: University Park, Penn

Burgoyne, J G (1976) *A Classified Bibliography of Some Research on Teaching Methods in Management Education and Some Inferences about the State of the Art* Management Teacher Development Unit Paper: University of Lancaster, UK

Burke, K (1969) *A Rhetoric of Motives* University of California Press: Los Angeles

Burns, T and Stalker, G M (1966) *The Management of Innovation* Tavistock Publications: London (second edition)

Burrell, G and Morgan, G (1979) *Sociological Paradigms and Organizational Analysis* Heinemann: London

Bush, T, Glatter, R, Goodey, J and Riches, C *eds* (1980) *Approaches to School Management* Harper and Row/The Open University: London

Byrne, E (1978) *Women and Education* Tavistock Publications: London

Cairns, G E (1984) Teacher burnout in New South Wales secondary schools: a review of the literature on occupational stress, the nature of teacher burnout and preventive measures in relation to teachers in New South Wales secondary schools. Unpublished MEd Admin dissertation. University of New England

Capie, W (1986) *Coming of Age: Systematic Performance Appraisal* Educational Measurement (forthcoming)

Carlson, R O (1964) Environmental constraints and organizational consequences: the public school and its clients *in* Griffiths (1984)

Carlson, R (1965) *Change Processes in the Public Schools* University of Oregon Centre for Advanced Study of Educational Administration: Eugene, Oregon

Charters, W W Jr and Jovick, T (1981) The gender of principals and principal teacher relations in elementary school *in* Schmuck *et al* (1981)

Cichon, D J and Koff, R H (1978) The teaching events stress inventory. ERIC Document ED 160 662

Coleman, J (1966) *Equality of Educational Opportunity* United States Department of Health, Education and Welfare: Washington, DC

Connell, R W, Ashendon, D J, Kessler, G W and Dowsett, G W (1982) *Making the Difference: Schools, Families and Social Division* Allen and Unwin: Sydney

Cooper, C L and Marshall, J (1978) *Understanding Executive Stress* Macmillan: London

Cooper, C L and Marshall, J eds (1980) *White Collar and Professional Stress* Wiley: Chichester

Cooper, C L and Payne, R (1978) *Stress at Work* Wiley: Chichester

Corbett, H, Dawson, J, Firestone, W (1984) *School Context and School Change* Teachers College Press: New York

Crandall, D P et al (1982) *People, Policies and Practices: Examining the Chain of School Improvement* (10 volumes) The Network: Andover, Mass

Crenson, M A (1971) *The Unpolitics of Air Pollution: A Study of Non-decision-making in the Cities* John Hopkins Press: Baltimore

Crewe, I ed (1974) *British Political Sociology Yearbook: Elites in Western Democracy* Croom Helm: London

Cuban, L (1976) *Urban School Chiefs Under Fire* University of Chicago Press: Chicago

Culbertson, J et al (1973) *Social Science Content for Preparing Educational Leaders* Merill: Columbus, Ohio

Cusick, P A (1973) *Inside High School* Holt, Rinehart and Winston: New York

Cusick, P A (1983) *The Egalitarian Ideal and the American High School* Longman: New York

Cuthbert, R (1984) *The Management Process* (Block 3, Part 2 of the Open University course Management in Post-Compulsory Education) The Open University Press: Milton Keynes

Dahl, R A (1972) *Who Governs? Democracy and Power in an American City* Yale University Press: New Haven

Dalin, P (1973) *Case Studies of Educational Innovation* **IV**: *Strategies for Innovation in Education* OECD/CERI: Paris

Dalin, P (1978) *Limits to Educational Change* Macmillan in association with the International Movement Towards Educational Change: London

Dalin, P and Rust, V D (1983) *Can Schools Learn?* NFER-Nelson: Windsor, Berks

Davies, B (1982) Organizational theory and schools *in* Hartnett (1982)

Davies, J L and Morgan, A W (1983) Management of higher education institutions in a period of contraction and uncertainty *in* Boyd-Barrett et al (1983)

Day, R and Day, J V (1977) A review of the current state of negotiated order theory *in* Benson (1977)

Deal, T E and Kennedy, A A (1982) *Corporate Cultures* Addison-Wesley: Reading, Mass

Denham, C and Lieberman, A eds (1980) *Time to Learn: A Review of the Beginning Teacher Evaluation Study* United States Department of Education, United States Government Printing Office: Washington, DC

Derr, B C (1986) *Managing The New Careerists: How to Direct Career Politics* Jossey-Bass: San Francisco, Cal

Dohrenwend, B S and Dohrenwend, B P (1974) *Stressful Life Events: Their Nature and Effects* Wiley: New York

Doyle, W (1978) Paradigms for research on teacher effectiveness *in* Schulman (1978)

Drabick, L W ed (1971) *Interpreting Education: A Sociological Approach* Appleton-Century-Crofts: New York

Dunham, J (1976) Stress situations and responses *in* National Association of Schoolmasters/Union of Women Teachers (1976)

Dwyer, D, Lee, G, Rowan, B and Bossert, S (1983) *Five Principals in Action: Perspectives on Instructional Management* The Far West Laboratory for Educational Research and Development: San Francisco

Edson, S (1981) If they can, I can: women aspirants to administrative positions in public schools *in* Schmuck et al (1981)

Ekholm, M (1979) *Research in Education — Does it Matter?* Report No 3 from School Leader Education, University of Linkoping: Linkoping, Sweden

Ekholm, M (1981) How does the headmaster put what he has learnt into practice? Experiences with the Swedish training programme for headteachers *in* Council of Europe: Council for Cultural Cooperation (1983)

Ekholm, M and Miles, M B (1985) Conclusions and recommendations *in* van Velzen *et al* (1985)

Elliott, G (1984) *Self Evaluation and the Teacher: An Annotated Bibliography and Report on Current Practice 1982 Part 5* School Curriculum Development Committee: London

Elliott, J (1983) *Teacher Evaluation and Teaching as a Moral Science* Cambridge Institute of Education: Cambridge (mimeo)

Ellis, A (1978) What people can do for themselves to cope with stress *in* Cooper and Payne (1978)

Elster, J (1978) *Logic and Society: Contradictions and Possible Worlds* Wiley: New York

Elster, J (1979) *Ulysses and the Sirens: Studies in Rationality and Irrationality* Cambridge University Press: Cambridge

Enders-Dragasser, U (1986) The privatization of school: women's unpaid work *in* Schmuck (1986) (forthcoming)

Erikson, E H (1950) *Childhood and Society* Norton: New York

Esp, G D (1980) *Selection and Training of Secondary School Headteachers in the Netherlands* Report on the author's AEC Trust Fellowship study visit ERIC/ED209179 Somerset Education Committee: Taunton

Etzioni, A ed (1969) *The Semi-Professions and Their Organization: Teachers, Nurses, Social Workers* The Free Press: New York

Everard, K B (1982) *Management in Comprehensive Schools: What Can Be Learned From Industry?* Centre for the Study of Comprehensive Schools: York

Everard, K B and Morris, G (1985) *Effective School Management* Harper and Row: London

Evers, C W (1985) Hodgkinson on ethics and the philosophy of administration *in* Rizvi (1985)

Ewald, W R ed (1968) *Environment and Change: The Next Fifty Years* Indiana University Press: Bloomington, Ind

Fenwick, P (1986) Women as educators in New Zealand *in* Schmuck (1986) (forthcoming)

Fiedler, F (1966) The contingency model: a theory of leadership effectiveness *in* Proshansky and Seidenberg (1966)

Filby, N N (1980) *What Happens in Smaller Classes* The Far West Laboratory for Educational Research and Development: San Francisco

Firestone, W and Corbett, H (1986) Organizational change *in* Boyan (1986) (forthcoming)

Fisher, C W (1980) Teaching behaviors, academic learning time, and student achievement: an overview *in* Denham and Lieberman (1980)

Francis, D and Woodcock, M (1982) *Fifty Activities for Self-Development* Gower Press: Aldershot

Freire, P (1972) *Pedagogy of the Oppressed* Penguin: Harmondsworth

Friedrich, C J (1963) *Man and His Government* McGraw-Hill: New York

Friedson, E (1975) *The Profession of Medicine* Dodd, Mead: New York

*Fullan, M (1982) *The Meaning of Educational Change* Teachers College Press, Columbia University: New York

Fuller, R Buckminster (1968) An operating manual for spaceship earth *in* Ewald (1968)

Galton, M, Simon, B and Croll, P (1980) *Inside the Primary Classroom* Routledge and Kegan Paul: London

Giddens, A (1979) *Central Problems in Social Theory: Action, Structure and Contradiction in Social Analysis* Macmillan: London

Gilbertson, M (1981) The influence of gender on the verbal interactions among principals and staff members: an exploratory study *in* Schmuck *et al* (1981)

Gill, D (1977) *Appraising Performance: Present Trends and the Next Decade* Institute of Personnel Management: London

Glass, G V (1977) A review of three methods of determining teacher effectiveness *in* Borich (1977)

Glass, G V and Smith, M L (1978) *Meta-Analysis of Research on the Relationship of Class-Size and Achievement* The Far West Laboratory for Educational Research and Development: San Francisco

Glatter, R (1983) Implications of research for policy on school management training *in* Hegarty (1983)

Glatter, R (1984) *Managing for Change* (Block 6 of the Open University course E324 Management in Post-Compulsory Education) The Open University Press: Milton Keynes

Goffman, E (1959) *The Presentation of Self in Everyday Life* Doubleday Anchor: Garden City, NY

Goffman, E (1975) *Frame Analysis* Peregrine Books: Harmondsworth

*Goffman, E (1976) *The Presentation of Self in Everyday Life* Penguin: Harmondsworth

Gonzalez-Tirados, R M (1983) A programme for the training of school directors at the Polytechnic University of Madrid *in* Hegarty (1983)

Good, T L and Grouws, D A (1977) Teacher effectiveness in fourth-grade mathematics classrooms *in* Borich (1977)

Goodlad, J A (1982) *A Place Called School — Prospects for the Future* McGraw-Hill: New York

Gouldner, A W (1955) *Wildcat Strike* Routledge and Kegan Paul: London

Gouldner, A W (1979) *The Future of the Intellectuals and the Rise of the New Class* Macmillan: London

Gray, H L ed (1982) *The Management of Educational Institutions: Theory Research and Consultancy* Falmer Press: Lewes, Sussex

Greenfield, T B (1975) Theory about organizations: a new perspective and its implications for schools *in* Hughes (1975)

Griffiths, D (1979) Another look at research on the behaviour of administrators *in* Immegart and Boyd (1979)

Griffiths, D E ed (1964) *Behavioural Science and Educational Administration* The 63rd Yearbook of the National Society for the Study of Education, The Chicago University Press: Chicago

Griffiths, D E (1959) *Administrative Theory* Appleton-Century-Crofts: New York

Gronn, P C (1979) *The Politics of School Management: A Comparative Study of Three School Councils* PhD Thesis: Monash University

Gronn, P (1983) *Rethinking Educational Administration: T B Greenfield and his critics (ESA 841) Theory and Practice in Educational Administration* The 63rd Yearbook of the National Society for the Study of Education, Chicago University Press: Chicago

Gross, N and Trask, A E (1976) *The Sex Factor and the Management of Schools* John Wiley: New York

Gross, N, Giaquinta, J and Bernstein, M (1971) *Implementing Organizational Innovations: A Sociological Analysis of Planned Educational Change* Basic Books: New York

Grossman, L (1976) *Fat Paper* McGraw-Hill: New York

Hall, V and Mackay, H (1983) *The Changing Role of the Secondary Headteacher: Project Outline* The Open University School of Education: The Open University

Halpin, A W ed (1958) *Administrative Theory of Education* Midwest Administration Center, University of Chicago: Chicago

Handy, C (1984) *Taken for Granted? Understanding Schools as Organizations* Longman for the Schools Council: York

Hanson, E M (1985) *Educational Administration and Organizational Behavior* Allyn and Bacon: Boston, Mass

Hargreaves, D H (1967) *Social Relations in a Secondary School* Routledge and Kegan Paul: London

Harris, H T B ed (1982) *The Commonwealth Case Book for School Administrators* Commonwealth Secretariat: London

Hartnett, A *ed* (1982) *The Social Sciences in Educational Studies* Heinemann: London

Havelock, R G (1973) *The Change Agent's Guide to Innovation in Education* Educational Technology Publications: New Jersey

Havens, E (1980) *Women in Educational Administration: The Principalship* National Institute of Education: Washington, DC

Hawes, H W R (1969) *Curriculum and Reality in African Primary Schools* Longman: London

Hawrylyshyn, B (1975) Management education — a conceptual framework *in* Taylor and Lippitt (1975)

Hegarty, S *ed* (1983) *Training for Management in Schools* Papers from an Educational Workshop organized by the National Foundation for Educational Research (NFER) at Windsor, 14-17 September 1982, under the auspices of the Council for Cultural Cooperation of the Council of Europe. NFER-Nelson for the Council of Europe: Windsor, Berks

Held, D (1980) *Introduction to Critical Theory: Horkheimer to Habermas* University of California Press: Berkeley and Los Angeles

Hirschman, A O (1981) *Essays in Trespassing: Economic Politics and Beyond* Cambridge University Press: Cambridge

Hodgkinson, C (1978) *Towards a Philosophy of Administration* Basil Blackwell: Oxford

Hodgkinson, C (1983) *The Philosophy of Leadership* Basil Blackwell: Oxford

Hoffman, J (1975) *Marxism and the Theory of Praxis* International Publishers: New York

Hollingshead, A B (1949) *Elmtown's Youth* John Wiley: New York

Hopkins, D (1984) *School Based Review for School Improvement: A Preliminary State of the Art* Centre for Educational Research and Innovation, OECD: Paris

Hopkins, D and Wideen, M *eds* (1984) *Alternative Perspectives on School Improvement* Falmer Press: Lewes, Sussex

Hord, S *ed* (1983) *A US Strategy for Research and Development Concerning the Principalship* OECD: Paris (mimeo CERI/SI/83.03)

Horney, K (1950) *Neurosis and Human Growth* W W Norton and Co: New York

Houle, C (1981) *Continuing Learning in the Professions* Adult Education Association of the USA: Washington, DC

House, E R (1974) *The Politics of Educational Innovation* McCutchan: Berkeley, Cal

House, E R (1981) Three perspectives on innovation: technological, political and cultural *in* Lehming and Kane (1981)

Hoy, W K and Miskel, C G (1978) *Educational Administration: Theory, Research and Practice* Random House: New York

Hoyle, E (1985) Educational research: dissemination, participation, negotiation *in* Nisbet, Nisbet and Megarry (1985)

Hoyle, E (1986) *The Politics of School Management* Hodder and Stoughton: London (forthcoming)

Hoyle, E and Megarry, J *eds* (1980) *The World Yearbook of Education: The Professional Development of Teachers* Kogan Page: London

Huberman, A M and Crandall, D (1983) *People, Policies and Practices: Examining the Chain of School Improvement* 9 *Implications for Action, a Study of Dissemination Efforts Supporting School Improvement* The Network: Andover, Mass

*Huberman, A M and Miles, M B (1984) *Innovation Up Close: How School Improvement Works* Plenum: New York

Hughes, M G *ed* (1975) *Administering Education: International Challenge* Athlone Press: London

Hughes, M G (1976) The professional as administrator: the case of the secondary school head *in* Peters (1976)

Hughes, M G (1983) The role and tasks of heads of schools in England and Wales: research studies and professional development provision *in* Hegarty (1983)

328   BIBLIOGRAPHY

Hughes, M G, Carter, J and Fidler, B (1981) *Professional Development Provision for Senior Staff in Schools and Colleges* Faculty of Education: University of Birmingham

Hunter, F (1963) *Community Power Structure* Anchor: New York

Immegart, G L and Boyd, W L *eds* (1979) *Problem Finding in Educational Administration* D C Heath: Lexington, Mass

Jaques, E (1951) *The Changing Culture of a Factory* Tavistock: London

Jaques, E (1955) Social systems as a defence against persecutory and depressive anxiety *in* Klein *et al* (1955)

Jaques, E (1970) *Work, Creativity and Social Justice* Heinemann: London

Jay, M (1973) *The Dialectical Imagination: A History of the Frankfurt School and the Institute for Social Research 1923-1950* Little, Brown and Co: Boston, Mass

Jencks, C (1972) *Inequality* Basic Books: New York

Jenkins, H O (1983) *Job Perceptions of Senior Managers in Schools and Manufacturing Industry* Unpublished PhD Thesis. Faculty of Education: University of Birmingham

Johnston, G S *ed* (1985) *Thought and Research in Educational Administration: The State of the Art* University Press of America: Lanham, Md

Jones, E and Montenegro, X (1982) *Recent Trends in the Representation of Women and Minorities in School Administration and Problems in Documentation* American Association of School Administrators: Arlington, Va

Joyce, B R, Hersh, R H and McKibbin, M (1983) *The Structure of School Improvement* Longman: New York

Kahn, R, Wolfe, D, Quinn, R, Snoek, J and Rosenthal, R (1964) *Organizational Stress: Studies in Role Conflict and Ambiguity* John Wiley: New York

Kanter, R M (1977) *Men and Women of the Corporation* Basic Books: New York

Kanter, R M (1983) *The Change Masters* Simon and Schuster: New York

Karabel, J and Halsey, A H *eds* (1977) *Power and Ideology in Education* Oxford University Press: New York

Karabel, J and Halsey, A H (1977) Educational research: a review and an interpretation *in* Karabel and Halsey (1977)

Kets de Vries, M R F and Miller, D (1984) *The Neurotic Organization: Diagnosing and Changing Counterproductive Styles* Jossey-Bass: San Francisco

Kindervatter, S (1983) *Learner-Centered Training for Learner-Centered Programmes* Training Notes Series No 1, Center for International Education: University of Massachusetts

Klein, S P *ed* (1985) *Handbook for Achieving Equity Through Education* Johns Hopkins University Press: Baltimore

Klein, S P and Alkin, M C (1977) Evaluating teachers for outcome accountability *in* Borich (1977)

Klein, M, Heimann, P and Money-Kyrle, R *eds* (1955) *New Directions in Psychoanalysis* Tavistock: London

Knowles, M (1973) *The Adult Learner: A Neglected Species* Gulf: Houston, Tex

Kolb, D (1974) On management and the learning process *in* Kolb, Rubin and McIntyre (1974)

Kolb, D, Rubin, I and McIntyre, J (1974) *Organizational Psychology — An Experiential Approach to Organizational Behaviour* Prentice Hall: London (second edition)

Kvist, P (1982) Leadership in schools: a Norwegian programme for improvement (Sheffield Papers in Educational Management No 27) Sheffield City Polytechnic: Sheffield

Kyle, R *ed* (1985) *Sourcebook for Effective Schools* National Institute of Education, United States Department of Education: Washington, DC

Lacey, C (1970) *Hightown Grammar* Manchester University Press: Manchester

Laird, D (1978) *Approaches to Training and Development* Addison-Wesley: Reading, Mass

Lakomski, G (1985b) Theory, value and relevance in educational administration *in* Rizvi (1985)

Landsbury, R D and Spillane, R (1983) *Organisational Behaviour: the Australian Context* Longman Cheshire: Melbourne

Larson, L L, Bussom, R S and Vicars, W M (1981) *The Nature of a School Superintendent's Work* Southern Illinois University: Carbondale, Ill

Lasswell, H D (1936) *Politics: Who Gets What, When, How* McGraw-Hill: New York

Lawrence, P R and Lorsch, J W (1967) *Organization and Environment* Harvard Graduate School of Business Administration: Cambridge, Mass

Lazarus, R S (1966) *Psychological Stress and the Coping Process* McGraw-Hill: London

Lehming, R and Kane, M eds (1981) *Improving Schools: Using What We Know* Sage: Beverley Hills, Cal

Leithwood, K A and Montgomery, D J (1986) *Improving Principal Effectiveness: the Principal Profile* OISE Press: Toronto

Levenson, H (1972) Distinctions within the concept of internal-external control: development of a new scale *in* American Psychological Association (1972)

Lewin, K (1935) *A Dynamic Theory of Personality* McGraw-Hill: New York

Lewin, K (1943) Forces behind food habits and methods of change *National Research Council Bulletin CVIII:* Washington, DC

Lightfoot, S (1983) *The Good High School: Portraits of Character and Culture* Basic Books: New York

Lipham, J (1964) Leadership and administration *in* Griffiths (1964)

Lipham, J M (1981) *Effective Principal, Effective School* National Association of Secondary School Principals: Reston, Va

Lippit, R, Watson, J and Westley, B (1958) *The Dynamics of Planned Change: A Comparative Study of Principles and Techniques* Harcourt, Brace & World Inc: New York

Litwak, E and Meyer, H J (1974) *School, Family and Neighbourhood* Columbia University Press: New York

Lortie, D C (1969) The balance of control and autonomy in elementary school teaching *in* Etzioni (1969)

Lortie, D C (1975) *School Teacher* University of Chicago Press: Chicago

Loucks-Horsley, S and Hergert, L F (1985) *An Action Guide to School Improvement* Association for Supervision and Curriculum Development, The Network: Andover, Mass

Louis, K (1980) *A Study of the R and D Utilization Program* Abt Associates: Cambridge, Mass

*Lukes, S (1974) *Power* Macmillan: London

Lyons, G (1974) *The Administrative Tasks of Head and Senior Teachers in Large Secondary Schools* Report to the School of Education, University of Bristol: Bristol

Lyons, G (1976) *Heads' Tasks: A Handbook of Secondary Administration* National Foundation for Educational Research: Slough

Lyons, G and Stenning, R (1985) *Managing Staff in Schools: A Handbook* Hutchinson Educational: London

Lyons, G, Stenning, R and McQueeney, J (1985) *Employment Relations in the Maintained Secondary Sector and the Training Needs of Headteachers* Report to the Department of Education and Science

McDonald, F J (1977) Research on teaching: report on phase II of the beginning teacher evaluation study *in* Borich (1977)

McGregor, D (1960) *The Human Side of Enterprise* McGraw-Hill: New York

McLeary, L and McIntyre, K (1974) *Competency Development and Methodologies of College Teaching in Principal In-Service: Where Will They Find It?* NASSP: Reston, Va

McMahon, A, Bolam, R, Abbott, R and Holly, P (1984) *Guidelines for Review and Internal Development in Schools (GRIDS): Primary and Secondary School Hand-Books* Longman for the Schools Council: York

Manley, F J, Reed, B W and Burns, R K (1961) *The Community School in Action: The Flint Program* Industrial Relations Center, Education-Industry Service, University of Chicago, Chicago

March, J G ed (1965) *Handbook of Organizations* Rand McNally: Chicago

March, J G (1984) How we talk and how we act: administrative theory and administrative life *in* Sergiovanni and Corbally (1984)

March, J G and Olsen, J P eds (1976) *Ambiguity and Choice in Organizations* Universistetsforlaget: Bergen, Norway

March, J G and Simon, H A (1958) *Organizations* Wiley: New York

Merton, R K (1973) *The Sociology of Science* University of Chicago Press: Chicago

Metcalfe, L (1981) Designing precarious partnerships *in* Nystrom and Starbuck (1981)

Meyer, J W ed (1978) *Organizations and Environments* Jossey-Bass: San Francisco, Cal

Meyer, J W and Rowan, B (1978) The structure of educational organizations *in* Meyer (1978)

Meyer, J W and Scott, W R eds (1983) *Organizational Environments: Ritual and Rationality* Sage: Beverley Hills, Cal

Meyer, J W, Scott, W R and Deal, T E (1983) Institutional and technical sources of organizational structure: explaining the structure of educational organizations *in* Meyer and Scott (1983)

Midwinter, E C (1972) *Priority Education: An Account of the Liverpool Project* Penguin: Harmondsworth

Miles, M B (1965) Planned change and organizational health *in* Carlson *et al* (1965)

Miles, M B and Ekholm, M (1985a) What is school improvement? *in* van Velzen *et al* (1985)

Miles, M B and Ekholm, M (1985b) School improvement at the school level *in* van Velzen *et al* (1985)

Mintzberg, H (1973) *The Nature of Managerial Work* Harper and Row: New York

Mitzel, H E ed (1982) *Encyclopedia of Educational Research* Macmillan and Free Press: New York

Morgan, C, Hall, V and Mackay, H (1984a) *The Selection of Secondary School Headteachers* The Open University Press: Milton Keynes

Morgan, C, Hall, V and Mackay, H (1984b) *A Handbook on Selecting Senior Staff for Schools* The Open University Press: Milton Keynes

Morgan, G ed (1983) *Beyond Method: Strategies for Social Research* Sage Publications: Beverley Hills, Cal

Morris, J and Burgoyne, J G (1973) *Developing Resourceful Managers* Institute of Personnel Management: London

Morris, V C, Crowson, R L, Porter-Gehrie, C and Hurwitz, E (1984) *Principals in Action* Charles E Merrill: Columbus, Ohio

Mulhauser, F (1983) Recent research on the principalship: a view from the National Institute of Education *in* Hord, S (1983)

Murray-Smith, S ed (1976) *Melbourne Studies in Education 1976* Melbourne University Press: Melbourne

Nias, J (1980) Leadership styles and job satisfaction in primary schools *in* Bush *et al* (1980)

Nisbet, J, Nisbet, S and Megarry, J eds (1985) *Research, Policy and Practice. World Yearbook of Education 1985* Kogan Page: London

Nuttall, D L (1981) *School Self Evaluation: Accountability With a Human Face?* Longman for the Schools Council: York

Nyerere, J K (1967) *Education for Self Reliance* Ministry of Information and Tourism: Dar-es-Salaam

Nystrom, P C and Starbuck, W H eds (1981) *Handbook of Organizational Design* Oxford University Press: New York

Oldroyd, D, Smith, K and Lee, J (1984) *School-based Staff Development Activities: A Handbook for Secondary Schools* Longman for the Schools Council: York

Olson, M (1965) *The Logic of Collective Action* Harvard University Press: Cambridge, Mass

Omari, I M, Mbise, A S, Mahenge, S T, Malekela, G A and Mbesha, M P (1983) *Universal Primary Education in Tanzania* International Development Research Centre: Ottawa, Canada

Ortiz, F (1982) *Career Patterns in Education: Women, Men and Minorities in Public School Administration* Praeger Press: New York

Ortiz, F and Marshall, C (1986) Women in educational administration *in* Boyan (1986) (forthcoming)

Orwell, G (1963) *Nineteen Eighty-four* Penguin: Harmondsworth

Ouchi, W G (1981) *Theory Z* Avon Books: New York

Paddock, S (1981) Male and female career paths in school administration *in* Schmuck *et al* (1981)

Parry, G and Morriss, P (1974) When is a decision not a decision? *in* Crewe (1974)

Parsons, T (1958) Some ingredients of a general theory of formal organization *in* Halpin (1958)

Peshkin, A (1978) *Growing Up American: Schools and the Survival of Community* University of Chicago Press: Chicago

Peters, R S ed (1976) *The Role of the Head* Routledge and Kegan Paul: London

Peters, T J and Austin, N (1985) *A Passion for Excellence* Random House: New York

Peters, T J and Waterman, R H (1982) *In Search of Excellence: Lessons from America's Best Run Companies* Harper and Row: New York

Peterson, P ed (1984) *The Social Context of Instruction: Group Organization and Group Processes* Academic Press: New York

Pfeffer, J (1982) *Organizations and Organization Theory* Pitman Publishing: Marshfield, Mass

Pfeiffer, J N and Jones, J F (1977) *Annual Handbook for Group Facilitators* University Associates: La Jolla, Cal

Pfeiffer, J N and Jones, J F (1977) An introduction to structured experiences *in* Pfeiffer and Jones (1977)

Phillipps, D and Thomas, A R (1982) Principals' decision making: some observations *in* Simpkins *et al* (1982)

Pocock, J G A (1972) *Politics, Language and Time* Methuen: London

Poster, C (1976) *School Decision Making* Heinemann: London

*Powell, M and Beard, J W (1984) *Teacher Effectiveness: An Annotated Bibliography and Guide to Research* Garland: New York

Presthus, R (1962) *The Organizational Society* Knopf: New York

Proshansky, H M and Seidenberg, B eds (1966) *Basic Studies in Social Psychology* Holt, Rinehart and Winston for the Psychological Study of Social Issues: New York

Pugh, D S and Hinings, C R eds (1976) *Organisational Structure, Extensions and Replications: The Aston Programme II* Saxon House: Farnborough, Hants

Ree, H (1985) *Education Extraordinary: The Life and Achievement of Henry Morris 1889-1961* Peter Owen: London

Rennie, J *et al* (1985) *British Community Primary Schools* Falmer Press: Lewes, Sussex

Renon, A G (1981) *The Functions of Education Administrators and the Training of Education Administrators* UNESCO EPP Report Studies TM/D2/2.1, UNESCO: Paris

Revans, R (1971) *Action Learning in Hospitals* McGraw-Hill: Maidenhead, Berks

Reynolds, C (1986) Too limiting a liberation: a case study on married women as teachers *in* Schmuck (1986) (forthcoming)

Rizvi, F ed (1985) *Working Papers in Ethics and Educational Administration* Deakin University: Victoria, Australia

Rockmore, T, Colbert, J G, Gavin, W J and Blakeley, T J (1981) *Marxism and Alternatives: Towards the Conceptual Interaction Among Soviet Philosophy, Neo-Thomism, Pragmatism and Phenomenology* D Reidel: Dordrecht, Holland

Rosenshine, B and Furst, N F (1971) Research on teacher performance criteria *in* Smith (1971)

Rowan, B (1981) The effects of institutionalized rules on administrators *in* Bacharach (1981)

Runciman, W G (1970) *Sociology and Its Place and Other Essays* Cambridge University Press: London

Rutherford, W L, Hord, S M, Huling, L L and Hall, G E (1983) *Change Facilitators: In Search of Understanding Their Role* Research and Development Center for Teacher Education, University of Texas at Austin: Austin, Tex (mimeographed)

Rutter, M (1983) Schools effects on pupil progress: research findings and policy implications *in* Schulman and Sykes (1983)

*Rutter, M, Maugham, B, Mortimer, P, Ouston, J and Smith, A (1979) *Fifteen Thousand Hours: Secondary Schools and Their Effects on Children* Open Books: London, and Harvard University Press: Cambridge, Mass

Sampson, S (1986) Teachers' careers and promotion in Australia *in* Schmuck (1986) (forthcoming)

Sarason, S (1971) *The Culture of the School and the Problem of Change* Allyn and Bacon: Boston, Mass

Schattschneider, E E (1960) *The Semi-Sovereign People* Holt, Rinehart and Winston: New York

Schein, E H (1985) *Organizational Culture and Leadership* Jossey-Bass: San Francisco

Schmitt, N et al (1982) *Criterion-Related and Content Validity of the NASSP Assessment Center* Research Report. Department of Psychology, Michigan State University: East Lansing

Schmuck, P (1975) *Sex Differentiation in Public School Administration* National Council of Administrative Women in Education: Arlington, Va

Schmuck, P ed (1986) *Women as Educators in the Western World* SUNY Press: New York (forthcoming)

Schmuck, P and Wyant, S (1981) Clues to sex bias in the selection of school administrators: a report from the Oregon network *in* Schmuck et al (1981)

Schmuck, P, Adkison, J, Peterson, B, Bailey, S, Glick, C, Klein, S, McDonald, S, Schubert, J and Tarason, S (1985) Administrative strategies for institutionalizing sex equality in education and the role of government *in* Klein (1985)

Schmuck, P, Charters, W W Jr and Carlson, R eds (1981) *Educational Policy and Management: Sex Differentials* Academic Press: New York

Schmuck, R A and Miles, M (1971) *Organizational Development in Schools* National Press Books: Palo Alto, Cal

Schön, D A (1983) *The Reflective Practitioner* Basic Books: New York

Schön, D A (1984) Leadership as reflection-in-action *in* Sergiovanni and Corbally (1984)

Scriven, M (1977) The evaluation of teachers and teaching *in* Borich (1977)

Seljelid, T (1982) *Handbook for the Working Environment and the Running of the School* (AMS) Project, Ministry of Cultural and Scientific Affairs: Oslo

Selye, H (1956) *The Stress of Life* McGraw-Hill: New York

Sergiovanni, T J (1984) Cultural and competing perspectives in administrative theory and practice *in* Sergiovanni and Corbally (1984)

Sergiovanni, T J and Corbally, J E (1984) *Leadership and Organizational Culture* University of Illinois Press: Urbana, Ill

Shakeshaft, C (1981) Women in educational administration: a descriptive analysis of dissertation research and paradigm for future research *in* Schmuck et al (1981)

Shapiro, D (1965) *Neurotic Styles* Basic Books: New York

Shulman, L E ed (1977) *Review of Research in Education* 5 Peacock Publishers: Itasca, Ill

Shulman, L E ed (1978) *Review of Research in Education* 6 Peacock Publishers: Itasca, Ill

Shulman, L E and Sykes, G eds (1983) *Handbook of Teaching and Policy* Longman: New York

Simpkins, W S, Thomas, A R and Thomas, E B eds (1982) *Principal and Task: An Australian Perspective* University of New England: Armidale, Australia

Smith, B O (1971) *Research in Teacher Education: A Symposium* Prentice-Hall: Englewood Cliffs, NJ

Smith, M A, Kalvelage, J and Schmuck, P (1980) *Sex Equity in Educational Leadership: Women Getting Together and Getting Ahead* Educational Development Center: Massachusetts

Soar, R S (1977) Teacher assessment: problems and possibilities *in* Borich (1977)

Stallings, J (1981) *Testing Teachers' In-class Instruction and Measuring Change Resulting from Staff Development* Teaching and Learning Institute: Mountain View, Cal

Steinbruner, J D (1974) *The Cybernetic Theory of Decision* Princeton University Press: Princeton, New Jersey

Stewart, R (1967) *Managers and their Jobs* Macmillan: London

Stewart, R (1976) *Contrasts in Management* McGraw-Hill: Maidenhead, Berks

Stewart, R (1982) *Choices for the Manager: A Guide to Managerial Work and Behaviour* McGraw-Hill: New York

Stockard, J, Schmuck, P, Kempner, K and Williams, P (1980) *Sex Equity in Education* Academic Press: New York

Sysiharju, A L (1986) Women as educators in Finland *in* Schmuck (1986) (forthcoming)

Tannenbaum, R, Weischler, I and Massarik, F (1961) *Leadership and Organisation: A Behavioural Science Approach* University of Illinois Press: Urbana, Ill

Taylor, B and Lippitt, G (1975) *Management Education and Training Handbook* McGraw-Hill: Maidenhead, Berks

Taylor, W (1969) *Heading for Change: The Management of Innovation in the Large Secondary School* Routledge and Kegan Paul: London

Tead, O (1965) *The Art of Administration* McGraw-Hill: New York

Thiagarajan, K M and Prahalad, C K (1969) *Some Problems in the Behavioural Science Education of Managers and Management Instructors in Developing Nations* Management Research Center, Rochester University: New York

Thompson, J D (1967) *Organizations in Action: Social Science Bases of Administrative Theory* McGraw-Hill: New York

Tung, R L and Koch, J L (1980) School administrators: sources of stress and ways of coping with it *in* Cooper and Marshall (1980)

Turner, G and Clift, P S (1985) *A First Review and Register of School and College Based Teacher Appraisal Schemes* Open University: Milton Keynes (mimeo)

Tyack, D and Hansot, E (1982) *Managers of Virtue: Public School Leadership 1820-1980* Basic Books: New York

Van der Vegt, R (1974) *Opleiden en Evalueren (Training and Evaluation)* Boom Uitgeverij: Meppel, The Netherlands

Van Essen, M (1986) Female teachers in the Netherlands, 1800-1865 *in* Schmuck (1986) (forthcoming)

Van Onselen, C (1976) *Chibaro: African Mine Labour in Southern Rhodesia 1900-1933* Pluto Press: London

*van Velzen, W G, Miles, M B, Ekholm, K, Hameyer, U and Robin, D (1985) *Making School Improvement Work: A Conceptual Guide to Practice* International School Improvement Project, Acco Pub: Leuven, Belgium

van Velzen, W G and Robin, D (1985) The need for school improvement in the next decade *in* van Velzen *et al* (1985)

Walker, S and Barton, L eds (1983) *Gender, Class and Education* The Falmer Press: Lewes, Sussex

Walker, W G (1965) *The Principal at Work: Case Studies in School Administration* University of Queensland Press: St Lucia, Queensland

Walker, W G (1970) *Theory and Practice in Educational Administration* University of Queensland Press: St Lucia, Queensland

Walker, W G and Crane, A R (1973) The selection of content for a theory-based perspective *in* Culbertson *et al* (1973)

Waller, W (1932) *The Sociology of Teaching* Wiley: New York

Walsh, K, Dunne, R, Stoten, B and Stewart, J D (1984) *Falling School Rolls and the Management of the Teaching Profession* NFER-Nelson: Windsor, Berks

Webb, H and Webb, D J (1967) *School Administration: A Casebook* International Textbook: Scranton, Pa

Webb, P C and Lyons, G (1982) The nature of managerial activities in education *in* Gray (1982)

Weick, K E (1979) *The Social Psychology of Organizing* Addison-Wesley: Reading, Mass

Weick, K E (1980) *Loosely coupled systems: relaxed meanings and thick interpretations* Cornell University Paper: Ithaca, NY

Weindling, R and Earley, P (1983) *The First Years of Headship in the Secondary School: Project Outline* National Foundation for Educational Research: Slough, Berks

Wheatley, M (1981) The impact of organizational structures and issues of sex equality *in* Schmuck *et al* (1981)

Willis, P (1977) *Learning to Labour: How Working Class Kids Get Working Class Jobs* Saxon House: Farnborough, Hants

Willower, D J (1971) The teacher subculture *in* Drabick (1971)

Willower, D J (1985) Mystifications and mysteries in thought and research in educational administration *in* Johnston (1985)

Wolcott, H F (1973) *The Man in the Principal's Office: An Ethnography* Holt, Rinehart and Winston: New York

Wood, A H (1976) M L C Melbourne, 1939-1966: A personal memoir *in* Murray-Smith (1976)

Woodcock, M and Francis, D (1982) *The Unblocked Manager: A Practical Guide to Self-development* Gower Press: Aldershot

Wragg, E C (1984) *Classroom Teaching Skills* Croom Helm: London

Wright Mills, C (1970) *The Sociological Imagination* Penguin: Harmondsworth

Wynn, R (1972) *Unconventional Methods and Materials for Preparing Educational Administrators* UCEA: Columbus, Ohio

Section II: Official publications

American Psychological Association (1972) *Proceedings of the 80th Annual Convention*

Association for Teacher Education in Europe and National Association of Head-teachers (1982) *Training for Heads (School Leaders) in Europe* Report of Conference, 12-14 March at Gatwick. ATEE: Brussels; NAHT: Haywards Heath, West Sussex

Commonwealth Council for Educational Administration (1980) *Commonwealth Directory of Qualifications and Courses in Educational Administration* Commonwealth Secretariat: London

Commonwealth Secretariat (1983) *The Commonwealth Casebook for School Administrators* Commonwealth Secretariat: London

Council of Europe: Council for Cultural Cooperation (1983) *School Management Training in Europe* Report of the 12th Council of Europe Teachers' Seminar, 21-26 September 1981, Donaueschingen. DECS/EGT(81)3-E. Council of Europe, Council for Cultural Cooperation: Strasbourg

Coventry Education Committee (1984) *Comprehensive Education for Life: A Consultative Document* Coventry Education Committee: Coventry

Department of Education and Science (1967) *Children and Their Primary Schools (The Plowden Report)* HMSO: London

Department of Education and Science (1972) *Educational Priority (The Halsey Report)* HMSO: London

Department of Education and Science (1977) *Ten Good Schools: A Secondary School Enquiry* HMSO: London

Department of Education and Science (1977) *A New Partnership for Our Schools (The Taylor Report)* HMSO: London

Department of Education and Science (1983) *Teaching Quality* (Cmnd 8836) HMSO: London

Department of Education and Science (1985) *Better Schools* (Cmnd 9469) HMSO: London

Florida Department of Education (1983) *Domains of the Florida Performance Measurement System* Office of Teacher Education, Certification and Inservice Staff Development: Tallahassee, Fla

Further Education Unit (1982) *Competency in Teaching: A Review of Competency and Performance Based Staff Development* FEU: London

Georgia Department of Education (1984) *Teacher Performance Assessment Instrument* Georgia Department of Education, Division of Staff Development: Atlanta, Ga

Halsey, A H *see* Department of Education and Science

Her Majesty's Inspectorate (1982) *The New Teacher in School: A Report by Her Majesty's Inspectors* HMSO: London

Her Majesty's Inspectorate (1985) *Quality in Schools: Evaluation and Appraisal* HMSO: London

*Hughes, M G (1981) *Leadership in the Management of Education: A Handbook for Educational Supervisors* Commonwealth Secretariat: London

Institute of Personnel Management/British Institute of Management (1980) *Selecting Managers — How British Industry Recruits* IPM information report 34. BIM Management Survey Report 49: London

Local Government Training Board (1984) *The Effective Manager: A Resource Handbook* EMAS Publishing: Budleigh Salterton, England

Malaysia, Government of (1956) Report of the Education Committee (The Razak Report). Government Printers: Kuala Lumpur

Manpower Services Commission (undated) *Management Self-development: A Practical Manual for Trainers* MSC Training Division: Sheffield

National Association of Schoolmasters and Union of Women Teachers (1976) *Stress in Schools* NAS/UWT: Hemel Hempstead, England

*Pareek, U and Rao, T V (1981) *Handbook for Trainers in Educational Management: with Special Reference to Countries in Asia and the Pacific* UNESCO, Roeap: Bangkok

Plowden, Lady (1967) *see* Department of Education and Science

Southern Rhodesia, Department of Native Education (1928) *Director's Report*

Suffolk Education Department (1985) *Those Having Torches . . . Teacher Appraisal: A Study* Suffolk Education Department: Ipswich, England

Taylor, T (1977) *see* Department of Education and Science

UNESCO EPP (1980) *The Co-ordination of Training Activities (Training Materials) in the Field of Educational Planning, Administration and Facilities* Workshop Report. Division of Educational Policy and Planning, UNESCO: Paris

UNESCO, Roeap (1979) *The Training of Educational Personnel* Report of a regional seminar, Thailand, October 1978. Regional Office for Education in Asia and Oceania, UNESCO: Bangkok

UNESCO, Roeap (1980) *Development and Testing of National Training Materials in Educational Planning and Management* Report of a consultative meeting. UNESCO, Bangkok

UNESCO, Roeap (1981) *Supporting Innovations in Education: Preparing Administrators, Supervisors and Other Key Personnel* Report of a technical working group meeting, 29 September — 11 October. UNESCO: Bangkok

UNESCO, Roeap (1983) *Training Education Personnel in Planning and Management Using Distance Teaching and Other Techniques* Report on an evaluation workshop. UNESCO: Bangkok

Western Australia, State School Teachers' Union of (1982) Teaching and stress. Position Paper: Perth

Zimbabwe, Government of (1983) *Annual Report of the Secretary for Education and Culture for the year ended 31 December 1982* Government of Zimbabwe

Section III: Articles, periodicals and working papers

Adams, B (1982) The staff burn-out syndrome: by way of a review *The North West Counsellors' Association Newsletter* 6 1: 37-41

Adkison, J A (1981) Women in school administration: a review of the research *Review of Educational Research* 51 3: 311-43

Administrative Science Quarterly (1983) Issue on organizational culture 28 3: 331-499

Aitken, M and Hage, J (1966) Organizational alienation: a comparative analysis *American Sociological Review* 31: 479-507

Allison, D J (1983) Toward an improved understanding of the organizational nature of schools *Educational Administration Quarterly* 19 4: 7-34

American Psychological Association (1972) *Proceedings of the 80th Annual Convention*

Anderson, C S (1982) The search for school climate: a review of the research *Review of Educational Research* 52 3: 368-420

Andrews, A G (1971) Ground rules for the great debate *Cambridge Journal of Education* 7 2: 90-94

Anstey, E (1971) The civil service administrative class: a follow up of post war entrants *Occupational Psychology* 45 1: 27-43

Archer, M S (1982) Morphogenesis versus structuration *British Journal of Sociology* 33 4: 455-83

Bacharach, S B and Mitchell, S M (1981) Critical variables in the formation and maintenance of consensus in school districts *Educational Administration Quarterly* 17 4: 74-97

Ballinger, E A (1985) *An Interim Analysis of Available Evaluation Reports on BASIC and OTTO Programs* National Development Centre for School Management Training, School of Education: University of Bristol

Barnes, S B (1969) Paradigms: social and scientific *Man* 4 1: 94-102

Barnett, B (1985) A synthesis for improving practice. Paper presented at the Annual Meeting of the American Educational Research Association: Montreal

Barr, A S (1935) The measurement of teaching ability *Journal of Educational Research* 28 8: 561-9

Bates, R (1981) Power and the educational administrator: bureaucracy, loose coupling or cultural negotiation. American Educational Research Association Annual Meeting Paper: San Francisco

Bates, R J (1980) Educational administration, the sociology of science, and the management of knowledge *Educational Administration Quarterly* 16 2: 1-20

Beckerman, T M and Good, T L (1981) The classroom ratio of high and low-aptitude students and its effect on achievement *American Educational Research Journal* **18** 3: 317-28

Bensky, J M, Shaw, S F, Grouse, A S, Bates, H, Dixson, B and Beane, W E (1980) Public law 94-142 and stress: a problem for educators *Exceptional Children* **47** 1: 24-29

Bentz, W K, Hollister, W G and Edgerston, J W (1971) An assessment of the mental health of teachers: a comparative analysis *Psychology in the Schools* **8** 1: 72-76

Bernstein, B (1967) Open schools, open society? *New Society* **14**

Bidwell, C E and Karsarda, J D (1980) Conceptualizing and measuring the effects of school and schooling *American Journal of Education* **88**: 401-30

Biklen, S K (1985) Teaching as an occupation for women: a case study of an elementary school. NIE GRANT G-81-007 Unpublished paper. Syracuse: New York

Blase, J J (1982) A social-psychological grounded theory of teacher stress and burnout *Educational Administration Quarterly* **18** 4: 93-113

Blase, J J (1984) A data based model of how teachers cope with work stress *Journal of Educational Administration* **22** 2: 173-91

Bossert, S T (1981) Understanding sex differences in children's classroom experiences *Elementary School Journal* **81** 254-66

Bossert, S T, Dwyer, D C, Rowan, B and Lee, G V (1982) The instructional management role of the principal *Educational Administration Quarterly* **18** 3: 34-64

Boyd, W L (1982b) The political economy of public schools *Educational Administration Quarterly* **18** 3: 111-30

Braddick, B and Casey, D (1981) Developing the forgotten army — learning and the top manager *Education and Development* **12** 3: 169-80

Bredeson, P V (1985) An analysis of the metaphorical perspectives of school principals *Educational Administration Quarterly* **21** 1: 29-50

Brophy, J E (1981) Teacher praise: a functional analysis *Review of Educational Research* **51** 1: 5-32

Brown, J S (1970) Risk propensity in decision making: a comparison of business and public school administrators *Administrative Science Quarterly* **15** 4: 473-81

Brown, R H (1978) Bureaucracy as praxis: towards a political phenomenology of formal organisations *Administrative Science Quarterly* **23** 3: 365-82

Burgoyne, J G (1976) Learning processes in the acquisition of managerial skills and qualities *Management, Education and Development* **7** 3: 205-08

Burke, B T (1982) Merit pay for teachers: Round Valley may have the answer *Phi Delta Kappan* **64** 4: 265-66

Burns, T (1955) The reference of conduct in small groups *Human Relations* **7** 4: 467-86

Byrne, C J (1983) Teacher knowledge and teacher effectiveness: a literature review, theoretical analysis and discussion of research. Strategy Paper presented to the 14th Annual Convocation of the Northeastern Educational Research Association: Ellenville, New York (October)

Carlson, R O (1961) Succession and performance among school superintendents *Administrative Science Quarterly* **6** 3: 220-27

Carter, P H (1979) Teacher stress: discipline, paperwork top the list of causes *Massachusetts Teacher* **59**: 7-11

Cichon, D J and Koff, R H (1980) Stress and teaching *National Association of Secondary Principals' Bulletin* **64** 34: 91-104

Clark, D L (1980) Factors associated with success in urban elementary schools *Phi Delta Kappan* **61** 7: 467-70

*Clark, D L, Lotto, L S and Astuto, T A (1984) Effective schools and school improvement: a comparative analysis of two lines of inquiry *Educational Administration Quarterly* **20** 3: 41-68

Coates, T J and Thoresen, C E (1976) Teacher anxiety: a review with recommendations *Review of Educational Research* **46** 2: 159-84

Cohen, M D, March, J D and Olsen, J P (1972) A garbage can model of organizational choice *Administrative Science Quarterly* **17** 1: 1-25

Coker, H, Medley, D M and Soar, R S (1980) How valid are expert opinions about
effective teaching? *Phi Delta Kappan* **62** 2: 131-49

Connors, D A (1983) The school environment: a link to understanding stress *Theory
into Practice* **22** 1: 15-20

Coughlan, R J (1970) Dimensions of teacher morale *American Educational Research
Journal* **1** 2: 221-34

Crane, A R (1980) Anxiety in organizations: explorations of an idea *Journal of
Educational Administration* **18** 2: 202-12

Crane, A R and Walker, W G (1976) Theory in the real world of the educational
administrator *UCEA Review* **17** 3: 1-40

Crowson, R L and Porter-Gehrie, C (1980) The discretionary behavior of principals
in large-city schools *Educational Administration Quarterly* **16** 1: 45-69

Daresh, J and Liu, C (1985) High school principals' perceptions of their instructional
leadership behavior. Paper presented at the Annual Meeting of the American Educational Research Association: Montreal

ᵇDarling-Hammond, L, Wise, A E and Pease, S R (1983) Teacher evaluation in the
organisational context: a review of the literature *Review of Educational Research* **53** 3: 285-328

Deal, T E (1985) National Commissions: blueprints for remodelling or ceremonies
for revitalizing public schools *Education and Urban Society* **17** 2: 145-56

Deal, T (1985) The symbolism of effective schools *Elementary School Journal*
85 5: 601-20

Deal, T E and Celotti, L D (1980) How much influence do (and can) administrators
have on classrooms? *Phi Delta Kappan* **61** 7: 471-3

Deal, T E and Kennedy, A (1983) Culture: a new look through old lenses. American
Educational Research Association Annual Meeting Paper: Montreal

Derr, B and Gabarro, J (1972) An organizational contingency theory for education
Educational Administration Quarterly **8**

Duignan, P (1980) Administrative behavior of school superintendents: a descriptive
study *Journal of Educational Administration* **18** 1: 5-26

Duke, D L and Imber, M (1985) Should principals be required to be effective?
School Organization **5** 2: 125-46

Duke, D L, Isaacson, N, Sagor, R and Schmuck, P (1983) The socialization of
administrators. American Educational Research Association Annual Meeting
Paper: Chicago

Dunham, J (1977) The effects of disruptive behaviour on teachers *Educational
Review* **29** 3: 181-87

Dunham, J (1980) An exploratory comparative study of staff stress in English and
German comprehensive schools *Educational Review* **32** 1: 11-20

Dunham, J (1981) Disruptive pupils and teacher stress *Educational Research* **23** 3:
205-13

Edgerton, S K (1977) Teachers in role conflict: the hidden dilemma *Phi Delta
Kappan* **59** 2: 120-22

Edmonds, R (1979) Effective schools for the urban poor *Educational Leadership*
37 1: 15-24

Ellström, P (1983) Four faces of educational organizations *Higher Education* **12**
2: 231-41

Emerson, R M and Messenger, S L (1977) The micro-politics of trouble *Social Problems* **25** 1: 121-34

Enns, F (1981) Some ethical-moral concerns in administration *Canadian Administrator* **20** 8: 1-8

Erickson, D A (1979) Research on educational administration: the state-of-the-art
Educational Researcher **8** 3: 91-4

Esp, D G (1980) Selection and training of secondary school senior staff: some European examples *Education* **156** 16: 1-4 (October)

Eubanks, E and Levine, D (1985) A first look at effective school projects at inner-city elementary schools. Paper presented at the Annual Meeting of the American Educational Research Association: Montreal

Evans, K M (1951) A critical survey of methods of assessing teaching ability *British Journal of Educational Psychology* **21** 2: 89-95

Farkas, J P (1982) Stress and the school principal: old myths and new findings *Administrator's Notebook* **30** 8: 1-4

Farrar, E, Neufeld, B and Miles, M B (1984) Effective schools programs in high schools: social promotion or movement by merit? *Phi Delta Kappan* **65** 10: 701-706 (June)

Fennell, M L, Barchas, P, Cohen, E, McMahon, A and Hildebrand, F (1978) An alternative perspective on sex differences in organizational settings: the process of legitimation *Sex Roles* **4** 4: 598-604

Feshback, N and Campbell, M (1978) Teacher stress and disciplinary practices in schools: a preliminary report ERIC Document ED 162 228

Flanders, N A (1977) Knowledge about teacher effectiveness *British Journal of Teacher Education* **3** 1: 3-26

Foster, W P (1980) Administration and the crisis in legitimacy: a review of Habermasian thought *Harvard Educational Review* **50** 4: 496-505

Friedman, M H (1978) School stress management training: an integrated approach. Unpublished paper presented at the Annual Meeting of the American Education Research Association

Friesen, D and Duignan, P (1980) How superintendents spend their working time *Canadian Administrator* **19** 5: 1-5

Fullan, M (1972) Overview of the innovative process and user *Interchange* **3** 2-3: 1-43, 70

Fullan, M (1985) Change processes and strategies at the local level *The Elementary School Journal* **85** 3: 391-421

Fullan, M and Newton, E (1985) High school principals as facilitators of instruction. Unpublished paper, Ontario Institute for Studies in Education: Toronto

Fullan, M and Pomfret, A (1977) Research on curriculum and instruction implementation *Review of Educational Research* **47** 1: 335-97

Getzels, J W and Cuba, E G (1957) Social behaviour and the administrative process *School Review* **65**: 423-41

Giroux, H A (1983) Theories of reproduction and resistance in the new sociology of education: a critical analysis *Harvard Educational Review* **53** 3: 257-93

Glatter, R (1982) The micropolitics of education: issues for training *Educational Management and Administration* **10** 2: 160-65

Gmelch, W H and Swent, B (1984) Management team stressors and their impact on administrators' health *Journal of Educational Administration* **22** 2: 192-205

Gorton, D (1982) Administrator stress: some surprising research findings *Planning and Changing* **12** 4: 195-99

Greenfield, T B (1978) Reflections on organization theory and the truths of irreconcilable realities *Educational Administration Quarterly* **14** 2: 1-23

Greenfield, T B (1980) The man who comes back through the door in the wall: discovering truth, discovering self, discovering organizations *Educational Administrative Quarterly* **16** 3: 26-59

Griffiths, D E (1975) Some thoughts about theory in educational administration *University Council for Educational Administration Review* **17** 1: 12-18

Griffiths, D E (1979) Intellectual turmoil in educational administration *Educational Administration Quarterly* **15** 3: 45-65

Gronn, P C (1983) Talk as the work: the accomplishment of school administration *Administrative Science Quarterly* **28** 1: 1-21

Gronn, P C (1984) 'I have a solution . . .': administrative power in a school meeting *Educational Administration Quarterly* **20** 2: 65-92

Haefele, D L (1978) The teacher perceiver interview: how valid? *Phi Delta Kappan* **59** 10: 683-84 (June)

Haefele, D L (1980 How to evaluate theee, teacher — let me count the ways *Phi Delta Kappan* **61** 5: 349-52 (January)

Hall, G E (1984) Three change-facilitator styles. Paper presented at the Annual Meeting of the American Educational Research Association: New York

Hall, G E and Hord, S M (1984) Analyzing what change facilitators do: the intervention taxonomy *Knowledge Creation, Diffusion, Utilization* **5** 3: 275-307

Hall, G E, Hord, S, Rutherford, W and Huling, L (1984) Change in high schools *Educational Leadership* **41**: 59-62

Hallinger, P and Murphy, J (1983) Instructional leadership and school socio-economic status: a preliminary investigation *Administrator's Notebook* **31** 5: 1-4

Hannaway, J and Sproull, L S (1979) Who's running the show?: coordination and control in educational organizations *Administrator's Notebook* **27** 9: 1-4

Hanson, E M and Brown, M E (1977) A contingency view of problem solving in schools: a case analysis *Educational Administration Quarterly* **13**

Hart, D (1973) Head complaints *The Times Educational Supplement* (23 September)

Hendrickson, B (1979) Is 'exhausted' an apt description of your present state of mind? *Learning* **1**: 37-9

Herriott, R E and Firestone, W A (1984) Two images of schools as organizations: a refinement and elaboration *Educational Administration Quarterly* **20** 4: 41-57

Hersey, P (1980) NASSP's Assessment Center: practitioners speak out *National Association of Secondary School Principals Bulletin* **64** 439: 87-117

Hiebert, B A (1983) A framework for planning stress control interventions *The Canadian Counsellor* **17** 2: 51-61

Hiebart, B and Farber, I (1984) Teacher stress: a literature survey with a few surprises *Canadian Journal of Education* **9** 1: 14-27

Hill, P and Schoubroeck, L V (1984) Stress and the school administrator: a survey of principals and deputy principals in government schools in Western Australia. Unpublished paper, Education Department of Western Australia: Perth

Hills, J (1980) A critique of Greenfield's 'new perspective' *Educational Administration Quarterly* **16** 1: 20-44

Holmes, T and Rahe, R (1967) The social readjustment rating scale *Journal of Psychosomatic Research* **11**: 213-18

Hosking, S and Reid, M (1985) Teacher stress — an organisational perspective. Unpublished paper, Victorian Teachers' Union: Camberwell

Hoy, W K, Blazovsky, R and Newland, W (1983) Bureaucracy and alienation: a comparative analysis *Journal of Educational Administration* **21** 2: 109-20

Hoyle, E (1965) Organizational analysis in the field of education *Educational Research* **7** 2: 97-114

Hoyle, E (1970) Planned organizational change in education *Research in Education* **3**

Hoyle, E (1982) Micropolitics of educational organizations *Educational Management and Administration* **10** 2: 87-98

Iwanicki, E F (1983) Towards understanding and alleviating teacher burnout *Theory into Practice* **22** 1: 27-32

Jick, T D (1979) Mixing quantitative and qualitative methods: triangulation in action *Administrative Science Quarterly* **24** 4: 602-11

Joyce, B and Showers, B (1980) Improving in-service training: the messages from research *Educational Leadership* **37** 5: 379-85

Jury, L E, Willower, D J and Delacy, W J (1975) Teacher self-actualization and pupil control ideology *Alberta Journal of Educational Research* **81** 4: 295-301

Katz, F E (1964) The school as a complex organization: a consideration of patterns of autonomy *Harvard Educational Review* **34** 3: 428-55

Kauchak, D (1984) Testing teachers in Louisiana: a closer look *Phi Delta Kappan* **65** 9: 626-68 (May)

Keavney, G and Sinclair, K E (1978) Teacher concerns and teacher anxiety: a neglected topic of classroom research *Review of Educational Research* **48** 2: 273-90

Kent Jennings, M (1968) Parental grievances and school politics *Public Opinion Quarterly* **32** 3: 363-78

Kmetz, J T and Willower, D J (1982) Elementary school principals' work behavior *Educational Administration Quarterly* **18** 4: 62-78

Koff, R, Laffey, J, Olson, G and Cichon, D (1979-80) Stress and the school administrator *Administrator's Notebook* **28** 9: 1-4

Kyriacou, C (1980) Coping actions and occupational stress among school teachers *Research in Education* **24**: 57-61

Kyriacou, C and Newson, G (1982) Teacher effectiveness: a consideration of research problems *Educational Review* **34** 1: 3-12

Kyriacou, C and Sutcliffe, J (1978) Teacher stress and satisfaction *Educational Research* **21** 2: 89-96

Lakomski, G (1985a) Critical theory and educational administration. American Educational Research Association Annual Meeting Paper: Chicago

Leach, D J (1984) A model of teacher stress and its implications for management *Journal of Educational Administration* **22** 2: 157-72

Leithwood, K A and Montgomery, D J (1982) The role of the elementary school principal in program improvement *Review of Educational Research* **52** 3: 309-39

Leithwood, K A and Montgomery, D J (1984) Patterns of growth in principal effectiveness. Paper presented at the American Educational Research Association Annual Meeting: New Orleans

Leithwood, K A, Stanley, K and Montgomery, D J (1984) Training principals for school improvement *Education and Urban Society* **17** 1: 49-72

Levi, L (1979) Occupational mental health: its monitoring, protection and promotion *Journal of Occupational Medicine* **21**: 26-32

Levine, V, Donellon, A, Gioia, D A and Sims, H P (1984) Scripts and speech acts in administrative behavior: the interplay of necessity, chance and free will *Educational Administration Quarterly* **20** 1: 93-110

Licata, J W and Hack, W G (1980) School administrator grapevine structure *Educational Administration Quarterly* **16** 3: 82-99

Lindblom, C E (1959) The science of muddling through *Public Administration Review* **19**

Little, J W (1982) Norms of collegiality and experimentation: workplace conditions of school success *American Educational Research Journal* **19** 3: 325-40

Little, J W (1984) Seductive images and organizational realities in professional development *Teachers College Record* **86** 1: 84-102

Little, J W (1985) What schools contribute to teachers' professional development. Paper presented at the Annual Meeting of the American Educational Research Association: Montreal

Litwak, E (1961) Models of bureaucracy which permit conflict *American Journal of Sociology* **67**

Lloyd, K (1981) Quality control in the primary school: the head's role in supervising the work of classteachers *School Organisation* **1** 4: 317-29

Lockheed, M E and Hall, K P (1976) Conceptualizing sex as a status characteristic: applications leading to leadership training strategies *Journal of Social Issues* **32** 3: 111-24

Lungu, G F (1983) Some critical issues in the training of educational administrators for developing countries of Africa *International Journal of Educational Development* **3** 1: 85-96

McDaniel, T R (1977) The NTE and teacher certification *Phi Delta Kappan* **59** 3: 186-88 (November)

McGregor, D (1957) An uneasy look at performance appraisal *Harvard Business Review* (September/October)

March, J G (1974) Analytical skills and the university training of educational administrators *Journal of Educational Administration* 12 1: 17-44

March, M E (1981) Control over educational decisions *Canadian Administrator* 21 3: 1-6

Marshall, D (1983) Critical decisions in the professional preparation and development of school administrators in developing areas. A discussion paper prepared for the CASEA section of the Canadian Society for the Study of Education

Martin, W J and Willower, D J (1981) The managerial behavior of high school principals *Educational Administration Quarterly* 17 1: 69-90

Medley, D M and Mitzel, H E (1959) Some behavioural correlates of teacher effectiveness *Journal of Educational Psychology* 50 6: 239-46

Meier, T K (1985) Leadership theories from industry: relevant to higher education? *Educational Administration and History* 17 1: 62-69

Meyer, J W and Rowan, B (1977) Institutionalized organizations: formal structure as myth and ceremony *American Journal of Sociology* 83 2: 340-63

Michaelson, J B (1981) The political economy of school district administration *Educational Administration Quarterly* 17 3: 98-113

Miles, M B (1983) Unravelling the mystery of institutionalization *Educational Leadership* 40 14-19 (November)

Mintzberg, H (1974) The manager's job — folklore and fact *Harvard Business Review*

Miskel, C and Cosgrove, D (1985) Leader succession in school settings *Review of Educational Research* 55 1: 87-106

Miskel, C, McDonald, D and Bloom, S (1983) Structural and expectancy linkages within schools and organizational effectiveness *Educational Administration Quarterly* 19 1: 49-82

Morgan, T (1973) Recent insights into the selection interview *Personnel Review* 4-13

Murphy, J, Hallinger, P and Mitman, A (1983) Problems with research on educational leadership: issues to be addressed *Educational Evaluation and Policy Analysis* 5 3: 297-305

Mykletun, R J (1984) Teacher stress: perceived and objective sources, and quality of life *Scandinavian Journal of Educational Research* 28 1: 17-45

Needle, R H, Griffin, T and Svedson, R (1981) Occupational stress: coping and health problems of teachers *The Journal of School Health* 51 3: 175-81

O'Dempsey, K (1976) Time analysis of activities, work patterns and roles of high school principals *Administrator's Bulletin* 7 8: 1-4

Ogawa, R T (1984) Teachers and administrators: elements of the information processing repertoires of schools *Educational Administration Quarterly* 20 2: 5-24

Olander, H T and Farrell, M E (1970) Professional problems of elementary teachers *Journal of Teacher Education* 21: 276-80

Peterson, K (1984) Mechanisms of administrative control over managers in educational organizations *Administrative Science Quarterly* 29 4: 573-97

Peterson, K D (1978) The principal's tasks *Administrator's Notebook* 26 8: 1-4

Peterson, P L and Janicki, T C (1979) Individual characteristics and children's learning in large-group and small-group approaches *Journal of Educational Psychology* 71 5: 677-87

Pettegrew, L S and Wolf, G E (1982) Validating measures of teacher stress *American Educational Research Journal* 19 3: 372-96

Phillipps, D and Thomas, A R (1983) Profile of a principal under stress *Primary Education* 14 6: 6-8, 31

Pink, W and Wallace, D (1984) Creating effective schools: moving from theory to practice. Paper presented at the Annual Meeting of the American Educational Research Association: New Orleans

Pitner, N J and Ogawa, R T (1981) Organizational leadership: the case of the school superintendent *Educational Administration Quarterly* 17 2: 45-65

Pratt, J (1978) Perceived stress among teachers: the effect of age and background of children taught *Educational Review* **30** 1: 3-14

Purkey, S and Smith, M (1983) Effective schools: a review *The Elementary School Journal* **83**: 427-52

Purkey, S and Smith, M (1985) School reform: the district policy implications of the effective schools literature *The Elementary School Journal* **85** 3: 353-90

Ratsoy, E W (1980) Environments, linkages and policy making in education *Canadian Administrator* **19** 7: 1-6

Reed, S (1979) What you can do to prevent teacher burnout *National Elementary Principal* **58** 3: 67-70

Richardson, J and Bennett, B (1984) Applying learning techniques to on-the-job development: Parts I, II and III *Journal of European Industrial Training* **8** 1: 3-7, 3: 5-10 and 4: 3-7

Rosenholtz, S and Simpson, C (1984) The formation of ability conceptions: developmental trend or social construction? *Review of Educational Research* **54**: 31-64

Rosenshine, B (1970) The stability of teacher effects upon student achievement *Review of Educational Research* **40** 5: 647-62

Rost, J C (1980) Human relations training in educational administration programs: a study based on a national survey *Group and Organization Studies* **5** 1: 80-95

Rowan, B (1983) Research on effective schools: a cautionary note *Educational Researcher* **12** 4: 24-31

Rowan, B and Denk, C (1984) Management succession, school socioeconomic context, and basic skills achievement *American Educational Research Journal* **21** 3: 517-37

Sander, B and Wiggins, T (1985) Cultural context of administrative theory: in consideration of a multidimensional paradigm *Educational Administration Quarterly* **21** 1: 95-117

Schwab, R L (1983) Teacher burnout: moving beyond 'psychobabble' *Theory into Practice* **22** 1: 21-26

Schwab, R L and Iwanicki, E F (1982) Perceived role conflict, role ambiguity, and teacher burnout *Educational Administration Quarterly* **18** 1: 60-74

Selye, H (1981) On executive stress *Executive Health* **18** 1: 1-6

Selye, H (1983) It's not the amount of stress you have, it's how you respond to it *Executive Health* **19** 5: 1-6

Shakeshaft, C and Nowell, I (1984) Research on theories, concepts and models of organizational behavior: the influence of gender *Issues in Education* **2** 3: 186-203

Showers, B (1985) Teachers coaching teachers *Educational Leadership* **42** 7: 43-9

Smedley, S R and Willower, D J (1981) Principals' pupil control behavior and school robustness *Educational Administration Quarterly* **17** 4: 40-56

Soar, R S, Medley, D M and Coker, H (1983) Teacher evaluation: a critique of currently used methods *Phi Delta Kappan* **65**: 239-46 (December)

Soubry, G (1978) France: the training of headmasters *Educational Administration* **7** 1: 15-32

Sousa, D A and Hoy, W K (1981) Bureaucratic structure in schools: a refinement and synthesis in measurement *Educational Administration Quarterly* **17** 4: 21-39

Sparks, G (1984) In-service education: the process of teacher change. Paper presented at the Annual Meeting of the American Educational Research Association: New Orleans

Spender, D (1984) Women as educational employees: a brief consideration of the principles and trends in Britain at a time of economic change. Paper presented at the Second International Interdisciplinary Congress on Women: Groningen, The Netherlands

Spillane, R (1983) Occupational stress and organisation development: a new research strategy. Unpublished paper presented at Seminar '83, Melbourne Organisation Development Network: Melbourne

Sproull, L S (1981) Managing educational programs: a micro-behavioural analysis *Human Organization* **40** 2: 113-22

Stallings, J (1980) Allocated academic learning time revisited, or beyond time on task *Educational Researcher* **9**: 11-16

Stetter, M W and Willower, D J (1985) School principals as threshold guardians: an exploratory study *Alberta Journal of Educational Research* **31** 1: 2-10

Stewart, R (1983) It's not what you do . . . it's the way that you do it *Personnel Management* (April)

Stewart, R (1984) The nature of management: a problem for management education *Journal of Management Studies* **21** 3: 323-30

Styles, K and Cavanagh, G (1977) Stress in teaching and how to handle it *English Journal* **66**: 76-79

Tenopyr, M L (1981) The realities of employment testing *American Psychologist* **36** 10: 1120-27

Tetreault, M K (1985) Stages of thinking about women: an experience derived evaluation model *Journal of Higher Education* (Summer)

Thomas, A R, Willis, Q and Phillipps, D (1981) Observational studies of Australian administrators: methodological issues *Australian Journal of Education* **25** 1: 55-72

Turner, G (1985) Nascent schemes for teacher appraisal *School Organisation* **5** 2: 155-61

Vanderberg, D (1982) Hermeneutical phenomenology in the study of educational administration *Journal of Educational Administration* **20** 1: 23-32

Virmani, K G (1980) Training for educational managers in India: a case for experiential learning methods *EPA Bulletin* **3** 2: 38-52

Walker, W G (1972) UCEA's bright son at morning: the Commonwealth Council for Educational Administration *Educational Administration Quarterly* **8** 2: 16-25

Walker, W G (1978) Values, unorthodoxy and the 'unscientific' in educational administration research *Educational Administration* **6** 2: 94-106

Walker, W G (1984) Administrative narcissism and the tyranny of isolation: its decline and fall, 1954-1984 *Educational Administration Quarterly* **20** 4: 6-24

Wall, G (1975) The concept of interest in politics *Politics and Society* **5** 4: 487-510

Weick, K E (1976) Educational organizations as loosely coupled systems *Administrative Science Quarterly* **21** 1: 1-19

Weick, K E (1982) Administering education in loosely coupled schools *Phi Delta Kappan* **63** 10: 673-76

Wellisch, J B, MacQueen, A H, Carriere, R A and Durk, G A (1978) School management and organization in successful schools *Sociology of Education* **51** 3: 211-26

Williams, R H and Willower, D J (1983) Female school superintendents on their work *Journal of Educational Equity and Leadership* **3** 4: 289-304

Willis, Q (1980) The work activity of school principals: an observational study *Journal of Educational Administration* **18** 1: 27-54

Willower, D J (1980) Contemporary issues in theory in educational administration *Educational Administration Quarterly* **16** 3: 1-25

Willower, D J (1981) Educational administration: some philosophical and other considerations *Journal of Educational Administration* **19** 2: 115-39

Willower, D J (1982) School organizations: perspectives in juxtaposition *Educational Administration Quarterly* **18** 3: 89-110

Willower, D J (1983) Evolution in the professorship: past, philosophy, future *Educational Administration Quarterly* **19** 3: 179-200

Willower, D J (1984) School principals, school cultures, and school improvement *Educational Horizons* **63** 1: 35-38

Wood, C J and Pohland, P A (1983) Teacher evaluation and the 'Hand of History' *Journal of Educational Administration* **21** 2: 169-81

Youngs, B B (1984) Drug use in the leadership area *The Canadian Administrator* **24** 1: 1-6

Zvobgo, R J (1980) Government missionary policies on African secondary education in Southern Rhodesia with special reference to the Anglican and Wesleyan Methodist churches. Unpublished PhD thesis, University of Edinburgh: Edinburgh

Section IV: Annotated bibliographies

Bailey, F G (1977) *Morality and Expediency: The Folklore of Academic Politics* Basil Blackwell: Oxford
An anthropological account of micro-political gamesmanship. Bailey draws on his own experience, his research and other published accounts to analyse the cut and thrust of university administration. Among the topics covered are committee dynamics, masks, reason and emotion and persuasive appeals resorted to by the actors. Written from a dramatistic or theatrical metaphor it elucidates the structure and function of 'arena' and 'elite' committee systems.

Barr, R and Dreeben, R (1983) *How Schools Work* University of Chicago Press: Chicago
This book presents one of the most carefully framed analyses of the school's production process. The authors argue that the division of labour and the allocation of resources to various subunits within the school are central to understanding school effects. Their analysis of elementary school classroom reading instruction demonstrates how decisions about assigning children to classrooms, within-classroom grouping practices, and the curriculum structure affect what and how much various students learn. Important implications for instructional management are reviewed. In addition, the book clearly articulates the theoretical rationale for studying schooling as a 'multilevel' phenomenon.

Borich, G D *ed* (1977) *The Appraisal of Teaching: Concepts and Process* Addison-Wesley: Reading, Mass
A collection of American papers on the techniques of appraising teaching. It places particular emphasis on the identification of teaching competencies. There are five sections: toward defining teacher competencies; measuring teacher performance; applications of performance appraisal systems; using appraisal techniques and procedures; and developing a valid appraisal system. The first part of the book discusses conceptual issues which relate to these five sections. Part two consists of collections of papers, several selected for each section, and reviewed briefly by the editor.

Buckley, J (1985) *The Training of Secondary School Heads in Western Europe* NFER-Nelson for the Council of Europe: Windsor, Berks
Commissioned by the Council of Europe, this study gives an overview of development in school management training in Western Europe. It contains chapters on the changing role of the secondary school head, the consequent training needs, five case studies of attempts to meet these training needs (France, Sweden, England, Netherlands and Norway), issues of methodology and issues of evaluation.

Clark, D L, Lotto, L S and Astuto, T A (1984) Effective schools and school improvement: a comparative analysis of two lines of inquiry *Educational Administration Quarterly* **20** 3: 41-68
This article is a review of two distinct traditions of educational inquiry which have evolved in the study of school effectiveness and school improvement. After years of equivocation about the role of schooling in student achievement, the school effectiveness literature has recently taken on a prescriptive tone; not only is schooling argued to matter, but also specific school characteristics are cited as associated with successful student outcomes. This perspective has emerged from the stimulus of

inquirers who have searched for and documented the characteristics of what have been termed instructionally effective schools. The school improvement literature is not characterized by the litany of factors associated with instructionally effective schools, but recent aggregations of the school improvement research indicate that agreement on variables affecting educational change programmes in schools and school systems is nearly as high as that in the school effectiveness literature. The history and the intra- and inter-literature consensus of these two lines of inquiry are examined in this review.

Darling-Hammond, L, Wise, A E and Pease, S R (1983) Teacher evaluation in the organisational context: a review of the literature *Review of Educational Research* **53** 3: 285-328
A fairly comprehensive and recent review of the literature on teacher evaluation. It presents a conceptual framework for examining the design and implementation of teacher evaluation processes in school organizations by examining research into teaching, organizational behaviour and policy implementation.

Fullan, M (1982) *The Meaning of Educational Change* Teachers College Press, Columbia University: New York
The Meaning of Educational Change makes sense of what happens – for better or worse – when educational innovations are attempted. 'Remarkably, it is only in the last twelve years (since about 1970) that we have come to understand how educational change works in practice. In the 1960s educators were busy developing and introducing reforms. In the 1970s they were busy failing at putting them into practice. Out of this rather costly endeavour (psychologically and financially) has come a strong base of evidence about how and why educational reform fails or succeeds.' Much of this evidence is very recent, and only now has it been brought together in a comprehensive framework. Professor Fullan shows that bringing about a successful change is a process involving factors that, while numerous and complex, are in no way incomprehensible. Those concerned with the improvement of schooling – at the national level, at the classroom level, or at any point between – will find in *The Meaning of Educational Change* guidelines for using the scarcer resources of the 1980s in programmes that genuinely benefit those they were designed to serve.

Goffman, E (1976) *The Presentation of Self in Everyday Life* Penguin: Harmondsworth
This book is perhaps the classic study of interpersonal behaviour. Goffman was a sociologist who drew on his fieldwork experience in a remote island rural community, literary works, diaries and memoirs to articulate a model of impression management. He shows how and why people project certain self images and identities, to whom and with what effect. The rules for managing self in 'back' and 'front' regions to audiences are elaborated in depth.

Griffiths, D E ed (1964) *Behavioural Science and Educational Administration: The Sixty-third Yearbook of the National Society for the Study of Education* Chicago University Press: Chicago
The 1964 Yearbook of the National Society for the Study of Education is a benchmark publication in the scientific study of the process of educational administration. The topics covered range from a history of the development of theorizing in the field to a discussion of contemporary theory based on a wide range of disciplines, especially the social sciences. The list of contributing authors reads like a 'who's who' of the most influential theorists and researchers in the field. Most remain active and visible today and are continuing to participate in dialogue in the field. The Yearbook is notable for the clarity of its expression and its avoidance of obfuscation. It is also a rich source of references for further reading by scholars.

Huberman, A M and Miles, M B (1984) *Innovation Up Close: How School Improvement Works* Plenum: New York
This book is a systematic, in-depth analysis of the improvement as it happened in 12 elementary and secondary school districts across the United States. The cases themselves are sampled from a nationwide study tracing the school improvement process from the federal down to the State level and then to some 146 school districts. Drawing on their expertise as specialists in the innovation process, and using a novel approach to single-case and cross-case analysis, Huberman and Miles provide a richly detailed yet clear account of innovation 'up close'. They examine the incentives, roles and actions of administrators, teachers, students and communities in the success or failure of such innovative programmes as remedial kindergartens, individualized reading and maths instruction, tailored vocational training and community-based civics. In lively, anecdotal accounts, the authors show precisely how innovations develop and stabilize over time and which factors account for their relative success.

Hughes, M G (1981) *Leadership in the Management of Education: A Handbook for Educational Supervisors* Commonwealth Secretariat: London
The handbook offers educational managers who have local or national training responsibilities some ideas on how aspects of educational management may be explored in an in-service training situation, the specific context of which will be determined locally. The publication includes examples of case studies and exercises, discussion of leadership issues, the planning and organization of in-service courses and evaluation procedures.

Lukes, S (1974) *Power* Macmillan: London
A very concisely written and persuasive overview of a long running acrimonious debate on power. Lukes spells out a three-dimensional framework for considering power and its forms. He shows how to get beyond the behaviourist political science attempt to measure and predict power and its effects. This book has been criticized by conservative and radical alike but it remains a masterly, succinct exposition of the central conceptual and empirical issues.

Pareek, U and Rao, T V (1981) *Handbook for Trainers in Educational Management: with special reference to countries in Asia and the Pacific* UNESCO, Roeap: Bangkok
The publication aims to develop training competencies and covers all aspects of training from training needs analysis to course design, materials selection and development, and evaluation. It is aimed at professional trainers and practitioners in educational management, and although most of the examples given are from countries in Asia and the Pacific, it has a much wider potential audience.

Powell, M and Beard, J W (1984) *Teacher Effectiveness: An Annotated Bibliography and Guide to Research* Garland: New York
This is an annotated bibliography of research published between 1965 and 1980 on teacher effectiveness — taking a very broad definition of the subject. The bibliography is preceded by an overview of the work included which explains the terms used and the issues discussed.

Rutter, M, Maugham, B, Mortimer, P, Ouston, J and Smith, A (1979) *Fifteen Thousand Hours: Secondary Schools and Their Effect on Children* Harvard University Press: Cambridge, Mass
An excellent example of the recent research on effective schools. Using a variety of methods, Rutter and his colleagues attempt to explain what makes some schools more successful than others. School ethos is a key factor. And the principal plays an active role in defining and maintaining a climate conducive to achievement. The book suggests numerous avenues for effective instructional management, especially in its case studies of certain successful schools.

van Velzen, W G, Miles, M B, Ekholm, M, Hameyer, U and Robin, D (1985) *Making School Improvement Work: A Conceptual Guide to Practice* International School Improvement Project. ACCO: Leuven, Belgium
This book is a valuable and well-written summary of concepts and findings relevant to school improvement. It resulted from the OECD/CERI International School Improvement Project (ISIP). It includes many case examples which are drawn on to illustrate its conclusions, and focuses on national, regional/local and institutional levels. The various chapters are concerned with: school improvement in the social context of the 1980s; the definition of school improvement; the 'context' that surrounds particular attempts at school improvement; designing strategies for school improvement; school improvement at the school level; the role of external support systems in school improvement; policy-making for school improvement; conclusions and recommendations for audiences at different levels.

Biographical notes on editors and contributors

Elisabeth Al-Khalifa (Chapter 17) is an advisory teacher in the City of Birmingham Multicultural Support Service. She has taught in secondary schools and has also worked in industry and commerce. Since 1979 she has led the Schools In-Service Unit, which works as a team of five, to provide school focused and classroom based in-service training in Birmingham schools in the field of anti-racist and multicultural education, with particular emphasis on classroom methodology and interaction. The team has experimented with in-service strategies in schools to facilitate an institutional basis for classroom change and the development of the school management team as part of this. She has recently completed an MEd dissertation at the University of Bristol on management development in schools.

Terry Astuto (Chapter 4) is Assistant Professor of Education, College of Education, Kansas State University, Manhattan, Kansas. She served as a teacher and administrator in the Milwaukee, Wisconsin Public Schools. Professor Astuto is currently President of the Organizational Theory Special Interest Group, American Educational Research Association. She is a codirector with Professor David Clark of the Policy Studies Center of the University Council for Educational Administration. They have recently released publications on merit pay for teachers and federal policy changes under the Reagan Administration. Their publications in organizational studies have dealt with effective schools, coupling as a variable in educational organizations, and the emergent paradigm shift in organizational theory.

Tony Bailey (Chapter 16) is a Reader in Education at the University of Sussex where he coordinates the regional school management training programme. He is currently Director of a nationally funded project, 'Support for the School Management Training Experience', and a member of the Steering Committee of the National Development Centre for School Management Training. For several years his work has focused on aspects of management and innovation in secondary schools and higher education.

Ray Bolam (Chapter 19) is Director of Further Professional Studies, University of Bristol, and Director of the National Development Centre for School Management Training. He taught English in a comprehensive school in London and then lectured in a teacher training college in Yorkshire. Since 1968 his work has been mainly concerned with action and evaluation research, particularly in the field of teacher education, and planned educational change. He has directed several projects, for example on: The Induction of Beginning Teachers; Local Educational Authority Advisers as Agents of Change; School-focused INSET; Self-evaluation in Schools; and External Support for Active Tutorial Work. He has been a consultant for OECD and the British Council. Currently he is working on the development and training of heads and senior staff.

Steven T Bossert (Chapter 8) is Professor and Chairman of the Department of Educational Administration at the University of Utah where he teaches courses on school effectiveness, organizational theory, and instructional supervision. His book, *Tasks and Social Relationships in Classrooms* (Cambridge University Press, 1979), and articles about the effects of activity structures on teacher-pupil and peer relationships, have contributed to the conceptualization of schooling and instructional effects. Dr Bossert's recent studies focus on instructional management and organizational effectiveness. Currently, he is preparing chapters for forthcoming volumes on school principals and on research in educational administration. Dr Bossert received his PhD in 1975 from the University of Chicago. He served as Assistant Professor of Sociology at the University of Michigan and as Director of Research and Development at Far West Laboratory in San Francisco. He is active in professional societies, publishing, research and consulting.

Chew Tow Yow (Chapter 21) is the Director of the National Institute of Educational Management, Ministry of Education, Malaysia. He began his career in education as a teacher in 1960. He taught in secondary schools and served as Deputy Principal and Principal of two secondary schools. In January 1970 he was posted to the Ministry of Education as an Assistant Director of Schools (primary schools). In 1973 he was reassigned as Project Coordinator to establish the Curriculum Development Centre of the Ministry of Education; subsequently he served as its Deputy Director when the Centre assumed full status as a division of the Ministry. In April 1979, on completion of his Doctoral studies, he was assigned to establish the National Institute of Educational Management. His academic interest is in curriculum theory and curriculum planning, while his practical experience has been in institutional building. He has also been on assignments for the UNESCO Regional Office at Bangkok as consultant in course development and in regional training workshops on educational planning and management.

David Clark (Chapter 4) is Professor of Education, School of Education, Indiana University, Bloomington, Indiana. He served as Dean of Education at Indiana and as an associate dean and faculty member at Ohio State. Prior positions were in the US Office of Education and in local school districts. Professor Clark is currently Vice President of the Division of Administration, American Educational Research Association. He is a codirector of the Policies Studies Centre of the University Council for Educational Administration.

Philip Clift (Chapter 9) is Lecturer in Education at the Open University. He is a member of the OECD International Schools Improvement Project and has contributed to publications arising from that project. His research interests are in school based review. He has written several journal articles on this subject, and is a member of Professor Nuttall's team writing a book about it. His other books include *Parental Involvement in Primary Schools* (NFER, 1979), *Record Keeping in Primary Schools* (Macmillan, 1982), and *Aims, Role and Development of Staff in the Nursery* (NFER, 1980).

Per Dalin (Chapter 22) is Director of the International Movement Towards Educational Change (IMTEC). He studied in universities in Norway, the United States and Germany and worked as a teacher, counsellor, and university lecturer before becoming Deputy Director of the Norwegian National Council for Innovation in Education, the Head of Research and Development in the Education Directorate of OECD, and then Director of IMTEC, initially with OECD and subsequently as an independent institution. His major interest is assisting educational institutions at various levels to achieve change. He has acted as consultant to 23 governments and has worked with many international organizations. He has published extensively in several languages and his most recent book (with Val Rust) *Can Schools Learn?* was published by NFER-Nelson in 1983.

Michael Fullan (Chapter 5) is a Professor of Sociology in Education and Assistant Director (Academic) at the Ontario Institute for Studies in Education (OISE). He has participated as researcher and consultant in a wide range of educational change projects with school systems, R & D institutes, and government agencies in Canada and internationally. His book *The Meaning of Educational Change* (Teachers College Press, New York; OISE Press, Toronto, 1982) has been widely acclaimed. His latest publication is: Change processes and strategies at the local level, in *The Elementary School Journal* **85**, 3: 391-421, published in 1985.

Kees J M Gielen (Chapter 20) is Director of Interstudie SO, the national in-service training institute for school managers of secondary schools in the Netherlands. Mr Gielen has been a teacher at a primary school, a teacher and head teacher at a teacher training college for primary education, member of staff of a national health service organization, and director of a local school guidance and service centre. He has been with Interstudie SO since 1977 and has been Director since 1979. Mr Gielen studied educational sciences. He is Chairman of the editorial board of *MESO*, a bi-monthly journal for school organization and educational management. He has published several articles on the work of school leaders, on network cooperation in education, etc. He is a member of the international editing board of ISIP Area 2 and, as such, is collaborating on two publications on school management development and school improvement in different countries. The address to contact is: Interstudie SO, Bothaplein 1, 6814 AJ Arnhem, The Netherlands; tel 085 454242.

Ron Glatter (Chapter 6) is Professor of Educational Administration and Management at the Open University. The Open University is a national distance learning institution, substantially supported by Government grant, which teaches through correspondence texts, television and radio programmes and face-to-face tutoring. (Over 2000 students, mostly teachers and educational administrators, followed degree level Open University courses in educational administration and management in 1985.) Professor Glatter previously worked at the University of London Institute of Education and the University of Manchester and was an educational administrator in London. He is current Chair of the British Educational Management and Administration Society (BEMAS) which is affiliated to the Commonwealth Council for Educational Administration (CCEA). His projects and publications have included the following areas: management development for the education profession and university staff; school governors; distance learning students.

Peter Gronn (Chapter 3) is Senior Lecturer in the Faculty of Education, Monash University, Melbourne, Australia. His teaching and research interests include politics, leadership, ethnographic and case study research methodology and psycho-biography. He has published in *Educational Administration Quarterly*, *Journal of Management Studies*, *Administrative Science Quarterly* and the *Australian Journal of Education*. His latest monograph is entitled The psycho-social dynamics of leading and following (1984), published by Deakin University Press, Australia.

Eric Hoyle (Guest Editor and Chapter 1) taught English in secondary schools from 1953 to 1961 before entering teacher education. Since 1971 he has been Professor of Education at the University of Bristol and is Dean of the Faculty of Education. His major interests are in the study of organizations, management, the teaching profession, the professional development of teachers and the relationship between research and policy. He was the founding co-editor of *Research in Education* and is on the editorial boards of various journals, including the *British Journal of Teacher Education*. He has served at various times on the Educational Research Board of the Social Science Research Council, the Executive of the Universities Council for the Education of Teachers and the County of Avon Education Committee. His latest book *The Politics of School Management* will be published in 1986.

Paul Hurst (Chapter 18) is Senior Lecturer in, and Chairman of, the Department of Education in Developing Countries of the Institute of Education of the University of London. He has extensive experience of education in Africa, Asia and the Middle East and frequently works as a consultant to aid agencies and national governments in the fields of policy analysis and implementation.

Geoffrey Lyons (Chapter 10) started his professional career as a teacher and has worked as a consultant on many educational projects in developing countries. He is currently on the staff of the Department of Education at the University of Hong Kong. He undertook the Heads Tasks and Teacher Career's projects for the Department of Education and Science and, with Ron Stenning, has recently completed the Staff Management project also for the Department of Education and Science. He is the author of *Heads Tasks* (NFER-Nelson, 1976), *Teacher Careers* (NFER-Nelson, 1981) and, with Ron Stenning, *Managing Staff in Schools* (Century-Hutchinson, 1986), as well as numerous articles and papers dealing with teacher and administrator development and with administration of schools.

Agnes McMahon (Assistant Editor and Chapter 7) is a Research Fellow in the University of Bristol School of Education. She is currently at the National Development Centre for School Management Training working on management development and training programmes for LEAs and schools. Prior to this she worked on the GRIDS Project, which is described in Chapter 7, and on training programmes for beginning teachers.

Obert Maravanyika (Chapter 15) is the inaugural and current Chairman of the Department of Curriculum Studies at the University of Zimbabwe. He did postgraduate work in curriculum studies at the Universities of London, Manchester and Zimbabwe. His current research interests include the role of historical antecedents in influencing curriculum decision making, use of qualitative methodologies in educational research, and general research methods in curriculum analysis.

His recent papers are on traditional African education and Western science, curriculum planning in Zimbabwean primary schools and on curriculum analysis and national development. He has recently completed a study of the curriculum in Dutch reformed primary schools in Zimbabwe as a basis for evolving a strategy of curriculum planning and development.

Colin Morgan (Chapter 11) is a Senior Lecturer at the Open University and Staff Tutor for Wales in the School of Education. He directed on a full-time basis the three-year Department of Education and Science-funded POST project on the appointment of secondary school head teachers in England and Wales. He has been a member of the Educational Policy Administration and Management group at the Open University since its founding, and is the author of many course units, TV and radio studies in educational management. His current research involvements are concerned with observing headship, methods of training head teachers and evaluating technical and vocational initiatives in secondary schools. His continuing interest in selection methods is currently focused on the appointment of assistant staff in schools.

Biddy Niblett (Bibliography) gained a Post-Graduate Diploma in Librarianship at the College of Librarianship, Wales. She worked for five years in the Research Department of Imperial Tobacco Company Limited. She is currently the Resources Officer for the National Development Centre for School Management Training, where she is developing a computerized database for information on school management training.

Desmond Nuttall (Chapter 9) is Professor of Educational Psychology and Director of the Centre for Curriculum and Professional Studies in the School of Education at the Open University. His interest in staff appraisal arose from his work on institutional self-evaluation, and he is currently leading a team who are writing a book bringing together all their work on that topic. He also leads the team conducting the national evaluation of the project funded by the Schools Council and the School Curriculum Development Committee entitled *Guidelines for Review and Internal Development in Schools.* His books include *School Self-Evaluation: Accountability with a Human Face?* (Longman for the Schools Council, 1981) and *Assessing Educational Achievement* (1986).

John Rennie (Chapter 12) has been Director of the Community Education Development Centre (CEDC), a national centre based in Coventry, since its establishment in 1981. Funded by two international foundations, it establishes development projects in many parts of the UK; offers training in different aspects of community education at all levels; conducts evaluation and research projects. Earlier, John Rennie taught for 10 years in secondary schools in Ellesmere Port and Manchester. He went on to teach in the Institute of Education, University of Nottingham, where he led the Schools Council Social Education Project. He became Community Education Adviser in Coventry in 1971 and Senior Adviser in 1979.

Susie Rodwell (Chapter 18) is Research Officer for the ODA-funded project Training Third World Educational Administrators — Methods and Materials, based in the Department of Education in Developing Countries of the Institute of Education of the University of London. Formerly an educational technology officer in the British Council media department, she has worked extensively in Asia and Africa undertaking field work, consultancy, media training and materials development activities, most recently in the field of educational administrator training.

Patricia Schmuck (Chapter 13) is an Associate Professor of Educational Administration in the Graduate School for Professional Studies, Lewis and Clark College, Portland, Oregon. She has been involved in education for 25 years as an elementary teacher, a school administrator, professor of education and as an author. With Richard Schmuck she is the co-author of *Group Processes in the Classroom* (1971), and *A Humanistic Psychology of Education* (1974). Her work on issues of gender in educational institutions began in 1975 with the publication of her dissertation, *Sex Differentiation in Public School Administration* (National Council of Administrative Women in Education, 1975). She was the Director of the Sex Equity in Educational Leadership Project at the University of Oregon from 1976 to 1979 which resulted in several publications such as *Sex Equity in Education*, and *Sex Equity in Educational Leadership: The Oregon Story* (Education Development Center, Mass, 1980). She is the founding mother of Northwest Women in Educational Administration, a support and advocacy group for women. She is currently editing a book, *Women as Educators in Western World Countries* (SUNY Press, NY, 1986).

A Ross Thomas (Chapter 14) is the Associate Professor of Educational Administration in the Centre for Administrative and Higher Education Studies, University of New England. He is a Fellow of the Australian College of Education and a member of the Australian Association for Research in Education, the Australian Council for Educational Administration, the American Educational Research Association, and Phi Delta Kappa. His research interests are in the fields of innovation, barriers to change, strategies of change, organizational climate of schools, observational studies of principals at work, principals' decision-making behaviour, and stress in principals. Professor Thomas is joint author and editor of *Explorations in Educational Administration, Educational Administration in Australia and Abroad,* and *Principal and Task: An Australian Perspective*, and also numerous journal articles and chapters. He is Editor of the *Journal of Educational Adminsitration.* In 1973-74 he was awarded a Canadian Commonwealth Visiting Fellowship to study preparation programmes for educational administrators in Canada. In October 1976 he represented Australia at the OECD-IMTEC bi-centennial seminar in the United States, the theme of which was the problems of urban education. He has been a Visiting Professor at the University of London Institute of Education, the Ontario Institute for Studies in Education and the Pennsylvania State University.

Glenn Turner (Chapter 9) is Research Fellow in the School of Education at the Open University. He is working on a research project investigating the 'nature, impact and effectiveness of schemes for teacher appraisal', directed by Professor Desmond Nuttall and Philip Clift, and funded by the Leverhulme Trust. His past work has included a study of pupil adaptations in a comprehensive school and evaluation of the impact of LEA-initiated schemes for school self-evaluation. He is also taking part in the national evaluation of the Schools Council GRIDS project. His publications include: *The Social World of the Comprehensive School: How Pupils Adapt* (Croom Helm, 1982) and (with Philip Clift) *A First Review and Register of School and College Based Teacher Appraisal Schemes* (Open University, Milton Keynes, 1985).

W G Walker (Chapter 23) is Emeritus Professor, Chief Executive and Principal of the Australian Administrative Staff College at Mount Eliza, Victoria. He was previously Professor of Educational Administration and for a time Acting Vice-Chancellor of the University of New England. A graduate of the Universities of Sydney (MA) and Illinois (PhD), he is a Member of the Order of Australia and an Honorary Fellow or Fellow of several learned and professional societies. He was founding editor of both *The Practising Manager* and the *Journal of Educational Administration* and is author of numerous books and articles on educational management. He was Foundation President of the Commonwealth Council for Educational Administration and is Immediate Past President of the Australian College of Education and President of the Society of Senior Executives. He is a member of Council of several university, institute and school bodies and serves on the Planning Council of the Congress on Education and Technology to be held at Vancouver in association with Expo '86. The William Walker Lecture, delivered annually in London for many years, was named in his honour.

Mike Wallace (Bibliography) was the Deputy Head Teacher of an 8-12 middle school before joining the staff of the National Development Centre for School Management Training in 1984. As a deputy head he conducted action research into his managerial work in school. He is currently interested in theories of learning for practical performance and their bearing upon methods of training for school management development.

Donald J Willower (Chapter 2) is Professor of Education in the Division of Education Policy Studies and Chairman of the Graduate Program in Educational Administration at the Pennsylvania State University. His work has centred on schools as organizations and on philosophical aspects of educational administration. He is the author of more than 120 publications on these topics, two of which received the Davis Award given by the *Educational Administration Quarterly*. He has been a Kellogg Fellow at the University of Oregon, a member of the National Commission on the Preparation of School Administrators of the American Association of School Administrators, President of the University Council for Educational Administration, and Distinguished Visiting Professor of the University of Alberta, Canada. He holds three degrees from the University of Buffalo, the BA and MA, both in philosophy, and the EdD in general administration.

Author index

Abbott, R 102
Abramowitz, S 32
Acker, S 176, 178, 180
Adams, B 191
Adkinson, J A 174, 176
Aiken, M 193
Albrecht, K 191
Al-Khalifa, E 21
Alkin, M C 130
Allen, B 139
Allison, G T 16, 39
Anderson, C S 32
Andrews, A G 189
Anstey, E 155
Apple, M 37
Archer, M S 50
Argyris, C 186
Astuto, T A 23, 31, 74, 88, 94,
    101
Austin, N 77

Bacharach, S B 35
Bachrach, P 47-8
Bailey, A J 215, 269
Bailey, F G 47
Ball, S J 17
Ballinger, E A 265
Baltzell, C 83, 158
Baratz, M S 47-8
Barnes, S B 47
Barnett, B 84
Baron, J 311
Barr, A S 128
Barr, R 116, 118
Barton, J 233
Bates, R 31, 37, 46
Beard, J W 128
Beckerman, T M 116
Beeby, C E 199
Bennett, B 220
Bensky, J M 190

Bentz, W K 189
Berman, P 77, 80, 91, 94, 96, 305
Bernbaum, G 143
Bernstein, B 17
Bidwell, C E 17, 31, 118
Biklen, S K 176, 180
Birchenough, M 101
Blakeley, T J 38
Blase, J J 191
Blazovsky, R 32
Block, J H 117
Bloom, S 32
Blumberg, A 34, 77, 113
Bolam, R 20, 101, 261
Borich, G D 128-9
Bossert, S T 23, 34, 76, 113, 115-18
Bowles, S 17, 30
Boyan, N J 31, 34, 38
Boyd, W L 30, 35, 39
Boydell, T 220
Braddick, B 218
Bredeson, P V 34
Brehmer, I 173
Bronfenbrenner, U 186
Brookover, W 113-14
Brophy, J E 117, 130-1
Brown, G W 188
Brown, J S 30
Brown, M E 19
Brown, R H 47, 50
Buckley, J 84, 92-3
Burford, C T 34
Burgoyne, J G 91, 223
Burke, B T 127
Burke, K 46-7
Burns, B 117
Burns, T 19, 48, 223
Burrell, G 15, 46
Bussom, R S 33
Byrne, C 132

Subject index